"The fate of those who have never heard [...] of our faith. Christians have long speculated about whether and now God may have spoken to those who have not been exposed to the church's preaching of salvation through Christ alone. This book deals respectfully with the different views of the subject which are found among evangelical believers while seeking to remain faithful to the teaching of Jesus himself. It is a model of how we should discuss such a delicate matter and come to a decision which upholds the uniqueness of the one and only Savior of mankind."

GERALD BRAY, RESEARCH PROFESSOR, BEESON DIVINITY SCHOOL

"For those who are more interested in faithful alignment with what Scripture says than in sentimentality on this extraordinarily challenging subject, this is now the book to read. Courteous in tone yet thoroughly engaged with those who take contrary positions, the contributors lead us with exegetical care, theological poise and pastoral sensitivity through a thicket of common objections. I warmly recommend this book."

D. A. CARSON, RESEARCH PROFESSOR OF NEW TESTAMENT, TRINITY EVANGELICAL DIVINITY SCHOOL

"No greater challenge faces the church of Jesus Christ than religious inclusivism—the belief that sincere people of many religions have enough truth to be saved from spiritual ruin. In age of tolerance for all that does not seem to hurt or inhibit, no note sounds more discordant than an exclusivistic requirement of faith in Jesus Christ. Yet—with patience, respect and biblical rigor—Morgan, Peterson et al. show such an exclusive claim is in the Bible. Nothing could be more insensitive and arrogant than repeating this claim—unless it is true. Then, nothing could be more gracious and necessary than this book's message."

BRYAN CHAPELL, PRESIDENT, COVENANT THEOLOGICAL SEMINARY

"A helpful, scholarly critique of inclusivism by various evangelical authors."

DONALD G. BLOESCH, PROFESSOR OF THEOLOGY EMERITUS, UNIVERSITY OF DUBUQUE THEOLOGICAL SEMINARY

"These thoughtful, irenic and informed essays provide an important response to more 'inclusivist' perspectives on the question of the destiny of the unevangelized. This is a helpful contribution to a complex and controversial set of issues."

HAROLD NETLAND, PROFESSOR OF PHILOSOPHY OF RELIGION AND INTERCULTURAL STUDIES, TRINITY EVANGELICAL DIVINITY SCHOOL

"Is personal faith in Jesus Christ the only way of salvation and what does this mean for this mission of the church in the twenty-first century? No two questions are more urgent on the evangelical agenda today, and this book deals honestly and forthrightly with both of them. A superb collection of essays reflecting biblical wisdom and churchly theology in the service of the gospel."

TIMOTHY GEORGE, FOUNDING DEAN, BEESON DIVINITY SCHOOL

"*Faith Comes by Hearing: A Response to Inclusivism* is a refreshing voice in an increasingly confusing evangelical literary output on matters pertaining to human religions. This timely book is a very helpful guide to Christians who want to seriously examine the biblical and theological issues for themselves. Useful to specialists and nonspecialists."

TITE TIÉNOU, DEAN AND PROFESSOR OF THEOLOGY, TRINITY EVANGELICAL DIVINITY SCHOOL

FAITH COMES BY HEARING

A Response to Inclusivism

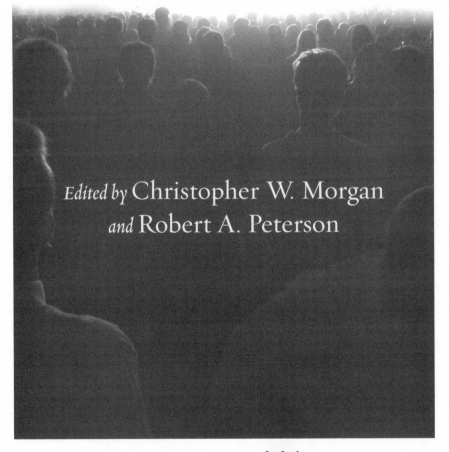

Edited by Christopher W. Morgan
and Robert A. Peterson

IVP Academic

An imprint of InterVarsity Press
Downers Grove, Illinois

Apollos
Nottingham, England

InterVarsity Press, USA
P.O. Box 1400, Downers Grove, IL 60515-1426, USA
World Wide Web: www.ivpress.com
Email: email@ivpress.com

APOLLOS (an imprint of Inter-Varsity Press, England)
Norton Street, Nottingham NG7 3HR, England
Website: www.ivpbooks.com
Email: ivp@ivpbooks.com

InterVarsity Press®, USA, is the book-publishing division of InterVarsity Christian Fellowship/USA®, a student movement active on campus at hundreds of universities, colleges and schools of nursing in the United States of America, and a member movement of the International Fellowship of Evangelical Students. For information about local and regional activities, write Public Relations Dept., InterVarsity Christian Fellowship/USA, 6400 Schroeder Rd., P.O. Box 7895, Madison, WI 53707-7895, or visit the IVCF website at <www.intervarsity.org>.

Inter-Varsity Press, England, is closely linked with the Universities and Colleges Christian Fellowship, a student movement connecting Christian Unions throughout Great Britain, and a member movement of the International Fellowship of Evangelical Students. Website: www.uccf.org.uk

Design: Cindy Kiple
Images: Bart Claeys/iStockPhoto

USA ISBN 978-0-8308-2590-5
UK ISBN 978-1-84474-252-3

Printed in the United States of America ∞

Library of Congress Cataloging-in-Publication Data

Faith comes by hearing: a response to inclusivism / edited by
Christopher W. Morgan and Robert A. Peterson.
   p. cm.
Includes bibliographical references and index.
ISBN-13: 978-0-8308-2590-5 (pbk.: alk. paper)
1. Assurance (Theology) 2. Salvation—Christianity. 3.
Christianity and other religions. 4. Salvation outside the church.
5. Religious tolerance—Christianity. I. Morgan, Christopher W.
1971- II. Peterson, Robert A., 1948-
BT785.F35 2007
234—dc22

                                                         2007038409

British Library Cataloguing in Publication Data

A catalogue record for this book is available from the British Library.

P	21	20	19	18	17	16	15	14	13	12	11	10	9	8	7	6	5	4	3	2	1
Y	26	25	24	23	22	21	20	19	18	17	16	15	14	13	12	11	10	09	08		

With gratitude, we warmly dedicate this book to our former students at California Baptist University, Biblical Theological Seminary and Covenant Theological Seminary who are serving Christ as pastors, church planters and missionaries.

Contents

Contributors

William Edgar (Dr. Théol., Université de Genève), Professor of Apologetics, Westminster Theological Seminary, Philadelphia

J. Nelson Jennings (Ph.D., University of Edinburgh), Associate Professor of World Mission, Covenant Theological Seminary

Walter C. Kaiser, Jr. (Ph.D., Brandeis University), Colman M. Mockler Distinguished Professor of Old Testament and President Emeritus, Gordon-Conwell Theological Seminary

Andreas J. Köstenberger (Ph.D., Trinity Evangelical Divinity School), Professor of New Testament and Greek, Southeastern Baptist Theological Seminary

Christopher W. Morgan (Ph.D., Mid-America Baptist Theological Seminary), Professor of Theology, California Baptist University

Robert A. Peterson (Ph.D., Drew University), Professor of Systematic Theology, Covenant Theological Seminary

Eckhard J. Schnabel (Ph.D., Aberdeen University), Associate Professor of New Testament, Trinity Evangelical Divinity School

Daniel Strange (Ph.D., University of Bristol), Lecturer in Religion, Culture and Public Theology, Oak Hill College, London

Stephen J. Wellum (Ph.D., Trinity Evangelical Divinity School), Professor of Christian Theology, Southern Baptist Theological Seminary

Acknowledgments

WE EXPRESS OUR GRATITUDE to Covenant Theological Seminary and California Baptist University for generously granting us sabbaticals to work on this project.

We thank many people for helping us to write this book.

Beth Ann Brown for first-rate editorial assistance.

Steve Jamieson, reference and systems librarian, and James Pakala, library director, both of the J. Oliver Buswell Jr. Library at Covenant Theological Seminary, and Barry Parker, reference and serials librarian of California Baptist University, for invaluable assistance in research.

Andy LePeau and Drew Blankman of IVP for their counsel, cooperation and flexibility.

Terrance L. Tiessen, author of *Who Can Be Saved? Reassessing Salvation in Christ and World Religions* (InterVarsity, 2004), for kindly reading and commenting on the manuscript.

Todd Bates, Tony Chute, Don Dunavant, Daniel Ebert and Jeff Mooney, colleagues, for offering suggestions.

Jeremy Ruch, Robert's teaching assistant, for compiling the author index.

Steve Lentz, Beth McCartney, Martie Thomas and Mary Pat Peterson, friends, for reading parts of the manuscript.

Shelley Morgan and Mary Pat Peterson, our wives, for their love, prayers and support.

I

Introduction

ROBERT A. PETERSON

Are those who, through no fault of their own, have never heard the gospel of Jesus Christ necessarily condemned to hell? Is there no possibility of salvation apart from explicitly responding to the gospel of Jesus Christ? These are deeply troublesome questions for all Christians who accept the uniqueness and normativity of Jesus Christ. No sensitive Christian who holds that salvation is available solely through the person and work of Jesus and who has been exposed to sincere followers of other religious traditions can fail to be distressed by the problem of those who have never heard.

There is a common perception among those outside the evangelical camp that evangelicals are agreed on all matters of doctrine, that in evangelical theology every question is definitively settled, and that there is no room for ambiguity or mystery. This, of course, is hardly the case. It is becoming increasingly evident that one issue upon which there is considerable disagreement among evangelicals is the question of the fate of those who have never been exposed to the gospel of Jesus Christ. And there are strong indications that this will be an even more controversial and divisive issue among evangelicals in the years to come. All evangelicals agree that this question is to be settled solely on the basis of the clear teaching of Scripture: All humankind stands condemned before God for its sin, not all persons will ultimately be saved, and God is entirely just and fair in his dealings with humankind. Evangelicals further agree that those who are saved are saved strictly on the basis of the person and work of Jesus Christ—salvation comes only through Jesus Christ.

But must one actually be confronted with the gospel of Jesus Christ and explicitly respond in faith in Christ in order to be saved? Or is it possible for some who have never heard of Jesus Christ nevertheless to benefit from the work of Christ and be saved? A variety of answers have been suggested.[1]

These words are truer today than when Harold Netland penned them in 1991.

---

[1]Harold A. Netland, *Dissonant Voices: Religious Pluralism and the Question of Truth* (Grand Rapids: Eerdmans, 1991), pp. 264-65.

Although evangelicals agree on the basics of Christianity, they disagree about many things, including the sensitive matter of the fate of the unevangelized. They agree that Jesus is the only Savior of the world, but are not unanimous on the answer to this question: Must one believe the gospel of Christ to be saved? Netland spoke prophetically: Disagreement over how to answer this question has intensified since he wrote. And this disagreement is the subject of this book, which respectfully takes issue with inclusivism and promotes exclusivism.

DEFINING KEY TERMS

It is important to define some key terms: *pluralism, exclusivism* and *inclusivism*. *Pluralism* is the view that all religions lead to God.[2] It denies that Jesus Christ is the world's only Savior. People may be saved, therefore, as adherents of Buddhism, Hinduism, or Islam, to cite the big three non-Christian religions as examples. Philosopher John Hick is one of the world's leading pluralists. The title of his book, *God Has Many Names*, speaks volumes, as Hick's adaptation of an ancient Indian religious poem (in another book) reveals:

> They call it Jahweh, Allah, Krishna, Param Atma,
> And also holy, blessed Trinity:
> The real is one, though sages name it variously.[3]

Although the essays in this volume will touch on pluralism and world religions, its main subject is the fate of those who have never heard the gospel. Pluralism must be distinguished from both exclusivism and inclusivism.

Exclusivism, sometimes called *restrictivism* or *particularism*, is the view that Jesus Christ is the only Savior of the world and that one must believe God's special revelation that culminates in the gospel of Christ in order to be saved. *Inclusivism* is the view that, although Jesus is the only Savior of the world, one does not have to believe the gospel to be saved. Exclusivism and inclusivism agree that Jesus is the only Savior of humankind; no human being will ever be saved from sin and hell by anyone other than Jesus. But exclusivism and inclusivism disagree on the necessity of unsaved persons to trust Christ for salvation. Exclusivists insist that faith in Christ is essential for salvation but inclusivists demur, saying faith in Christ is the best way, but not necessarily the only way, for human beings to ap-

---

[2]Pluralist sources include, beside John Hick's *God and the Universe of Faiths* (Basingstoke, U.K.: Macmillan, 1988), his *God Has Many Names*, (London: Macmillan, 1980); Paul F. Knitter, *No Other Name? A Critical Survey of Christian Attitudes toward the World Religions* (Maryknoll, N.Y.: Orbis Books, 1985). Books opposing pluralism include Harold A. Netland's *Dissonant Voices*, as well as his *Encountering Religious Pluralism: The Challenge to Christian Faith and Mission* (Downers Grove, Ill.: InterVarsity Press, 2001); Lesslie Newbigin, *The Gospel in a Pluralist Society* (Grand Rapids: Eerdmans, 1989).
[3]Hick, *God and the Universe of Faiths*, p. 140.

propriate the benefits of Jesus' death and resurrection. Said differently, inclusivism agrees with exclusivism that in terms of ontology (the order of being) only Jesus saves. But inclusivism parts ways with exclusivism in terms of epistemology (the order of knowing) when it maintains that unsaved persons can be saved by Jesus without hearing his name in this life.

IDENTIFYING KEY PLAYERS AND BOOKS

It is helpful to identify some of the key players in the debate between exclusivism and inclusivism. The recent history of inclusivism perhaps begins with Raimundo Pannikar's *The Unknown Christ of Hinduism,*[4] which as the title indicates proposed an unwitting following of Jesus Christ by Hindus. Evangelical studies in the West commence with Sir Norman Anderson's *Christianity and Comparative Religion* (1970), in which he opposed pluralism but opened the door to inclusivism.[5] While treating other themes, Clark Pinnock promoted inclusivism and challenged "the influence of the restrictivist [exclusivist] standpoint among fellow evangelicals" in *A Wideness in God's Mercy.*[6]

In 1992, John Sanders wrote one of the two most important books espousing inclusivism: *No Other Name: An Investigation into the Destiny of the Unevangelized.*[7] In 300 pages, he seriously treated the Bible, theology, and history, and set the stage for ongoing discussion. Sanders rejected what he regarded as the two extremes of universalism (the view that all would be saved) and restrictivism (exclusivism) and preferred instead "wider hope views." These included universal evangelization before death, universal opportunity at death, the view that God decides based upon what he knows people's response to the gospel would have been (middle knowledge), evangelism after death, and Sanders's preference—"inclusivism: universally accessible salvation apart from evangelization."[8]

In the 1990s evangelical publishers contributed multiauthor books to the discussion. Baker Book House led off in 1991 with *Through No Fault of Their Own? The Fate of Those Who Have Never Heard,* edited by William V. Crockett and James G. Sigountos, in which twenty contributors explored theological, biblical and missi-

---

[4]Raimundo Pannikar, *The Unknown Christ of Hinduism* (London: Darton, Longman & Todd, 1964). A revised and enlarged edition was published almost two decades later: *The Unknown Christ of Hinduism: Towards an Ecumenical Christophany* (Maryknoll, N.Y.: Orbis, 1981).
[5]A second edition, titled *Christianity and World Religions: The Challenge of Pluralism,* was published by Inter-Varsity Press (Leicester, U.K., and Downers Grove, Ill., 1984).
[6]Clark H. Pinnock, *A Wideness in God's Mercy. The Finality of Jesus Christ in a World of Religions* (Grand Rapids: Zondervan, 1992), p. 181.
[7]John Sanders, *No Other Name: An Investigation into the Destiny of the Unevangelized* (Grand Rapids: Eerdmans, 1992).
[8]Ibid., p. 215.

ological issues related to hell, pluralism, exclusivism and inclusivism. InterVarsity Press in 1995 added *What About Those Who Have Never Heard? Three Views on the Destiny of the Unevangelized*, edited by John Sanders, in which essays appeared promoting inclusivism (Sanders), a chance after death for the unreached (Gabriel Fackre) and exclusivism (Ronald H. Nash). Also in 1995, Zondervan Publishing House issued *More Than One Way? Four Views on Salvation in a Pluralistic World* edited by Dennis L. Okholm and Timothy R. Phillips, with essays defending pluralism (John Hick), inclusivism (Clark Pinnock) and two types of exclusivism (Alister E. McGrath; and Douglas Geivett and Gary Phillips).

A second book promoting inclusivism (while also dealing with world religions) which merits a place of importance alongside Sanders's *No Other Name* is Terrance L. Tiessen's 500-page *Who Can Be Saved? Reassessing Salvation in Christ and World Religions.*[9] Tiessen's book is fresh, clear and insightful. Three features set it apart from those of previous evangelical inclusivists. First, he avoids some errors committed by inclusivists before him. Second, he presents a more thorough argument. Third, unlike the previous evangelical inclusivists, who wrote from within an Arminian (synergistic) theological framework, Tiessen is Calvinistic (monergistic) in his theological commitments.[10]

Exclusivists were not reluctant to enter the discussion. In 1994, Ronald H. Nash penned *Is Jesus the Only Savior?* He spends one half of the book rejecting the pluralism of John Hick, and the other half rejecting the inclusivism of Clark Pinnock and John Sanders.[11] Also in 1996, D. A. Carson wrote a powerful critique of religious pluralism titled *The Gagging of God.*[12] Although the book ranges far and wide in its topics, pages 278-314 offer a vigorous critique of inclusivism. In 2002, Daniel Strange wrote *The Possibility of Salvation Among the Unevangelised: An Analysis of Inclusivism in Recent Evangelical Theology.*[13] In a book that has not received the attention it deserves in America, Strange, arguing from Scripture and systematic theology, capably takes to task Clark Pinnock's version of inclusivism.

---

[9]Terrance L. Tiessen, *Who Can Be Saved? Reassessing Salvation in Christ and World Religions* (Downers Grove, Ill.: InterVarsity Press, 2004).

[10]Another Reformed scholar who inclines toward inclusivism is R. Todd Mangum, "Is There a Reformed Way to Get the Benefits of the Atonement to 'Those Who Have Never Heard'?" *Journal of the Evangelical Theological Society* 47/1 (March 2004): 121-36.

[11]Ronald H. Nash, *Is Jesus the Only Savior?* (Grand Rapids: Zondervan, 1994).

[12]D. A. Carson, *The Gagging of God: Christianity Confronts Pluralism* (Grand Rapids: Zondervan, 1996).

[13]Daniel Strange, *The Possibility of Salvation Among the Unevangelised: An Analysis of Inclusivism in Recent Evangelical Theology*, Paternoster Biblical and Theological Monographs (Waynesboro, Ga.: Paternoster, 2002).

CITING THE MAJOR INCLUSIVIST ARGUMENTS

As Netland predicted, then, the past fifteen years have witnessed a spirited debate concerning the merits and demerits of both exclusivism and inclusivism. At this point an important question must be posed: What major arguments do inclusivists advance to support their position? There are five such arguments, although not all inclusivists employ all of them.

First, inclusivists argue that God's revelation of himself in creation and conscience not only condemns but also saves. Accordingly, persons may be saved, without hearing of Jesus, by responding positively to general revelation.

Second, most inclusivists raise the issue of God's justice: It would be unjust of God to condemn people merely because they have never heard the gospel of Christ. For God to be merciful and just there must be other ways of coming to him.

Third, some inclusivists, not all, have argued that adherents of the world's non-Christian religions may be saved apart from believing the gospel. It is not that these religions themselves teach the way of salvation, but that God in his grace accepts those who sincerely repent and seek him within the confines of their religions.

Fourth, it is common for inclusivists to point to Old Testament believers as examples of persons saved without the message of Jesus. Inclusivists also put in this category "holy pagans," biblical figures such as Melchizedek and Cornelius, whom they claim were saved apart from special revelation. Those today who have never heard of Christ are "informationally B.C." and God accepts them, if they, like Old Testament saints and holy pagans, turn to him.

Fifth, all inclusivists claim that in Scripture some persons are saved not by specific faith in Jesus Christ but by a more generic faith principle. Unreached people today, in similar fashion, can be saved apart from the gospel, by this same faith principle.

PREVIEWING THIS BOOK

The five main chapters of this book (chapters three through seven) address these five inclusivist arguments. In chapter two, Christopher Morgan, professor of theology at California Baptist University, discusses varieties of exclusivism and inclusivism in detail. Then Daniel Strange, lecturer in religion, culture, and public theology at Oak Hill College, London, argues that general revelation is insufficient for salvation. William Edgar, professor of apologetics at Westminster Theological Seminary, Philadelphia, demonstrates that exclusivism is consistent with a biblical view of God and his justice. Eckhard Schnabel, associate professor of New Testament at Trinity Evangelical Divinity School, argues that Paul did not believe that first-century adherents of non-Christian religions could be saved by Jesus without hearing the gospel. Walter Kaiser, professor of Old Testament and president emeritus at Gordon-Conwell Theological Seminary, contends that Old Testament saints were saved by believing in special revelation and that there are not "holy pagans" in Scripture. Stephen Wellum, professor of Christian theology at Southern Baptist Theological Seminary, argues that, according to Scripture, saving faith is faith in God's special, covenantal revelation, culminating in the gospel of Christ. To claim that persons can be saved today without explicit faith in Jesus is to turn the Bible's story on its head, to overturn the flow of redemptive history from the Old Testament to the New. In chapter eight, Robert A. Peterson, professor of theology at Covenant Theological Seminary, contrasts exclusivist and inclusivist exegesis of the key debated passages, attempting to show that exclusivism does a better job of explaining the biblical text and that inclusivism falls short.

Because this book is a response to inclusivism, these six chapters are largely (though not entirely) devoted to answering inclusivist arguments. But it is also important to present exclusivism positively, and that is just what Andreas Köstenberger and J. Nelson Jennings do in chapters nine and ten. Köstenberger, professor of New Testament and Greek at Southeastern Baptist Theological Seminary, sets forth the good news about Christ as the gospel for all nations. Jennings, associate professor of world mission at Covenant Theological Seminary, argues that an exclusivist theology of mission better fits the Bible's story than an inclusivist theology of mission.

In the final chapter, the coeditors succinctly answer the eight most important questions that have been asked throughout the book.

We have sought to introduce readers—even those with little background—to the discussion between exclusivism and inclusivism. But these matters are complex and this chapter has erred on the side of oversimplifying a complex discussion. The next chapter will seek to remedy this situation by exposing readers to the nuances of the various exclusivist and inclusivist positions while working toward a new and improved system of classifying them.

2

Inclusivisms and Exclusivisms

CHRISTOPHER W. MORGAN

FEELINGS SOMETIMES RUN DEEP in the debate between those who claim that Jesus saves some who do not hear the gospel (inclusivism) and those who hold one must believe the gospel to be saved (exclusivism).

> If God really loves the whole world and desires everyone to be saved, it follows logically that everyone must have access to salvation. . . . They cannot lack the opportunity merely because someone failed to bring the Gospel of Christ to them. . . . The Bible does not teach that one must confess the name of Jesus to be saved. . . . Evangelicals often try to prevent this biblical truth from being taken seriously. . . . What does "evangelical" mean when applied to those who seem to want to ensure that there is as little Good News as possible?[1]

> Inclusivism has become an enormously influential position among evangelicals at the end of the twentieth century. . . . It certainly makes a powerful appeal to our emotions. . . . The acceptance of this biblically unsupportable opinion carries an enormously high theological cost. One hopes that large numbers of evangelicals already committed to inclusivism will see these dangers and recognize the weaknesses of the position they have accepted in such a careless and unthinking way.[2]

God made us emotional beings and something would be wrong if our convictions did not affect our feelings. It is normal to have deep feelings about such important matters as the fate of the unevangelized. But certain factors have produced misunderstanding on both sides that has sometimes led to unfair descriptions of the "opposition," and even name-calling. And perhaps nothing has stirred confusion into this debate more than problems in categorizing the views. Ian Markham offers wise counsel:

---

[1]Clark H. Pinnock, *A Wideness in God's Mercy: The Finality of Jesus Christ in a World of Religions* (Grand Rapids: Zondervan, 1992), pp. 157-58, 162-63.
[2]Ronald Nash, *Is Jesus the Only Savior?* (Grand Rapids: Zondervan, 1993), p. 175.

Organization and classification of material is essential as an aid to effective communication. Good teachers and writers will use labels to organize material, which play a
valuable role in simplifying a debate. They provide a way in for the student or reader.
However, this organization and classification of material is not a neutral and objective
enterprise. One's classification will hide certain basic distinctions and options.[3]

Classification is both essential and biased, as the following survey of the development of the traditional classification system of exclusivism-inclusivism-
pluralism reveals. It is essential because all parties have expressed frustration with
the traditional classification system. And because it is biased, we will cautiously
suggest an improved classification that displays the emerging spectrum of views
and delineates the various forms of inclusivism and exclusivism. Our goal is to
bring clarity and perspective to this important discussion in evangelicalism.

THE TRADITIONAL CLASSIFICATION

Exclusivism: Jesus is the only Savior of the world, and one must believe God's special revelation culminating in the gospel of Christ to be saved.

Inclusivism: Jesus is the only Savior of the world, but one does not have to believe the gospel
to be saved.

Pluralism: All paths are valid and lead to God.

Figure 1. What about those who have never heard the gospel?

Its origin and development. Though John Hick overviewed three major approaches to other religions in 1980,[4] the threefold classification of exclusivism, inclusivism, and pluralism seems to come from his student Alan Race in 1982.[5] In
1986, Gavin D'Costa used the same threefold classification in his *Theology and Religious Pluralism: The Challenge of Other Religions*[6] and the trajectory for this tax-

---

[3]Ian Markham, "Creating Options: Shattering the 'Exclusivist, Inclusivist, Pluralist,' Paradigm," *New Blackfriars* 74, no. 867 (January 1993): 33; see also the response of Gavin D'Costa, "Creating Confusion: A Response to Markham," *New Blackfriars* 74, no. 867 (January 1993): 41-47; Tim Perry, "Be-
yond the Threefold Typology: The End of Exclusivism, Inclusivism, and Pluralism?" *Canadian Evangelical Theological Review* 14 (Spring 1997): 1-8.
[4]John Hick, *God Has Many Names* (Philadelphia: Westminster Press, 1980), chap. 2.
[5]Alan Race, *Christians and Religious Pluralism: Patterns in the Christian Theology of Religions* (Maryknoll, N.Y.: Orbis, 1982). Harold Netland and Stanley Grenz both suggest this. See Harold A. Netland, *Encountering Religious Pluralism: The Challenge to Christian Faith and Mission* (Downers Grove,
Ill.: InterVarsity Press, 2001), p. 46; Stanley J. Grenz, *Renewing the Center: Evangelical Theology in a
Post-theological Era* (Grand Rapids: Baker, 2000), p. 252. Grenz's bibliography on the classification
systems was also helpful.
[6]Gavin D'Costa, *Theology and Religious Pluralism: The Challenge of Other Religions* (New York: Oxford
University Press, 1986).

onomy began. When addressing the subject, leading evangelicals such as Harold Netland (1991), Ronald Nash (1993) and Alister McGrath (1994) continued using this threefold classification.[7] Interestingly, in their later works, D'Costa and Netland each expressed their frustration with it. The threefold approach was also met with criticism. Some felt the model was inadequate to describe the varied views. As early as 1985, Mark Heim found it problematic.[8]

In 1992, John Sanders in *No Other Name: An Investigation into the Destiny of the Unevangelized* categorized the debate around restrictivism (another term for exclusivism), universalism and universally accessible salvation, which includes inclusivism, universal evangelization (with three subviews—before death, at death and middle knowledge), and eschatological evangelization.[9] Sanders's work quickly became the inclusivist standard. His selection of *universalism* rather than *pluralism* displays his focus on the question of the unevangelized and not the broader questions surrounding world religions. Sanders's inclusion of the universal evangelization views also demonstrates his desire to nuance the traditional threefold classification.

In 1993 Ian Markham asserted that the theology of religions debate has been "stifled by an overemphasis on the standard three-fold paradigm."[10] He believed that the paradigms blend three issues: the conditions for salvation, whether the world religions are worshiping the same God, and the truth about the human situation.[11]

In 1995, Sanders edited *What About Those Who Have Never Heard? Three Views on the Destiny of the Unevangelized.*[12] Though the book focused on the views of inclusivism, "divine perseverance" (commonly called "postmortem evangelism"), and restrictivism, Sanders offered multiple perspectives on the destiny of the unevangelized. Categories that he added to his previous taxonomy were pluralism, complete agnosticism (that there was insufficient biblical material to warrant a conclusion), optimistic agnosticism and pessimistic agnosticism.[13]

The year 1995 was a popular one for this issue. Not only did InterVarsity Press

[7]Harold Netland, *Dissonant Voices: Religious Pluralism and the Question of Truth* (Grand Rapids: Eerdmans, 1991); Nash, *Is Jesus the Only Savior?* pp. 9-25; Alister McGrath, *Christian Theology* (Oxford: Blackwell, 1994).
[8]S. Mark Heim, *Is Christ the Only Way?* (Valley Forge, Penn.: Judson Press, 1985), pp. 111-27.
[9]John Sanders, *No Other Name: An Investigation into the Destiny of the Unevangelized* (Grand Rapids: Eerdmans, 1992; reprint, Eugene, Ore.: Wipf & Stock, 2001).
[10]Markham, "Creating Options," p. 33.
[11]Ibid., pp. 33-41.
[12]John Sanders, ed., *What About Those Who Have Never Heard? Three Views on the Destiny of the Unevangelized* (Downers Grove, Ill.: InterVarsity Press, 1995). Sanders defended inclusivism, Gabriel Fackre made the case for "divine perseverance," and Ronald Nash argued for restrictivism.
[13]Ibid., pp. 12-14.

publish *What About Those Who Have Never Heard? Three Views on the Destiny of the Unevangelized* but Zondervan also released *More Than One Way? Four Views on Salvation in a Pluralistic World*, edited by Dennis Okholm and Timothy Phillips. Okholm and Phillips organized the debate around four major positions: pluralism, inclusivism, and two kinds of "particularism" (their term for exclusivism).[14] Okholm and Phillips also shared their aversion for the traditional labels, which were crafted by those opposing exclusivism:

> As before, these categories are rhetorical instruments that frame the debate through their often hidden theological agendas. Clearly, terms are rhetorical tools, they aid in selling a case to the audience by linking their vocabulary with the culture's sensitivities, thereby suppressing certain questions. Indeed, the harsh attacks and caricatures in the current theological debate regarding other religions feature all the color of a political campaign, where rhetoric is just as important as substance. Before compliantly accepting these categories, one needs to expose them as rhetorical devices.[15]

Because *exclusivism* and *restrictivism* suggest narrowmindedness, intolerance and dogmatism to many in our culture, Okholm and Phillips proposed "particularism," a term that was used interchangeably with exclusivism prior to the early 1980s.[16]

In 1996, Millard Erickson in *How Shall They Be Saved? The Destiny of Those Who Do Not Hear of Jesus* interacted with six perspectives: traditional Roman Catholic exclusivism, Protestant exclusivism, classical universalism, pluralism, Roman Catholic inclusivism and Protestant inclusivism. In another section, he addressed postmortem evangelism.[17]

Recently, evangelical scholars have been increasingly unwilling to accept the traditional classification of exclusivism-inclusivism-pluralism. In his valuable *Encountering Religious Pluralism: The Challenge to Faith and Mission* (2001), Harold Netland admits his struggle with the threefold classification. He concurs with Okholm and Phillips in their assessment that the label "exclusivism" is pejorative

---

[14]Dennis L. Okholm and Timothy R. Phillips, eds., *More Than One Way? Four Views on Salvation in a Pluralistic World* (Grand Rapids: Zondervan, 1995).

[15]Ibid., pp. 14-15.

[16]Ibid., pp. 16-17. Okholm and Phillips, *Four Views*, cite Paul Tillich, *Christianity and the Encounter of the World Religions* (New York: Columbia University Press, 1962), pp. 35-44; Gerald H. Anderson and Thomas F. Stransky, C.S.P., eds., *Christ's Lordship and Religious Pluralism* (Maryknoll, N.Y.: Orbis, 1981), pp. 148-52.

[17]Millard J. Erickson, *How Shall They Be Saved? The Destiny of Those Who Do Not Hear of Jesus* (Grand Rapids: Baker, 1996). Two other important works addressing this debate published in 1996 are Vinoth Ramachandra, *The Recovery of Mission: Beyond the Pluralist Paradigm* (Grand Rapids: Eerdmans, 1996); and D. A. Carson, *The Gagging of God: Christianity Confronts Pluralism* (Grand Rapids: Zondervan, 1996).

and brings unflattering connotations.[18] Like them he opts for "particularism" as a better alternative.

In *The Possibility of Salvation Among the Unevangelized: An Analysis of Inclusivism in Recent Evangelical Theology* (2002), Daniel Strange examines inclusivism from the perspective of systematic theology.[19] In what is arguably the best work by an exclusivist to date, Strange places inclusivism in the context of discussions of the tensions between the themes of particularity and universality. Strange moves beyond the traditional threefold classification and suggests an overall theological scheme that is discerning, although complicated.[20] Strange then addresses nine positions of particular accessibility and universal accessibility: Reformed hard restrictivism (Carl Henry), Reformed agnostic restrictivism (Okholm and Phillips), Reformed soft restrictivism (Shedd), the Reformed view of general revelation serving as a preparation of the gospel (Piper), soft inclusivism/opaque exclusivism (Paul Helm), non-Reformed restrictivism, postmortem evangelism (Gabriel Fackre), the middle knowledge view (William Lane Craig) and positive agnosticism (Stott).[21]

In *Beyond the Impasse: Toward a Pneumatological Theology of Religions* (2003), Amos Yong criticized the threefold classification:

> In sum, then, the exclusivist-inclusivist-pluralist categories may have outlived their usefulness. They represent one approach to the theology of religions but not self-evidently the least problematic or most productive one. Is it not true, for example, that many of us are exclusivist, inclusivist, and pluralist in different respects? . . . Further, the categories themselves are becoming murky through a variety of qualifications.[22]

---

[18]Netland, *Encountering Religious Pluralism*, pp. 46-48.
[19]Daniel Strange, *The Possibility of Salvation Among the Unevangelised: An Analysis of Inclusivism in Recent Evangelical Theology*, Paternoster Biblical and Theological Monographs (Waynesboro, Ga.: Paternoster, 2002), pp. 304-31.
[20]Here is his scheme:

Divine Salvific Will
B1: Particular—B2: Universal
Divine Salvific Provision
B3: Particular—B4: Universal
Salvific Hope
B5: Pessimistic—B6: Optimistic
Salvific Accessibility
B7: Particular—B8: Universal
Salvific Means
B9: Special Revelation—B10: Special & General Revelation
Salvific Eschatological Opportunity
B11: Determined in this life—B12: Possible opportunity after death

[21]Strange, *The Possibility of Salvation*, pp. 304-31.
[22]Amos Yong, *Beyond the Impasse: Toward a Pneumatological Theology of Religions* (Grand Rapids: Baker, 2003), p. 28.

In 2004 Terrance Tiessen published the most significant work by an inclusivist
since John Sanders. In *Who Can Be Saved? Reassessing Salvation in Christ and
World Religions* Tiessen sought to clarify the discussion by renaming and redefin-
ing the categories. Appropriating the term from William Lane Craig, Tiessen labels his brand of inclusivism as "accessibilism."[23] He suggests five categories in his
classification system: ecclesiocentrism (exclusivism), agnosticism, accessibilism
(his term for an inclusivism that denies that other religions are a means of salvation), religious instrumentalism (his term for an inclusivism that holds that other
religions are a possible means of salvation) and relativism.[24] Tiessen makes a significant contribution to the discussion of taxonomy. He proposes a new term for
exclusivism: *ecclesiocentrism*. He acknowledges the reality of the agnostic category.
Most important, Tiessen differentiates two major kinds of inclusivism—and not
simply by referring to one as Roman Catholic and the other as Protestant. He observes that the issue that distinguishes them is whether God uses other religions
as a means of faith and salvation.

   Its inadequacies. Despite all their differences, pluralists, inclusivists and exclusivists can agree that the traditional threefold classification system is inadequate.
World religions inclusivists such as Mark Heim and pluralists such as Gavin
D'Costa have a problem with the question itself.[25] Evangelical inclusivists are
often troubled by the designation "inclusivism" since their view is sometimes
equated with Karl Rahner's "anonymous Christianity" and with others who hold
that world religions may lead to salvation.[26] And exclusivists are bothered by their
pejorative assigned label. Moreover, exclusivists of the stricter kind and those of
the softer kind are not always happy to be grouped together.

   An even greater problem with the traditional taxonomy is that it is used to provide perspectives on two separate questions: the salvation of the unevangelized and
world religions. And though these are related issues, they are distinct; and using
the same classification for both creates confusion. Thus, it seems there is a need
for two classification systems—one for the fate of the unevangelized and another
for a theology of religions.

---

[23]Terrance L. Tiessen, *Who Can Be Saved? Reassessing Salvation in Christ and World Religions* (Downers
   Grove, Ill.: InterVarsity Press, 2004), p. 33 n. 6.
[24]Ibid., pp. 31-47.
[25]S. Mark Heim, *Salvations: Truth and Difference in Religion* (Maryknoll, N.Y.: Orbis, 1995); idem,
   The Depth of the Riches: A Trinitarian Theology of Religious Ends (Grand Rapids: Eerdmans, 2001).
   Gavin D'Costa, ed., *Christian Uniqueness Reconsidered: The Myth of a Pluralistic Theology of Religions*
   (Maryknoll, N.Y.: Orbis, 1990); idem, *The Meeting of Religions and the Trinity* (Maryknoll, N.Y.: Orbis, 2000). See also Klaus Runia, "The Gospel and Religious Pluralism," *Evangelical Review of Theology* 14, no. 4 (1990): 363-67.
[26]For example, see Tiessen, *Who Can Be Saved?* pp. 33-34.

Because of the confusion mentioned above, it is crucial to know which question is being discussed when using the label "exclusivist." If the question pertains to other religions, an exclusivist is one who regards Christianity as the only valid means of salvation among the world's religions. If the question concerns the fate of the unevangelized, then an exclusivist is one who holds to the necessity of persons believing the gospel for salvation. Exclusivism used in this sense is a precise label, maintaining that special revelation is necessary for salvation. Yet, exclusivism when applied to other religions may include every response to the fate of the unevangelized except world religions inclusivism or pluralism. To demonstrate the height of confusion, we note that some evangelicals could call themselves exclusivists when discussing the question of other religions and inclusivists concerning the question of the fate of the unevangelized; Clark Pinnock labels himself this way in *A Wideness in God's Mercy!*[27]

This is why more distinctions are necessary. Some scholars suggest that the terms *exclusivism* and *particularism* are synonymous, while *restrictivism* is properly used only in the context of the fate of the unevangelized. When introducing *What About Those Who Have Never Heard?* John Sanders offered the following clarification:

> It should be noted that Nash uses the term exclusivism as synonymous with restrictivism. This is legitimate for our purposes so long as readers keep in mind that not all people agree with equating the two terms. In the literature on religious pluralism, exclusivism designates the view that Christianity offers the only valid means of salvation; other religions are completely ineffectual for divine salvation, and God does not make use of them. Though exclusivism affirms the particularity and finality of Jesus, it does not necessarily entail restrictivism, since some exclusivists are universalists, while other exclusivists affirm an opportunity after death for salvation. Both Karl Barth and Carl F. H. Henry are exclusivists regarding the relationship between Christianity and other religions, but they disagree strongly when it comes to the destiny of the unevangelized. Henry is a restrictivist, while Barth hoped for universal salvation.[28]

In his footnote, Sanders elaborated, "This is the reason I coined the term *restrictivism* in my book *No Other Name: An Investigation into the Destiny of the Unevangelized*. . . . Another term was needed in order to distinguish exclusivism from the

---

[27]Pinnock, *A Wideness in God's Mercy*, p. 15. With the blurring of the classification systems, one could be an exclusivist regarding world religions and inclusivist regarding the salvation of the unreached, an exclusivist and universalist, an exclusivist and a proponent of postmortem evangelism, or an exclusivist and an exclusivist.

[28]Sanders, *What About Those?* pp. 12-13. Sanders cited Carl F. H. Henry, "Is It Fair?" in *Through No Fault of Their Own? The Fate of Those Who Have Never Heard*, ed., James Sigountos and William Crockett (Grand Rapids: Baker, 1991), pp. 245-55; and Karl Barth, *Church Dogmatics* 4/3 (Edinburgh: T & T Clark, 1936-69), pp. 461-78.

belief that salvation is restricted to those who hear the gospel."[29]

Harold Netland concurred:

> Whereas restrictivism is a view about a specific soteriological issue (the necessary
> conditions for salvation as this relates to the unevangelized), particularism is a per-
> spective about a broader set of issues having to do with Christianity and other reli-
> gions. Thus, while all restrictivists are particularists, not all particularists are
> restrictivists.[30]

When both of these questions were largely undeveloped in evangelical theology, this did not present much of a problem. But now that scholars have begun to
address both questions more precisely, they are helpfully distinguishing the questions. It therefore seems wise to offer distinctive classification systems for both
questions.[31]

This may partially account for Tiessen's new taxonomy. He is wise to seek a new
term for exclusivism. It is also good that he allows for a variety of positions on this
issue. For example, he insightfully differentiates two kinds of inclusivism—accessibilism and religious instrumentalism. But while his delineations are helpful in
some ways, in others they are problematic. He tends to blend the two questions
together in the same taxonomy—the first three classifications focus on the salvation question and the latter two on the question of other religions. To his credit he
acknowledges this predicament.[32]

Further, although Tiessen's desire to coin a new term for exclusivism is wise, his
designation of it as "ecclesiocentrism" is unsatisfying. This may be an appropriate
term for Roman Catholic exclusivism as held by Cyprian and the Fourth Lateran
Council, but does not ring true as an accurate presentation of evangelical exclusivism.

Tiessen's term for his own position, *accessibilism*, is also simultaneously beneficial and confusing. Significantly, in using the term, Tiessen effectively distinguishes between his kind of inclusivism and the world religions variety. Yet readers

---

[29]John Sanders, *What About Those?* p. 157 n. 4, italics original. Dennis Okholm and Timothy Phillips
agreed. They asserted that particularism "includes a range of positions," from what they call "hard
restrictivism" to "optimistic agnosticism," *More Than One Way?* pp. 19-20.

[30]Netland, *Encountering Religious Pluralism*, p. 50.

[31]This chapter focuses on the soteriological question and its classification. Hopefully, others will more
carefully develop the classification concerning world religions. For one detailed investigation and
classification, see Veli-Matti Kärkkäinen, *An Introduction to the Theology of the Religions: Biblical, Historical and Contemporary Perspectives* (Downers Grove, Ill.: InterVarsity Press, 2003), pp. 165-352.
His analysis is helpful, even if its terminology tends to distortion. Concerning the world religions
question, positions 1-5 and 7 in the emerging spectrum would be types of particularism/exclusivism,
position 6 would be a type of inclusivism, and position 9 would be pluralism. Position 8 (universalism) could be located in any of the three positions depending on how one delineates it.

[32]Tiessen, *Who Can Be Saved?* p. 32.

could get the impression that Tiessen presents a new kind of inclusivism. And that is not the case. Later in the book he refers to Pinnock, Sanders and Yong as accessibilists.[33] Tiessen essentially follows Sanders and the majority of evangelical inclusivists who are open to general revelation being sufficient for salvation, while rejecting world religions as a means of salvation. His inclusivism differs from Sanders not in his conclusions about inclusivism itself but in the theological framework that supports it—Tiessen is a middle knowledge Calvinist and Sanders is an open theist Arminian.[34]

THE EMERGING SPECTRUM

Such inadequacies with the threefold classification point to the need for an improved taxonomy. Creating an entirely new taxonomy would overturn twenty-five years of traditional terminology and might result in further confusion. And such a bold move may be unnecessary. Instead of trying to dispose of the threefold classification, it seems wiser to build on the insights of previous scholars and pursue a nuanced classification.

Such a classification would need to be accurate, showing the existing distinctions, while not creating artificial ones. The classification would also have to be fair. Pluralists and inclusivists tend to put unwarranted labels on exclusivists. And exclusivists sometimes return the favor. As a remedy, our proposed classification will allow inclusivists and exclusivists to label their own views. Tiessen's distinctions between the two types of inclusivism will be followed with minimal rewording. As exclusivists we will distinguish three types of exclusivism.

Such a classification would also need to offer clarification. It would acknowledge that on the question of the fate of the unreached, Terrence Tiessen's position is not identical to Karl Rahner's, and John Stott's is not identical to D. A. Carson's. Unlike Stott, who is agnostic on the fate of the unevangelized, Carson is not.[35] A good classification should also refrain from labeling agnostic or inclusivist all who raise the theoretical possibility of God using extraordinary means to bring people to faith.[36]

A nuanced classification, then, would faithfully communicate the existence of an emerging spectrum of perspectives on the question of the fate of the unevangelized.

---

[33]Ibid., p. 41, 41 n. 33, 65.
[34]Other reformed evangelicals have also shown an openness toward inclusivism. See R. Todd Mangum, "Is There a Reformed Way to Get the Benefits of the Atonement to 'Those Who Have Never Heard'?" *Journal of the Evangelical Theological Society* 47, no. 1 (March 2004): 121-36.
[35]Tiessen mistakenly places Carson in the agnostic category.
[36]Gerald R. McDermott, *Can Evangelicals Learn from World Religions? Jesus, Revelation, and Religious Traditions* (Downers Grove, Ill.: InterVarsity Press, 2000), p. 213, erroneously calls Erickson an inclusivist.

Forcing everyone into one of three categories is simplistic. Netland offers help:

> But we should not think of these as three clear-cut categories so much as three points
> on a broader continuum of perspectives, with both continuities and discontinuities
> on various issues across the paradigms, depending on the particular question under
> consideration. Within each paradigm there is considerable diversity on subsidiary is-
> sues, and we must recognize that, as discussions become increasingly sophisticated
> and nuanced, it is often quite difficult to locate particular thinkers in terms of the
> three categories.[37]

A word about methodology is in order. Instead of trying to force everyone into
the three categories, we first observe how thinkers regard the fate of the unevangelized. Then, we categorize the major views and seek accurately to label them.

So, then, what are the main responses to the question "Is there any basis for
hope that those who do not hear of Christ in this life will be saved?" Although,
when answering this question most theologians assume the traditional threefold
framework: exclusivism-inclusivism-pluralism, we uncovered nine distinct responses.[38] We will use many quotations in an effort to advance a fair and accurate
presentation of all positions. Here is the spectrum of responses that emerged to
the above question.[39]

1. Church exclusivism
2. Gospel exclusivism
3. Special revelation exclusivism
4. Agnosticism
5. General revelation inclusivism
6. World religions inclusivism
7. Postmortem evangelism
8. Universalism
9. Pluralism

This book focuses on the issues related to views two through six, though it addresses concerns related to all nine positions.

---

[37]Netland, *Encountering Religious Pluralism*, p. 47. We prefer the term spectrum to continuum because
the latter implies a scale whereas the former suggests a less ordered variety of perspectives.

[38]The theologians do not always speak to recent issues and sometimes refute opponents rather than directly answering certain questions, so categorizing them is not always simple. Furthermore, many of the
writers we cite do not specifically address all of the questions we are raising or are not operating with
the spectrum of categories that we propose here. Therefore, the placement of a proponent within one
category does not absolutely rule out that he or she might also agree with elements in another category.

[39]The labels for the exclusivist and inclusivist positions are our own shorthand and do not necessarily
reflect the terminology of their proponents. Furthermore, multiple versions of many positions on the
spectrum exist. This classification, therefore, recounts the major positions and does not claim to be
exhaustive.

Below are nine responses to the question "Is there any basis for hope that those who do not hear of Christ in this life will be saved?"

1. *Church exclusivism.* One of the earliest responses to this question in Christian history is, "No, 'outside the church there is no salvation.' " Cyprian (ca. 200-258), bishop of Carthage, made this statement with reference to heretics, schismatics and apostates from the church.[40] Fulgentius of Ruspe (468-533) applied this teaching to Jews and pagans and this extended application was accepted and formalized by the Council of Florence (1431-1438). The Fourth Lateran Council (1215) firmly announced: "There is indeed one universal Church of the faithful outside which no one at all is saved."[41]

This is the traditional exclusivist position of the (pre-Vatican II) Roman Catholic Church.[42] We suggest a modification of Tiessen's term "ecclesiocentric exclusivism" that we will call "church exclusivism." Some may prefer to call it pre-Vatican II Roman Catholic exclusivism. No matter the term, this was a Roman Catholic form of exclusivism and is inadequate to describe most evangelicals.[43] Tiessen makes the mistake of placing Cyprian and Carl Henry in the same category.[44] That is inaccurate and potentially misleading. Lutheran theologian Carl Braaten offers help: "If, traditionally, Roman Catholic theology has taught 'outside the church there is no salvation,' Lutheran theology has taught 'outside of Christ there is no salvation.' "[45] Most evangelicals would be uncomfortable being assigned the designation "ecclesiocentric exclusivism."

2. *Gospel exclusivism.* A second major response is, No, they must hear the gospel and trust Christ to be saved. James Borland, a proponent of this position, asserts, "Everyone must hear and believe the gospel to be saved."[46] Borland states that the content of faith in the Old Testament was special revelation, but in the progress of revelation and since the cross of Christ, the gospel is the content of faith.[47]

---

[40]Strange, *The Possibility of Salvation;* Tiessen, *Who Can Be Saved?* and Sanders, *No Other Name* were particularly helpful for this section.

[41]Tiessen, *Who Can Be Saved?* p. 36; see also Jacques Dupuis, *Toward a Christian Theology of Religious Pluralism* (Maryknoll, N.Y.: Orbis, 1997), pp. 92-94.

[42]This is not to suggest that the Roman Catholic Church was monolithic on this point.

[43]Exceptions include many of the nondenominational Churches of Christ of the American restoration movement.

[44]Tiessen, *Who Can Be Saved?* pp. 36-38.

[45]Carl Braaten, "Lutheran Theology and Religious Pluralism," *Lutheran World Federation* 23-24 (January 1988): 122; idem, *No Other Gospel! Christianity Among the World's Religions* (Minneapolis: Fortress, 1992), pp. 65-82. See also Sanders, *No Other Name*, pp. 188-90.

[46]James Borland, "A Theologian Looks at the Gospel and World Religions," *Journal of the Evangelical Theological Society* 33 (March 1990): 3-11.

[47]Ibid.

John Piper also holds this view:

> The question we have been trying to answer in this section is whether some peo-
> ple are quickened by the Holy Spirit and saved by grace through faith in a mer-
> ciful Creator even though they never hear of Jesus in this life. Are there devout
> people in religions other than Christianity who humbly rely on the grace of a
> God whom they know only through nature or non-Christian religious experi-
> ence?
>
> The answer of the New Testament is a clear and earnest No. Rather, the mes-
> sage throughout is that with the coming of Christ a major change has occurred
> in redemptive history. Saving faith was once focused on the mercy of God known
> in His redemptive acts among the people of Israel, and in the system of animal
> sacrifices and in the prophecies of coming redemption. . . .
>
> But now the focus of faith has narrowed down to one Man, Jesus Christ, the
> fulfillment and guarantee of all redemption and all sacrifices and all prophecies.
> It is to his honor now that henceforth all saving faith shall be directed to him.[48]

Piper later clarifies that general revelation may be used as one step in the process
of salvation but that it still serves as a preparation for the gospel.[49]

We call this position "gospel exclusivism" because it emphasizes the necessity
of the gospel as the sole means for people coming to saving faith. When possible,
we will also label the types of exclusivism and inclusivism so as to highlight the
particular means involved.

3. *Special revelation exclusivism.* Third, some answer, No, unless God chooses to
send them special revelation in an extraordinary way—by a direct revelation from
the Lord through a dream, vision, miracle, or angelic message. Due to the emphasis on salvation being through special revelation alone, we call this "special revelation exclusivism." That also distinguishes it from gospel exclusivism.

William Shedd advocated this position, teaching that the unreached are voluntary transgressors, worthy of eternal punishment, and have no claim on divine

---

[48]John Piper, *Let the Nations Be Glad! The Supremacy of God in Missions* (Grand Rapids: Baker, 1993),
p. 163. Robertson McQuilkin agrees. See *The Great Omission* (Grand Rapids: Baker, 1984), pp. 42-
53.

[49]Ibid., 142-47. Piper adds: "My suggestion is that Cornelius represents a kind of unsaved person
among an unreached people group who is seeking God in an extraordinary way. And Peter is saying
that God accepts this search as genuine (hence "acceptable" in Acts 10:35) and works wonders to
bring that person the gospel of Jesus Christ the way he did through the visions of both Peter on the
housetop and Cornelius in the hour of prayer" (p. 146). An interesting twist to this approach to seeking comes from William Lane Craig, who holds a middle knowledge version, in which God sees to
it that all who would trust Christ receive the gospel. See William Lane Craig, "No Other Name: A
Middle Knowledge Perspective on the Exclusivity of Salvation through Christ," *Faith and Philosophy*
6 (April 1989): 172-88.

mercy.[50] He also concluded that the church must focus its efforts on evangelism and missions, the God-ordained "ordinary" means taught in Scripture to bring people to faith in Christ. Shedd added a caveat, however, suggesting that in his sovereignty the Holy Spirit may choose to use "extraordinary" means to bring people to salvation. These are unusual and not normal.

To show he stood within the Reformed tradition, Shedd cited the Second Helvetic Confession (1566): "We recognize that God can illuminate whom and when he will, even without the external ministry, for that is in his power" (1.7). Shedd also cited the Westminster Confession of Faith (1646): "God, in his ordinary providence, maketh use of means, yet is free to work without, above, and against them at his pleasure" (5.3); and "Elect infants, dying in infancy, are regenerated and saved by Christ, through the Spirit, who worketh when, and where, and how he pleaseth: so also are all other elect persons who are incapable of being outwardly called by the ministry of the Word" (10.3). While many interpret this as referring to those severely mentally challenged, Shedd followed those who interpret it as also including the unevangelized.[51]

Bruce Demarest is a more recent example of a theologian who espouses this position. He puts forward "the possibility that Christ may choose to reveal himself specially to a person who has not previously heard the Good News."[52] But Demarest clarifies his view:

> What is special and different here is not the content of the Gospel message, but the manner in which the message is revealed. Of course, in acknowledging God's freedom to reveal himself savingly to a human soul, we do not legitimize all alleged "experiences of God." The reader should note that the view presented is not that of a person casting himself on the mercy of God as a result of his own searchings. The possibility we hold open is that of a supernatural and contentful revelation of Christ to the soul, which elicits the free response of faith and commitment. In such a case the person is saved through a personal encounter with Jesus Christ.[53]

In a previous work, Demarest states:

> The overwhelming biblical dictum is that all people are lost and need to come to Christ for salvation. Let the church be reminded that in the plan of God the cus-

---

[50]William G. T. Shedd, *Dogmatic Theology* (New York: Scribners, 1888-1894), 2:706-8. See also the third edition edited by Alan Gomes: William G. T. Shedd, *Dogmatic Theology*, 3rd ed. (Phillipsburg, N.J.: Presbyterian & Reformed, 2003), pp. 337-40, 906-11. In personal correspondence, Gomes helpfully confirmed this interpretation of Shedd. Daniel Strange, *The Possibility of Salvation*, pp. 312-16, was also insightful in his analysis of Shedd's approach to exclusivism.

[51]Shedd, *Dogmatic Theology*, pp. 706-8.

[52]Bruce A. Demarest, *The Cross and Salvation* (Wheaton: Crossway, 1997), p. 90.

[53]Ibid.

tomary means by which sinners should come to know and love God is through the preached message of the cross. The number of those who might be brought to Christ through extraordinary means is small at best. . . . Let the Church know that if the heathen are to be saved, in overwhelming measure it will be through the instrumentality of the message entrusted to it.[54]

Timothy George also holds to this form of exclusivism. He criticizes inclusivism:

From the standpoint of biblical theology, however, this theory trivializes the tragic consequences of the Fall and thus exalts too highly the possibilities of common grace. The specific message of Jesus Christ, his cross and resurrection is not an extra "add-on" to what is already present to the human psyche through creation and culture. Rather, it is an absolutely decisive factor in bringing lost sinners into right relationship with God. . . . Should we then dogmatically declare that no one could be saved apart from the preaching of the gospel through human missionaries and evangelists? Biblical particularists who believe in the sovereignty of God will be cautious in making such a blanket claim. God is God and can work by extraordinary as well as ordinary means to accomplish his purpose.[55]

George then cites the Second London Confession of 1689, a Baptist confession which closely parallels the Westminster Confession of Faith on this issue, and speaks of the salvation of elect infants and "other elect persons, who are incapable of being outwardly called by the ministry of the Word." He then reasons that if the risen Christ appeared to Saul and if an angelic messenger can bring the gospel (2 Cor 11:14; Gal 1:8), then it is theoretically possible that "special communications of the gospel" could be "extended in the gracious providence of God."[56] George clarifies that there is nothing in Scripture that indicates that this actually occurs but that if it did the content of the communications would be identical with that of the apostolic witness—salvation by grace alone, received by faith alone, and on the basis of Christ's finished death on the cross alone.

4. *Agnosticism*. The fourth response is that we cannot know for certain the answer to this question. Tiessen appropriately labels this view "agnosticism," though such a designation unfortunately conjures up the agnostic position related to the existence of God.[57]

Those sometimes designated "pessimistic agnostics" sound much like exclusiv-

---

[54]Bruce A. Demarest, *General Revelation: Historical Views and Contemporary Issues* (Grand Rapids: Zondervan, 1982), pp. 259-62.

[55]Timothy George in "Forum Discussion on Inclusivism," in *Who Will Be Saved? Defending the Biblical Understanding of God, Salvation, and Evangelism*, ed. Paul R. House and Gregory A. Thornbury (Wheaton, Ill.: Crossway, 2000), pp. 145-48.

[56]Ibid.

[57]Tiessen, *Who Can Be Saved?* pp. 38-39.

ists. Such proponents often maintain that though a theoretical possibility exists that those who have never heard the gospel could respond to God via general revelation, there is little biblical warrant to expect that people actually do. In fact, many who hold to this position emphasize that the biblical evidence shows that people reject the communications of God in general revelation (Rom 1:18-32). J. I. Packer speaks to this possibility:

> We may safely say (i) if any good pagan reached the point of throwing himself on his Maker's mercy for pardon, it was grace that brought him there; (ii) God will surely save anyone he brings thus far (cf. Acts 10:34f; Rom 10:12f); (iii) anyone thus saved would learn in the next world that he was saved through Christ. But what we cannot safely say is that God ever does save anyone this way.[58]

Packer stresses that the Fall has rendered us unable to respond to God in faith apart from divine grace but he remains agnostic concerning the remote possibility that God may save this way. Yet he is clear that "we have no warrant to expect that God will act thus in any single case where the gospel is not known or understood."[59] Moreover, Packer asserts, "Living by the Bible means assuming that no one will be saved apart from faith in Christ, and acting accordingly."[60]

Millard Erickson shares Packer's reservations about the potential effectiveness of general revelation. Can those who have never heard the gospel respond to God through general revelation? Yes, Erickson suggests.[61] But will they? He answers:

> Rather commonly, the Scripture seems to indicate, sinners fail to know God correctly and accurately from general revelation, instead distorting and confusing what is revealed there. The effect of sin on human noetic capability is everywhere presupposed. . . . There are no unambiguous instances in Scripture of persons who became true believers through responding to general revelation alone. Scripture does not indicate how many, if any, come to salvation that way.[62]

Harold Netland similarly concludes:

> It seems to me that the wisest response to this perplexing issue is to recognize that we cannot rule out the possibility that some who never hear the gospel might nevertheless, through God's grace, respond to what they know of God through general revelation

---

[58]J. I. Packer, *God's Words* (Downers Grove, Ill.: InterVarsity Press, 1981), p. 210. Packer referred to himself as a "conscientious agnostic" on this subject in a telephone interview on June 15, 2007.

[59]J. I. Packer, "Good Pagans and God's Kingdom," *Christianity Today,* January 17, 1986, p. 25.

[60]J. I. Packer, "Evangelicals and the Way of Salvation," in *Evangelical Affirmations,* ed. Kenneth S. Kantzer and Carl F. H. Henry (Grand Rapids: Zondervan, 1990), pp. 121-23.

[61]Erickson, *How Shall They Be Saved?* pp. 130-39, 147-58. Erickson confirmed that this is his position in a telephone interview on June 18, 2007.

[62]Ibid., p. 158. See also idem, "Hope for Those Who Haven't Heard? Yes, But . . . ," *Evangelical Missions Quarterly* 11 (April 1975): 124-25.

and turn to him in faith for forgiveness. But to go beyond this and to speculate about how many, if any, are saved this way is to move beyond what the Scriptures allow. . . . Indeed the clear pattern in the New Testament is for people first to hear the good news of Jesus Christ and then respond by God's grace to the gospel in saving faith.[63]

Thus, some say that though it is possible that people might respond in faith through general revelation, there is no biblical warrant to affirm that it actually happens. This version of this position proves difficult to label. Okholm and Phillips call it "pessimistic agnosticism," whereas Carson refers to such a view as "soft inclusivism," Tiessen, "agnosticism," and Helm, "opaque exclusivism."[64] Okholm's and Phillips's label is beneficial in that proponents are pessimistic about the prospects of people coming to Christ in this way; Carson's term is appropriate in so far as these scholars do not completely shut the door to inclusivism; Tiessen's is helpful in that advocates stress that the Bible does not provide sufficient evidence to form a firm conclusion on the matter; and Helm's is fitting because it shows that those holding this view are largely exclusivist, even if in a qualified manner.

Others holding this position are more hopeful. John Stott exemplifies this "optimistic" version:

> I believe the most Christian stance is to remain agnostic on this question. . . . The fact that God, alongside the most solemn warnings and about our responsibility to respond to the gospel, has not revealed how he will deal with those who have never heard it. . . . [H]owever, I am imbued with hope. I have never been able to conjure up (as some great Evangelical missionaries have) the appalling vision of the millions who are not only perishing but will inevitably perish. On the other hand . . . I am not and cannot be a universalist. Between these extremes I cherish the hope that the majority of the human race will be saved.[65]

5. *General revelation inclusivism.* A fifth view answers, Yes, they can respond to God through seeing enough of who he is in general revelation. This is traditional inclusivism. As exclusivist Daniel Strange makes clear in his chapter on general

---

[63]Netland, *Encountering Religious Pluralism,* p. 323.

[64]Carson, *The Gagging of God,* p. 279; Tiessen, *Who Can Be Saved?* pp. 38-40; Paul Helm, "Are They Few That Be Saved?" in *Universalism and the Doctrine of Hell,* ed. Nigel M. de S. Cameron (Grand Rapids: Baker, 1992), pp. 278-79.

[65]David L. Edwards and John R. W. Stott, *Evangelical Essentials: A Liberal-Evangelical Dialogue* (Downers Grove, Ill.: InterVarsity Press, 1988), p. 327. Michael Green's views closely resemble those of Stott. He asserts that humans are not in a position to judge such cases but should leave these matters to God who is "utterly fair" and "passionately loving." He then suggests that those who have never heard "may well be" analogous to Old Testament believers who were saved by a more general faith. His tone is hopeful, "Such people may well be saved, not because of their religion, but because of what Christ has done for all." See Michael Green, *"But Don't All Religions Lead to God?" Navigating the Multi-Faith Maze* (Grand Rapids: Baker, 2002), p. 81.

revelation and as this chapter will develop later, inclusivism has multiple variations. John Sanders is a proponent who carefully delineates his position and that
of other inclusivists:

> Some advocates of the wider hope maintain that some of those who never hear the
> gospel of Christ may nevertheless attain salvation before they die if they respond in
> faith to the revelation they do have. . . . Inclusivists believe that appropriation of
> salvific grace is mediated through general revelation and God's providential work-
> ings in human history. Briefly, inclusivists affirm the particularity and finality of sal-
> vation only in Christ but deny that knowledge of his work is necessary for salvation.
> That is to say, they hold that the work of Jesus is ontologically necessary for salvation
> (no one would be saved without it) but not epistemologically necessary (one not need
> be aware of the work in order to benefit from it). Or in other words, people can re-
> ceive the gift of salvation without knowing the giver or the precise nature of the
> gift.[66]

With conclusions similar to Sanders but holding a different theological framework, Terrance Tiessen proposes that Jesus Christ is God's sole means of salvation
and that salvation is "accessible" to people who do not receive the gospel. He believes that non-Christians can be saved, but is emphatic that he and many evangelical inclusivists conclude that other religions are not to be viewed as God's instrument in their salvation.[67] Tiessen states that while other religions are not
means of salvation, people in them may be saved through general revelation even
while remaining in them: "Given the perspective that I have put forward, I grant
that the member of another religion *may* be personally in saving relationship to
God, in spite of the fact that their religion, as such, is erroneous and, as a system,
is counterproductive for people seeking God."[68]

Desiring to distance himself and others from the view that world religions are
a sufficient means that God uses to bring people to saving faith, Tiessen prefers
the label, "accessibilism." Tiessen's distinguishing of the two types of inclusivism
is valid and helpful. The term he chooses for this view, however, is confusing.
Many assumed Tiessen was offering a new position. But, he includes Pinnock,
Sanders, and Yong as advocates of accessibilism. He thus stands in continuity with
other inclusivists who hold that God may save some through the means of general
revelation.[69] To clarify this point and to continue to label according to means
whenever feasible, we suggest the name "general revelation inclusivism."

6. *World religions inclusivism.* A sixth answer to the question is, Yes, they can

---

[66]Sanders, *No Other Name*, pp. 215-16.
[67]Tiessen, *Who Can Be Saved?* p. 33.
[68]Ibid., p. 441, emphasis original. For a similar statement by Tiessen, see ibid., p. 393.
[69]Ibid., p. 41 n. 33. See also ibid., p. 65.

respond to God through general revelation or their religion, since their religion contains truth from general revelation and possibly remnants of special revelation. This position too is often called "inclusivism" and is similar to the fifth position in regarding general revelation as a possible means of salvation. But this position differs from the fifth in holding that world religions too are a sufficient means of God bringing people to saving faith. We, therefore, call this "world religions inclusivism" and follow Tiessen in distinguishing it from what we call "general revelation inclusivism."[70]

Proponents of this view assert God has chosen to use world religions as a means of salvation.[71] Roman Catholic theologian Karl Rahner's "anonymous Christianity" is an example of this position:

> Therefore no matter what a man states in his conceptual, theoretical and religious reflection, anyone who does not say in his heart, "there is no God" (like the "fool" in the psalm) but testifies to him by the radical acceptance of his being, is a believer. . . . And anyone who has let himself be taken hold of by this grace can be called with every right an "anonymous Christian."[72]

Hans Küng was even stronger. He proposes an "ordinary" way of salvation within world religions and an "extraordinary" way within the Christian church.[73]

> Since God seriously and effectively wills that all men should be saved and that none should be lost unless by his own fault, every man is intended to find his salvation within his own historical condition . . . within the religion imposed on him by society. . . . A man is to be saved within the religion that is made available to him in his historical situation. Hence it is his right and duty to seek God within that religion in which the hidden God has already found him.[74]

7. *Postmortem evangelism.* A seventh reply is, Yes, those who have never heard the gospel will have an opportunity to trust Christ after death. This view is traditionally called "postmortem evangelism." It concurs with exclusivism when it stresses that faith is a conscious and explicit trust in Christ but sides with inclusivism when it contends that the love and justice of God require that everyone be given an opportunity to trust Christ. J. P. Lange urges: "Holy Scripture nowhere

---

[70]Tiessen, *Who Can Be Saved?* pp. 43-45, calls this "religious instrumentalism."

[71]For a valuable summary of this type of inclusivism, see ibid. See also Erickson, *How Shall They Be Saved?* pp. 103-20.

[72]Karl Rahner, *Theological Investigations*, trans. Karl and Boniface Kruger (Baltimore: Helicon, 1969), 6:395.

[73]Tiessen, *Who Can Be Saved?* p. 44.

[74]Hans Küng, "The World Religions in God's Plan of Salvation," in *Christian Revelation and World Religions*, ed. Josef Neuner (London: Burns & Oates, 1965), pp. 51-53. We first saw this quotation in Tiessen.

teaches the eternal damnation of those who died as heathens or non-Christians; it rather intimates in many passages that forgiveness may be possible beyond the grave, and refers the final decision not to death, but to the day of Christ."[75] Though preferring the designation "divine perseverance," Gabriel Fackre concurs: "Sinners who die outside the knowledge of the gospel will not be denied the hearing of the Word."[76] Donald Bloesch and Jerry Walls offer similar proposals.[77]

8. *Universalism.* The eighth opinion is, Yes, everyone will ultimately be saved. Historically known as "universalism," this view exists in multiple forms, but in each the outcome is the same: Every human being whom God has created will finally come to enjoy the everlasting salvation into which Christians enter here and now.[78]

Universalists such as John A. T. Robinson argue that the biblical revelation of God's love for his world entails a purpose of saving everyone, and that God must achieve that purpose. Novelist Madeleine L'Engle states this idea clearly:

> I know a number of highly sensitive and intelligent people in my own communion [i.e., Anglicanism] who consider as a heresy my faith that God's loving concern for his creation will outlast all our willfulness and pride. No matter how many eons it takes, he will not rest until all of creation, including Satan, is reconciled to him, until there is no creature who cannot return his look of love with a joyful response of love. . . . I cannot believe that God wants punishment to go on interminably any more than does a loving parent. The entire purpose of loving punishment is to teach, and it lasts only as long as is needed for the lesson. And the lesson is always love.[79]

Another recent proponent is Jan Bonda, who holds that God wants to save all people and that he will accomplish that purpose. None will suffer endlessly in hell, he maintains.[80]

---

[75]John Peter Lange, *First Peter* (New York: Scribner, 1868), p. 75. For a helpful evaluation of this position, see Erickson, *Who Shall Be Saved?* pp. 159-75.

[76]Gabriel Fackre, "Divine Perseverance" in Sanders, *What About Those?* p. 84; Fackre, *The Christian Story: A Narrative Interpretation of Basic Christian Doctrine* (Grand Rapids: Eerdmans, 1984), pp. 232-34.

[77]Donald Bloesch, *Essentials of Evangelical Theology*, 2 vols. (New York: Harper & Row, 1982), 1:244-45; 2:225-30. Jerry Walls, *The Logic of Damnation* (South Bend, Ind.: University of Notre Dame Press, 1992).

[78]For an insightful critique of the forms of universalism, see J. I. Packer, "Universalism: Will Everyone Ultimately Be Saved?" in *Hell Under Fire*, ed. Christopher W. Morgan and Robert A. Peterson (Grand Rapids: Zondervan, 2004), pp. 169-94.

[79]Madeleine L'Engle, *The Irrational Season* (New York: Seabury, 1977), p. 97. We owe this quotation to Packer, "Universalism," p. 179.

[80]Jan Bonda, *The One Purpose of God: An Answer to the Doctrine of Eternal Punishment*, trans. Reinder Bruinsma (Grand Rapids: Eerdmans, 1993).

9. *Pluralism.* The ninth major response to the question is, Yes, those who have never heard may experience "salvation" as they understand it because each embraces their version of the real, though the question is erroneous because it assumes that Christianity is ultimate. Whereas universalism teaches that everyone will be saved, while maintaining the uniqueness and finality of Christianity, pluralism contends that all major religions are equally valid and thus denies the uniqueness of Christianity. Pluralist John Hick explains:

> The great world faiths embody different perceptions and conceptions of, and correspondingly different responses to the Real [the religious ultimate] from within the major variant ways of being human; and that within each of them the transformation of human existence from self-centeredness to Reality-centeredness is taking place. These traditions are accordingly to be regarded as alternative Soteriological "spaces" within which, or "ways" along which, men and women find salvation/liberation/ultimate fulfillment.[81]

Paul Knitter, Gordon Kaufman and Langdon Gilkey, among others, also represent this pluralist viewpoint.[82]

"Is there any basis for hope that those who do not hear of Christ in this life will be saved?" Here is a summary of the nine major responses to the question:

1. Church exclusivism: No, outside the church there is no salvation.

2. Gospel exclusivism: No, they must hear the gospel and trust Christ to be saved.

3. Special revelation exclusivism: No, they must hear the gospel and trust Christ to be saved, unless God chooses to send them special revelation in an extraordinary way—by a dream, vision, miracle, or angelic message.

4. Agnosticism: We cannot know.

5. General revelation inclusivism: Yes, they can respond to God in saving faith through seeing him in general revelation.

6. World religions inclusivism: Yes, they can respond to God through general revelation or their religion.

7. Postmortem evangelism: Yes, they will have an opportunity to trust Christ after death.

8. Universalism: Yes, everyone will ultimately be saved.

9. Pluralism: Yes, many will experience "salvation" as they understand it because they embrace their version of the real.

---

[81]John Hick, *An Interpretation of Religion* (New Haven: Yale University Press, 1989), p. 240. See also Hick, "Pluralism," in Okholm and Phillips, *Four Views on Salvation*, pp. 27-91.
[82]For insightful critiques of pluralism, see Carson, *The Gagging of God*, and Netland, *Encountering Religious Pluralism*.

In figure 2 the circles represent the means God uses to bring people to salvation. The larger the concentric circle, the broader the means of salvation. Thus, beginning with the largest circle, world religions inclusivism embraces all of the means God uses to bring people to salvation. General revelation inclusivism holds that God's means of salvation may include the church, gospel, special revelation, and general revelation, but not world religions. And so forth. Similarly, the smaller the concentric circle, the narrower the means of salvation. Therefore, beginning with the smallest circle, church exclusivism holds that outside the church there is no salvation. And gospel exclusivism broadens the means to include the gospel. And so on.

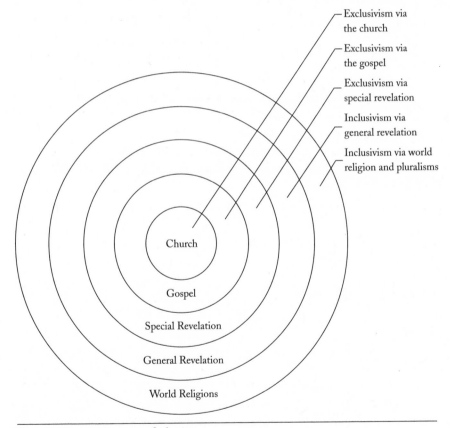

Figure 2. Views on the means of salvation

CONCLUSIONS

Varieties of both inclusivism and exclusivism are developing. Subsets of each tend to diverge over the matter of the means God uses to bring people to salvation. First, while the broader concept of inclusivism remains an important category, particular inclusivisms merit differentiation. Tiessen's division of inclusivism into two distinct forms is helpful and persuasive. One form, which we have called general revelation inclusivism, maintains that God may save through general revelation. The other, which we have called world religions inclusivism, adds the possibility of world religions serving as a means for salvation. The two forms differ primarily concerning the possible means God uses to save.

General Revelation Inclusivism:	People may come to saving faith by means of general revelation but not by world religions.
World Religions Inclusivism:	People may come to saving faith by means of general revelation and/or world religions.

Figure 3. Inclusivisms and means of salvation

The use of means in general, and the role of world religions in particular, arguably stand as the most important issues right now for inclusivists. Inclusivists concur in viewing the gospel, special revelation, and general revelation as means God employs to save. They increasingly disagree, however, over the role and value of world religions in salvation. In fact, many inclusivists are now suggesting that the question should not be the fate of the unevangelized but the role and value of world religions. Because inclusivists believe that the unevangelized can be saved, they naturally ask: By what means are they saved? Does the Spirit use only general revelation, or does he also use world religions in bringing people to faith? If the latter, what role do other religions play in salvation?

For example, in *Renewing the Center: Evangelical Theology in a Post-theological Era* (2000), Stanley Grenz asserts that the primary question facing inclusivists is, "Do other religions play a providential role in salvation?"[83] Gerald McDermott agrees. In *Can Evangelicals Learn from World Religions?* (2000), McDermott seeks to develop an evangelical theology of religions that "addresses not the question of salvation but the problem of truth and revelation, and takes seriously the normative claims of other traditions."[84] In *Beyond the Impasse: Toward a Pneumatological Theology of Religions* (2003), Amos Yong follows this trend, arguing that while the soteriological question is not unimportant, the question that should occupy evangelicals is the broader question of the theology of religions.[85] That same year Veli-Matti

---

[83]Grenz, *Renewing the Center*, pp. 268-69.
[84]McDermott, *Can Evangelicals Learn from World Religions?* p. 12.
[85]Amos Yong, *Beyond the Impasse*, pp. 25-29.

Kärkkäinen in *An Introduction to the Theology of the Religions: Biblical, Historical and Contemporary Perspectives* offers a significant analysis of the major responses to the world religions question. Many inclusivists themselves, then, indicate that their focus needs to shift from possible means to the role of world religions.

Second, particular exclusivisms also need to be distinguished. Three distinct forms exist and they too diverge over means. Church exclusivism maintains that outside the church there is no salvation. Gospel exclusivism teaches the necessity of hearing and believing the gospel of Christ. Special revelation exclusivism agrees with gospel exclusivism but also proposes that God may use extraordinary means of special revelation to bring people to Christ.

Church Exclusivism: People cannot be saved outside the church.

Gospel Exclusivism: People cannot be saved apart from hearing the gospel.

Special Revelation Exclusivism: People cannot be saved apart from special revelation.

Figure 4. Exclusivisms and means of salvation

Thus, for both exclusivists and inclusivists the primary questions revolve around the means God uses for bringing people to saving faith. In debating each other, the central issue lies in whether or not the truths of general revelation are sufficient for salvation. Within exclusivism, the major differences of opinion concern how God gives special revelation: Does it come only through the human messenger of the gospel? Does God occasionally use extraordinary means? Is there a theoretical possibility of people seeking God through general revelation but a practical impossibility?[86] Within inclusivism, the internal dispute surrounds the value of and possible divine use of world religions in bringing people to faith in God.

In sum, two signs indicate that the discussion surrounding exclusivism and inclusivism is maturing. Representatives from both sides agree that the exclusivism-inclusivism-pluralism paradigm is insufficient. Moreover, exclusivists and inclusivists are not only debating each other but are generating internal discussions. Hopefully, these external and internal discussions will advance the debate and yield further insights.

---

[86]One issue that appears neglected in this internal discussion is the role of general revelation in salvation. Exclusivists agree that it is insufficient for salvation. But what role does it play in the process of salvation? How is it preparatory? For partial answers to these questions see Daniel Strange's essay, pp. 40-70 and the conclusion, pp. 247-48.

3

General Revelation
Sufficient or Insufficient?

DANIEL STRANGE

For various reasons, however, this general revelation is not sufficient.
On this point, too, Christian theologians are unanimous.

HERMAN BAVINCK

What kind of God is he who gives man enough knowledge
to damn him but not enough to save him?

DALE MOODY

IT IS WITH SOME FEAR AND TREMBLING that I attempt to cut my way
through the jungle that is marked on my theological map as general revelation. I
have gleaned enough local knowledge to know that in terms of biblical exegesis,
systematic formulation, and apologetic application, the terrain is both vast, and at
times impenetrably dense and disorientating (but needing, ironically, a scalpel and
not a machete to understand the theological nuance and sophistication). I am also
aware that this ground has been the scene of some bloody family feuds, the "worlds
within worlds" of theology, be it the intra neo-orthodox Barth and Brunner debate, or between all those wishing to trace their lineage back to Calvin.[1] However,

---

[1] For the most comprehensive one volume treatment of general revelation, see Bruce Demarest, *General Revelation: Historical View and Contemporary Issues* (Grand Rapids: Zondervan, 1982).

I know that such a journey is unavoidable, as general revelation is a foundational doctrine of theological prolegomena, and its formulation will inevitably have profound systematic consequences for the rest of one's theological paradigm.

Considering the context of this present volume, though, one might be excused for thinking the above paragraph somewhat melodramatic. As your tour guide on this particular journey through "general revelation," are we not all actually on a well-worn path that is pretty straightforward and that should grant us a safe and smooth passage to our destination?

First, we are limiting our scope to those broadly within the evangelical constituency. This means we are working on the assumption that, however we define it objectively, subjectively appropriate it, or relate it to other revelatory modes, general/natural revelation *does* exist, that is to say that God has freely and purposively chosen to reveal himself in creation and/or history.

Second, we are not focusing our interest primarily on general revelation in terms of some of the broader questions pertaining to an evangelical theology of religions—whether there is truth, revelation, or good in non-Christian worldviews/religions;[2] or whether there is a universal natural law which can be the basis for public policy and cobelligerence;[3] or even the missiological and apologetic concerns of points of contact and contextualization. While these are *extremely* important questions demanding urgent and detailed attention by evangelical theologians, our particular focus here pertains to general revelation and its relation to soteriology: is there exegetical and theological warrant to claim that God can and does save people who only have access to general revelation?

Third, we are, I hope, all now familiar with at least some of the theological and philosophical issues generating our question: for example, the fact of religious pluralism, biblical axioms of universality and particularity, the fairness and justice of God, the depth of sin, the nature of faith, etc. I also presume familiarity with some of the biblical passages pertinent to general revelation and soteriology: Psalm 19; John 1:9; Acts 14:15-17; 17:22-31; Romans 1:18-32; 2:14-16; 10:17-18.

In light of the above delineations, is there not and has there not always been a consensus of opinion when it comes to relating evangelical theology and the doctrines of general revelation and soteriology? What is this consensus? Boldly speak-

---

[2]For a helpful introduction to these questions, see Harold A. Netland, *Encountering Religious Pluralism: The Challenge to Christian Faith and Mission* (Downers Grove, Ill.: InterVarsity Press, 2001); pp. 308-48; Terrance L. Tiessen, *Who Can Be Saved? Reassessing Salvation in Christ and World Religions* (Downers Grove, Ill.: InterVarsity Press, 2004), pp. 297-476.
[3]For contrasting views on this, see, for example, Stephen J. Grabill, *Rediscovering the Natural Law in Reformed Theological Ethics* (Grand Rapids: Eerdmans, 2006); Peter Leithart, *Natural Law: A Reformed Critique*. Biblical Horizons Occasional Paper 25 (Niceville, Fla.: Biblical Horizons, 1996).

ing, it is that however rich, variegated, and nuanced a doctrine of general revelation we have, soteriologically speaking, general revelation is insufficient to save but
sufficient to condemn and "render without excuse." Or, to put it a different way,
God does not save people through the revelation of himself in creation and that
what is needed is a more effectual revelation:

> In the divine mercy this came through the revealed utterances of certified prophets
> and apostles and through the life and teachings of the incarnate Christ, all of which
> are preserved in inspired Scripture. This fuller knowledge of God's nature and re-
> demptive purposes provides the objective basis for faith's informed decision.[4]

The very existence of this chapter included in this volume demonstrates that no
such consensus exists. There is a dissenting view with regard to the salvific capac-
ities of general revelation; indeed part of the dissenting view is to question whether
there was *ever* a historical consensus on the matter.[5]

While it would be both naïve and presumptuous to simply bypass historical
evangelical thinking in this area, this chapter is not meant to be a descriptive piece
of historical theology, but rather a prescriptive attempt at some theological evaluation and construction that will attempt to move discussion forward and not simply rehearse what has been written previously. My aim is to show *how* and *why*
general revelation is insufficient for salvation (but sufficient for what God has pur-
posed for it), by placing it within the larger context of both the history of revelation and the revelation of history.

The chapter has two parts. First, I will briefly describe three different types of
position, which all to a greater or lesser degree allow the possibility that God may
save people through general revelation alone. I label these three positions according to their theological framework: synergistic inclusivist, monergistic accessibilist, and missiological experiential. Second, I return to some of the seminal biblical texts, making some exegetical and hermeneutical comments. I then place
these passages within a wider systematic theological context that makes sense of
the relational dynamic between general revelation and special revelation. In conclusion, I nuance my overall thesis and suggest some further areas for discussion.

GENERAL REVELATION AS SUFFICIENT FOR SALVATION

I have already hinted that inclusivists are keen to show a historical theological
tradition of soteriological inclusivity. However, I hope it is not contentious to

---

[4]Bruce Demarest, "General and Special Revelation," in *One Lord, One God: Christianity in a World of
Religious Pluralism*, ed. Andrew D. Clarke and Bruce W. Winter (Grand Rapids: Baker, 1992), p. 199.
[5]See, for example, John Sanders, *No Other Name: Can Only Christians be Saved?* (Grand Rapids: Eerdmans, 1992); Tiessen, *Who Can Be Saved?* pp. 48-70.

note that the current debate over inclusivism appeared in embryonic form about twenty-five years ago. The salvific potential of general revelation was tentatively trailed by a number of evangelical scholars in the 1980s. One seminal work was Norman Anderson's *Christianity and World Religions.*[6] Packer quotes Anderson in a short article Packer himself wrote on the subject in 1986:

> But could God, in particular cases, work with and through the light of general revelation—light that comes to every human being—to evoke repentance and faith, and thus to bring about the salvation of some to whom no verbal message about God forgiving sins has ever come? . . . In *Christianity and World Religions*, Sir Norman Anderson states the question as it relates to non-Christian worshipers: "Might it not be true of the follower of some other religion that the God of all mercy has worked in his heart by his Spirit, bringing him some measure to realise his sin and need for forgiveness, and enabling him, in his twilight as it were, to throw himself on God's mercy?" The answer seems to be yes, it *might* be true.[7]

Based on these rough sketches, a number of scholars have developed more detailed and confident proposals.

Synergistic inclusivism. Within this section I will focus on the work of Clark Pinnock and John Sanders. The wider context of their inclusivism is their espousal of the theological paradigm known as the Trinitarian Openness of God, which in terms of soteriology is synergistic in orientation with its strong belief that human responsibility must entail libertarian freedom.[8] As well as championing openness theology they have also been at the forefront of discussions concerning the fate of the unevangelized and an evangelical theology of religions. Their inclusivist proposals have been two of the most detailed theological constructions.

Clark Pinnock. Pinnock's argument for the salvific potential of general revelation is necessitated by prior theological commitments. Pinnock's inclusivism is founded on the two inseparable axioms of particularity and universality which he believes are able to resist the twin errors of restrictivism and pluralism. Particularity refers to the uniqueness and finality of Jesus Christ. Universality consists of three elements: God's universal salvific will, the doctrine of unlimited atonement, and what Pinnock calls the "hermeneutic of hopefulness"—that Scripture, theology and history are optimistic as to the breadth and inclusivity of salvation in Jesus

---

[6]Norman Anderson, *Christianity and World Religions* (Downers Grove, Ill.: InterVarsity Press, 1984).

[7]J. I. Packer, "Good Pagans and God's Kingdom," *Christianity Today*, January 17, 1986, p. 25.

[8]Both were contributors to the original openness volume, Clark Pinnock et al., eds., *The Openness of God: A Biblical Challenge to the Traditional Understanding of God* (Downers Grove: Ill.: InterVarsity Press, 1994).

Christ.[9] From here Pinnock makes a logical step from universality to universal accessibility of salvation, based not so much on God's universal salvific will (which
could be frustrated by a shortcoming of the missionary mandate), but on God's
universal offer of salvation in the life, death, and resurrection of Christ: "the opportunity must be given for all to register a decision about what was done for
them."[10] Pinnock endorses Hackett's statement that

> if every human being in all times and ages has been objectively provided for through
> the unique redemption in Jesus, and if this provision is in fact intended by God for
> every such human being, then it must be possible for every human individual to be-
> come personally eligible to receive that provision—regardless of his historical, cul-
> tural, or personal circumstances and situation, and quite apart from any particular
> historical information or even historically formulated theological conceptualiza-
> tion—since a universally intended redemptive provision is not genuinely universal
> unless it is also and for that reason universally accessible.[11]

Here then is the conundrum which Pinnock seeks to solve: how can salvation
be shown to be universally accessible? Pinnock's argument is what I have previously called "pneumatological inclusivism"[12] founded on a "cosmic covenant" involving two movements: God's universal offer of salvation through the omnipres-
ent Spirit, and humanity's response by faith on the basis of God's universal
revelation.

> The cosmic breadth of Spirit activities can help us conceptualize the universality of
> God's grace. The Creator's love for the world, central to the Christian message, is
> implemented by the Spirit. . . . There is no general revelation or natural knowledge
> of God that is not at the same time gracious revelation and a potentially saving
> knowledge. All revealing and reaching out are rooted in God's grace and are aimed
> at bringing sinners home.[13]

On the God-ward side of this covenant, Pinnock stresses the cosmic breadth
of the Spirit present from creation and constantly offering relationship to creatures. Rather than thinking in terms of *extra ecclesiam nulla salus* (outside the

---

[9]For a more detailed account of Pinnock's proposal, see Daniel Strange, *The Possibility of Salvation
Among the Unevangelised: An Analysis of Inclusivism in Recent Evangelical Theology* (Waynesboro, Ga.:
Paternoster, 2002), pp. 41-127.

[10]Clark H. Pinnock, *A Wideness in God's Mercy: The Finality of Jesus Christ in a World of Religions* (Grand
Rapids: Zondervan, 1992).

[11]Stuart Hackett, *The Reconstruction of the Christian Revelation Claim* (Grand Rapids: Baker, 1984), p.
244. This is a question for all Arminians to answer.

[12]See part 2, "The 'Pneumatological Inclusivism' of Clark H. Pinnock" in Strange, *The Possibility of Salvation*, pp. 41-127.

[13]Clark Pinnock, *Flame of Love: A Theology of the Holy Spirit* (Downers Grove, Ill.: InterVarsity Press,
1996), p. 187.

church, there is no salvation), we should rather affirm *extra gratium nulla salus* (outside grace there is no salvation):[14] "The Spirit is present in all human experience and beyond it. There is no special sacred realm, no sacred-secular split—practically anything in the created order can be sacramental of God's presence."[15] Other features in Pinnock's formulation include a reworking of the Wesleyan doctrine of prevenient grace combined with a protestantizing of Karl Rahner's "supernatural existential," a rejection of the *filioque* clause, and an adoption of Irenaeus's phrase "the two hands of God," which sees Christology from the perspective of pneumatology. Pinnock says, "access to grace is less of a problem for theology when we consider it from the perspective of the Spirit, because whereas Jesus bespeaks particularity, Spirit bespeaks universality. The incarnation occurred in a thin slice of Palestine, but its implications touch the furthest star."[16]

On the human side of this covenant, Pinnock argues that all humanity can respond to God's offer in faith based on the revelation people have received. At this point we see the entrance of general revelation into Pinnock's argument:

> Inclusivism believes that God can use both general and special revelation in salvific ways. Western theology since Augustine has been pessimistic about admitting God's grace outside the church and salvific divine revelation outside of Christ. This tradition has said that general revelation provides a rudimentary knowledge of God and creates significant points of contact for missionaries, but it does not create the possibility of redemption. This implies that God reveals himself to all people not to help them, but to make their condemnation more severe. . . . What kind of God is it who would reveal himself in order to worsen the condition of sinners and make their plight more hopeless? . . . There is a witness in creation and providence that God uses for human good. God reveals himself to all peoples and never leaves himself without witness (Acts 14:17). Revelation is embodied in other religions. The revelation in creation is capable of mediating knowledge of God. God, the compassionate Father of our Lord Jesus Christ, is always and everywhere seeking the lost sheep. What we call general revelation and common grace contains not merely natural but supernatural and gracious elements.[17]

John Sanders. Sanders's use of general revelation is part of a cumulative case for an inclusivist soteriology. Like Pinnock, John Sanders is critical of two forms of restrictivist argument that claim that general revelation is sufficient to condemn

---

[14]Ibid., p. 194.

[15]Ibid., p. 62.

[16]Ibid., p. 188.

[17]Clark H. Pinnock, "An Inclusivist View" in *More Than One Way? Four Views of Salvation in a Pluralistic World*, ed. Dennis L. Okholm and Timothy R. Phillips (Grand Rapids: Zondervan, 1995), pp. 117-18.

but not sufficient to save. The first form argues that there may well be enough objective revelation in creation to be saved but that subjectively human sinfulness means we do not appropriate this revelation. Sanders describes the second form thus:

> Some restrictivists pose a yet more troubling problem by arguing that the unevangelised are justly condemned for rejecting that light of general revelation and that even a total acceptance of that revelation would still be insufficient for salvation. . . . By this logic the unevangelised are truly damned if they do and damned if they don't.[18]

Sanders's critique is that this use of general revelation is erroneous on two accounts:

> First, revelation, whether in the Bible or in creation, neither condemns nor saves. It is God who condemns and saves. And God can work through any means he sees fit to use in order to reach those he loves. Second, saying that the God known through creation condemns while the God known through the Bible saves, sounds as though there are two Gods—one damning and one saving. But there is one God, whose Holy Spirit is actively seeking the lost wherever they may be.[19]

Sanders is quick to note that such a view does not imply Pelagianism; it is the Spirit's work in the world to convict people of sin and turn them towards God. Second, it is the righteousness of Christ which is accounted to us on the basis of faith in God, "whether that God be known as Creator or as the Incarnate one. The Holy Spirit seeks to develop faith in us regardless of the revelation we have."[20] Third, Sanders does not ignore the fact that the unevangelized are sinners. However, "it is not beyond the Spirit's wisdom or power to reach sinners."[21]

In his personal defense of inclusivism, Sanders concentrates on Paul's argument in Romans 1–3. For Sanders, Paul's argument is not against those who believe in works righteousness but rather those who set Jew apart from Gentile. It is a boundary marker dispute, arguing that simply possessing the public badges of national identity does not guarantee salvation. Indeed, "faith is the only badge that Paul allows."[22] He writes:

> The justification of all ungodly people by the work of Christ leads Paul to see humanity in a radically new light. Paul now understands that God loves all sinners, that God has taken care of human sin with the death and resurrection of Jesus, and that

---

[18]Sanders, *No Other Name*, p. 69.
[19]John Sanders, "Inclusivism," in *What About Those Who Have Never Heard?* ed. John Sanders (Downers Grove, Ill: InterVarsity Press, 1995), p. 42.
[20]Ibid., p. 43.
[21]Ibid.
[22]Ibid., p. 51.

anyone can benefit from that work through faith in God (Rom 4:24—5:18). God is looking for those who will trust him, and Gentiles can trust God even if they remain ignorant of special revelation. . . .

For Paul, all who love their neighbours demonstrate that they have the law written on their hearts (Rom 2:14-15) and so fulfil what God wanted (Rom 13:8). A genuine faith in God manifests itself in love of both God and neighbour. Such faith and love is not limited to those within the visible boundaries of synagogue or church. . . . There is only one God for Paul (Rom 3:30), and that God is related to all people as Creator. He seeks the response of creaturely dependence from humanity, and such faith is possible, under the leading of the Spirit, for Jew or Gentile, evangelized or unevangelized. . . . Some ask, "If general revelation can save, why did God bother to provide special revelation?" Again, revelation does not save—God does. Furthermore, as was said above, the Christian enjoys many blessings that the believer does not experience. Though walking will get you from Chicago to Seattle, there are many blessings to going by plane.[23]

Finally, Sanders makes some comments on Romans 10:9, 14-18.[24] First he claims that restrictivists are guilty of eisegesis and fallacious logic. Using the logic that "If A, then B" does not necessarily mean "If not A, then not B," Sanders argues that 10:9—"if anyone receives Christ, then he will be saved"—does not logically entail "if anyone does not receive Christ, then he is lost." Second, on 10:13 Sanders notes that "in Scripture, the word 'name' usually refers to a person's character rather than to a title identifying an individual. To 'call upon the name of the Lord' refers to asking God for forgiveness and help."[25] General revelation contains enough informational content for someone to throw themselves upon the mercy of God. Third,

restrictivists commonly overlook Paul's appeal to the creation revelation in Romans 10:18. Quoting the great creation hymn Psalm 19, Paul says that the "gospel" has gone out to all the world. Inclusivists argue that what Paul is saying here is that all who respond to the revelation they have by calling out to God will be saved by Jesus Christ, since calling out to God is, in fact, calling upon the Lord Jesus.[26]

It is important to reiterate, that given the Arminian/Openness presuppositions of Pinnock and Sanders, enshrined in Pinnock's universality axiom, universal accessibility is a *necessary* consequence, which therefore means a certain theological pressure to then prove how salvation is universally accessible. Having rejected a number of other possibilities,[27] general revelation becomes the release mechanism

[23]Ibid., p. 49.
[24]Sanders, *No Other Name*, pp. 67-68.
[25]John Sanders, "Is Belief in Christ Necessary for Salvation?" *Evangelical Quarterly* 60 (1988): 247.
[26]Ibid., p. 68.
[27]For example, middle knowledge or a post-mortem evangelistic encounter with Christ.

to solve this conundrum, but which for these thinkers is clearly evidenced in Scripture and missiological experience (on this more shortly). Despite all their caveats concerning lack of assurance and continuing necessity of mission, for Pinnock and Sanders, there is sufficient objective informational content in general revelation and sufficient subjective ability in humanity to appropriate this revelation and for God to save those without special revelation, which he graciously does.

Monergistic accessibilism. I have attempted to note the theological context of Pinnock's and Sanders's use of general revelation, and the systematic connections between their inclusivism and their wider commitments. We might say that for these thinkers, their foundations are presuppositions concerning universality and God's openness, and their actual building is their inclusivist argument proper of which a central beam is the salvific potential of general revelation.

Ironically, noting such contexts and connections has made the ensuing debate somewhat opaque. While critique has focused on many different points, it is Pinnock's and Sanders's strong Trinitarian Openness and therefore synergistic construal of inclusivism which has dominated discussion, being as much a focus of critique as the original question of whether there can be salvation outside the preaching of the gospel by a human messenger in this life. To put it another way, is it possible to "save" the saving potential of general revelation from its Arminian/ Openness context and transfer it into a Calvinist/Reformed context?

Recently certain scholars have attempted to do just that. Here I adapt the title used by Terrance Tiessen and call such positions monergistic and accessibilist, that is, that God can sovereignly save those who do not hear the gospel from a human messenger in this life. I will briefly outline two advocates of this position, R. Todd Mangum, and Tiessen himself.

R. Todd Mangum. Mangum holds to classically Reformed soteriology, affirming the doctrines of total depravity and particular redemption. At the level of theological foundations he is "unfazed" by "any number of stock inclusivist-Arminian arguments" concerning the Reformed soteriological structure.[28] However, he does not think that this necessarily means the rejection of the central inclusivist tenet that Jesus is ontologically necessary for salvation but not epistemologically necessary: there can be gradations of "accurate *understandings* of what is the real (ontological) means of their having been brought into favorable relationship with God."[29] Indeed, Mangum has been impelled to look at some of the biblical texts

---

[28]R. Todd Mangum, "Is There a Reformed Way to Get the Benefits of the Atonement to 'Those Who Have Never Heard'?" *Journal of the Evangelical Theological Society* 47, no. 1 (March 2004): 123.
[29]Ibid., p. 124.

that inclusivists highlight which "have . . . stimulated different tracks of thought that have nuanced my own thoroughly Reformed soteriological perspective."[30] Again, one of his main arguments is the adequacy of general revelation for salvation.

Mangum notes the Reformed consensus regarding the insufficiency of general revelation to save:

> Reformed thinkers do not deny that general revelation *per se*, is abundant in the accurate and poignant information it makes available about God. General revelation "should" be a powerful communicative force that "should" draw people to God effectively. Reformed theologians have no reservations about this. The failure is not God's failure to communicate clearly or to reveal himself sufficiently. The problem is the human response—or, more precisely, the depraved human *inability* to respond.[31]

At this point he strongly criticizes sentimental inclusivist anthropology, which denies the depravity and wickedness of human nature in sin and which questions God's justice towards these "innocent" human beings whom God does not give a fair chance. He says "inclusivist arguments that seek to ameliorate this point—*argumenta ad misericorda*—at best can come dangerously close to 'loving the wicked' in a way that the God of the Bible expressly 'prohibits.'"[32] However, instead of asking theologically loaded questions, Mangum rephrases it, "If God has his elect in remote portions of the world, could he use general revelation to reach them? Put this way, it seems to me that a Reformed thinker's answer would have to be more ambivalent."[33] First (and like Sanders), he notes that Reformed theologians have moved too quickly to the conclusion that

> though the light of general revelation communicates accurate information about God that is sufficient to render human beings inexcusable, it is insufficient to serve as viable salvific revelation even if human beings responded and acquiesced completely to it. This inference Romans 1 does not support and, I suggest, is an inference that actually runs counter to the direction of the Romans 1 argument. If the content of revelation described in Romans 1 were inherently insufficient for initiating a salvific relationship with God, the passage would be portraying God as condemning people for failing to cross a bridge that would have collapsed had they tried to use it anyway. This dubious idea . . . ends up suggesting that general revelation is really designed by God to damn—which at best, is an inference not addressed by Romans 1, and at worst, turns the passage on its head.[34]

---

[30]Ibid., p. 125.
[31]Ibid., pp. 125-26.
[32]Ibid., p. 127.
[33]Ibid.
[34]Ibid., pp. 127-28 n. 16.

Second, more positively, he looks again at Romans 10 and Paul's use of Psalm 19. Like Sanders, he criticizes the way this passage has been dealt with by those critical of inclusivism, claiming that those who think Paul is only talking about special revelation are guilty of coming close to proof by emphatic assertion. Rather it is "Paul himself who reopens the question in verse 18, when he says: 'But have they never heard?'—deliberately undermining, in part, his earlier rhetorical question, 'How shall they hear without a preacher?' They may hear, apparently (and extraordinarily), through the consistent testimony of general revelation."[35]

> Paul's argument [in Rom 9–11] is that God is gracious to whom he will be gracious and that he is capable of reaching people and establishing a relationship with people who have been exposed to a lot less special revelation than the more obvious "covenant community." . . . [I]nclusivists are right on this point: God may be more gracious toward those outside the visible covenant community than that he has fully disclosed. Romans 10:18 sanctions speculation, at least, as to whether a "wider hope" may be warranted. Of course, people in remote sections of the world will not respond to the revelation to which they are exposed unless the Holy Spirit works in their heart and mind in an extraordinary way. But is this not true in any case? All Reformed thinkers recognize that, unless the Holy Spirit overrides, supersedes, and transforms the depraved human will, no one will respond. The real question is whether God needs special revelation to do this work. Given the sufficiency of "information" in general revelation, it is not implausible to think that, given a miraculous work in the mind and heart of a person in a remote section of the world, that person could respond to the information they have.[36]

Terrance Tiessen. Tiessen's overall argument for a Reformed accessibilism is multifaceted containing historical, exegetical, and theological arguments enshrined in sixteen theses.[37] Thesis 7 is most relevant to our study:

> Salvation has always been by grace through faith, but the faith that God expects (and gives) is appropriate to the revelation of himself that he has given to a particular individual. God requires people who receive general revelation to honor him as the Creator and Provider, to be thankful to him, to obey their consciences and to cast themselves on his mercy when they are aware of their failure to do what is right. If the Spirit of God were to elicit this response in anyone's heart, they would be saved.[38]

Tiessen's use of general revelation here is similar to that of Mangum's but there are a few variations worth noting. After affirming that salvation is only by grace through faith, Tiessen notes that the content of faith that justifies has not

---

[35]Ibid., pp. 128-29.
[36]Ibid., p. 129.
[37]Tiessen, *Who Can Be Saved?* pp. 22-30.
[38]Ibid., p. 138.

always been the same and then asks what faith looks like for those who only have access to general revelation. Soteriologically the crucial question is this: "Is it possible that God may have given some revelation that was sufficient to constitute them justly condemned but insufficient to permit them to be saved?"[39] He notes the usual response from Romans 1:18-32, that general revelation is sufficient to condemn but insufficient to save and that special revelation is necessary. He writes:

> But the implications of that position have troubled many Christians. If Scripture teaches it, we must accept it, however disturbing we find it; but should we not examine God's word carefully to be sure that this is a necessary burden to carry? Are we sure that there are people who have no revelation other than what God gives in creation? Much more importantly, does the Bible categorically assert that *none* of the people who have creational revelation *ever* honour God as Creator or are thankful to him.[40]

Looking again at Romans 1:18-32, Tiessen thinks it is pushing Paul's argument too far to suggest a blanket universality of wicked suppression. Certainly those who do suppress the truth and do not honor God are without excuse and yet "the most negative statement we could make from Romans 1, therefore, is that 'there may be some who respond positively, but Paul makes no mention of them.' This is different from hearing a positive *assertion* that no one does respond."[41] Here he concurs with David Clark and Millard Erickson:

> David Clark hits the right note with his suggestion that Romans 1:18-23 is "consistent with the claim that natural revelation fails to bring salvation to those who are rebellious and wicked, but potentially leads to salvation for those who respond to it." I think that Clark is correct to observe that those who find in Romans 1:18-23 a demonstration that special revelation is necessary for salvation "do so because they assume on some other ground that only those with special revelation can be saved. . . . If we portray God's judgment in ways that run counter to everything we expect on proper human jurisprudence, we will have to provide good explanation for doing so . . . Millard Erickson's approach strikes me as much more plausible. He writes concerning Romans 1:20,
>
> > If they are condemnable because they have not trusted God through what they have, it must have been possible somehow to meet his requirements through this means. If not, responsibility and condemnation are meaningless. . . . If individuals, on the basis of the inner law, come to realise their own sin-

[39]Ibid., p. 140.
[40]Ibid., p. 141.
[41]Ibid., italics original.

fulness, guilt and inability to please God, then that law would also have the effect of bringing them grace.[42]

What would be the cognitive content of saving faith through general revelation? Tiessen argues that Romans 1:21 suggests a worship of the Creator God and thankfulness for his provision, and Romans 2 suggests obedience to the law, "these people are not justified by their works, but this righteousness gives evidence of the work of God in their lives."[43]

After offering several extrabiblical instances of those who have shown faith without evidence of special revelation, Tiessen issues a note of caution, admitting that "I find no biblical examples of people who were saved through general revelation alone."[44] He also then goes on to argue that "evangelicals who have spoken optimistically about the salvific potential of general revelation may have underestimated the extent to which special revelation is experienced."[45] Despite these caveats, Tiessen's conclusion is that "in principle . . . it is possible that God might graciously save someone through general revelation by eliciting the appropriate kind of faith in that person's mind and heart."[46]

Missiological experiential. In support of their exegetical and theological claims concerning the salvific sufficiency of general revelation, Sanders and Tiessen both note and reinterpret the anthropological findings of those who have encountered the religious other on the mission field, most noticeably Don Richardson in his popular book *Eternity in Their Hearts*.[47] Based on his understanding of the Abram/Melchizedek encounter in Genesis 14, Richardson believes Melchizedek to be a type of "general revelation" and Abram a type of "special revelation."[48] His thesis is that general revelation includes "redemptive analogies" embedded in religious cultures throughout history and which can be *preparatio* for the gospel message. Richardson himself stops short of claiming that these analogies in themselves are salvific, distinguishing them as "redemptive" rather than "redeeming"—they contribute to redemption rather than culminating it. He says further, " 'redemptive

---

[42]Ibid., p. 142. Tiessen is quoting David K. Clark, "Is Special Revelation Necessary for Salvation?" in *Through No Fault of Their Own?* ed. William V. Crockett & James G. Sigountos (Grand Rapids: Baker, 1991), pp. 40-41; and Millard Erickson, *How Shall They Be Saved?* (Grand Rapids: Baker, 1996), p. 194.

[43]Tiessen, *Who Can Be Saved?* p. 145.

[44]Ibid., p. 149.

[45]Ibid., p. 150. He gives eight reasons for this.

[46]Ibid., p. 164.

[47]Don Richardson, *Eternity in Their Hearts* (Ventura, Calif.: Regal, 1981).

[48]Ibid., p. 31. Richardson asks what made Melchizedek greater in spiritual rank than Abram. His answer is that Melchizedek, as a representative of general revelation, was greater than Abram who represented special revelation, as general revelation "is older and it influences 100 percent of mankind (Psalm 19) instead of just a small percentage!" (p. 31).

lore' contributes to the redemption of a people solely by facilitating their understanding of what redemption means."[49]

What is important to note is that Richardson includes all of this "redemptive" data under general rather than special revelation, and so far in all the above descriptions, these two forms of revelation have been clearly distinguished from each other. A different categorization comes from Gerald McDermott.[50] McDermott's inspiration comes from his historical research on Jonathan Edwards, which has concentrated on Edwards's response to the religion of the Enlightenment: Deism. Focusing on Edwards's understanding of typology and his extensive notes concerning other faiths, McDermott, in his own work, argues for a category of revelation that is neither general (because this revelation is not universal) nor special (because it does not reveal salvation through Christ). Rather it is a category he calls "revealed types" originating from a *"prisca theologia,"* the idea of an ancient tradition of revelation passed down through tradition over generations:

> The *prisca theologia* was developed first by Clement of Alexandria, Origen, Lactantius, and Eusebius to show that the greatest philosophers had borrowed from the Chosen people. . . . In his own appropriation of the *prisca theologia*, Edwards said that the heathen learned these truths by what could be called a trickle-down process of revelation. In the "first ages" of the world the fathers of the nations received revelation of the great religious truths, directly or indirectly, from God himself. These truths were then passed down, by tradition, from one generation to the next. Unfortunately, there is also a religious law of entropy at work. Human finitude and corruption inevitably cause the revelation to be distorted, resulting in superstition and idolatry. . . . Edwards was always quick to note that heathen religion and philosophy contained "many absurdities" (e.g., *Misc.* 1350). But he learned from the *prisca theologia* that among the absurdities there were enough "scraps of truth" to show the way to salvation (*Misc.* 1297; *NS,* 387). Edwards found one way, then, to respond to the scandal of particularity the reports from the East has posed. He agreed with the deists that the problem could not be ignored and disagreed with Reformed scholastics who saw nothing beyond knowledge of God the Creator in non-Christian religions. God's justice and goodness were not sufficiently protected by the received tradition, so Edwards appropriated an old tradition to make Reformed history anew. In Edwards' new history God was still good, in the context of the new knowledge of plu-

---

[49]Ibid., p. 59.
[50]See Gerald R. McDermott, *Can Evangelicals Learn from World Religions?* (Downers Grove, Ill: InterVarsity Press, 2000); idem, *Jonathan Edwards Confronts the Gods* (New York: Oxford University Press, 2000); idem, "What if Paul Had Been from China? Reflections on the Possibility of Revelation in Non-Christian Religions" in *No Other Gods Before Me?* ed. John G. Stackhouse (Grand Rapids: Baker, 2001), pp. 17-35.

ralism, because knowledge of God the Redeemer has been available from the beginning.[51]

Edwards suggested that animal sacrifices, found in almost all world religions, were "shadows" or "images" of Jesus' great and final sacrifice that would eliminate the need for all subsequent sacrifices. Even idol worship and human sacrifice were hints of the incarnation and the Father's sacrifice of the Son. . . . [A]s Edwards has argued, it suggests that the world is full of types that point to the triune God—just as traditional theology has claimed that all the world is full of general revelation. My claim is that among the religions are scattered promises of God in Christ and that these promises are revealed types planted there by the triune God.[52]

McDermott lists a number of reasons why God would provide such types.[53] Although he only dwells on the point briefly, he does note that there are many who would want to push a soteriological purpose: "perhaps God might use this revelation, however incomplete, to save those who have not heard rightly about Jesus."[54]

GENERAL REVELATION AS SUFFICIENT, BUT *NOT* FOR SALVATION

We have now surveyed three different approaches, all of which claim exegetically, theologically, and phenomenologically that under certain conditions, general revelation can be a sufficient means through which God saves those who never hear the gospel. The question we must ask is whether general revelation can deliver these expectations. In the remaining part of this essay I wish to give a "character reference," arguing both exegetically and systematically, that general revelation is an unsuitable candidate for the "promotion" it has been given by these scholars, and that while general revelation serves a crucial role in the sovereign purposes of God, in and of itself it is insufficient to bring salvation. God has prescribed the way of salvation which is faith in Jesus Christ in special revelation ordinarily through the hearing of the gospel message through a human messenger in this life. Before we proceed I should declare my own Reformed/Calvinistic presuppositions with regard to God's sovereignty in salvation. While these presuppositions will become apparent in my argumentation, the purpose of this essay cannot be another simple rehearsal of the debate between Calvinism, Arminianism and now, Open Theism. I hope I have shown already that while these presuppositions do play a foundational role, the argument for general revelation's sufficiency is seen in all

---

[51]McDermott, *Jonathan Edwards Confronts the Gods*, pp. 94-95.
[52]McDermott, "What if Paul Had Been from China?" p. 28.
[53]One of these purposes is McDermott's thesis that these types can teach Christians by reminding them of aspects of their tradition which they have forgotten, or even "another providential purpose for revealed types may be that non-Christian religions contain aspects of the divine mystery that the Bible does not equally emphasize." ("What if Paul Had Been from China?" p. 33.)
[54]McDermott, *Can Evangelicals Learn*, p. 115.

three soteriological frameworks. Those who disagree with my presuppositions will have to adjust my argument accordingly.

For the sake of clarity it will help to make a number of distinctions which will act as scaffolding as I construct my argument.[55] First, we must distinguish between God's revelation of himself in nature and history and God's revelation of himself in the gospel. Second, we must distinguish between God's revelation of himself in his works and his words. Third, we must distinguish between God's revelation in nature manifested externally of persons and internally within persons. Fourth, we must distinguish between objective revelation and subjective appropriation or illumination of that objective revelation. Fifth, we must distinguish the time before the Fall (prelapsarian) and after the Fall (postlapsarian). Finally we must distinguish between the general operations of the Holy Spirit in the world and the particular work of the Holy Spirit in regeneration. While it is not possible to comment on every possible combination of these delineations, a number of key relationships can be noted.

In what follows I will first mark out some exegetical "dots" commenting briefly on those passages most relevant to the topic. Second, I will outline a more detailed profile by drawing together some systematic theological observations. Finally, I will offer some possible ways forward that I hope will deepen evangelical thinking in this area.

Exegetical dots.

Psalm 19:1-6. Let us return to Psalm 19:1-6, "considered the OT *locus classicus* for the subject of general revelation."[56] My intention here is to demonstrate a major incongruity between the nature, function and context of general revelation as portrayed in the psalm and the inclusivist use of general revelation.

What is the medium and message of God's revelation in verses 1-6? God's glory is declared by the work of his hands. Elohim's glory expresses weightiness and importance but is to be contrasted with the "Glory of the YHWH" which is associated with God's particular revelation at Sinai.[57] The glory in verse 1 is proclaimed by God's handiwork. Here the NIV is unhelpful as it seems to smooth out a strange paradox in its translation of verse 3: "There is no speech or language *where* their voice is not heard." However, other versions retain a more literal sense. Here is the NRSV:

---

[55]This is scaffolding that is somewhat artificial as will be shown below when it is taken away.

[56]James K. Hoffmeier, "'The Heavens Declare the Glory of God': The Limits of General Revelation," *Trinity Journal* 21NS (2000): 17.

[57]For more on this distinction see ibid., p. 20.

The heavens are telling the glory of God;
and the firmament proclaims his handiwork.
Day to day pours forth speech,
and night to night declares knowledge.
There is no speech, nor are there words;
their voice is not heard;
yet their voice [or line] goes out through all the earth,
and their words to the end of the world.

We can say here that the "medium is the message," for in the context of the psalm as a whole, this "wordless speech" (what Hoffmeier calls "veiled information about God") is contrasted, complimented, and supplemented by God's words in Torah (Psalm 19:7-14).[58] As Craigie notes in his commentary:

> The poet draws out the paradox of "inaudible noise." On the one hand there is no speech, no noise from a literal or acoustic perspective (v. 4); on the other hand, there is a voice that penetrates to the furthest corners of the earth. The poet conveys something of the subtlety of nature's praise of God: it is there, yet its perception is contingent upon the observer. To the sensitive, the heavenly praise of God's glory may be an overwhelming experience, whereas to the insensitive, sky is simply sky and stars are only stars; they point to nothing beyond. In this hymn of praise, it is not the primary purpose of the psalmist to draw upon nature as a vehicle of revelation, or as a source of the knowledge of God apart from the revelation in law (or Torah v. 8); indeed, there is more than a suggestion that the reflection of God's praise in the universe is perceptible only to those already sensitive to God's revelation and purpose.[59]

Here we witness a wonderful unity to God's revelation in creation and Torah, but a unity in which there is not only a definite qualitative difference between the two modes of revelation, but also an inseparability and "order," which presupposes that it is only in context of special revelation and salvation that God's general revelation of himself in creation can be truly understood. This is Hoffmeier's conclusion in his close textual work on the psalm:

> In the second paragraph, the divine name occurs six times, and a seventh is found in the closing prayer. The absence of the divine name in the opening section as compared to the ubiquity in 19:7-11 is poignant. . . . The association of the divine name in this psalm, first with the law (19:7) and then with the salvific terms in v. 14, suggests that salvation derives from a covenant relationship with *YHWH*.[60]

A delicate balance is necessary in the need to affirm both the objectivity of gen-

---

[58]Ibid.
[59]Peter Craigie, *Psalms 1-50*, Word Biblical Commentary (Waco, Tex.: Word, 1983), p. 181.
[60]Hoffmeier, "'The Heavens Declare the Glory of God,'" pp. 21ff.

eral revelation and the subjectivity of its appropriation, rejecting both those who wish to construct a natural theology apart from special revelation and those who contend that no revelation is communicated through nature. In his own exposition of the nature psalms and what they teach with regard to general revelation, Berkouwer argues that it is fundamental that we understand the nature psalms within the context of the already regenerated, redeemed, and particular community of Israel:

> What does this special attention for the cosmic mean *in the realm of the salvation of the Lord?* Because *this* is unconditionally evident, that nature is not seen isolated from the salvation of the God of Israel. With the psalms on nature we touch upon Israel's psalmodies and upon the songs of praise of *the Lord's people.*[61]
>
> It is wholly justified when again and again it is emphasised that it is *Israel* that sings these psalms. In this emphasis the characteristic principle is distinguished which in all correct *evaluation* of creation is of decisive importance. The thing which is needed here is *eyes* which are able to see and discover. And there are those that seeing, do *not* see. *Israel* does hear the voice of God in nature and in the thunderstorm. . . . This understanding, and seeing, and hearing, is possible only in the communion with him, in the enlightening of the eyes by the salvation of God, and by the Word of the Lord. But this seeing and hearing is *not* a *projection* of the believing subject, but an actual *finding*, and *seeing*, and *hearing!* Here nothing is "read into" but it is only an *understanding* of the *reality* of revelation.[62]

Having noted this need for subjective illumination, we must not lose the objective nature of this creation revelation, which is still a *universal* declaration. Verse 4 conveys this objectivity, for the handiwork is God's "line," as in a measuring line, which is universally revealed. This term is often associated with God's justice and judgment; "the 'line' of God's revelation through creation could thus conceivably be interpreted to signify a measuring rod which brings his justice to bear upon the nations in agreement with how they interact with it."[63]

Romans 1:18-32. With the psalmist's words echoing in our ears, we continue drawing our portrait as we return to the seminal passage of Romans 1:18-32. Some general comments are in order. First, in terms of the overall flow of argument in this section, I remain unconvinced by John Sanders et al. that this is a "boundary marker dispute" rather than that of "works righteousness." Rather Paul is moving, as Moo outlines, "inward through a series of concentric circles: from the whole of humanity (Rom 1:18), to humanity apart from special revelation—mainly, then, Gentiles (Rom 1:19-32), to the 'righteous' person—but mainly the

---

[61]G. C. Berkouwer, *General Revelation* (Grand Rapids: Eerdmans, 1955), p. 128.
[62]Ibid., pp. 131-32, italics original.
[63]Christopher R. Little, *The Revelation of God Among the Unevangelized* (Pasadena, Calif.: William Carey Library, 2000), pp. 13-14.

Jew (Rom 2:1-16), to the Jew explicitly (Rom 2:17–3:8)"[64] placing all under the condemnation of God. With regard to those who only have access to general revelation, I fail to see Paul's line of argumentation being positive and optimistic, but rather deeply negative and pessimistic, a line Paul's Jewish readers would all agree on, but which, as Schreiner notes, is Paul's strategy: "Paul attacked the Gentiles first, and while the Jews are saying 'amen' he shockingly indicts them as well."[65]

Second, I wish to respond to the cluster of arguments put forward by Tiessen, Clark and Erickson who are critical of a "restrictivist eisegesis" in traditional interpretations of this passage, which claim a blanket universal condemnation and, which for them, Paul never positively asserts. As Clark summarizes:

> The claim that natural revelation renders one without excuse but cannot save is not required by Romans 1:18-23, although it is consistent with it. Romans 1:18-32 is also consistent with the claim that natural revelation fails to bring salvation to those who are rebellious and wicked, but potentially leads to salvation for those who respond to it. Romans 1:18-32 is therefore circumstantial evidence for the traditional Reformed view. And those who find it demonstrative do so because they assume on some other ground that only those with special revelation can be saved.[66]

While I agree with Clark that the case both for and against the salvific sufficiency of general revelation is not built on this one text alone, again and simply at the level of overview this "softening" of Paul's position would seem to go directly against the flow of argument in this section:

> To posit that anyone could experience the saving righteousness of God through natural revelation would run roughshod over the intention of this text. The conclusion of this section (Rom. 3:9-20) demonstrates that sin exercises universal power. The argument is not that most people are under the power of sin, but that all people, without exception, are under the dominion of sin. Faith becomes a reality only through the preached word (10:14-17).[67]

Tiessen's and Clark's "implicit" and "inferential" reading of this text seems to me to be a defensive move that seeks to neuter a strong argument against their position rather than offer a positive argument for their position. We might ask what is motivating their hermeneutic here. Underlying their exegesis appears to be an uneasiness with the implication that God is unjust if he gives sufficient revelation to condemn but not sufficient revelation to save. Revelation that condemns must also have the potential to save. While I intend to come back to this issue later on,

---

[64]Douglas Moo, *The Epistle to the Romans* (Grand Rapids: Eerdmans, 1996), p. 92.
[65]Thomas R. Schreiner, *Romans* (Grand Rapids: Baker, 1998), p. 82.
[66]Clark, "Is Special Revelation Necessary for Salvation?" pp.40-41.
[67]Schreiner, *Romans*, pp. 85-86.

in terms of a reading of Romans 1:18-32, the problem for Tiessen, Clark, Erickson et al. is that an "explicit," "natural" reading appears to focus *only* on the condemnatory function of general revelation. There is no mention of salvation here. But *must* salvation be an implicit potentiality in general revelation? Turretin argues not, for there is fundamental asymmetry between condemnation and salvation:

> That which is sufficient to render inexcusable does not therefore suffice for salvation if used properly; for more things are requisite for the obtainment of salvation than for incurring damnation justly and without excuse. For evil arises from some defect, but the good requires a whole cause. For example, he who offends in one point is guilty of all (Jam. 2:10); but not, therefore, he who does well in one point is just in all. The commission of one sin can render a man inexcusable, but the performance of one good work is not sufficient to save him. Thus the Gentiles were inexcusable because they substituted gods without number in place of that one God whom they could know from the light of nature; but we cannot infer from this that the knowledge of one God is sufficient absolutely for salvation. Thus this inexcusableness must be restricted to the subject matter of which the apostle treats (viz., to idolatry), which was sufficient for their condemnation, although the avoidance of it would not suffice for their salvation.[68]

Moving onto more detailed comments on Romans 1:18-32 we can learn from the Dutch missiologist J. H. Bavinck who brilliantly exegetes this passage within the larger context of his expertise in the theology of religions and a life spent studying and interacting with the religious other on the mission field.[69]

In terms of content, what are we to understand by "God's eternal power and divine nature" (Rom 1:20)? There is true knowledge of God manifested but it is of a "general" and limited kind. Visser summarises Bavinck's thinking at this point.

> God's invisible qualities refer to God's virtues, to that which is inaccessible to human eyes. His "eternal power" and "divine nature" denote the two virtues which determine the essential relationship of man to God. The term "eternal power" points to the fact that God is the bearer of all things, that man lives by the might of God, and this that man's relationship to God is one of total dependency. The concept "divine nature" signifies the wholly otherness of God which always entails an I-Thou relationship, a relationship of responsibility between man and God.[70]

---

[68]Francis Turretin, *Institutes of Elenctic Theology*, 3 vols. (Phillipsburg, N.J.: Presbyterian & Reformed, 1992), 1:12.

[69]See J. H. Bavinck, *The Church Between Temple and Mosque* (Grand Rapids: Eerdmans, 1966); idem, *An Introduction to the Science of Missions* (Grand Rapids: Baker, 1960); idem, "General Revelation and the Non-Christian Religions," *Free University Quarterly* 4 (1944): 43-55.

[70]Paul J. Visser, *Heart for the Gospel, Heart for the World: The Life and Thought of a Reformed Pioneer Missiologist Johan Herman Bavinck (1895-1964)* (Eugene, Ore.: Wipf & Stock, 2003), p. 122.

This corresponds well to the heaviness of glory of Psalm 19:1. Added to this is the nature of general revelation. Here Bavinck stresses its dynamic, personal and relational character.

> The Greek *nooumena*, literally "being intelligently observed," emphasises that seeing with the eye is not intended in this verse; but at the same time it does not mean that seeing God's everlasting power and Godhead is attained by a process of reasoning. It is reached not as a logical conclusion, but in a moment of vision. It suddenly comes upon a person; it overwhelms him.[71]
>
> If we wish to use the expression "general revelation" we must not do so in the sense that one can conclude God's existence from it. This may be logically possible, but it only leads to a philosophical notion of God as the first cause. But that is not the biblical idea of general revelation. When the Bible speaks of general revelation it means something quite different. There it has a much more personal nature. It is divine concern for men collectively and individually. God's deity and eternal power are evident; they overwhelm man; they strike him suddenly, in moments when he thought they were far away. They creep up on him; they do not let go of him, even though man does his best to escape them.[72]

What is mankind's reaction to this revelation? The first thing to note is that there is a reaction; general revelation "does not simply slide off man ineffectually like a raindrop glides off a waxy leaf tree."[73] Visser comments:

> In Bavinck's view, when God manifests himself to man through general revelation, man becomes knowledgeable in a *de jure* (juridical) sense but proves, in that revelatory encounter with God, to be so profoundly sinful that *de facto* (actual) attainment of knowledge does not occur. Man "is a knower who does not know, a perceiver who does not perceive."[74]

Here Bavinck focuses on Paul's use of the words "suppression" *(katechontōn)* and "exchange" *(allassō/metallassō)*. Again it is important to note the dynamic nature of what is going on. Suppression carries with it the sense of violently holding down. The sinner constantly suppresses general revelation and is therefore without excuse. One illustration might be that of a child playing with an inflatable ball in the water. He tries to push the ball under the water with all his might and thinks he has succeeded, but the ball always pops up to the surface again for the child to try again, and so on. Here is the "game" between revelation and suppression. Bavinck notes "this repression occurs so immediately, so spontaneously, so si-

[71]Bavinck, *Church Between Temple and Mosque*, p. 120.
[72]Ibid., p. 124.
[73]Visser, *Heart for the Gospel*, p. 142.
[74]Ibid., p. 144. He is quoting Bavinck from *Religiieus besef en christelijk geloof* [Religious Consciousness and Christian Faith] (Kampen, 1949) still not translated into English.

multaneously with understanding a perception that at the very same moment he sees, he no longer sees, at the very moment he knows, he no longer knows."[75]

Along with suppression comes substitution. General revelation is not obliterated totally but rather perverted, twisted and distorted, "the sparse, totally decontextualized elements deriving from it that do manage to stick in the conscious mind form nuclei around which complexes of a totally deviant nature crystallize."[76] Here Bavinck evocatively uses the illustration of dreaming:

> In the dreaming state, too, all sorts of objective and real phenomena, such as the sound of running water in an eaves trough, the flash of the headlights of a car going by, the rumble of a train passing in the distance, or the monotonous ticking of an alarm clock, are registered but immediately torn out of context, endlessly magnified, and turned into fulcrums for chains of thought which differ radically from the reality of the phenomena which occasioned them. In the world of dreams we see the processes of "repression" and "substitution" in intimate association. Reality is smothered and at one and the same time this muted reality manifests created power. The result is one huge fantasy, a colourful collection of confused images from which the objective elements on which they are built can be disentangled with only the very greatest of difficulty.[77]

Finally in his exposition, Bavinck adds a crucial nuance to his argument. While all humanity is guilty of suppression and substitution, there is no uniformity but a great variety in the depth of suppression and substitution. The reason for such variation is not the "goodness" of man but rather the restraining grace of God through the operation of the Holy Spirit:

> The history of religion is not always and everywhere the same; it does not present a monotonous picture of only folly and degeneration. There are culminating points in it, not because human beings are much better than others, but because every now and then divine compassion interferes, compassion which keeps man from suppressing and substituting the truth completely.[78]

Romans 2:14-16. I would suggest that the epistemological paradigm outlined above can be applied to and make sense of the much discussed Romans 2:14-16. Sanders claims that Paul is here talking about those who demonstrate saving faith outside the boundaries of the visible church. But again the text, as well as context, seems to lead in precisely the opposite direction. In terms of context the universality and depth of sin is pervasive throughout this section of the letter and both

---

[75]Bavinck, *Religiieus besef en christelijk geloof,* p. 172; quoted in Visser, *Heart for the Gospel,* p. 145.
[76]Bavinck, *Religiieus besef en christelijk geloof,* p. 179; quoted in Visser, *Heart for the Gospel,* p. 146.
[77]Visser, *Heart for the Gospel,* p. 145.
[78]Bavinck, *Church Between Temple and Mosque,* p. 126.

begins (Rom 1:18) and ends Paul's argument (Rom 3:20). Moo (*contra*
Snodgrass)[79] argues that for Paul even to argue for a grace inspired "works-based"
(as opposed to a "flesh-based") soteriology would be inconsistent with the climax
of his argument in chapter 3, where he stresses justification by faith alone and by
grace alone. Moo says, "Romans 2 cannot mean that people are saved apart from
faith or apart from the gospel."[80]

If this passage is not referring to salvation, then to what is it referring? There
are two dominant ways to understand this text, both of which rule out a soteriologically inclusivist/accessibilist position. Some commentators argue that Paul is
talking about Gentile Christians[81] (which would, of course, invalidate the inclusivist argument), but I am still persuaded that Paul is referring to Gentile unbelievers who do not have special revelation but general revelation, in terms of morality, which condemns and does not save:

> As sinners, these Gentiles seek to keep down the testimony of the Spirit of God within
> and about them. Even so, as in the case of knowledge (Rom. 1:20) so in the case of
> morality (Rom. 2:14, 15), he cannot wholly keep the Spirit's testimony from being ef-
> fective. There is an incidental and involuntary conformity to some of the requirements
> of the law in their moral reactions. . . . Paul does not here say that the law is written in
> the hearts of men. It is true that they have the law written in their hearts. Their own
> make-up as image-bearers of God tells them, as it were, in the imperative voice, that
> they must act as such. All of God's revelation to man is law to man. But here we deal
> with man's response as an ethical being to this revelation of God. All men, says Paul,
> to some extent, do the *works* of the law. He says that they have the *works* of the law
> written in their hearts. Without a true motive, without a true purpose, they may still
> do that which externally appears to be acts of obedience to God's law. God continues
> to press his demands upon man, and man is good "after a fashion" just as he "knows
> after a fashion."[82]

> The natural man accuses or else excuses himself only because his own utterly de-
> praved consciousness continues to point back to the original state of affairs. The prod-
> igal son can never forget the father's voice. It is the albatross forever about his neck.[83]

---

[79]Klyne R. Snodgrass, "Justification By Grace—to the Doers: An Analysis of the Place of Romans 2
in the Theology of Paul," *New Testament Studies* 32 (1986): 72-93.

[80]Douglas Moo, "Romans 2: Saved Apart from the Gospel?" in *Through No Fault of Their Own?* p. 140.

[81]For example, C. E. B. Cranfield, *A Critical and Exegetical Commentary on the Epistle to the Romans*,
ICC, 2 vols. (Edinburgh: T & T Clark, 1975), 2:159-63; N. T. Wright, "Romans," in *The New Interpreter's Bible Commentary*, vol. 10 (Nashville: Abingdon, 2002), pp. 441-42. For a fuller discussion,
see Little, *The Revelation of God Among the Unevangelized*, pp. 34-40.

[82]Cornelius Van Til, *An Introduction to Systematic Theology*, vol. 1 (Phillipsburg, N.J.: Presbyterian &
Reformed, 1974), p. 105.

[83]Cornelius Van Til, "Nature and Scripture," in *The Infallible Word: A Symposium*, ed. N. B. Stonehouse
and Paul Woolley (Phillipsburg, N.J.: Presbyterian & Reformed, 1946), p. 275.

Romans 10: 9, 14-18. Finally we come to Romans 10:9, 14-18. That we are subjecting this passage to scrutiny may seem somewhat perverse, for as Tiessen himself notes, "it is a text that has been widely used within the evangelical tradition of missionary motivation to argue for the necessity of the preaching of the gospel for people to be saved."[84] However, as already described above, Sanders, Tiessen, and Mangum all make use of this text in various ways to support their claims concerning the possibility of salvation through general revelation. What are we to make of their exegeses? Before we consider verses 14-18, I wish to briefly reiterate both Nash's and Carson's critique of Sanders's argument regarding verse 9—"That if you confess with your mouth, 'Jesus is Lord,' and believe in your heart that God raised him from the dead, you will be saved" does not necessarily entail that those who do not confess will not be saved because "If A, then B" does not necessarily mean "If not A, then not B."[85] Nash and Carson note that such logic is sound *except* if all members of A are precisely identical to all members of B, then "If not A (if you do not confess with your mouth) then not B (you will not be saved)." Carson continues:

> In other words, what Sanders has done is *assume* that the two classes do not precisely coincide—which is, of course, nothing other than assuming his conclusion. Of course, exclusivists for their part must not simply assume the opposite. But in fact, it can be shown that the perfect coincidence of the two classes is precisely what Paul presupposes. This is clear not only from Paul's treatment of the entire biblical story-line, but from this chapter of the epistle to the Romans. . . . For Paul, it is impossible to call on the true God without believing in Jesus.[86]

Regarding verses 14-18, and not unlike the other passages in Romans we have considered, there are some possible legitimate variations in interpretation among evangelical biblical scholars. But it is my contention that, even from within these different readings, Paul is not speaking of the possibility of salvation through general revelation.

First, we must consider the context of these verses and to whom Paul is referring. Sander's and Erickson's isolation of verse 18 (Paul's use of Psalm 19:4) to argue for a "gospel according to nature,"[87] whereby one can be ontologically saved by Christ while being epistemologically unaware of Christ, depends on the focus being on Gentiles (who have no access to special revelation). However, the major

---

[84]Tiessen, *Who Can Be Saved?* p. 265.

[85]See Ronald Nash, *Is Jesus the Only Savior?* (Grand Rapids: Zondervan, 1994), pp. 144-45; D. A. Carson, *The Gagging of God: Christianity Confronts Pluralism* (Grand Rapids: Zondervan, 1996), pp. 312-13.

[86]Ibid., p. 313.

[87]This is Little's phrase in *Revelation of God Among the Unevangelized*, p. 40.

contemporary evangelical commentaries on Romans all argue that Paul is referring to either Israelites exclusively or primarily. If this is the case then this passage becomes somewhat irrelevant to our discussion because Israelites are not only recipients of general revelation but of special revelation. This is Little's position:

> The Jews had heard the gospel through special revelation. Initially, they received it in their own scriptures before Paul's missionary activity ever began. It was presented to them in Isa. 53, the same book which Paul quotes, years before. They may not have understood it, but nevertheless, they did hear it. This is why Paul can retort: "But I say, surely they have never heard, have they? Indeed they have." And ultimately, they hear the gospel through the widespread apostolic ministry of Paul and others.[88]

Second, and with the above in mind, we must comment on Paul's use in Romans 10:18 of Psalm 19:4, a section of the psalm that, we already argued, refers to God's general revelation. Is Paul referring here to general revelation? Is Paul saying that through a gracious work of the Spirit there is enough information in general revelation for people to be saved? We recall that according to Mangum, although Paul seems to have restricted the means to salvation to the hearing of the gospel through a human messenger in verses 13-15, Paul's quoting of Psalm 19, reopens the possibility of salvation through general revelation in verse 18.

Again this abrupt change of direction in Paul's flow of argument appears totally unnatural and out of context with Paul's argument. To my mind the most persuasive exegeses argue that Paul is not using Psalm 19 to directly refer to general revelation (while noting that there are degrees of hesitancy as to just how Paul *is* using the psalm). Here I note the comments of Moo, Murray and Wright regarding this verse, which are all variations on a theme:

> The implied object of the verb "heard" in Paul's question must be "the word of Christ"; "their voice" and "their words" in the Psalm verse must then refer to the voices and words of Christian preachers. . . . Paul is not, then, simply using the text according to its original meaning. His application probably rests on a general analogy: as God's word of general revelation has been proclaimed all over the earth, so God's word of special revelation in the gospel, has been spread all over the earth. His intention is not to interpret the verse of the Psalm, but to use its language, with the "echoes" of God's revelation that it awakes, to assert the universal preaching of the gospel.[89]

> It has raised a difficulty that the psalmist here speaks of the work of creation and providence and not to special revelation. Was this due to a lapse of memory or to in-

[88]See ibid., p. 41.
[89]Moo, *Epistle to the Romans*, pp. 666-67.

tentional artifice? It is not necessary to resort to either supposition. We should remember that this psalm deals with general revelation (vss. 1-6) and with special
revelation (vss. 7-14). In the esteem of the psalmist and in the teaching of Scripture
throughout these two areas of revelation are complementary. This is Paul's own conception (cf. Acts 17:24-31). Since the gospel proclamation is now to all without distinction, it is proper to see the universality of general revelation and the unity of the
gospel. The former is the pattern now followed in the sounding forth of the gospel
to the uttermost parts of the earth. The application which Paul makes of Psalm 19:4
can thus be seen to be eloquent not only with this parallel but also of that which is
implicit in the parallel, namely the widespread diffusion of the gospel of grace.[90]

It is also possible that, if Paul has the rest of Psalm 19 in mind, he may have taken
vv. 1-6, as well as vv. 7-11, as referring to Torah, in which case he could be celebrating the fact that the "word" of Deut. 30:14 was not freely available to all, as God always intended. This link between the occurrences of *rhēma in vv. 8* and 17-18 seems
to point in this direction.[91]

Finally I wish to simply note Tiessen's use of this passage in his accessibilist
case. Unlike others we have mentioned, he does not attempt to relate this passage
to general revelation. Rather his appeal is to the *irrelevancy* of this passage in the
debate, attempting to counter those who wish to use verse 15 to argue for the necessity of a human messenger to proclaim the word of Christ. His conclusion is
that verse 15 is not a normative principle but refers to a particular historical
context:

> Paul's point is that Israel is without excuse for their failure to experience the "right-
> eousness that is by faith" in Jesus because the gospel was taken to them by divinely
> commissioned preachers and they refused to believe. Paul is not making a statement
> about whether they would have been guilty of unbelief if they had not heard the gos-
> pel. The point is that they *did* hear it and so they were guilty.[92]

Regarding Psalm 19:4, Tiessen states, "Paul does not quote it as a proof-text or
as a fulfilled prophecy (note the absence of specific reference to Scripture), but he
uses the words to refer to the Christian mission of the diaspora."[93]

Perhaps what is most surprising here is that Tiessen cites Calvin in support of
his exegesis:

> John Calvin's commentary on Romans 10:14 is both interesting and significant.
> Calvin observes that it is "necessary to have the word, that we have a right knowledge

[90]John Murray, *The Epistle to the Romans* (Grand Rapids: Eerdmans, 1968), 2:61.
[91]Wright, "Romans," p. 669.
[92]Tiessen, *Who Can Be Saved?* p. 268. His quotations from Calvin are taken from *Calvin's Commentaries* (Wilmington, Del.: Associates Publishers & Authors, n.d), pp. 1469-70, italics original.
[93]Tiessen, *Who Can Be Saved?* p. 267.

of God." But notice how Calvin continues: "No other word has he mentioned here but that which is preached, because it is the *ordinary* mode which the Lord has appointed for conveying his word. But were any on this account to contend that God cannot transfer to men the knowledge of himself, except by the instrumentality of preaching, we deny that to teach this was the Apostle's intention; for he had in view the *ordinary* dispensation of God, and did not intend to prescribe a law for the distribution of his grace." . . . To insist that Romans 10:14-15 teaches an exclusive instrumentality of the preached gospel on God's saving program would require one to deny that saving faith is ever elicited by the many instances of God's direct encounter with individuals.[94]

Joining the exegetical dots. Let us start to join up some of these exegetical points in our portrait of general revelation. The first characteristic to note about general revelation, as it pertains to God's revelation in nature—before we take into consideration the debilitating effects of sin—is that general revelation is a revelation of God's works and that, as a mode or instrument of God "speaking," works by themselves are hermeneutically ambiguous needing further revelatory supplementation to make them clear. I would assert that Psalm 19 is a microcosm of the symbiotic relationship between general and special revelation. My purpose is not to drive a wedge between general and special revelation or to denigrate God's general revelation but simply to note that God's purpose in general revelation has never been for it to function independently of his "worded" special revelation. God's "words" have always been needed to interpret and supplement God's "works." This important insight was made by Vos, elaborated by Van Til, and brought out well by Peter Leithart in his analysis and mild critique of Calvin's view of natural law, which occupies the same theological territory. In *Institutes* 1.4.1 Calvin states: "As experience shows, God has sown a seed of religion in all men, but scarcely one man in a hundred is met with who fosters it, once received, in his heart, and none in whom it ripens—much less shows fruit in season."[95] Leithart comments thus:

> Calvin's reference to "scarcely one man in a hundred" should be understood as "no one"; the whole thrust of Calvin's argument in the opening chapters of the *Institutes* is that no man can, without the aid of special revelation, be fruitful in the knowledge of God. Still, implicit in his argument is the belief that theoretically (*si integer stetisset Adam*) men could have arrived at a true and proper knowledge and worship of God by nourishing the innate seed alone. Theoretically, the innate knowledge of God and general revelation are sufficient for a true and obedient knowledge of him.
>
> Contrary to the implications of Calvin's statement, it is clear from Scripture that

[94]Ibid., pp. 267-68.
[95]John Calvin, *Institutes of the Christian Religion*, trans. Ford Lewis Battles, 2 vols (Philadelphia: Westminster Press, 1960), 1.4.1.

supernatural revelation, special revelation was necessary even before the Fall. Adam could never have deduced the prohibition on the tree of knowledge either from his innate knowledge or from the appearance of the tree itself. . . . One inference to be drawn is that general revelation was never intended to function without special revelation. Looking at the issue from another direction, special revelation is necessary not in the contingent sense that the incarnation is necessary, special revelation is absolutely necessary to man as man. Without special revelation, even prelapsarian Adam would not have been able fully to obey and know God or correctly interpret the world around him. Calvin, however, tied his doctrine of Scripture, and hence his doctrine of special revelation, so closely to the Fall, that he failed to see the absolute necessity of special revelation. Or, to put it more whimsically, Calvin had not read the works of Geerhardus Vos and therefore lacked a category of "preredemptive" special revelation.

The consequences of this oversight for Calvin's theology as a whole are quite significant. By failing to recognise the necessity of special revelation in the prelapsarian situation, Calvin granted general revelation a degree of autonomy that Scripture itself never permits.[96]

General revelation lacks the specificity of special revelation. God's words have always been needed to interpret, supplement and therefore compliment God's works; these two modes of revelation were never meant to be separated from one another or to work independently of each other.

This is not all, though, for this objective epistemological insufficiency of general revelation becomes intensely more acute after the Fall. First, there is an increased complexity and potential hermeneutical ambiguity in the objective external revelation; for what is revealed now is not only God's glory and goodness but his wrath and judgment as well (Rom 1:18). Second, this revelation of wrath is revealed both externally in the world and internally within mankind. Here we must keep in mind both God's original judgment in linear history from the Fall of Adam and Eve, and also the present continuing cyclical nature of God's wrath in his "handing over": "God does not simply let the boat go—he gives it a push down downstream. Like a judge who hands over a prisoner to the punishment his crime has earned, God hands over the sinner to the terrible cycle of ever-increasing sin."[97] For those with eyes to see, both blessing and wrath reveal God, but for those dead in sin, the wicked suppression and substitution of God's blessing and wrath in general revelation means that they do not truly know God—even as Creator. As Van Til notes:

---

[96]Peter J. Leithart, "That Eminent Pagan: Calvin's Use of Cicero in *Institutes* 1.1-5," *Westminster Theological Journal* 52 (1990): 12-13.
[97]Moo, *Epistle to the Romans*, p. 111.

It is accordingly no easier for sinners to accept God's revelation in nature than to accept God's revelation in Scripture. They are no more ready of themselves to do the one than to do the other. From the point of the view of the sinner, theism is as objectionable as Christianity. Theism that is worthy of the name is Christian theism. Christ said that no man can come to the Father but by him. No one can become a theist unless he becomes a Christian. Any God that is not the Father of our Lord Jesus Christ is not God but an idol. It is therefore the Holy Spirit bearing witness by and with the Word in our hearts that alone effects the required Copernican revolution and makes us both Christians and theists.[98]

After the Fall what sinners need is the regenerating power of the gospel to know God as Creator and Redeemer, and general revelation is an inappropriate vehicle because knowledge of the gospel of our Lord Jesus Christ is not contained in it: "Man the sinner, as Calvin puts it, through the testimony of the Spirit receives a new power of sight by which he can appreciate the new light given in Scripture. The new light and the new power of sight imply one another. The one is fruitless for salvation without the other."[99] Greg Johnson echoes this:

> Special revelation is needed because special grace is needed. An intense knowledge of one's own unworthiness and a determination to do better, even *with* the gospel is not salvific. Faith must be consciously placed in the gospel of Jesus. The difference here is the difference between knowing the standard for which man was made and receiving God's provision for the standard breaker. It is the difference between law and gospel.[100]

Turretin does as well (with reference to Rom 1):

> It is falsely asserted that in that which may be known of God . . . there is given objectively a revelation of grace, and a Redeemer sufficient for salvation, if not clear and explicit, at least obscure and implied, inasmuch as in it God is known as merciful and therefore, in a certain although confused manner, as a Redeemer who will accept a satisfaction, may call to repentance and promise remission of sin. For in the first place, to be able to know God as merciful by a general mercy tending to some temporal good and delay of punishment is far different from being able to know him as merciful by a mercy special and saving in Christ after a satisfaction has been made. To be able to know him as placable and benign is different from being able to know him as actually to be appeased or certainly to be appeased.[101]

Unlike special revelation, general revelation simply does not contain the truth

---

[98]Van Til, "Nature and Scripture," p. 280.
[99]Ibid., p. 281.
[100]Greg Johnson, "The Inadequacy of General Revelation for the Salvation of the Nations" (1996): <http://gregscouch.homestead.com/files/Generalrev.html> (accessed January 23, 2007).
[101]Turretin, *Institutes*, 1:12.

content necessary for saving faith and so is not an appropriate vehicle for the Spirit's saving work of regeneration.[102]

Looking at the bigger picture. What then is the purpose of general revelation if it is not salvific? Here, once more, fundamental theological presuppositions come into play. I am working within an understanding that affirms both exhaustive divine foreordination and human responsibility. Considered independently the purpose of general revelation is unclear, but when related to special revelation and the wider purposes of God it serves a crucial purpose. On this point Van Til's analysis is particularly helpful. First, he notes the "problem" associated with the "dividing" of God's revelation, a criticism made, ironically, by both Sanders and Pinnock in their inclusivist frameworks:

> The first point that calls for reflection here, is the fact that it is, according to Scripture itself, the same God who reveals himself in nature and in grace. . . . Contemplation of this fact seems at once to plunge us into great difficulty . . . saving grace is not manifest in nature; yet it is the God of saving grace who manifests himself by means of nature. How can these two be harmonized? The answer to this problem must be found in the fact that God is "eternal, incomprehensible, most free, most absolute." Any revelation of himself that God gives of himself is therefore absolutely voluntary. Herein precisely lies the union of the various forms of God's revelation with one another. God's revelation in nature, together with God's revelation in Scripture, form God's one grand scheme of covenant revelation of himself to man. The two forms of revelation must therefore be seen as presupposing and supplementing one another. They are aspects of one general philosophy of history.[103]

This philosophy of history concerns the historical "process of differentiation that works toward redemption and reprobation."[104] In other words the purpose of general revelation is to provide the background or scaffolding for God's redemption in Christ: "here then is the picture of a well-integrated and unified philosophy

---

[102]Faith cannot maintain its fully orbed character of *notitia, fiducia,* and *assensus* if the object changes from Christ to God, as it is a knowledge of who Christ is and what he has done that defines saving faith. Looking outside ourselves to the objective work of Christ tells us also something of the role of faith and its efficacy. As John Murray writes: "It is to be remembered that the efficacy of faith does not reside in itself. Faith is not something that merits the favour of God. All the efficacy unto salvation resides in the Saviour, . . . it is not faith that saves but faith in Jesus Christ; strictly speaking, it is not even faith in Christ that saves but Christ that saves through faith. Faith unites us to Christ in the bonds of abiding attachment and entrustment and it is this union which insures that the saving power, grace, and virtue of the Saviour become operative in the believer. The specific character of faith is that it looks away from itself and finds its whole interest and object in Christ. He is the absorbing preoccupation of faith." John Murray, *Redemption Accomplished and Applied* (Grand Rapids: Eerdmans, 1955), p. 112.
[103]Van Til, "Nature and Scripture," p. 266.
[104]Ibid., p. 268.

of history in which revelation in nature and revelation in Scripture are mutually meaningless without one another and mutually fruitful when taken together."[105] Mirroring the traditional qualities of Scripture, Van Til goes on to speak about the necessity, authority, sufficiency, and perspicuity of general revelation. What Van Til says about the sufficiency of general revelation is particularly pertinent. Natural revelation was never meant to function by itself and was insufficient without special revelation. But it was historically sufficient:

> After the Fall of man natural revelation is still historically sufficient. It is sufficient for such as have in Adam brought the curse of God upon nature. It is sufficient to render them without excuse. Those who are in prison and cannot clearly see the light of the sun receive their due inasmuch as they have first abused the light. . . . At every stage in history God's revelation in nature is sufficient for the purpose it was meant to serve, that of being the playground of differentiation between those who would and those who would not serve God.[106]

Here we must return to Romans 1:20 "so that men are without excuse." Exegetically the preposition *eis* can be interpreted in a consecutive sense ("so that") and so the clause is one of result: "the meaning is then that man is without excuse as an immanent consequence of his conduct: though having eyes to see and ears to hear, people fail to see and hear, therefore they are without excuse."[107] Alternatively, the *eis* could be final ("in order that"), which would make the clause one of purpose: "The sense would be that God reveals himself in order that man would not be able to plead ignorance, that he discloses himself with the aim of making it impossible for people to have an excuse for failing to recognise what can be known about him. He wants those who do not acknowledge him to be bereft of any alibi for their behaviour."[108] In his commentary, Murray takes *eis* as indicating result rather than design, although he still helpfully notes God's overall sovereignty:

> Objection to this view fails to take account of the benignity and sufficiency of the revelation which renders men inexcusable. The giving of revelation *sufficient* to constrain men to worship and glorify the Creator and given with the design that they would be without excuse, if they failed to glorify, cannot be unworthy of God. Besides, even if we regard the clause in question as expressing result rather than design, we cannot eliminate from the all-inclusive ordination and providence of God the design which is presupposed on the actual result. If inexcusableness is the result, it is the designed result from the aspect of decretive ordination.[109]

---

[105]Ibid., p. 269.
[106]Ibid.
[107]Visser, *Heart for the Gospel*, p. 131.
[108]Ibid.
[109]Murray, *Epistle to the Romans*, 1:40.

Standing back and looking at general revelation from the perspective of God's "all-inclusive ordination and providence" is helpful. I think it suggests a possible answer to the protest (raised by Sanders in synergist form and Mangum in monergist form) that those who only have general revelation are "damned if they do, and damned if they don't," a point even Paul Helm in his sympathetic analysis of Calvin calls a "logical oddity or curiosity," when looking at Calvin's commentary on Acts 17.[110]

The question of those who never hear the gospel is often emotively framed as those who do not hear "through no fault of their own." This claim rests on the assumption that those without special revelation are not responsible for their lack of special revelation, hence the pressure falls on general revelation to provide sufficient knowledge. However, I would like to suggest that both theologically and historically the precise opposite is true. In light of what we have noted about the nature of general revelation and its inseparability from and meaning within God's special revelation, we are in a position to suggest some implications regarding those in the history of the world who potentially[111] have *only* had access to general revelation. If general revelation and special revelation were, in the preceptive will of God, always meant to be understood together before the Fall, and if special revelation is even more necessary after the Fall to correct and interpret general revelation, then *if* there are those in history who *only* have general revelation, are they not those who have fallen outside of God's preceptive (but not decretive) will? Despite protests as to the narrowness of those who fall within special revelation, historically speaking we have seen that there was a time when special revelation was indeed as universally known and accessible as general revelation.[112] The entrance of sin has consequences for the accessibility of revelation. In the sovereign providence of God, he has preserved and sustained redemptive knowledge of himself within some streams of humanity and not within others. McDermott (from Edwards) is right to talk of a religious law of entropy:

> Throughout the work of redemption, degeneration set in whenever progress was made. By what I have called religious entropy, the revelations given to human beings were immediately and then continually attacked by corruption and distortion. God's intermittent recharging of the battery of revelation, as it were, was inevitably followed by loss of religious energy. The final result of thousands of years of such renovation and destruction was an entire world of heathen peoples hopelessly lost in idolatry.[113]

---

[110]Paul Helm, *John Calvin's Ideas* (New York: Oxford University Press, 2004), p. 215.
[111]For what I mean by "potentially," please see below.
[112]This is *contra* Richardson.
[113]McDermott, *Jonathan Edwards Confronts the Gods*, p. 97.

Romans 1:18-32 shows us the "inner workings" of all this. In humanity's universal but variegated suppression of the truth, God has judicially "let go" and "given over" peoples according to his purposes. Instrumentally the withdrawal of special revelation from a people, with its important corrective to salvifically insufficient general revelation, is already a demonstration of God's righteous judgment, a cyclical degenerative process of sin and judgment continuing over generations. In other words it is precisely "through their own fault" that some may find themselves devoid of special revelation and the gospel. Such an interpretation, of course, requires us to broaden our hermeneutic of Western individualism and to understand that God deals not just with humanity as individuals, but as families, peoples, nations and cultures. There is a corporate responsibility here, the most universal "unity" being our guilt in Adam.

GENERAL REVELATION AS AN INSUFFICIENT CATEGORY?

My intention in this essay has been to demonstrate that general revelation is insufficient for salvation both in terms of its medium and its message. I have also attempted to show the sufficiency of general revelation in the wider purposes of God. Within the framework of exhaustive foreordination and human responsibility, I have argued that if there are people in the world who only have general revelation, then they evidence, in an extreme form, a divine judicial abandonment. In this concluding section I wish to offer three constructive caveats to this thesis, which I hope will nuance what I have already said as well as advance the debate in this area.

First, we must remember that the judgment and punishment of unbelievers is always according to the revelation they have received. Those who have suppressed both general and special revelation will be judged more harshly than those who have received only general revelation. This appears to be the meaning behind texts like Luke 12:47-48 with its "few blows" and "many blows," and also Jesus' words in sending out the seventy-two in Luke 10:12, "I tell you, on that day it will be more tolerable for Sodom than for that town."

My second caveat might appear odd in light of what I have already argued. Throughout this chapter I have been at pains to erect a scaffold that carefully separates and distinguishes general revelation from special revelation. While this separation and distinction is absolutely necessary, there is a sense in which it is somewhat abstract and artificial. Our theological categorization of revelation, general and special, as hermetically sealed compartments can be shown to be rather inadequate. John Frame demonstrates this in his re-categorization of God's revelation from general and special categories into: the word that comes through nature and history, the word that comes through persons, and the word written. Regarding nature and history he notes:

> One thing is lacking in God's revelation through nature. Scripture never indicates that it teaches people the way to salvation. . . . So we might say that nature teaches only law not gospel. Nevertheless, the gospel is revealed through history, specifically through redemptive history, those events in which God saves his people from sin. Those events form the content of gospel preaching. So history as a whole does convey the gospel. But only those in proximity to redemptive events can learn from them the way of salvation.[114]

He expands this point in a footnote:

> On the whole, my category of "revelation given through nature and history" is identical to the traditional category of "general revelation." But there is a difference. Revelation given through nature and history, taken as a whole, includes both law and gospel, for the gospel is a segment of history, that segment we call redemptive history. But general revelation understood in the traditional way, is that portion of God's revelation in nature and history that does not include the gospel. Redemptive history is hard to classify. . . . Since God's revelation in redemptive history is revelation in event, rather than word, we are inclined to want to call it general. But since it has redemptive content, we are inclined to call it special. To some extent these are artificial categories, and it doesn't matter much which we use to describe redemptive history. But we should be aware of the ambiguity of this category of revelation.[115]

Here a complementary historical point can be made. I have already noted the *prisca theologia*, that is, special revelation present from the creation of man, which has been passed from Adam and his progeny down through generations, perverted and distorted yes, but still an echo of true knowledge. Bavinck calls this "proto-

---

[114]John Frame, "The Organism of Revelation," in part 3 of *The Doctrine of the Christian Life*, pp. 127-28:<http://reformedperspectives.org/newfiles/joh_frame/DCL9,_The_Organism_of_Revelation.pdf> (accessed January 23, 2007).

[115]Ibid. Leithart makes a similar point, "The Bible teaches that God reveals His character in creation, in history, and in Scripture. If we wish to know God, we have to seek Him as He has revealed Himself through these media. We cannot know God by peeking 'behind' the screen of history and Scripture; we come to know him *through* His words and works. History, Scripture and creation are the 'books' of God, and if we would know Him we must open the books. There is fuller revelation in one or another of God's books. For example we know about God's provision in Christ from Scripture rather than from creation. Yet it is the same God who writes to us in each. Each book, in fact, is large enough to include the others. If we open God's book of creation, we realize that the creation is not static but in motion, that creation has a history; this God's revelation in creation includes His revelation in history. And since Scripture exists in history, it too forms a chapter in God's book of creation and history. History is the story of God's actions, which manifest His character, and Scripture is largely a record of those actions, that story." Peter Leithart, *Heroes of the City of Man* (Moscow, Idaho: Canon Press: 1999), pp. 33-34.

word" revelation.[116] Added to this is what Bavinck calls the radiation or inflow of special revelation into another religious tradition (e.g., Plato being influenced by the prophets, Thomas preaching in India, Nestorian influence in China),[117] to which I would add the strong possibility that Muhammad came into contact with some form of Christianity.[118] On similar lines, Leithart makes a plausible case that moral consensus between Christians and non-Christians does not originate in general revelation, as is often assumed, but rather originates in a mixture of general and special revelation.[119]

This "messiness" in the history of revelation and the revelation of history means that it is difficult, if not impossible, to excavate the history of a religious tradition and separate out the influence of general revelation and special revelation. I commented earlier on those who have *only* come into contact with general revelation. In light of the influence of special revelation in the history of the world, this may be far less people than often imagined. Because of human suppression and substitution, and without the regenerating work of God, this once true knowledge of God becomes atrophied through a divine providential law of entropy and rather than becoming a means to salvation, it becomes a further basis for judgment. However, this "wideness" and original universality of special revelation means the basis of judgment will be on a rejection of more than just a "pure" form of general revelation. As Van Til comments:

> We have brought the elements of God's revelation in nature as it is now in close re-
> lation to the fact of man's original perfection, as well as with whatever contact the

---

[116]Bavinck, "General Revelation and Non-Christian Religions," p. 51.

[117]Ibid., p. 52.

[118]See Peter Leithart, "Mirror of Christendom": <http://www.marshillaudio.org/resources/pdf/Leithart .pdf> (accessed January 23, 2007).

[119]Leithart's thesis is as follows: "I hope to make a plausible case that much of what has been identified as a moral consensus based on natural revelation is more accurately seen as a product of general and special revelation. Pagans hold to certain moral principles that are compatible with Christian morality not only because they are inescapably confronted with God's revelation in creation, but also because they have been directly or indirectly exposed to an influence by the Spirit operating through special revelation and the other means of grace. Whatever moral consensus exists is thus not a product of pure 'common grace' (devoid of all contact with revelation), nor of 'special grace' (saving knowledge of God through Christ and his word), but what I call . . . 'middle grace' (non-saving knowledge of God and his will derived from both general and special revelation). To put it another way, because of the cultural influence of the Bible, unbelievers in America are more Christian than unbelievers in Irian Jaya. To put it another way, there is not and has never existed a pure 'common grace' cultural situation. This is no cause for arrogant Western imperialism and superiority. Cultures and nations rise and fall. Indeed it is conceivable to posit that the West is currently experiencing God's judicial abandonment which entails a gradual 'de-civilization,' as the growth and spread of Christianity in the non-Western world entails a gradual 'civilizing.'" Peter Leithart, "Did Plato Read Moses? Middle Grace and Moral Consensus," *Biblical Horizons Occasional Paper* 23 (1995): 4-5.

world has had with the principle of redemption. These should never be mechanically separated. We should not think of someone now in the midst of a non-Christian country and imagine him looking up into the sky or round about him in nature in order to see what he can learn about God from such an observation, only afterwards to consider whether there is any other material to be taken into consideration, and that from the very outset. When we think of the responsibility of men who have only the light of nature, we must think of all the facts that have bearing on this situation. There is in the first place, the fact of the present revelation of God in nature. It is this that Paul emphasizes in the first chapter of Romans. But there is in the second place, also the equally important fact that mankind was originally represented in Adam. . . . Even in the first chapter, Paul brings these two into contact with one another when he says that the invisible things of God have been known by man "since the creation of the world." These two should never be separated. Paul teaches both. . . . Hence we should not think of the revelation of God in nature and seek to establish man's responsibility from that alone, as though nothing else were to be taken into consideration. No concrete case exists in which man has not more than the revelation of God in nature. It is no doubt true that many have *practically* nothing else, inasmuch as in their case the tradition of man's original estate has not reached them and no echo of the redemptive principle has penetrated their vicinity. Yet it remains true that the race as a whole has once been in contact with the living God, and that it was created perfect. Man remains responsible for these facts. Back of this arrangement is the Creator and, therefore, the sovereign God.[120]

The difficulty in clearly demarcating general revelation and special revelation leads to my concluding caveat which, in a chapter that has been largely negative, is an attempt to be more positive and constructive. While general revelation may be insufficient for salvation, this does not necessarily lead to parsimony with regard to salvation, for it is argued, for example by Little and Tiessen, that special revelation has multiple modalities. This means we can be positive with regard to God's salvific communication of himself and the gospel message throughout the world even if general revelation is insufficient. Little argues for seven such modalities: oral tradition, miraculous events, dreams, visions, angels, human messengers, and the written word of God.[121] He writes:

We must recognise that God is not limited either by the activity of the Church or the spread of the Bible to accomplish His redemptive purposes in history. Just as He

---

[120]Van Til, *Introduction to Systematic Theology*, p. 78.

[121]See Little, *Revelation of God Among the Unevangelized*, chs. 3-5; idem, "Toward Solving the Problem of the Unevangelized," *Africa Journal of Evangelical Theology* 21, no. 1 (2002): 45-62. For more on dreams and visions, see John K., "Dream Encounters in Christian and Islamic Societies and Its Implication for Christian Ministry and Mission": <http://www.globalmissiology.org/english/index.html> (accessed January 23, 2007).

employed the modalities of special revelation throughout redemptive history as recorded in Scripture, He is able to utilize them today in view of His desire to call a
people unto himself (Rev. 5:9). As Alister McGrath explains, "God's saving work
must never be exclusively restricted to human preaching, as if the Holy Spirit was
silent or inactive in God's world, or as if the actualization of God's saving purposes
depended totally on human agencies. The Creator is not dependent on His creation
in achieving His purposes." Hence, we are not as important as we sometimes like to
think we are.[122]

Knowing the response of those who stress the necessity of the human messenger from Romans 10:14, Little argues that Paul is "simply highlighting our human
responsibility as Christ's ambassadors, nothing more and nothing less."[123] We
have already noted Tiessen's support of this position.

Certainly this opens another whole area of discussion, an area which I have attempted to categorize and analyze elsewhere.[124] There are good reasons to be more
cautious and nuanced than Little and Tiessen in their espousal of multi-modali-
ties. First, there is the question (usually contextualized in the question of *charis-
mata* and rehearsed between continuationists and cessationists) as to how God
chooses to speak today and the relationship between the *historia salutis* and the
ordo salutis. Second, with regard to proto-word revelation, oral tradition, and the
inflow of special revelation into other traditions, I have already indicated the sinful
human propensity to pervert and distort the truth of God's revelation and which
becomes a basis for further judgment and not a *preparatio evangelica*. Third, in all
the biblical accounts of conversion, it appears that at some point all people come
into contact with a human messenger. Commenting on the Cornelius incident in
Acts 10, Helm notes that it is "unacceptedly abstract and hypothetical to say . . .
if Cornelius had not met Peter he would be saved. Scripture does not invite us to
break up the causal nexus of events as revealed as to speculate about each link in
the chain."[125] Is missionary contact normative or exclusively necessary for salvation? The whole tenor of the book of Acts and the sending of the church into the
world seems to strongly prioritize the modality of the human messenger, although
I might tentatively suggest that if God does use other modalities then they can be
seen as providentially pre-evangelistic and part of God's wonderful sovereignty in

---

[122]Little, "Toward Solving the Problem of the Unevangelised," p. 60. He is quoting McGrath's essay,
"A Particularist View: A Post-Enlightenment Approach," in *More than One Way?* p. 176.

[123]Little, "Toward Solving the Problem of the Unevangelised," p. 60.

[124]See Appendix 1: "Evangelical Responses to the Fate of the Unevangelised" in Strange, *The Possibility
of Salvation*, pp. 294-331.

[125]Paul Helm, "Are They Few That Be Saved?" in *Universalism and the Doctrine of Hell*, ed. Nigel M.
de S. Cameron (Grand Rapids: Baker, 1992), p. 280.

calling his people to himself. Certainly if God's common grace (or middle-grace) is the reason for the variegated nature of suppression and substitution, then we can say that common grace serves special grace, what John Murray calls the "long lines of preparation in the realms of common grace,"[126] "the vestibule of faith," for "faith does not take its genesis in a vacuum, it has its antecedents and presuppositions both logically and chronologically in the operations of common grace."[127]

On this note I finish with a boldly beautiful statement from J. H. Bavinck who encapsulates both the need of a gospel messenger but also the wonderful, personal, relational, triune God revealed supremely in the Lord Jesus who seeks and saves the lost:

> We can say that natural man is ever busy repressing or exchanging. But does he always succeed to the same degree? That depends on the strength with which God approaches him. God can at times, as it were, stop the noiseless engines of repression and exchange and overwhelm man to such an extent that he is powerless for a moment. There is, also, the silent activity of the Holy Spirit inside man, even if he resists him constantly. . . . When a missionary or some other person comes into contact with a non-Christian and speaks to him about the gospel, he can be sure that God has concerned himself with this person long before. That person had dealings more than once with God before God touched him, and he experienced the two fatal reactions—suppression and substitution. Now he hears the gospel for the first time. As I have said elsewhere, "we do not open the discussion, but we need only to make it clear that the God who has revealed his eternal power and Godhead to them, now addressed them in a new way, through our words. The encounter between God and that man enters a new period. It becomes more dangerous but also more hopeful. Christ now appears in a new form to him. He was, of course, already present in this man's seeking; and, because he did not leave himself without a witness, Christ was wrestling to gain him, although he did not know it. . . . In the preaching of the gospel, Christ once again appears to man, but much more concretely and in audible form. He awakes man from his long disastrous dream. At last suppression and substitution cease—but this is possible only in faithful surrender.[128]

---

[126]John Murray, "Common Grace," in *Collected Writings*, 4 vols. (Edinburgh: Banner of Truth, 1977), 2:115.

[127]Ibid.

[128]Bavinck, *Church Between Temple and Mosque*, pp. 125-27.

4

Exclusivism

Unjust or Just?

WILLIAM EDGAR

ANYONE WHO ENGAGES IN APOLOGETIC discussions with skeptics will experience that uncomfortable moment when the question is asked, "How is it fair that those who have never even heard the gospel should be condemned to the desolation of an eternity without God?" Indeed, if we are honest, it is likely that we believers have asked the same question. The quandary may come in a different form: "How is it that the death of Jesus of Nazareth, a Jew from the first century, can be the only access to the salvation of mankind?" Or even, "How can one religion be true, when there are so many other faiths on our planet?" As many on both sides of the issue have pointed out, the Christian faith seems so scandalously particular!

Lurking around these troubling questions about justice is what we call the problem of evil. The concern about the fate of the unevangelized is in a way a subset of the larger question of *theodicy.* This technical, somewhat dry term, is derived from Greek roots, *theos* (God) and *dik-* (justice), and raises the matter of God's justice, seeking to affirm that somehow he is just, despite appearances to the contrary. What we are discussing might be called the "soteriological problem of evil."[1] Why does not God provide everyone with at least the opportunity to repent and believe? Gabriel Fackre makes an explicit connection between the fate of the unevangelized and theodicy, because they display similar concerns to hold up God's power, his goodness, and the reality of evil at the same time. For him, it is sin that keeps the gospel from reaching every corner of the world before people die, and so there should be a way of overcoming that roadblock. (His solution is what he calls "post-mortem evangelism," that is, God will make sure that everyone has the opportunity to hear the gospel, even if it is after death.)[2]

---

[1]The term used in Daniel Strange's excellent study, *The Possibility of Salvation Among the Unevangelised: An Analysis of Inclusivism in Recent Evangelical Theology* (Waynesboro, Ga.: Paternoster, 2002), p. 20.
[2]See John Sanders, ed., *What About Those Who Have Never Heard?* (Downers Grove, Ill.: InterVarsity Press, 1995), pp. 71-95.

A popular position that argues against the idea of restricting salvation to the evangelized is known as *inclusivism*. One of the most articulate representatives of this view is John Sanders.[3] For him, there is a tacit injustice in any view that would restrict salvation. *Restrictivists*, as he calls his opponents, cannot square the love of God and his desire that none should perish with a limited audience for the gospel. He says, "Does God truly love *all* people enough genuinely to desire that they be saved? Restrictivists would seem to be saying that he does not, since they teach that he has not provided an opportunity for all people to benefit from the redeeming work of the Son."[4] For Sanders, this is a question of fairness. He objects to the view that presents general revelation (available to all) as only a vehicle for condemnation, whereas to gain access to salvation one needs special revelation (available only to some). On the restrictivist interpretation of Romans 1—3, the unevangelized are justly condemned for rejecting the light of general revelation, and yet, "even a total acceptance of that revelation would still be insufficient for salvation. This is like telling my daughter," he continues, "that I am angry with her for not washing the dishes and then acknowledging that I would still be angry with her even if she had washed them. By this logic, the unevangelized are truly damned if they do and damned if they don't."[5]

The larger theodicy problem can be stated as a metaphysical issue. David Hume asked in a formal, philosophical sense, how God could be both good and all-powerful in the face of the reality of evil. We feel the weight of his conundrum. More recently, Georges Sorel has challenged philosophers in our time to accomplish a "great task," which is to "revamp the theory of evil."[6] It should be noted in passing that this is not just a problem for theists. Whether persons are atheists, materialists, or simply believe good and evil exist, they must grapple with these tough questions, unless they wish to resort to the view that the world is some kind of sick joke.[7]

Although the problem is philosophical, it is far more often an emotional issue. Catastrophes involving the fate of thousands of people are often the occasion for sharpening the discussion. Numerous reflections about the problem of evil naturally arose surrounding the two world wars, the Holocaust, mass forced starva-

---

[3]Sanders prefers the term *wider hope* to inclusivism, and argues that there are several kinds, each with different emphases.

[4]John Sanders, *No Other Name: An Investigation into the Destiny of the Unevangelized* (Grand Rapids: Eerdmans, 1992), p. 60.

[5]Ibid., p. 69.

[6]See Georges Sorel, *Reflections on Violence*, ed. Jeremy Jennings (Cambridge: Cambridge University Press, 1999).

[7]N. T. Wright, *Evil and the Justice of God* (Downers Grove, Ill.: InterVarsity Press, 2006), p. 19.

tions, and the cruelties of so-called reforms, which were thinly veiled extermina-
tion campaigns, such as the Cultural Revolution, various genocides, and ethnic
cleansings.[8] As if these were not enough, we should remember that famine, pov-
erty, and disease affect far more people, in proportion, than any of these single disastrous events. Still, it is individual calamities that most often trigger emotional
reactions. For example, such deliberations are rife in the aftermath of the 9/11 disaster. And while Americans and Europeans took extraordinary measures to in-
crease their "homeland security," terrorists managed to surprise the cities of
Madrid and London. Surely there is more to come.

Even the most dispassionate thinkers were shocked by such events. Jacques
Derrida, though well aware of the mind-set that condemns American insensitiv-
ities to what is sacred in Islam, finds the "bin Laden effect" unacceptable, not only
for its cruelty, disregard for human life, poor treatment of women, and its use of
modern technology to foster religious fanaticism, but for something else. In his
words, "No, it is above all the fact that such actions and such discourse *open onto
no future and, in my view, have no future.*"[9] Not inclined to approve either American or British political posture, nevertheless Derrida cannot accept the "bin
Laden" refusal to interact with anyone else in view of a common cause. As many
others have noted, there is a central irony to this kind of terrorist tactic. Its interpretation of Islam, though on the surface anti-modern, is only possible within a
thoroughly modern bias. For Derrida, the greatest sin is to refuse to enter into discourse with other traditions. For most of us, his view is hopelessly spineless, but
yet it shows that even the most analytical and detached thinkers can be piqued.

What brings about the shock is the violent contrast between our assumptions
and the events. But are those assumptions warranted? While, in a way, major di-
sasters are never comparable, yet nothing is absolutely new under the sun. Today
we think of the great Tsunami of South East Asia, or Hurricane Katrina. Yesterday
it was the earthquake at Lisbon.

PROGRESS INTERRUPTED

We can understand why the Deist movement developed in Europe in the centuries
after the Reformation. Embarrassed by the narrowness of the doctrine of salva-

---

[8]See the work of Benjamin Lieberman on ethnic cleansings in post-war Europe in *Terrible Fate: Ethnic
Cleansing in the Making of Modern Europe* (Chicago: Ivan R. Dee, 2006). He tracks the horrendous
number of deportations and exterminations after World War II. He makes the significant point that
at this time 14 million or more Germans made up the largest case of involuntary migrations in modern European history.
[9]Giovanna Borradori, *Philosophy in a Time of Terror: Dialogues with Jürgen Habermas and Jacques Derrida* (Chicago: University of Chicago Press, 2003), p. 113, italics original.

tion, which was limited to a single mediator, Jesus Christ, many thinkers began to affirm that God should be conceived of principally as the Creator. They believed that this approach was a guarantee of good moral conduct and of good providential government in the world. At the same time, traditional enumerations of dogma, including the Trinity and the atonement of Christ, were considered incompatible with universal reason. We may think of Edward Herbert of Cherbury (1583-1648) who held that common notions *(notitae communes)* can be arrived at through unaided reason (albeit arranged for us by divine providence). Such key concepts as God's oneness, repentance for sin, and the reality of the afterlife, can be arrived at by anyone with a sound mind, he argued, not simply by Christian people who claim unique access to divine revelation in Scripture.

While Deism was not intended to oppose Christian faith, it was meant to give it a reduced place, one that is less exclusive, and to place it within a broader worldview, one which includes numerous religions and philosophies. Deism came and went, but its heirs built on the implications of the legacy and became even more relativizing than their fathers. Years later, Deism in its original form has largely been eclipsed, yet we have inherited the idea that religions should be judged by science or human reason rather than by appeals to authoritative revelation. This approach has seen many variants. In the nineteenth century the discipline known as the "science of the history of religions" became prominent. The premise was that no one religion or philosophy had the right to call others to account. In our own times, the proclamation of the "universal rights of man" and the push for constitutional democracies where everyone is meant to have equal opportunities regardless of their creed lends plausibility to limiting the exclusive authority of one religion.[10]

The issue of fairness is at the center of the evangelical debates over the issue of the fate of the unevangelized. Carl F. H. Henry, writing for the anthology *Through No Fault of Their Own?* asks, "Is It Fair?"[11] He proceeds to raise several penetrating issues about the assumptions behind the question, including, "Is any human being totally 'unreached' by truth about God and his ways?" And, most significantly for our purposes, "How is 'fairness' to be defined, and by whom?"

The question is actually an old one, though not always put in strictly the same terms. For that matter, it is raised in the Bible itself. Some of these same sensitivities are expressed in the Scriptures, from a mind-set that we think could only have

---

[10]Of course, it is only *plausibility*, since ensuring equal rights before the law is not meant to be a judgment for or against a particular religion. Indeed, most Christians would argue that such rights flow out of the biblical teaching on the *imago Dei*.

[11]Carl F. H. Henry, "Is It Fair?" in *Through No Fault of Their Own? The Fate of Those Who Have Never Heard*, ed. William V. Crocket and James G. Sigountos (Grand Rapids: Baker, 1991), pp. 245-55.

arisen in modern times. Again, much of it surrounds the question of "fairness" in God's dealings. "How odd of God to choose the Jews," Ogden Nash once quipped. Why should Israel be called to drive out the nations? The book of Deuteronomy records that God used the people of Israel in the destruction of the corrupt nations of Canaan not because they were better or more significant, but simply because he loved them (Deut 7:7). They were the chosen people. But how is that fair? In Romans 9 Paul walks the reader through the same difficulty. If God chooses some and not others, "Then why does God still blame us? For who resists his will?" (Rom 9:19). This seems a reasonable point, at least at first blush.

Perhaps the most passionate outcry against what appeared utterly unjust in the providence of God was voiced by Job:

> Even today my complaint is bitter;
> His hand is heavy in spite of my groaning.
> If I only knew where to find him;
> If only I could go to his dwelling!
> I would state my case before him
> And fill my mouth with arguments. (Job 23:2-4)

The Old Testament is replete with such sentiments. Habakkuk, perplexed by what seems to be overly harsh judgment on Israel through a barbarous people, complains to the Lord, whom he knows to be just and fair, "Your eyes are too pure to look upon evil. . . . Why then do you tolerate the treacherous? Why are you silent?" (Hab 1:13). Elie Wiesel could not have put it more poignantly, trying to understand the Holocaust: "Where is God? Is he not silent? Why?"[12]

Historians remember how the shock of the devastating earthquake at Lisbon in 1755 was followed by a metaphorical earthquake in the philosophical world. Of the city's quarter million people, over ninety thousand were killed. Around 85 percent of its buildings were destroyed. This catastrophe burst in on an otherwise rather optimistic Enlightenment period. Consider the popular philosophy known as "optimism." The chief architect was G. W. Leibniz (1646-1716), who actually coined the term *theodicy* and taught that God had created the best of all possible worlds. In this same vein, Alexander Pope could write, in his *Essay on Criticism:*

> First follow Nature, and your judgment frame
> By her just standard, which is still the same;
> Unerring Nature, still divinely bright,
> One clear, unchanged, and universal light.

---

[12]These three questions permeate the works of Elie Wiesel. See, for example, *Night* (New York: Bantam, 1982), pp. 32, 62; and *After the Darkness* (New York: Schocken, 2002).

These lines were written in 1711, and followed by similarly buoyant epics such as the *Rape of the Lock* and, most significantly, *The Essay on Man* (1733-1734), with its celebration of the great chain of being and the famous conclusion, "Whatever is, is right." It is scarcely likely that such lines could have been penned after Lisbon. Voltaire, who otherwise admired Pope, wrote his powerful *Poem on the Disaster of Lisbon*, which attacked this unrealistic philosophy of optimism. It contained these lines: "O miserable mortals! O deplorable earth! . . . Mistaken philosophers who cry, 'All is well.' Run, look at these awful ruins, this debris."[13]

Yet the hidden presupposition of progress and the goodness of human reason is very tenacious. Many of us, especially in the West, tend to carry it in our subconscious. Strange, is it not, considering so much evidence to the contrary? Indeed, much of Western modernity is built upon this foundation. Philosophically, so many of the key Enlightenment figures believed in some version of progress. In addition to Leibniz and Pope, consider Condorcet (1743-1794), who firmly believed that the human race was progressing toward greater and greater perfection. If only we could apply the certainties of mathematics to moral and political life, we would see growth toward the greatest happiness for all.[14] Kant himself believed in the immortality of the person, which should lead everyone to perfect virtue through the perfection of generic reason. He taught that ethics was based on the quest for a single supreme principle of morality that could be attained, because it binds all rational creatures.

The notion of progress has found its way into popular discourse as well. How many politicians who end their term in ambiguity will appeal to *history* as a final court of appeals? The idea is that while today we may not be satisfied with a particular policy, tomorrow we will understand how significant it was. Only on the supposition that we are progressing does this argument make sense. When an office installs a new computer network and it does not work well, we hear the cynical mantra, "This must be progress!" Much of modern liberalism (I am referring to social and political liberalism, not theological liberalism) is based on the unspoken assumption of the natural goodness of the human being. If we could only have

---

[13]O malheureux mortels! ô terre déplorable! O de tous les mortels assemblage effroyable! D'inutiles douleurs éternel entretien! Philosophes trompés qui criez: "Tout est bien"; Accourez, contemplez ces ruines affreuses, Ces débris, ces lambeaux, ces cendres malheureuses, Ces femmes, ces enfants l'un sur l'autre entassés, Sous ces marbres rompus ces membres dispersés; Cent mille infortunés que la terre dévore.

[14]His views are best represented in his essay, *Sketch for a Historical Picture of the Progress of the Human Mind* (1795). T. R. Malthus would later attack this essay but without relinquishing the notion of progress altogether.

more funding or a better work environment, things would go better. Why did this person go wrong? It is in his background (not his nature).

HOPEFUL REALISM

The assumption of optimism that characterized the Enlightenment position was not tenable then, and it is no more credible today. Once we begin to see this, the Christian answer becomes more plausible. But how can we hold to the reality of evil without blaming God?

Why are these evils so appalling to us? Why do they affect our emotional and psychological life, perhaps even more than our metaphysical worries? I would submit that, first, it is because we are right to be outraged. So indeed is God! But if that is the case, how can he claim to be good and loving—what kind of justice would tolerate such wrongs for such a long time? We need to ask that question with courage, neither by diminishing the outrage of evil nor by ruling the Christian answer out of court on grounds of our concept of fairness, without a full hearing. There is bound to be mystery here, but we should not, as it were, so mystify the issue that we will remain agnostic. In what follows I will argue that arriving at some clarity on the problem of evil will take us a long way toward understanding the claim of exclusivity with respect to Christ's salvation.

So, is it fair? It is always crucial to examine one's presuppositions when going into a discussion such as this. Without diminishing our outrage at injustice, can we possibly contain it within an explanatory matrix which will bring us some measure of comfort? We shall now look at four critical areas in order to understand the problem of evil more clearly.

The composition of evil. What exactly is the nature of evil? One of the most basic distinctions we may put forward is between evil *endured* and evil *committed*. When we endure evil, we are afflicted. While we may experience evil in the form of suffering, there is something more at stake than simple pain. Simone Weil reminds us, "In the realm of suffering, affliction is something apart, specific, and irreducible. It is quite a different thing from simple suffering. It takes possession of the soul and marks it through and through with its own particular mark, the mark of slavery."[15] When we experience such affliction we feel violated. Or we feel despair. Behind those feelings is the conviction that this should not be. When a child is ill or an accident takes the life of a bystander, we sense an injustice. Innocent people have been sullied.

When we commit evil, on the other hand, it is we who inflict pain on others.

---

[15]"The Love of God and Affliction," in Simone Weil, *Waiting for God*, trans. Emma Craufurd (New York: HarperCollins/Perennial, 2001), p. 67.

Our intentions and actions render us guilty and shameful. This form of evil is condemnable; we are not dealing with innocent victims, but with perpetrators who are liable. Here is the crux of the matter. Can such a distinction really hold up? Put another way, is there any endured evil that is truly undeserved? Here, the biblical answer is twofold.

At one level, no evil is endured by purely innocent people. This is surely one of the most difficult ideas to understand, let alone accept. Yet the Bible is unrelenting here. When a number of Galileans were murdered by Pilate, Jesus' hard question was, "Do you think that these Galileans were worse sinners than all the other Galileans, because they suffered in this way? No, I tell you; but unless you repent, you will all likewise perish" (Lk 13:2-3). And he followed it up in the same terms by commenting on eighteen people who had perished from the falling tower of Siloam: "Do you think that they were worse offenders than all the others who lived in Jerusalem? No, I tell you; but unless you repent, you will all likewise perish" (Lk 13:4-5).

The working assumption of those who heard the Lord was no doubt the same as ours. We are basically good, or at least not guilty of particular sins deserving such retribution. Maybe no one is perfect, but our imperfections are a contradiction to our basic natures, which are good.

Is this assumption altogether wrong? If it is, how can we feel optimistic so much of the time? I would suggest that a certain kind of optimism is a reflection of our (true) understanding that God is good and has a felicitous purpose for history. Yet our positive outlook is only one side of the story. Taken by itself, it cannot make sense of the world. The Bible tells us that while God is good, humankind is fallen. We are flawed. The apostle Paul goes far in support of this diagnosis: "For we have already charged that all, both Jews and Greeks, are under the power of sin, as it is written: 'None is righteous, no, not one'" (Rom 3:9-10).

Is this some kind of Pauline pessimism, or could it possibly be true? And how could we be expected to decide such a thing? The answer is that it is not we who must decide. It is God himself. Of course, we must be persuaded. But the Scripture claims that what is fundamentally wrong with the world is that humanity has turned against God. Evil, then, cannot be limited to horizontal, human affliction but needs to have its more basic definition in relation to God. Is this so preposterous? Each person must examine his conscience and decide. Ask yourself this: If no one were looking, not even God (presuming you believe in God), what would you really be capable of doing? Or this: Given enough provocation, how far might you go in your cruelty?

One of the most powerful accounts of a man who changed his mind about the human condition, and thus his own condition, is the story of W. H. Auden (1907-

1973).[16] I had the privilege of meeting Auden while I was in college. He was without a doubt one of the greatest poets of the twentieth century. Born in York, and
educated at Oxford, he spent a considerable part of his life in America. One incident in his life shook his optimistic philosophy to the core. His earlier work was
characterized by a simple humanism, a trust in the goodness of human nature.
One evening in 1939, he went to the movies in Yorkville, the German section of
New York City. The film was *Sig im Poland*, the story of Hitler's invasion of War-
saw. As the account unfolded Auden could hear in the German-sympathizing audience shouts of "Kill them!" He would later comment on this: "I wondered then,
why I reacted as I did against the denial of every humanistic value. The answer
brought me back to the church." Why? Because he knew these outcries were a sign
of malevolence, though he did not yet know the reason to call the Nazis evil. His
biographer says, "It was not just a question of shattered optimism: the whole
ground of his outlook had shifted beneath his feet. If humanity were innately
good, then on what basis could he legitimately object to the murderous shouts
of the Germans in that cinema audience, or indeed the behaviour of Hitler
himself?"[17]

Auden had to find some objective ground to call Hitler utterly wrong and he
could not find it in his lazy humanism. He quipped, "The English intellectuals
who now cry to Heaven against the evil incarnated in Hitler have no heaven to cry
to." He then began to read theology books, and eventually came to the conclusion
that all human beings were sinful, not just the Nazis. His reasoning was that God,
the absolute judge, declares it so. Pessimistic? Not ultimately, because only when
you have such an objective accusation is there hope for a remedy. If I am only a
little flawed, I only need to do better. But when I cannot, what is there left for me
to hope in? How can I explain deep evil all around, and even in me, if I am honest?
But if I am flawed through and through, then there is nothing I can even hope for.
But I can turn to the one who conquers evil, the one who defines it in the first
place.

At the same time, it is just as important to stress that in a fallen world, good
and evil are not distributed equally and according to deserts. The reason certain
catastrophes call into question our sense of fairness is because they are dispropor-
tionate. Faced with the unjust suffering of a child, Dostoyevsky could say, "I would
persist in my indignation even if I were wrong."[18] Hovering over the limp body of

---

[16]The following is taken from Os Guinness, *The Journey: Our Quest for Faith and Meaning* (Colorado
Springs: NavPress, 2001), pp. 75-78. This episode is in turn taken from Humphrey Carpenter, *W. H.
Auden: A Biography* (New York: Houghton Mifflin, 1982).
[17]Ibid., p. 76.
[18]Fyodor Dostoyevsky, *The Brothers Karamazov* (New York: Bantam, 1972), bk. 4, chap. 7.

her fatally wounded husband in the limousine in Dallas, Jacqueline Kennedy could be overheard to say, or rather to cry out, "No! No!" Outrage was mixed with denial, both the result of a profound sense of the scandal of such palpable evil.

Again, we are in good company. The psalmist admits:

> But as for me, my feet had almost stumbled,
> My steps had nearly slipped.
> For I was envious of the arrogant
> When I saw the prosperity of the wicked.
> For they have no pangs until death;
> Their bodies are fat and sleek.
> They are not in trouble as others are;
> They are not stricken like the rest of mankind. (Ps 73:2-5)

For now, then, justice does not prevail in the world. Rather, we face daily, flagrant injustices. But it is crucial to see things in the proper light. Such unbalanced distribution is not a sign of the injustice of God but of the way things are in a fallen world. They are meant to signal that there is something wrong with the world, not with God. And they are meant to drive us to cry out to God for answers.

The main answer is the certainty of judgment. Our psalmist teetered on the edge of despair, until he walked into God's sanctuary, and began to realize the final picture (Ps 73:17-20). Then he saw that justice delayed is not justice denied. It drove him closer to the Lord, who works within his own timetable.

What, then, is the nature of evil? The heart of the matter is this: Evil is not simply an affliction on innocent people. Evil is the universal rejection of God the Creator. To return to Paul's argument in Romans, each of us knows God but refuses to acknowledge him as we should. His language is strong:

> For what can be known about God is plain to them, because God has shown it to them. For his invisible attributes, namely, his eternal power and divine nature, have been clearly perceived, ever since the creation of the world, in the things that have been made. So they are without excuse. For although they knew God, they did not honor him as God nor give thanks to him. (Rom 1:19-21)

The very center of evil, then, is a refusal before God. It is by definition wrong to turn against God, since God defines who we are and what our purpose is. He has made a covenant arrangement with us, according to which we enjoy our liberty and our way of life, and his intentions toward us are only good. There is no reason to transgress his covenant—yet we have.

So, what about people who have never heard of God, especially the Christian God? Strictly speaking, there are not any. As Romans argues, and as the sermons in the book of Acts confirm, everyone knows God, and knows a great deal about him. They not only know his nature and his standards, but they know he is patient and long-suffering (Rom 2:4; Acts 14:15-17; 17:30). One of my challenges as a Christian apologist is to help people see the culpable disconnect between their actual claims and their true understanding. The ethicist Peter Singer is famous for declaring that elderly people who no longer serve a useful purpose may be dispensable, as they cost society a great deal. But his own mother is a victim of Alzheimer's, and Singer spends a great deal on her care. All of us are like Peter Singer. We make claims about ideas, such as the low value of life, but cannot live with them because we *know* better. This renders us guilty before a holy God.

All of us are lost before a righteous God and deserve his anger. It is *fair* for God to be angry with the world, as we saw, because we have transgressed his covenant and committed cosmic treason.[19] If the Word of God does not convince us of that, our own testimony about ourselves should. Again, as Paul puts it in Romans, "Therefore you have no excuse, O man, every one of you who judges. For in passing judgment on another you condemn yourself, because you, the judge, practice the very same things" (Rom 2:1). So, in *fairness*, God could judge the whole world and not be tainted with one small spot of guilt. But in *mercy* he saves many from their condition.

The origin of evil. Where, then, does evil come from? Even if it is our *fault*, can a sovereign God have no ultimate responsibility for it? Certainly one of the most difficult philosophical problems about the origin of evil centers on how God could have worked it into the creation. A full discussion of that issue would require more space than we have at present. For now we can only say the following.

1. Once again, evil is utterly and radically incompatible with God's nature. God cannot be tempted by evil, nor can he tempt anyone, because in him resides only goodness. He is the Father of lights, "with whom there is no variation or shadow due to change" (Jas 1:12-17). Scripture over and over again declares evil to be against God, even to the point of making the average reader weary with the repetition. "You . . . are of purer eyes than to see evil and cannot look at wrong," the prophet declares (Hab 1:13).

To be sure, now that evil is in the world, God may use it for his purposes. In his judgments, by chastising his people, and most poignantly by sending his only Son to die on the gibbet of torture, he shows his sovereignty over all things, including evil. Occasionally he sends an "evil spirit from the LORD" (1 Sam 16:14; 18:10; 19:9). But we may never suggest, indeed it is blasphemous to do so, that God is complicit with evil. Such a proposition amounts to calling evil good, and

---

[19] I first heard this expression from R. C. Sproul. It captures well the sense of the enormity of the sin of our representative, Adam, and of our own sin.

deserves total condemnation (Is 5:20).

2. So, where does evil *come* from? We do not exactly know, at least altogether. God does, of course. But we do know two things which help in the discussion. The first is that God is absolutely sovereign over all things. His counsel is the ultimate cause of all things. Nothing escapes his will. Thus, somehow—strangely and mysteriously—he planned evil to have its role in the history of the world. We cannot escape this conclusion, even though it makes us shudder. And, nothing we say about the ultimate origins of evil should ever suggest a justification of it.[20] Evil remains the unjustified horror. Second, and this is crucial: God is in no way accountable for evil. Whatever that original cause may entail, it does not imply liability. One of the great confessional documents of the seventeenth century, the *Westminster Confession of Faith*, reflects on this problem.[21] In its attempt to clarify different kinds of causes, it uses the term "authorship" of evil. And it insists that God cannot be the author of evil. At the same time it acknowledges that God ultimately ordains all things. How can this be? We must make distinctions within the concept of causality that we are not used to making. There is an ultimate cause which nevertheless does not carry with it guilt or accountability.

3. How do these things relate? Or, to put it theologically, what kind of compatibility is involved? To cut to the chase: God is so great, and his counsel so wise and good, that he can make a world where evil is real, and it comes as the result of human choice, without God being accountable. When God created the world he could give it its own sovereignty, its own freedom, without giving up one bit of his own sovereign power. Contrary to "kenotic" models, he did not have to give up any portion of his deity in order to do this.

The Westminster Confession, mentioned above, describes this compatibility so well that it is worth quoting one of the relevant sections in full: "God from all eternity did, by the most wise and holy counsel of his own will, freely and unchangeably ordain whatsoever comes to pass: yet so, as thereby neither is God the author of sin, nor is violence offered to the will of the creature, nor is the liberty or con-

---

[20]Henri Blocher takes great pains to avoid any concession to a divine purpose for evil. This would, in his terms, amount to a justification, if not an excuse, for evil. To cover his bases, he goes so far as to deny the classical view of eschatology before the fall, using the probation as a means to the end of eternal life, a move we find unnecessary. See *Evil and the Cross* (Downers Grove, Ill.: InterVarsity Press, 1994), pp. 84-104; and *In the Beginning: The Opening Chapters of Genesis* (Downers Grove, Ill.: InterVarsity Press, 1984), chap. 6.

[21]The Westminster Confession (1646) is the fruit of the labors of divines commissioned to produce standards which could unite Scotland and England. Adopted by the Church of Scotland in 1647, it was subsequently accepted by most Presbyterian churches, and many Congregationalist and even Baptist churches, with appropriate modifications. It is often considered to be the culmination of Protestant confessional theology, stressing themes such as the covenant, God's sovereignty and human responsibility, criteria for true worship, and the like.

tingency of second causes taken away, but rather established" (3.1). It would be hard to state either side of the equation more strongly. Everything that happens goes back to God's will—not just his knowledge (which would be ineffective if there were not the power to carry things out), but his decree. And yet the entire responsibility for sin falls upon the creature. The reality and liability for that human decision is ensured by the covenant that establishes the world in the first place.

The link between the divine and the created must go back to some kind of heavenly accommodation. By his good providence God sustains the process as well as the proximate causes which give the world its authenticity. Again, as the Confession puts it in 5.4, describing original sin, God's power extends itself even to the fall, not by bare permission but by determination, and yet "so as the sinfulness thereof proceeds only from the creature, and not from God." This compatibility affects everything about the world, not only evil things but good things as well. As 7.1 tells us, "The distance between God and the creature is so great, that although reasonable creatures do owe obedience unto him as their Creator, yet they could never have any fruition of him as their blessedness and reward, but by some voluntary *condescension* on God's part, which he has been pleased to express by way of covenant." There is wonderful mystery here. For our purposes what we need to retain is God's innocence of all evil, indeed, his right to judge it, yet at the same time the wonderful reality of this world, its power, and its capacity for rebellion.

God is utterly God. The world is utterly real. That is only possible because God made the world and continues to relate to it, to ensure its reality, by accommodation.

4. Thus, while God is the one who assures the reality of earthly causes, humankind is the author of sin, because of its freedom. Humans are responsible. And that responsibility is somehow tied in to their liberty. What is human liberty in the biblical picture? Non constraint. That is, human action, or agency, is *real*. How can that be? We are responsible for our decisions and actions, because, for one, our agency is worthy of approbation or blame. Human choice belongs to us, our wills are our own, and are not controlled by an external force. This is true, while divine foreordination is true at the same time. To be sure, these are limiting concepts. But one cannot rob the other of its reality. Indeed, the one insures the other.

John Calvin pointed out that when man fell he did not lose his will but the *health* of his will. In other words, we may have free will, but that will is "so enslaved that it can have no power for righteousness."[22] What then determines our actions? This is difficult to say, without falling either into anarchy or determinism. As Rob-

---

[22]*Institutes* 2.2.7.

ert Lewis Dabney points out, we are a dispositional complex, which includes various tendencies, desires, motives, etc. All of these determine our actions. As the heart goes, so goes the man, we might say.[23] This leaves room for influences, environment, parents, even "extenuating circumstances," but still the responsibility ("authorship") is on the choice-maker. Put another way, it is *I*, not external coercion, which determines my action. If I am inclined to go one way, nothing can force me to do the opposite.

Earlier, we mentioned Romans 9:19, where the reader asks rhetorically for Paul, If God's will is final, why does he still find fault? Though Paul does say that the question is out of order, pretentiously challenging the Creator, he does provide some insight. Paul's helpful metaphor here is that of the potter and the clay. He asks whether or not the potter has the right to make out of the same lump of clay one vessel for "honored" use and another for "dishonorable" use (Rom 9:21). In keeping with his imagery we must not confuse this language with determinism. A lump of clay, as used here by Paul, is already weakened because of the fall. In other words, we are not dealing with good ingredients which God may use for destruction. We are dealing with evil ingredients, which God in his mercy may single out for salvation.

5. One question in this discussion will surely be raised. How is it that sin came into the world through one man, Adam, at the dawn of human history? At first this would seem an arbitrary arrangement. Why should one person be able to drag the entire human race down with him? But that is not a helpful way to frame the question. In the structure of creation, the way God put things together, humanity relates to God by a particularly faceted covenant. God has made us so that we are represented by a covenant head. Our identity as human beings is not only individual, but collective, through the one head. Adam failed the test in Eden, and a curse was put on his progeny, because that is the way we relate to God. Had we related to God merely as individuals starting from neutrality, as the modern mindset would have it, then of course some might be good and some might be bad. But as it is, we all are inclined to evil.

And yet, still, we are responsible for our choices. This covenant arrangement is not one that allows us to say, I am not guilty because my forefather Adam put me in this position. The guilt may take a particular shape because of solidarity with Adam, but it cannot be displaced to him. In Romans, this covenant headship is not even mentioned until chapter 5. Chapters 1-3 demonstrate our responsibility and failure without having to go back to Adam. This arrangement may strike the individualist modern reader as odd, but it is in fact a wonderful expression of hu-

---

[23]Robert L. Dabney, *Lectures in Systematic Theology* (Grand Rapids: Zondervan, 1972), pp. 128-30.

man solidarity, ironically, an elusive value much sought after by our contemporaries.

The conquest of evil. In the midst of all this, is there any good news? Of course, once we see how radically evil we are, then the gospel answer comes not as a matter of fairness, but as a wonderful surprise. God has not only retained his full right to be angry with our sin, and thus to place a curse upon the world, but he has determined to save multitudes from their plight because of his love. This is the gospel, the good news, that by mutual agreement the eternal Son of God became a man, who both perfectly obeyed the Father and also took all of the guilt for sin upon himself as a substitute for his people. Not only that, but whoever turns to the Lord for mercy shall be saved. And we have a new covenant head, Jesus Christ—the last Adam, the second man—who leads us in righteousness.

Though space forbids fuller treatment here, it needs to be said that the atonement of Christ was the only way reconciliation between God and his people was possible. The Lord's concern was to find a way to forgive sinners, of course. But his deeper concern was to find a way to satisfy himself, a righteous and holy God, whose very nature requires anger against the sinner. When Paul refers to us as enemies of God, he is not only concerned to remind us of our status before a holy God, but of God's status before us. Due to our sins, it is *he* who is *our* enemy. The death (and resurrection) of Christ, as horrible, bloody, and excruciating as it had to be, was the only way to cover the face of God from the reality of our sin. Jesus Christ, God-man, had to obey God's law perfectly (his active obedience) but also to submit perfectly to the sanctions of the law (his passive obedience) if reconciliation were to occur.

One of the most important arguments for the exclusivity of Christ as the way to salvation is this bloody cross. Only if a worthy substitute could be found, one who would experience the terror of abandonment ("My God, My God, why have you forsaken me," he cried [Mt 27:46]) could our eternal abandonment from God be remedied. In no other religion is there anything remotely close to this extraordinary move: God became human in order to die and be raised for the guilt of his people, and thus to give them the gift of forgiveness. How could anyone even suggest another way, or alternate religions, when this most costly sacrifice was proffered by God himself?

It is quite indecent to suggest that Christ's resurrection is simply one way to our justification and life. It has to be the only way (Rom 4:25; 8:11). Without it, God cannot remain "just and the justifier of the one who has faith in Jesus" (Rom 3:26). Consequently, our response in faith is not an optional requirement. To have access to justification, there must be faith. And for there to be an object of faith worthy of this response, there must be a full content, revealed, and accessible to "whosoever" would believe that Jesus is Lord (Rom 10:9-10).

To repeat, then, the fact that God has chosen to save many people is not a question of fairness or justice but one of grace and mercy. If God had saved no one at all, he would still be entirely fair. But the fact that he has saved many—a great multitude according to the last book in the Bible—is a matter of mercy and love (Rev 5:11-14; 7:9-10).

The status of the unevangelized. We are now ready to look directly at the question, how can it be fair for God to give *opportunity* to some, but not to all? Why did he not give everyone a chance to hear and decide? Even if we admit he did not have to save everyone, should he not have provided everyone the same opportunity to repent and believe? And why at first did the gospel move across the Roman Empire, then Europe, but not Asia or South America? What of the "soteriological problem of evil?" So, now, we come back to the beginning. "How can it be fair that those who have never even heard the gospel should be condemned to the desolation of an eternity without God?" The answer, as I see it, involves a couple of steps.

1. It is crucial at the outset to remember that condemnation is not based on hearing the *gospel* and refusing it, but on knowing God and refusing him. Certainly we should not be judged based on something we never knew. But we do know. As we saw, according to Romans 1—2, we know a great deal. Now, it may be that some hear the gospel itself and refuse it. I suppose their condemnation is greater. Perhaps also there is greater condemnation for those who live in countries with a long Christian history and with access to the Bible than for those in relatively unevangelized places. It is not certain what is meant by the distinction Jesus made between those who receive a "severe beating," and those who receive a "light beating." But it is clear that to whom much has been given, much will be required (Lk 12:47-48). "Human beings are judged in God's sight for the response they make to whatever light they have—and no human being is without light."[24]

Those representing the more inclusivist or *wider hope* views deem this approach unacceptable. To return to John Sanders, for him there is an injustice in the view that apart from special revelation one cannot be moved by the Holy Spirit to repent and be saved. He asks, "If an individual's rejection of the truth of general revelation is counted as an implicit rejection of Jesus, then why is it that an individual's conviction of sin and desire for God through the leading of the Holy Spirit are not counted as implicit acceptance of Jesus?"[25] But this is contrary to how Scripture frames the issue. When an unbeliever rejects general revelation, it is not counted as an implicit rejection of Jesus, but as an explicit rejection of what is clearly known. The spirit of Romans 1—3, as we have been arguing, is not that

---

[24]Carl Henry, "Is It Fair?", p. 247.
[25]Sanders, *No Other Name*, pp. 69-70.

unbelievers are rejecting something they cannot know directly. Rather, it is that *truth* is being suppressed by actions that are culpable (Rom 1:18). What is this truth? It is that God in all his divinity and power is there, that he deserves to be honored and thanked (Rom 1:20-21). He is a God worthy to be known and placed at the center of life. He is not only a just God, but a patient and merciful God. Instead of acknowledging him, unbelievers have chosen foolishness, idolatry and shameful lusts (Rom 1:23-32). Sanders greatly underestimates the radical evil in our hearts, which drives us to utter foolishness.

Furthermore, where does the idea that the Holy Spirit can lead people to an implicit acceptance of Jesus come from? Emotionally this possibility appears attractive. But, going back to Romans, and to the rest of Scripture, what is clearly taught is that the Holy Spirit works explicitly to lead people to Christ, and the means he uses is preaching. Sanders argues that Romans 10:9 states "nothing more than that the confession of Christ is *one* sure way to experience salvation."[26] In his view it simply does not comment on people who have not heard of Christ. But a frank look at Romans 10 tells us something different. Paul asks, rhetorically, "How can they believe in the one of whom they have not heard?" Of course, they cannot. Paul says it in no uncertain terms, "Faith comes from hearing the message" (Rom 10:17). Interestingly, as the chapter progresses, he stresses that the gospel does not come to good people who have almost arrived at salvation, but to bad people on whom, nevertheless, God has compassion. Quoting Isaiah, he adds, "I was found by those who did not seek me, I revealed myself to those who did not ask for me" (Rom 10:20). The clear emphasis here is on a God who reveals himself not to people who are led by the Spirit to accept Jesus implicitly, but to rebels who want nothing of it.

The view known as exclusivism is not unjust, though it is willing to uphold the requirements of a just God. It is also full of mercy on those for whom pure justice would require condemnation. The wider hope view confuses the two attributes. It appears to turn mercy into an act of justice. To be sure, for mercy to be genuine, a just resolution of the problem of sin must be available, which it is in the finished work of Christ. But that is different from saying that mercy is required by justice.

2. We should also remember the passion of God himself for reaching lost people. The story recounted in Scripture over and over is one of a God pleading with his people to turn to him: "As I live, declares the Lord GOD, I have no pleasure in the death of the wicked, but that the wicked turn from his way and live; turn back, turn back from your evil ways, for why will you die, O house of Israel?" (Ezek 33:11). This is not an isolated Old Testament appeal; we hear it in the New Testament as

[26]Ibid., p. 67.

well (see 1 Tim 2:4, 6; 2 Pet 3:9). Who is more busy gathering up his sheep from all over the world than our Savior (Jn 10:16)? The reason why the church must be a disciple-making body is that it follows the urgent call of its Master (Mt 28:18-20). This is why the apostles tirelessly went to evangelize the world. Paul asks, "How are they to believe in him of whom they have never heard?" They cannot, so they need a preacher who is sent to them (Rom 10:14-15). Evangelism, not undue anxiety about the fate of the unevangelized, is the mandate of the church.

3. How does he call his people to himself? By seeking them and saving them. By calling them by name. This means the spread of the gospel in many different ways to various parts of the world is a process governed by God's providence. Could he have called out to the whole world at once, perhaps with a loud voice from heaven? We do not know, but the way he actually does call is far more persuasive. He shows respect for people's dignity, for their culture and language, and for the process of history. For example, the extraordinary work of Bible translators is one moving testimony to the lengths to which the Lord is willing to go to reach the lost. The process may seem long and involved to us, but the fact is that in the two millennia since the coming of Christ, the church has grown from a relatively modest minority into more than two billion, and is still growing fast. Ironically, for those inclined to think a European Christian civilization is unfair, today one is more likely to hear the gospel clearly proclaimed in South America or in Africa than in Europe or possibly North America.

4. Who are God's people? Not random respondents, but his carefully, lovingly chosen ones. God, from all eternity, has elected many to be the objects of his love. His providence is only the means to carry out his electing love. Thus, the fact that not everyone has the opportunity to hear the gospel is not an indication of unfairness, but the way the Lord carries out the realization of his sovereign, loving choice made in eternity. Reformed theology has always recognized God's plan to save some but not all according to his free and wise plan. True, there has been an important debate between those who believe he decreed to elect his people *before* his decision to create and permit the fall (supra-lapsarianism), and those who believe he decreed to elect his people *after* his decision to create and permit the fall (infra-lapsarianism). But for our purposes the ultimate decision, and then its realization in history, is what is crucial. The reason, in any scenario, is not fate, nor chance, but electing love.

Again, his providence is a means of carrying out his purpose of choosing some but not all. To put it positively, he knows his sheep by name and will make arrangements for them to hear and respond. Negatively, he has determined to pass others by and leave them in the place we all deserve to be. The fact that some do not hear the gospel is one of the providential means of his passing them by. This may be a hard saying, emotionally, but it only follows from the fact that all deserve death, yet many are saved.

5. Are there any exceptions at all to the normal way of being saved? Could it ever be that some who have not heard the gospel, and thus have not been able to articulate a response, can be justified and reconciled to God? I can think of at least one possible case.[27]

a. Believers before Christ came who were called by God but did not know the full story of the coming of Immanuel were saved because the benefits of Christ were reckoned to them in anticipation. This is surely the case of the Jews in the Old Testament, and of others like Melchizedek who were in their same situation. They were saved by Christ though not having full knowledge of his person and work. As recipients of divine revelation, they knew about sacrificial atonement, and they understood the need for divine forgiveness, and maybe much else besides, but they did not have access to the whole picture as we do on this side of Calvary.

b. Handicapped or severely challenged persons. Again, to cite the Westminster Confession, "So also are [regenerated and saved by Christ] all other elect persons, who are incapable of being outwardly called by the ministry of the word" (10.3). Is this a kind of "inclusivism" before its time? The proof-texts to the Confession here are 1 John 5:12, which states that whoever does not "have the Son of God" does not have life, and Acts 4:12, which says there is no other name given whereby we can be saved. The concern of the framers of the Confession is no doubt two-fold. On the one hand they meant to acknowledge the obvious problem of those who are *incapable* of properly hearing the gospel, and thus of giving an informed response. They are not speculating on *providential* incapacity because missionaries had not yet arrived, or something of the sort. Rather, they are thinking of those whose mental condition prevents them from making sense of the words of the preached gospel. On the other hand, they wanted to underscore the need to come through Christ and him alone. Contemporary inclusivists have attempted to see this as an open door toward any kind of exception including unevangelized people, but it is not possible to draw such a conclusion from this exception in the Confession. It simply was not the intention of the framers to speculate on a general category of unevangelized persons (see chap. 25).

GO AND MAKE DISCIPLES

In conclusion, the truths we have presented should reassure us about the certainty of salvation for God's people. He has not offered the *possibility* of salvation, but the sure fact of salvation. If this means some of the unevangelized will not find

---

[27]The possibility of children dying in infancy comes to mind.

faith that should not drive us to anxiety but to missions! Because God is utterly fair in his judgments, but yet has also revealed his love for the lost—indeed his longing over them, finding a way to save them without impugning his own holiness—then we should not complacently be entertaining theories of inclusivism or second chances, which bring more problems than answers. Instead, we should gladly accept the call to evangelism, the call to the church as ambassador of Christ in a world of alienation and darkness. That is one of the most urgent calls of the church today.

5

Other Religions
Saving or Secular?

ECKHARD J. SCHNABEL

WHEN WE DEFINE RELIGION IN THE MOST general terms as "a particular system of faith and worship," and when we place this definition in the context of the faith and worship of both Israel and the early Christians, a crucial question arises: Who sets up the perspectives, the principles, and the promises of the particular "system" of faith and worship?

Israel was convinced that it was Yahweh, the Creator of the world and the Lord of history, who determines what people must believe and how they must worship if he is to be pleased. Similarly, the early Christians were convinced that it was the one true God, the Creator of the world and the Lord of history, who had revealed himself in Jesus, the crucified and risen Messiah and Savior, who determines what people must believe and how they must worship if he is to be pleased. Both Israel and the early Christians were convinced that faith that saves, i.e., that delivers from sin and its consequences and guarantees fellowship with God, and its consequent worship cannot be framed, defined, or constructed by human beings. All such efforts remain human attempts which are tainted by the human predicament of having rebelled against God and of having been shut out from the delight of living in God's presence. The unalterable fact that "God is in heaven, and you are on earth" (Eccles 5:2)[1] entails on the one hand that God must reach out to human beings if there is to be any possibility of reconciliation. And it implies, on the other hand, that human beings must accept God's way out of the wilderness of the human condition.

Both Israel and the early Christians were convinced that God had indeed provided a path to salvation, a path that is inextricably linked with the divine revela-

---

[1]Scripture quotations in this essay are from the NRSV.

tion of the perspectives, principles, and promises of faith and worship that please God. Both Israel and the early Christians were convinced that such a divine revelation had taken place in Israel. Jews were convinced that such a saving revelation had occurred in the history of the descendants of Abraham. And the early Christians were convinced that the climax of God's saving revelation had taken place in the person and history of Jesus of Nazareth, the messianic Son of Man. Both Israel and the early Christians held that other systems of faith and worship were human—grounded in human concerns, framed by human beings, and controlled by human ideas about deities and sacrifices. In contemporary parlance, Israel and the early Christians regarded other systems of faith and worship, devised by human beings, as "secular" religions.[2]

In order to establish the view of the apostle Paul concerning secular religions, we will probe Romans 1:18-32 and Acts 17:22-31, two texts in which Paul comments explicitly on what he believes to be the realities of the systems of faith and worship of people who have not responded in obedience to God's revelation. Then, and much more briefly, we will examine Romans 2:1—3:31 and 1 Corinthians 1:18—2:5, two texts in which Paul emphasizes that salvation can be found only through faith in Jesus Christ, the crucified and risen Messiah-Savior.

THE REALITY OF SECULAR RELIGIONS

Romans 1:18-32. Paul was arguably better informed about the various deities and cults and their particular traditions and requirements of faith and worship than specialists in Greek and Roman religion are today. As Paul lived and worked in cities such as Tarsus, Antioch, Thessalonica, Philippi, Athens, Corinth and Ephesus, he would have walked past hundreds of temples, altars, and statues of various deities every day. Visitors to Rhodes could see 73,000 statues, and the theater in Ephesus displayed 120 of Nike and Eros alone (Pliny *Naturalis historia* 34.36 lectio varia).[3] In any given city, thousands of inscriptions announced the presence and

---

[2]Note the definition of *human* in the *Oxford English Dictionary:* "Belonging or relative to human beings as distinguished from God or superhuman beings; pertaining to the sphere or faculties of mankind (with implication of limitation or inferiority); mundane; secular. (Often opposed to *divine*.)" The basic definition of *secular* is "of or pertaining to the world."

[3]On Greek and Roman religion see Kurt Latte, *Römische Religionsgeschichte*, 2nd ed.; reprint, 1992; Handbuch der Altertumswissenschaft 4/4 (München: Beck, 1967); Ramsay MacMullen, *Paganism in the Roman Empire* (New Haven: Yale University Press, 1981); Walter Burkert, *Greek Religion: Archaic and Classical* (Oxford: Blackwell, 1985); Mary Beard et al., *Religions of Rome. Vol. 1: History. Vol. 2: A Sourcebook* (Cambridge: Cambridge University Press, 1998); Hans-Josef Klauck, *The Religious Context of Early Christianity: A Guide to Graeco-Roman Religions,* Studies of the New Testament and Its World (Edinburgh: T & T Clark, 2000).

extolled the virtues of the various deities that citizens, freedmen, and slaves worshiped.

In Athens, Paul "observed with sustained attention" (*theōreō*, Acts 17:16) the numerous images of deities which were on display in the city, he "looked carefully" (*anatheōreō*, Acts 17:23) at their sanctuaries, and he took notice of their altars, among them an altar with the dedication, "To an unknown god" (*agnōstō theō*, Acts 17:23). Archaeological, epigraphical, and literary sources show that the people of Athens worshiped in temples devoted to Anubis, Aphrodite, Apollo, Ares, Artemis, Asclepius, Athene, Cybele Demeter, Dionysos, Harpocrates, Hekate, Hephaistos, Hera, Heracles, Hermes, Hestia, Isis, Pan, Poseidon, Sarapis, the Twelve Gods, and Zeus, and in temples dedicated to the veneration of the emperor. People also worshiped abstractions such as the Demos (the People of Athens) and Nike (Victory), as well as heroes such as Antiochos, Ajax, Aigeus, Akamas, Aristogeiton, Epitegios, Erechtheus, Eurysakes, Harmodios, Hippothoon, Iatros, Kallistephanos, Kekrops, Leos, Oineus, Pandion, Strategos and Theseus.

Paul was not an academic, teaching students and reading and writing books, but a working missionary who was in constant contact with people—free citizens and slaves, men and women, Jews and Greeks (and Scythians and other "barbarians," cf. Col 3:11)—people whom he instructed to turn from their idols to the living and true God and to have faith in the crucified and risen Christ who will return as the judge of humankind (1 Thess 1:9-10).

The most extensive comments on the faith and worship of people who do not acknowledge the one true God and his revelation of salvation are found in Romans 1:18-32.[4] Paul argues that pagans know the rightful claims of God the Creator, but they suppress the truth and the reality of God (Rom 1:18). God has revealed to all people everything that "can be known about God" (Rom 1:19). He has revealed himself in the works of creation and through his interventions in history, thus providing humankind the opportunity to perceive him (Rom 1:20). The pagans refused to honor God as God and they refused to thank him for his gracious revelation (Rom 1:21).

As a result, the "thinking" *(dialogismos)* of pagans has become "futile" (*mataioō*, Rom 1:21), i.e., their "calculating consideration"[5] about the world and about God has proven to be incapable of producing lasting, reliable and useful

---

[4]For the following exposition, see Eckhard J. Schnabel, *Early Christian Mission* (Downers Grove, Ill.: InterVarsity Press, 2004), 2:1336-44, besides the standard commentaries on Paul's letter to the Romans.

[5]G. Petzke, *"dialogismos," Exegetical Dictionary of the New Testament*, ed. Horst Robert Balz and Gerhard Schneider (Grand Rapids: Eerdmans, 1990-1993), 1:308.

results. This "futility" consists in an "understanding of reality in contrast to the only valid reality of God," an understanding which Paul calls senseless.[6]

Which aspects of pagan religiosity does Paul have in mind? If he could have referred to the *Metamorphoses* of Apuleius, a philosopher and rhetorician of the second century, he might have referenced the words of the goddess Isis when she responds to Lucius, who has just interpreted the rise of the moon as the theophany of the goddess:

> Behold, Lucius, moved by your prayers I have come, I the mother of the universe, mistress of all the elements, and first offspring of the ages; mightiest of deities, queen of the dead, and foremost of heavenly beings; my one person manifests the aspect of all gods and goddesses *(deorum dearumque facies uniformis)*. With my nod I rule the starry heights of heaven, the health-giving breezes of the sea, and the plaintive silences of the underworld. My divinity is one, worshipped by all the world under different forms, with various rites, and by manifold names *(cuius numen unicum multiformi specie, ritu vario, nomine multiiugo totus veneratur orbis)*. (Apuleius, *Metam.* 11.5)[7]

Isis presents herself as the one deity of all being, combining in her appearance all gods and goddesses which are worshiped by the various peoples under different names and with different rites—Apuleius mentions the Phrygians, Attica, Cyprians, Cretans, Sicilians, Eleusis, Ethiopia and the Egyptians. Even though the deity has innumerable names, she claims that there is one name which truly describes her, a name that is known only among the Egyptians and the Ethiopians: "The people of the two Ethiopias,[8] who are lighted by the first rays of the Sun-God as he rises every day, and the Egyptians, who are strong in ancient lore, worship me with the rites that are truly mine and

---

[6]H. Balz, "*mataios*," *EDNT* 2:396. In the LXX, idols are often referred to as *mataia* (Lev 17:7; 2 Chron 11:15; Is 28:29; Hos 12:2; cf. 2 Sam 17:15; Jer 2:5; 51:17 [LXX 28:17]), i.e., as "mere useless nothings"; cf. C. E. B. Cranfield, *The Epistle to the Romans*, 2 vols., International Critical Commentary (Edinburgh: T & T Clark, 1975-79), 1:117. On papyri evidence for *mataios* meaning "futile, vain, worthless," cf. P.Lond. VII 1941,4; P.Cair.Zen. I 59060,2-3; P.Oxy. VII 1027,10; cf. Peter Arzt-Grabner et al., *1. Korinther* Papyrologische Kommentar zum Neuen Testament 2 (Göttingen: Vandenhoeck & Ruprecht, 2006), p. 158.

[7]Apuleius, *Metamorphoses. Latin and English*, ed. and trans. J. A. Hanson; LCL (Cambridge, Mass.: Harvard University Press, 1989), pp. 298-301; cf. Reinhold Merkelbach, *Isis regina–Zeus Sarapis. Die griechisch-ägyptische Religion nach den Quellen dargestellt* (Stuttgart: Teubner, 1995), §484. For the following comments see Jan Assmann, "Isis bei den Griechen," in *Antike Randgesellschaften und Randgruppen im östlichen Mittelmeerraum*, ed. H.-P. Müller and F. Siegert; Münsteraner Judaistische Studien 5 (Münster: Harrassowitz, 2000), pp. 29-45. On Apuleius and the cult of Isis, cf. John Gwyn Griffiths, ed., *Apuleius: The Isis-Book* (*Metamorphoses*, Book 11); Etudes préliminaires aux religions orientales dans l'Empire romain 39 (Leiden: Brill, 1975).

[8]Philae, the major cult site of Isis in the late Egyptian period, was regarded as belonging to Nubia (= Ethiopia).

call me by my real name, which is Queen Isis."[9]

An early second century invocation of Isis (P.Oxy XI 1380)[10] includes an elaborate list of the titles that are employed to worship Isis in towns or nomes of Egypt (lines 1-76) and in towns, districts, and countries in other parts of the world (lines 76-119)—a total of 122 places are mentioned, of which 55 are outside Egypt, ranging from Rome in the West to India in the East. The text mentions the various names which are used in worship, names which are interpreted as referring to Isis, the one goddess:

> at Aphroditopolis One . . . at Pemphris Isis, ruler, Hestia, lady of every country . . . at Buto skilled in calculation . . . at Thonis love . . . at Menouthis warlike . . . at Pelusium bringer to harbour . . . in Arabia great, goddess; in the Island giver of victory in the sacred games; in Lycia Leto; at Myra in Lycia sage, freedom; at Cnidus dispeller of attack, discoverer; at Cyrene Isis; in Crete Dictynnis; at Chalcedon Themis; at Rome warlike . . . among the Indians Maia; among the Thessalians moon; among the Persians Latina . . . at Sidon Astarte; at Ptolemaïs understanding; at Susa in the district by the Red Sea Sarkounis.

After further titles (lines 119-142), which include the line "the beautiful life of all gods" (line 126-127),[11] the invocation presents a long hymn of praise addressed to Isis (lines 142-298).

An inscription dating to the first or second century, found in Capua in Italy, honors Isis in a pantheistic fashion: "Arrius Balbinus dedicates [the statue] to you, goddess Isis, who are One and All (*una quae es omnia dea*), because my wish has been fulfilled" (CIL X 3800).[12] Plutarch mentions a statue that can be seen in Saïs,

---

[9]On the cult of Isis in general, cf. Hendrik S. Versnel, *Ter unus. Isis, Dionysos, Hermes: Three Studies in Henotheism.* Inconsistencies in Greek and Roman Religion 1 (Leiden: Brill, 1990), pp. 39-95; Merkelbach, *Isis regina*; Sarolta A. Takács, *Isis and Sarapis in the Roman World.* RGRW 124 (Leiden: Brill, 1995); Reginald E. Witt, *Isis in the Ancient World* (Baltimore: Johns Hopkins University Press, 1997); Malcolm D. Donalson, *The Cult of Isis in the Roman Empire: Isis Invicta.* Studies in Classics 22 (Lewiston: Mellen, 2003); Laurent Bricault, ed., *Isis en occident.* Actes du IIème Colloque international sur les études isiaques, Lyon III 16-17 mai 2002; RGRW 151 (Leiden: Brill, 2004).

[10]The *editio princeps* was published by Bernard P. Grenfell and Arthur S. Hunt, *The Oxyrhynchus Papyri Part XI. Edited with Translations and Notes* (London: Egypt Exploration Fund, 1915), pp. 190-220; text and translation ibid., pp. 196-203 (= P.Oxy XI 1380); cf, Merkelbach, *Isis regina*, §165.

[11]Grenfell and Hunt translate the phrase *theōn hapantōn to kalon zōon* "the beautiful animal of all the gods," while Assmann translates "das schöne Leben aller Götter."

[12]Ladislav Vidman, *Sylloge inscriptionum religionis Isiacae et Sarapiacae.* Religionsgeschichtliche Versuche und Vorarbeiten 28 (Berlin: De Gruyter, 1969), No. 502; Vincent Tam Tinh Tran, *Essai sur le culte d'Isis à Pompéi* (Paris: Boccard, 1964), p. 17; Françoise Dunand, "Le syncrétisme isiaque à la fin de l'époque hellénistique," in *Les Syncrétismes dans les religions de l'antiquité.* Colloque de Besançon, 22-23 octobre 1973; ed. F. Dunand and Pierre P. Lévêque; Études préliminaires aux religions orientales dans l'Empire romain 46 (Leiden: Brill, 1975), pp. 79-83, here p. 82; Merkelbach, *Isis regina*, §169 ("die du als die Eine [auch zugleich] Alles bist"). Verity Platt, "Viewing, Desiring, Believing: Confronting the Divine in a Pompeian House," *Art History* 25 (2002): 87-112; 112 n. 69 translates the phrase *una quae es omnia dea* as "the one goddess who is all goddesses."

depicting "Athena, whom they believe to be Isis," bearing the inscription: "I am all that has been, and is, and shall be (*egō eimi pan to gegonos kai ōn kai esomenon*), and my robe no mortal has yet uncovered" (Plutarch *Isis and Osiris* 9.9-10 [Mor. 354C]). This version of the inscription combines pantheism and mystery:[13] The revelation of truth ultimately eludes human beings.[14]

The monotheism of the Hellenistic cult of Isis, where one deity is worshiped with the names and in the languages of other nations, based on the claim that all gods are, ultimately, only names of One, is not even close to the monotheism of Israel which the early Christians shared.[15] Paul's was an exclusive monotheism which denied the existence of any god beside the God of Abraham who revealed himself in Jesus Christ. It was a monotheism that rejected female deities. It was a monotheism that did *not* regard as divine the mother of a "son of god" who brings salvation.[16] It was a monotheism that did not require initiation into the mysteries of a god.[17] It was a monotheism that was convinced that the one true and living God has revealed himself in an intelligible manner. Paul would have regarded any assertions to the contrary, whether related to Isis or to Zeus or to any other God, hero, or emperor as "futile," as it contradicted the only valid reality of the living God.

In Romans 1, Paul implicitly follows Old Testament precedent in using the first commandment of the Decalogue as the fundamental criterion for a critical evaluation of pagan religiosity:[18] There is no God besides Yahweh, the Creator of the universe:

> I am the LORD your God, who brought you out of the land of Egypt, out of the house of slavery; you shall have no other gods before me. You shall not make for

---

[13]In Proclus, *In Platonis Timaeum commentaria* 30, the phrase "my robe no mortal has yet uncovered" refers to the notion that Isis has brought forth the sun without male participation; cf. John Gwyn Griffiths, *Plutarch's De Iside et Osiride* (Cardiff: University of Wales Press, 1970), p. 283.

[14]Cf. Assmann, "Isis," p. 44, with reference to the theory of the Egyptian mystery religions which accepts the principle that ultimately truth remains a mystery, as truth can be grasped only in a veiled manner in images, myths, allegories, and riddles (cf. the expression of this principle in neo-Platonism, in hermetic literature, and in gnosticism). According to Plutarch, Isis-Athena is identical with Psyche; see *Isis and Osiris* 60, 62 [Mor. 375-376]; cf. Merkelbach, *Isis regina*, pp. 259-61.

[15]Cf. John E. Goldingay and Christopher J. H. Wright, "'Yahweh our God Yahweh One': The Old Testament and Religious Pluralism," in *One God, One Lord in a World of Religious Pluralism*, ed. A. D. Clarke and B. W. Winter (Cambridge: Tyndale House, 1991), pp. 34-52; J. Gordon McConville, "Yahweh and the Gods in the Old Testament," *European Journal of Theology* 2 (1993): 107-17.

[16]On the iconography of Isis lactans (Isis nursing the child Horus), cf. Jan Bergman, *Ich bin Isis. Studien zum memphitischen Hintergrund der griechischen Isisaretalogien*. Acta Universitatis Upsaliensis Historia Religionum 3 (Stockholm: Almqvist & Wiksell, 1968).

[17]On the mysteries of Isis, cf. Merkelbach, *Isis regina*, pp. 266-303.

[18]Paul is more explicit in 1 Thess 1:9; 4:5; 1 Cor 12:2; 8:4-6. See Richard Bauckham, *God Crucified: Monotheism and Christology in the New Testament* (Grand Rapids: Eerdmans, 1999).

yourself an idol, whether in the form of anything that is in heaven above, or that
is on the earth beneath, or that is in the water under the earth. You shall not bow
down to them or worship them; for I the LORD your God am a jealous God. (Deut
5:6-9)

The Mosaic law prohibits worshiping the sun, the moon, and the stars. Deuteronomy 4:19 states unambiguously: "And when you look up to the heavens and
see the sun, the moon, and the stars, all the host of heaven, do not be led astray
and bow down to them and serve them, things that the LORD your God has al-
lotted to all the peoples everywhere under heaven." The same emphasis is maintained in the various traditions of the second temple period. The author of the War
Scroll uses the expressions "sons of darkness," "nations of wickedness" and "nations
of futility" to describe the Gentiles (1QM I,1; IV,12; VI,6; XI,9; XIV,7; XV,2). In
the Jewish Hellenistic work Wisdom of Solomon, the Gentiles are described as
serving nameless and lifeless idols, an activity that is "the beginning and cause and
end of every evil" (Wisdom 14:27); God's punishment will fall upon the Gentiles
"because they thought wickedly of God in devoting themselves to idols, and because in deceit they swore unrighteously through contempt for holiness" (Wisdom
14:30).

Another result of humankind's rejection of the one true God is the fact that
people's "hearts" *(kardia)* have become "dark" *(skotizō)* and therefore "senseless" *(asynetos,* Rom 1:21). Paul asserts here that the seat of reasoning,
thought, and will—the center of human personhood—has become devoid of
life and truth. As people did not allow their thinking to be illuminated by the
light of God's self-revelation, they have no hope of finding the way home to
God on their own accord, as darkness makes the destination of the path to true
life invisible. The maxim "the journey is the destination," if understood as a
general principle of human existence, tries to hide the fact that humankind is
lost—a journey without a destination is not a journey but a random movement
in space and time, and a journey that fails to arrive at the intended destination
is a nightmare.[19]

The "darkness" of pagan religiosity implies a lack of orientation and thus a lack
of salvation. This conviction could have been illustrated by Paul with reference to

---

[19]Note the ritual for expulsion from the Community (Joseph M. Baumgarten, in *Damascus Document
II, Some Works on the Torah, and Related Documents,* ed. James H. Charlesworth, PTSDSSP 3 [Tübin-
gen: Mohr-Siebeck, 2006], p. 3) at the end of the Damascus Document in which the priest blesses
the Almighty God who "established peoples in accordance with their families and tongues for their
nations, but made them go astray in a trackless void. But our ancestors you did choose and to their
descendant(s) you gave your truthful statutes and your holy precepts, which (if) a person does, he
shall live" (4Q266 11,9-12; translation Baumgarten, ibid., p. 69).

the mythological paintings in the House of D. Octavius Quartio on the Via Abbondanza (Pompeii 2.2.2-5).[20] These paintings are arranged around a raised portico which overlooks a long ornamental water channel, flanked by an *aedicula* (small shrine) with dining couches on the east side (biclinium), and a small room (room f) on the west that is decorated with a panel depicting a priest of Isis (the niche may have held a cult image of the goddess).[21] The *aedicula* is framed by a painting of Narcissus who is entranced by his reflection and a painting of Thisbe committing suicide over the dying body of Pyramus, while the entrance to the Isiac chamber is framed by a painting of Actaeon being attacked by his hounds and a painting of a crouching nude Diana. V. Platt comments that "all three scenes depict a problematic confrontation, a meeting of gazes, between two individuals (in the case of Narcissus, between himself and his reflection), which results in death."[22] This "narrative of transgressive viewing (Narcissus, Pyramus and Thisbe, Actaeon and Diana)" is followed by the salvation offered by the cult of Isis. "It is precisely when the viewer enters the chamber, as he passes between Diana and Actaeon and undergoes a potentially transgressive viewing of the naked goddess in the painting, that he comes face to face with a three-dimensional goddess who exists in his own space." The inscription beneath the painting of the priest of Isis suggests to the viewer that salvation with the help of Isis is possible in Pompeian society.[23] However, Isis, understood as Isis Panthea (Universal Goddess),

> does not only proffer the possibility of salvation, but through her association with Venus and Diana also embodies those forces of desire which draw us into the dangerous dialectics which destroyed Narcissus, Pyramus, Thisbe and Actaeon. Her presence does not, then, necessarily guarantee that the viewer is safe from the perils of the gaze. . . . (Isis) may, as an all-embracing embodiment of the Other, testify to that paranoid consciousness of the general gaze which seems to imbue Roman society of the Imperial era. . . . Erotic desire and religious anxiety are yoked together in

---

[20]Vittorio Spinazzola, *Pompei alla luce degli scavi nuovi di Via dell' Abbondanza* [*anni 1910-1923*] (Rome: Libreria della Stato, 1953), 1:369-434 (on the paintings, ibid., pp. 391-94, 402-3); Francesca C. Tronchin, "An Eclectic *Locus Artis*: The Casa di Octavius Quartio at Pompeii," Ph.D. dissertation (Boston University, 2006). On account of electoral inscriptions on the exterior walls of the house, some associate the house with Loreius Tiburtinus; cf. Matteo Della Corte, *Pompeii: The New Excavations* [*Houses and Inhabitants*], rev. ed. (Pompei: Scuola Tipografica Pontifica Bartolo Longo, 1944), pp. 92-9 [No. 493].

[21]For the following description, see Platt, "Confronting the Divine"; Tronchin, "Casa di Octavius Quartio," pp. 17-20, pp. 252-65.

[22]Platt, "Confronting the Divine," p. 88; the following quotations, ibid., pp. 103-4.

[23]The reading of the inscription is contested. V. Spinazzola reads the name "Amilius Faventinus Tiburtinus" and interprets the priest as coming hailing from the Tiber region, whereas M. Della Corte reads "Amplus Alumnus Tiburs" ("Tiburs, the magnificent propagator [of the cult of Isis in Pompeii]," interpreting the priest as an ancestor of Loreius Tiburtinus who owned the house.

each image in a manner which represents the Other at its most beguiling, and yet its most dangerous."[24]

Thus, one could argue, Isis does not save after all but leaves her devotees perplexed, bewildered, and confused—not only on account of the potential fate of transgression and destruction, embodied by Diana, but also because the viewer eventually must leave the potential safety of the Isis chamber and return to the portico in order to re-enter the house, passing again the three models of the dangerous options of human reality. There is no assurance of salvation, only possibilities of relief in the midst of powerful forces that can and will lead to destruction and death.

Paul asserts that people claim to be wise (sophoi), without recognizing that they have become fools (Rom 1:22). This evaluation is linked with people's claim that they have the light of wisdom while they sit in darkness as well as with their claim that they know the living God while they worship objects made of stone, wood, or metal. Instead of worshiping the living God, the pagans worship "images resembling a mortal human being or birds or four-footed animals or reptiles" (Rom 1:23), which are "idols that cannot speak" (1 Cor 12:2). In other words, they are images that have no life.

Most deities were portrayed in male or female human form. Zeus (Jupiter) is generally depicted as a mature adult male, bearded and with flowing hair.[25] Early images often show him hurling a thunderbolt. Classical representations show him seated on a throne. His iconography includes a thunderbolt, scepter, scales, ram and the lion. Artemis (Diana), the goddess of wild animals, of hunting and of young virgin women is portrayed as an athletic young woman (more attractive than Athena, less voluptuous than Aphrodite), wearing a short (thigh-length) hunting dress. Her attributes include bow and arrows or quiver, a hair ribbon, deer or wild goat, bear, quail and a torch. Personifications of abstractions were portrayed in human form as well: Concordia, the goddess of unity and agreement, was portrayed on coins with a patera in right hand and her left elbow resting on a statue of Spes, cornucopiae under chair. Iustitia, the goddess of justice,

---

[24]Platt, "Confronting the Divine," pp. 105-6. Tronchin, "Casa di Octavius Quartio," pp. 51-52, 279, offers a less speculative interpretation of room f and of the portrait of a priest of Isis: "The concentration of Egyptian iconography in room f and the garden might suggest that the residents of this area of the house were devoted to the cult of Isis. The cult was especially popular among Roman women. Given the 'feminine' iconography of room f—which includes female personifications of the seasons and Venus—it may be argued that this was a space primarily used by the matriarch of the family who may have also been a member of the popular Isiac cult in Pompeii. . . . The name and the portrait most likely refer to a son or grandson who had dedicated his life to the Egyptian goddess and gone to live in her temple as other priests of Isis did."

[25]See <http://web.uvic.ca/grs/bowman/myth/gods/zeus_i.html> (with links to images).

was portrayed with an olive twig, patera, and scepter. Pax, the goddess of peace, was portrayed as a young woman carrying a cornucopia, an olive branch or a sheaf of grain, or with a branch upward in her right hand and a scepter in her left hand. Pietas, the goddess of piety, is portrayed as sprinkling incense with her right hand over an altar, with a box of perfumes in her left hand.[26] Animal gods are attested for Egypt, where the divine was worshiped in the form of monkeys, birds and crocodiles.[27]

Was Paul aware of the possibility that pagans did not worship the statues of deities as such, but that statues made of stone or wood were dedicatory gifts and symbolic representations? Porphyry from Tarsus, the last great defender of pagan religiosity, attacked the (as he calls them) "surprisingly ignorant" people who were not aware of this difference.[28] Paul, who does not discuss such objections to the Christian view of the pagan worship of images, would probably counter such arguments with references to God's invisibility, glory and immortality.[29] At any rate, Paul insists that while pagans certainly have a "religious" experience when they place their faith in an image (e.g., of Zeus/Jupiter) which they worship, they never hear a response and thus they remain trapped in the darkness of their own thoughts, hopes, and desires, without receiving orientation from the living God who alone can grant salvation.

For Paul, the religious practices of the nations are the result of a twofold refusal. They refuse to acknowledge the presence of the light and power of God's reality (Rom 1:21), and they refuse to participate in God's glory as people who have been created in the image of God. Instead, they have turned this glory "into the likeness of an image of his creatures," and they have accepted the transient nothingness of idol images that depict people and animals (Rom 1:23).[30] The religious experiences of the pagans thus consist in exchanging "the truth about God for a lie" and in worshiping and serving "the creature rather than the Creator" (Rom 1:25).

---

[26]Other female personifications include Abundantia, Aeternitas, Clementia, Constantia, Fecunditas, Felicitas, Fortuna, Hilaritas, Indulgentia, Providentia, Pudicita, Securitas and Victoria. Male abstract personifications include Aequitas (god of fair dealing), Honus (god of military honor), Liberalitas (god of generosity), and Virtus (god of prowess).

[27]Lucian *Deorum concilium* 10-11; *De sacrificiis* 14-15. Cf. MacMullen, *Paganism*, pp. 75-78, on the "analytical theology" of pagan critics of contemporary religious rites such as Plutarch, Lucian, Lucian and Porphyry.

[28]Porphyry *Peri agalmatōn* 1; cf. further Celsus, in Origen *Cels.* 7.62.

[29]Cf. Rom 1:20, 23; cf. James D. G. Dunn, *Romans*, Word Biblical Commentary 38A-B (Dallas: Word, 1988), 1:63. Athenagoras, Origen, Eusebius and Athanasius later argued that even though educated pagans are aware of this difference, the vast majority of idol worshipers are not.

[30]This argument agrees with a broad biblical and Jewish tradition, cf. Ps 106:20 LXX; Jer 2:11; Is 44:9-20; Wisdom 11:15; 12:24; 13:10-14; 14:8; 15:18-19.

108 FAITH COMES BY HEARING

The ethical and social realities of the Greek and Roman cities are the consequence of this rebellion against the reality of the one true God who continues to be present in his creation as he judges the Gentiles.[31] God's wrath and the self-destruction of men and women "are closely connected. Men and women pay for their perversion of the truth of God, and the community and fellowship of people suffers as well."[32] A prime indicator of the alienation from the living God is the "impurity" *(akatharsia)* of people's desires *(epithymiai)*, evidenced by the degradation of their bodies (Rom 1:24) and of their passions (*pathē atimias* Rom 1:26). This degradation becomes visible in homosexual behavior, which exchanges the divine order with a self-imposed order that contradicts nature (Rom 1:26-27). The moral contentment of Greco-Roman society which accepted pre- and extra-marital sexual activity, including homosexual activity, is the result of people's failure to recognize the consequences of their behavior on the Day of Judgment. Paul's missionary preaching did not present a solution to a moral crisis that his pagan listeners would have perceived as such. Rather, Paul's preaching revealed that their moral contentment was the result of their failure to recognize the consequences of their behavior on the Day of Judgment.[33]

As the pagans exclude the reality and the claims of the true and living God from their everyday lives, their reasoning lacks norms and moderation *(adokimos nous)*. They are no longer able to distinguish between right and wrong, and thus, by necessity, they do "things that should not be done" (Rom 1:28). Everything becomes possible, and they do not even recognize that they destroy themselves. Paul sees paganism as "a self-destructive mode of being human."[34] God allowed the pagans to leave the restricted area protected by his good and perfect will and gave them up to their self-chosen desires. This can be observed in countless specific modes of behavior: injustice and wickedness, greed and corruption, envy and murder and strife and deceit and craftiness, gossip and slander, hatred of God and arrogance, pride and smugness, ever new inventions of evil, disobedience of parents, foolishness and instability, heartlessness and mercilessness, and the active support

---

[31]Note the phrase "therefore God gave them up" *(dio paredōken autous)* in Rom 1:24, 26, 28.

[32]Otto Michel, *Der Brief an die Römer,* Kritisch-exegetischer Kommentar über das Neue Testament 4 (Göttingen: Vandenhoeck & Ruprecht, 1978), p. 104.

[33]Note that in the lists of vices in 1 Cor 5:10, 11; 6:9, 10; 10:8; 2 Cor 12:21; Gal 5:19; 1 Thess 4:3; Eph 5:3; and Col 3:5, immoral behavior is generally mentioned first. Stephen J. Chester, *Conversion at Corinth: Perspectives on Conversion in Paul's Theology and the Corinthian Church.* Studies of the New Testament and Its World (Edinburgh: T & T Clark, 2003), p. 147, points out that these "vices" represented accepted behavior in Greco-Roman society, and that Paul's missionary preaching did not present a solution to a moral crisis that his pagan listeners would have perceived as such. Rather, Paul seeks to move his pagan listeners "from false contentment to crisis to security in Christ."

[34]N. T. Wright, *What Saint Paul Really Said. Was Paul of Tarsus the Real Founder of Christianity?* (Grand Rapids: Eerdmans, 1997), p. 89.

of these destructive patterns of behavior (Rom 1:29-32). The terms that Paul uses
to describe non-Jews in Romans 1 and in other passages—"unjust" *(adikos)*, "unbelieving" *(apistos)*, "nations, gentiles, polytheists" *(ethnē)*, "uncircumcised, gentiles" *(akrobustia)*—imply various negative connotations: lawlessness, sin, unbelief, hostility against God, idolatry, moral dereliction, nonmembership in the
people of God.[35]

Paul's diagnosis of contemporary Greco-Roman society was highly critical. His
negative assessment of pagan life, thought, and spirituality results from the fact
that he writes as a missionary, theologian, and pastor, not as a neutral observer
who describes anthropological data. Paul describes human behavior and cultural
patterns in the context of the reality of God the Creator and the coming Judgment
Day when everyone will be held accountable for their behavior by the one true and
living God. This is the reason why positive or neutral statements on pagans or on
pagan society are rare.[36]

Paul's subsequent discussion explains the "secular" religious cults of the Greco-
Roman world not simply as religious ignorance. Rather, he regards the pagan cults
as a deliberate rebellion against God that leads to the worship of idols and to immoral behavior. In Romans 5:12-21 Paul links the sin of humankind with the behavior of Adam. Adam's sin cannot be explained away as more or less innocent ignorance. Rather, it was deliberate disobedience in the face of advance knowledge.
Paul takes the individual pagan and his actions seriously: everyone is responsible
for his actions. Thus he argues that the religious actions of the pagans are futile,
as their (im)moral behavior demonstrates: They are far removed from the light of
the life of the one true God.

Acts 17:22-31. When Paul engaged in missionary outreach in the marketplace
of Athens, speaking to people who happened to be there (Acts 17:17),[37] Epicurean
and Stoic philosophers initiated a discussion with him concerning the deity that
he proclaimed (Acts 17:18). They eventually took him to the Council of the Areopagus where he was asked to explain the "new teaching" concerning the strange,
astonishing gods which he was heard to propound (Acts 17:19-20). The speech
which Luke provides at this point in his account (Acts 17:22-31) allows Paul to

---

[35]Cf. Rolf Dabelstein, *Die Beurteilung der "Heiden" bei Paulus*, BET 14 (Frankfurt: Lang, 1981), pp. 15-
60; cf. also Ulrich Heckel, "Das Bild der Heiden und die Identität der Christen bei Paulus," in *Die
Heiden. Juden, Christen und das Problem des Fremden*, ed. R. Feldmeier and U. Heckel, WUNT 70
(Tübingen: Mohr-Siebeck, 1994), pp. 269-96, 270-74.

[36]We find such positive statements exclusively in ethical contexts where Paul reminds Christian believers of social norms for proper behavior; cf. 1 Thess 4:12; 1 Cor 10:32; Col 4:5; cf. also the reference
to what is "good" in 1 Thess 5:15; Rom 12:9; 13:3; 14:16; 15:2; 16:19.

[37]See Schnabel, *Early Christian Mission*, 2:1169-79.

develop and explain his concept of God in front of an intellectual audience.[38] The Council evidently inquired whether Paul wanted to introduce deities that were unfamiliar to the Athenians.[39] Even in the cosmopolitan Hellenistic period with its syncretistic tendencies, "There were nonetheless manifest symptoms of reservations against foreign gods and cults. . . . In both classical and Hellenistic times the introduction of foreign cults and rites required the official authorization of the state."[40] An Athenian decree stipulates: "The king archon shall fix the boundaries of the sanctuaries/sacred precincts in the Pelargikon, and in the future no one shall found altars, cut the stones from the Pelargikon or take out earth or stones without (the authorization of) the council and the demos."[41] Isocrates praises the Athenians for guarding "against the elimination of any of the ancestral sacrifices and against the addition of any sacrifices outside the traditional ones" (*Areopagiticus* 30). Josephus relates that Ninos, a priestess of the Phrygian god Sabazios, was put to death by the Athenians "because someone accused her of initiating people into mysteries of foreign gods; this was forbidden by their law, and the penalty decreed for any who introduced a foreign god was death" (Josephus *Against Apion* 2.267).[42] Maecenas's speech to Augustus suggests that this aversion to foreign and new cults persisted well into the first century, as the emperor is advised:

> Do you not only yourself worship the divine Power everywhere and in every way in accordance with the traditions of our fathers, but compel all others to honour it.

---

[38]In other words, the so-called Areopagus speech is not an example of missionary preaching before Gentiles—which then can be faulted for lacking an exposition of the person and the significance of Jesus Christ; cf. recently Stanley E. Porter, *The Paul of Acts: Essays in Literary Criticism, Rhetoric and Theology,* WUNT 115 (Tübingen: Mohr-Siebeck, 1999), p. 124. For the following comments, cf. Schnabel, *Early Christian Mission,* 2:1392-1404. On questions of authenticity see Colin J. Hemer, "The Speeches of Acts II. The Areopagus Address," *Tyndale Bulletin* 40 (1989): 239-59; Ben Witherington III, *The Acts of the Apostles: A Socio-Rhetorical Commentary* (Grand Rapids: Eerdmans, 1998), p. 519, with n. 205.

[39]On the deities that were worshiped in Athens, cf. John McK. Camp, *Gods and Heroes in the Athenian Agora* (Princeton, N.J.: American School of Classical Studies at Athens, 1980); see the summary in Schnabel, *Early Christian Mission,* 2:1175-77. On the role of the Council of the Areopagus concerning religious affairs and Acts 17, see Daniel J. Geagan, *The Athenian Constitution after Sulla.* Hesperia 12 (Princeton, N.J.: American School of Classical Studies at Athens, 1967), p. 50; David W. J. Gill, "Achaia," in *The Book of Acts in Its Graeco-Roman Setting,* ed. D. W. J. Gill and C. Gempf; *The Book of Acts in Its First-Century Setting,* vol. 2 (Exeter, U.K.: Paternoster, 1994), pp. 433-53.

[40]Versnel, *Ter unus,* pp. 121-22. On Athenian law against foreign gods, cf. ibid., pp. 123-46. See also Robert Garland, *Introducing New Gods: The Politics of Athenian Religion* (Ithaca, N.Y.: Cornell University Press, 1992).

[41]IG I³ 78 (I² 76; ca. 422 B.C.); Franciszek Sokolowski, *Lois sacrées des cités grecques* (Paris: Boccard, 1969), No. 5; Eran Lupu, *Greek Sacred Law: A Collection of New Documents.* Religions in the Graeco-Roman World 152 (Leiden: Brill, 2005), p. 36.

[42]Versnel, *Ter unus,* pp. 115-17, 127. Demosthenes 19.281 refers to this incident, which took place sometime in the fourth century, as well, without mentioning the name Ninos.

Those who attempt to distort our religion with strange rites you should abhor and punish, not merely for the sake of the gods (since if a man despises these he will not pay honour to any other being), but because such men, by bringing in new divinities in place of the old, persuade many to adopt foreign practices, from which spring up conspiracies, factions, and cabals, which are far from profitable to a monarchy. (Cassius Dio 52.36)[43]

The introduction of a deity into a city would prompt the magistrates to ascertain the novelty of the cult, the desirability of allowing it, and its requirements, such as the need for a temple or an altar, sacrifices, festivals, and processions. A good example is the decree permitting Kitians to found a temple of Aphrodite in Athens:

Gods. When Nikokratos was archon, in the first prytany (that of the tribe Aegeis): Theophilos from the deme Phegous, one of the Proedroi, put this matter to the vote: The Council decided (after Antidodos, son of Apollodoros, from the deme Sypalletos made the motion):

Concerning the things that the Citians say about the foundation of the temple to Aphrodite, it has been voted by the Council that the Proedroi, the ones to be chosen by lot to serve as Proedroi at the first Assembly, should introduce the Citians and allow them to have an audience, and to share with the People the opinion of the Council, that the People, having heard from the Citians concerning the foundation of the temple, and from any other Athenian who wants to speak, decide to do whatever seems best. When Nikokrates was archon, in the second Prytany (that of the tribe Pandionis): Phanostratos from the deme Philaidai, one of the Proedroi, put this matter to the vote: The People decided (after Lycurgus, son of Lycophron, of the deme Boutadai made the motion): Concerning the things for which the Citian merchants resolved to petition, lawfully, asking the People for the use of a plot of land on which they might build a temple of Aphrodite, it has seemed best to the People to give to the merchants of the Citians the use of a plot of land on which they might build a temple of Aphrodite, just as also the Egyptians built the temple of Isis. (IG II^2 337)[44]

[43]On religious laws in Greece and Rome, see Franciszek Sokolowski, *Lois sacrées de l'Asie Mineure*. Travaux et mémoires 9 (Paris: Boccard, 1955); idem, *Lois sacrées des cités grecques. With Supplément* (Paris: Boccard, 1962); idem, *Lois sacrées des cités grecques*; R. C. T. Parker, "What Are Sacred Laws?" in *The Law and the Courts in Ancient Greece*, ed. E. M. Harris and L. Rubinstein (London: Duckworth, 2004), pp. 57-70; Lupu, *Greek Sacred Law* (read with the review by J. M. Carbon, *Bryn Mawr Classical Review* 2005.04.07); Stephen D. Lambert, "Athenian State Laws and Decrees, 352/1 - 322/1: II Religious Regulations," *ZPE* 154 (2005): 125-59. There are laws regulating cult calendars, the foundation of a cult, sacred land or property (statues, dedications, etc.), sacrifices, pre- and post-sacrifice procedures, such as purification rites, festival regulations (processions, etc.), religious offices, disciplinary penalties and funerals.
[44]Cf. Lambert, "Athenian State Laws and Decrees II," p. 153 fig. 3.

When we read Acts 17:22-31 in this context,[45] the main thrust of Paul's speech is his emphasis that he is not introducing a new deity to Athens; rather, he proclaims the deity who is honored at the altar with the inscription, "To an unknown god" (Acts 17:23). He points out that the god whose spokesman he is does not want to acquire a piece of land on which a sanctuary or an altar for cultic veneration should be erected, as this god neither lives in temples nor has a need for festivals or sacrifices (Acts 17:24-26).

While Paul clarifies that he does not seek the permission of the Council and of the people of Athens to introduce a deity to be added to the pantheon of gods that are worshiped in the city, he does advance a legal argument. Always the missionary who seeks to lead people to faith in God's salvific revelation, he points out that they—the honorable members of the venerable Council of the Areopagus—must repent as everybody else must repent of deficient religious beliefs and practices, since God has fixed the Day of Judgment, drawn up the rules for the trial and for the verdict that will be pronounced, and appointed the judge.[46]

Luke's summary of Paul's speech is often interpreted in terms of parallels in Greek philosophy. This "Greek interpretation" of biblical revelation is taken by some critics to prove that the Areopagus speech in Acts 17 could not have been given by Paul but reflects, rather, the thinking of the author of the book of Acts.[47] Evangelical scholars generally explain the Greek or Hellenistic elements of the speech as an example of contextualization. In the words of F. F. Bruce: "Paul knew the wisdom of adapting his tone and general approach to the particular audience or readership being addressed at the time."[48] Several studies have shown that the Areopagus speech contains not only "points of contact" with Paul's pagan and intellectual audience which included Stoic and Epicurean philosophers,[49] but at the

---

[45]Cf. Bruce W. Winter, "On Introducing Gods to Athens: An Alternative Reading of Acts 17.18-20," *Tyndale Bulletin* 47 (1996): 71-90.

[46]Winter, "Introducing Gods," p. 85.

[47]Most prominently Martin Dibelius, *Studies in the Acts of the Apostles* (New York: Scribner's, 1956), pp. 26-77.

[48]F. F. Bruce, *The Book of the Acts*, rev. ed. New International Commentary on the New Testament (Grand Rapids: Eerdmans, 1988), p. 334; Dean E. Flemming, *Contextualization in the New Testament: Patterns for Theology and Mission* (Downers Grove, Ill.: InterVarsity Press, 2005), pp. 72-84.

[49]For a summary of the points of contact, see Schnabel, *Early Christian Mission*, 2:1396-98; cf. Abraham J. Malherbe, *Paul and the Popular Philosophers* (Minneapolis: Fortress, 1989), pp. 147-63; David L. Balch, "The Areopagus Speech: An Appeal to the Stoic Historian Posidonius against Later Stoics and the Epicureans," in *Greeks, Romans, and Christians: Essays in Honor of Abraham J. Malherbe*, ed. D. L. Balch et al. (Minneapolis: Fortress, 1990), pp. 52-79; Bruce W. Winter, "In Public and in Private: Early Christian Interactions with Religious Pluralism," in *One God, One Lord in a World of Religious Pluralism*, ed. A. D. Clarke and B. W. Winter (Cambridge: Tyndale House, 1991), pp. 112-34.

same time "points of contradiction."[50] The latter demonstrate that Paul does not regard the Athenians' various systems of faith and worship as more or less identical with, or at least similar to, the Christians' convictions concerning God, the world, humankind, history, and salvation. He does not argue for an essential continuity between the revelation of the God whom he proclaims and the convictions of pagan poets and philosophers. Instead, he disputes the Athenians' understanding of the divine.

The reference to the "unknown god" (Acts 17:23), understood in the context of Isaiah 45:15, 18-25, implies a censure of pagan religious convictions. The prophet Isaiah, after repeating Israel's monotheistic confession, "Truly, you are a God who hides himself, O God of Israel, the Savior" (Is 45:15), narrates a speech of Yahweh in which he seeks to convert the people to worshiping the one true God. If Israel's God appears to be hidden and thus an unknown God, Yahweh's words prove that he is indeed not in hiding at all: "For thus says the LORD, who created the heavens (he is God!), who formed the earth and made it (he established it; he did not create it a chaos, he formed it to be inhabited!): I am the LORD, and there is no other. I did not speak in secret, in a land of darkness; I did not say to the offspring of Jacob, 'Seek me in chaos.' I the LORD speak the truth, I declare what is right" (Is 45:18-19). Yahweh goes on to state that the nations "have no knowledge" and that "those who carry about their wooden idols" are praying to "a god that cannot save" since "there is no other god besides me, a righteous God and a Savior; there is no one besides me" (Is 45:20-21). This truth leads to an invitation: "Turn to me and be saved, all the ends of the earth! For I am God, and there is no other. By myself I have sworn, from my mouth has gone forth in righteousness a word that shall not return: 'To me every knee shall bow, every tongue shall swear'" (Is 45:22-23). Read in the light of this dialogue between Yahweh and the nations, the reference to the religiosity of the Athenians and to the altar of an "unknown god" in Acts 17:23 may be a complimentary introduction on the surface only.[51]

---

[50]Bertil Gärtner, *The Areopagus Speech and Natural Revelation* (Lund: Gleerup, 1955), and David W. Pao, *Acts and the Isaianic New Exodus* (WUNT 2/130; Tübingen: Mohr-Siebeck, 2000), pp. 193-208, emphasize the Old Testament background of Paul's speech. See also Richard J. Gibson, "Paul and the Evangelization of the Stoics," in *The Gospel to the Nations: Perspectives on Paul's Mission: In Honor of Peter T. O'Brien*, ed. P. Bolt and M. Thompson (Downers Grove, Ill.: InterVarsity Press, 2000), pp. 309-26. For the following summary, see Schnabel, *Early Christian Mission*, 2:1398-1401.

[51]Bruce, *Acts*, p. 335, asserts with reference to Lucian *Anacharsis* 19 that it was forbidden to use complimentary exordia in addressing the Areopagus court, hoping to secure its goodwill. Since Lucian (second century A.D.) describes practices at the time of Solon (sixth century B.C.), it is unclear whether this reference can be taken to describe the practices of the Court of the Areopagus in the first century.

Paul acknowledges that the Gentiles seek God (Acts 17:27). However, the next clause shows that he is skeptical concerning the actual outcome of this search: Uncertainty is indicated first in the introduction by *ei ara ge* ("in the hope that"[52]), second by the optative mood of the verbs *(psēlaphēseian* and *heuroien)*, and third by the choice of the verb *psēlaphaō* ("to touch by feeling and handling" or, as here, to look for something in uncertain fashion, "to feel around for, grope for").[53] The Jewish author of Wisdom of Solomon 13:5-6 voiced similar doubts: "For from the greatness and beauty of created things comes a corresponding perception of their Creator. Yet these people are little to be blamed, for perhaps they go astray while seeking God and desiring to find him."

When Paul states that God "is not far from each one of us" (Acts 17:27), listeners who are aware of Jewish convictions based on Scripture[54] would indeed wonder whether this is a reference to Stoic notions of the presence of the divine in everything that exists,[55] or a critical comment on unsuccessful attempts to find God who is "near" but not quite present. If the prepositional expression *en autō* in Acts 17:28 is understood not in a spatial sense ("in him"),[56] but in an instrumental sense ("by him"), the triadic formulation is not an argument for humankind's kinship with God but a theological statement about God's past and present sovereignty in creation: human beings owe their existence and the circumstances of their life to God—"by him we live and move and have our being."

While the quotation from Aratos (*Phaenomena* 5)[57] in Acts 17:28 ("For we too are his offspring") can be understood as an accommodation to the philosophical convictions of the audience in the Council of the Areopagus,[58] the context of Paul's scriptural view of creation is again significant. In *this* context, the statement about people being God's offspring refers to Israel's conviction that the one true

---

[52]Walter Bauer et al., *A Greek-English Lexicon of the New Testament and Other Early Christian Literature*, ed. F. W. Danker, 3rd ed. (Chicago: University of Chicago Press, 2000), p. 278 s.v. *ei* 6a (cf. ibid., p. 127 s.v. *ara* 3).

[53]BDAG 1098, with reference to Philo *De mutatione nominum* 126.

[54]Note Ps 145:18: "The LORD is near to all who call on him, to all who call on him in truth," with the emphasis on the second part of the sentence.

[55]Seneca formulates that "God is near you, with you, in you" (*prope est a te deus, tecum est, intus est*; Seneca *Epistulae morales* 41.1).

[56]A spatial understanding of *en autō* would lead the Stoic philosophers in the Council to interpret the triadic formulation in terms of the life, the movement, and the being of humankind "in god" in a pantheistic sense as the immanence of man in the all-pervasive deity; cf. the quotation from Seneca *Epistulae morales* 41.1. Cf. Rudolf Pesch, *Die Apostelgeschichte*, Evangelisch-Katholischer Kommetar zun Neuen Testament 5/1-2 (Zürich/Neukirchen-Vluyn: Benziger/Neukirchener, 1986), 2:139.

[57]Aratos (315-240 B.C.) of Soloi, a port city in Cilicia, was one of the most important Hellenistic poets. His *Phaenomena* was the most widely read poems after Homer's *Iliad* and *Odyssey*.

[58]For details, see C. K. Barrett, *The Acts of the Apostles*, International Critical Commentary (Edinburgh: T & T Clark, 1994-1998), 2:847-48.

God created "the one ancestor" from whom he made all people (Acts 17:26). The knowledge of the poets is partial; it becomes more fully relevant only in the context of the truth of God's revelation of his activity as the Creator of "the world and everything in it" (Acts 17:24).[59] The reference to the one ancestor in Acts 17:26 ("From one ancestor he made all nations to inhabit the whole earth") is an unambiguous reference to the biblical tradition of the beginning of all human existence in the creation of Adam, the first man whom God brought into being (Gen 1:26-27; 2:7). There is no clear parallel in Greek thought and mythology to this conviction that the human race can be traced back to one man who was created by God. Paul's use of the language of the Bible in his reference to the creation narrative of the book of Genesis conveys a biblical critique of popular polytheism and idolatry.[60]

Paul criticizes the pagan religious notion that God lives in man-made houses of worship. His critique of temples in Acts 17:24 (God "does not live in shrines made by human hands") certainly reminded his listeners on the Areopagus of Epicurean arguments.[61] At the same time this critique of pagan religious belief and practice reflects the words of the prophet Isaiah, that the one true God insists that "heaven is my throne and the earth is my footstool; what is the house that you would build for me, and what is my resting place? All these things my hand has made, and so all these things are mine, says the LORD" (Is 66:1-2). Paul also criticizes the pagan practice of sacrifices and the underlying belief that God must be "served by human hands" (Acts 17:25).

The Epicureans rejected the offering of sacrifices for the gods, arguing that a god does not need human things.[62] Paul's critique is again biblically informed, when he asserts that God "is not served by human hands, as though he needed anything, since he himself gives to all mortals life and breath and all things." The prophet Isaiah proclaims, "Thus says God, the LORD, who created the heavens and stretched them out, who spread out the earth and what comes from it, who gives breath to the people upon it and spirit to those who walk in it" (Is 42:5). In Israel's worship, the people were regularly reminded of God's sovereign independence of human beings: "If I were hungry, I would not tell you, for the world and all that is in it is mine. Do I eat the flesh of bulls, or drink the blood of goats?" (Ps 50:12-13).

After condemning temples and sacrifices, Paul also disparages the images

---

[59]Pesch, *Apostelgeschichte*, 2:139.

[60]Barrett, *Acts*, 2:842.

[61]The Epicureans argued that the gods do not live in man-made temples. Plutarch *Moralia* 1034b writes that "one should not build temples of the gods."

[62]Philodemus *Pros eusebeias* Frag. 38; Plutarch *Moralia* 1052a; cf. Plato *Timaeus* 33d, 34b.

which pagans worship: "Since we are God's offspring, we ought not to think that the deity is like gold, or silver, or stone, an image formed by the art and imagination of mortals" (Acts 17:29). The reference to "the times of human ignorance" (Acts 17:30) makes the conclusion inescapable that we have here a clear indictment of popular pagan piety. Both the Stoic and the Epicurean philosophers had come to an arrangement with popular religious practices, conceding the reality of contemporary religiosity as it was expressed in the cultic activity in the temples of the cities. The philosopher Epicurus was convinced that popular piety was misguided, but he did not attempt to prevent his followers nor the people at large from participating in the local cults. An Epicurean text, written around A.D. 50, asserts that piety cannot be proved by the offering of sacrifices, and then argues that sacrificing to the gods is permitted since it is in agreement with religious traditions (P.Oxy II 215). Plutarch accuses the Stoics of contradicting their philosophical position when they visit the mysteries in the temples, when they ascend the acropolis to honor the idol statues, and when they lay down wreaths in the sanctuaries despite their convictions (Plutarch *Mor.* 1034B-C). Paul explicitly rejects any accommodation of his convictions to the religiosity of the population.[63] He uses the quotation from Aratus ("For we too are his offspring," Acts 17:28) as argument against such a rapprochement with the religious pluralism of Greco-Roman culture: "Since we are God's offspring, we ought not to think that the deity is like gold, or silver, or stone, an image formed by the art and imagination of mortals" (Acts 17:29). If human beings owe their existence to God, then it is ridiculous to portray God in the form of statues made of gold, silver, or marble and to worship these representations. This condemnation of pagan worship of statues again takes up biblical traditions and their sometimes rather polemical verdicts on pagan idol worship.[64]

Paul goes on to assert that the story of Athens is a record of "times of ignorance" *(chronoi tēs agnoias)* which God has so far "overlooked" (Acts 17:30).[65] The religious pluralism of the Athenians, far from being a positive reality, makes them guilty before God: One cannot ignore truth for too long without being responsible for one's behavior. The statement that God "overlooked" or "ignored" this ignorance is, on the one hand, a reference to God's merciful patience in not suppressing false religious worship, and, on the other hand, an indictment of the Athenians: God never approved of their "ignorant" idolatrous worship. Consider-

---

[63]Cf. Winter, "Religious Pluralism," pp. 122, 126-30.
[64]Cf. Is 40:18-19; 44:9-20; 45:15-24; 46:5-7; see also Wisdom 13:1-19.
[65]Cf. Barrett, *Acts*, 2:830, who comments that "from nature the Greeks have evolved not natural theology but natural idolatry."

ing the fact that the cultic veneration of the deceased emperors was an increasingly important element of Roman culture in the larger cities,[66] Paul's rejection of the Athenians' religious pluralism was ill-advised from the point of view of the principle of accommodation, detrimental for his missionary project in Athens, and potentially dangerous to himself and to future followers of Jesus Christ in the city.[67]

Paul's response to the religious convictions and practices of his pagan audience was, in the end, not accommodation but confrontation. While he uses terminology that is immediately understood by the members of the Council of the Areopagus, and while many of his statements and assertions are acceptable at least for some members of the Council, depending on their philosophical convictions, Paul leaves no doubt that he unambiguously rejects the plurality of gods and cults and the proliferation of temples, altars, and statutes in the city of Athens. That Paul's main concern is not the accommodation of his beliefs to the convictions of his audience but rather the truth of the message which he proclaims becomes obvious at the end of the speech. Paul declares that the one God who created the world "now commands all people everywhere to repent, because he has fixed a day on which he will have the world judged in righteousness by a man whom he has appointed, and of this he has given assurance to all by raising him from the dead" (Acts 17:30-31). Paul not only advances philosophical and logical arguments for the necessity to abandon the religious convictions and practices that have characterized the history and the life of the city of Athens. He also establishes the necessity of changing religious convictions and cultic activities with a reference to the divine judgment "by a man" (Acts 17:31). Paul emphasizes that God will judge the "world"

---

[66]On the emperor cult in general, cf. Manfred Clauss, *Kaiser und Gott. Herrscherkult im römischen Reich* (Stuttgart: Teubner, 1999); Ittai Gradel, *Emperor Worship and Roman Religion*, Oxford Classical Monographs (Oxford, New York: Clarendon Press, 2002); Hubert Cancik and Konrad Hitzl, eds., *Die Praxis der Herrscherverehrung in Rom und seinen Provinzen* (Tübingen: Mohr Siebeck, 2003).

[67]Shortly after 27 B.C. the Athenians erected a small temple east of the Parthenon on the Acropolis in which Roma and Julius Caesar were venerated. A series of thirteen small altars, most of which were discovered in the vicinity of the *agora*, provide evidence for vitality of the emperor cult in the lower city as well. Claudius was worshiped as Apollo Patroos, and Tiberius was honored with an inscription that dedicated to him the large bronze quadriga of the second century BC that stood in front of the Stoa of Attalos. On the emperor cult in Athens cf. Michael C. Hoff, "The so-called Agoranomion and the Imperial Cult in Julio-Claudian Athens," *Archäologischer Anzeiger* (1994): 93-117; Michael C. Hoff, "The Politics and Architecture of the Athenian Imperial Cult," in *Subject and Ruler: The Cult of the Ruling Power in Classical Antiquity*, ed. A. Small, Journal of Roman Archaeology Sup 17 (Ann Arbor, Mich.: Journal of Roman Archaeology, 1996), pp. 185-200; Antony J. S. Spawforth, "The Early Reception of the Imperial Cult in Athens: Problems and Ambiguities," in *The Romanization of Athens*, ed. Michael M.C. Hoff and S. I. Rotroff, Oxbow Monograph 94 (Oxford: Oxbow Books, 1997), pp. 183-202; Fernando Lozano, *La religión del poder el culto imperial en Atenas en época de Augusto y los emperadores Julio-Claudios*, BAR International Series 1087 (Oxford: Hedges Archaeopress, 2002).

(*oikoumenē*) and that he has already appointed a judge who will carry out the divine judgment. According to Luke's (summary) account, Paul avoids mentioning the name of Jesus, perhaps because he wants to avoid the impression that he proclaims "foreign divinities" (Acts 17:18).[68] When Paul points out that this divinely appointed judge was a man who had lived, died, and was raised from the dead by God (Acts 17:31), the reaction of the audience was divided: Some members of the Council wanted to hear more, while others scoffed. The notion of a physical resurrection from the dead was foreign to both the Epicureans and the Stoics who taught that the "art of dying" meant to teach people to accept their mortality.[69] Paul is convinced, and he states as much, that the religious activities of the Athenians are evidence of ignorance, as none of the deities or cults of the city are able to guarantee salvation on the day of universal judgment.

THE EXCLUSIVE SALVATION IN JESUS MESSIAH

Romans 2:1—3:31. Paul's argument in Romans 2:1—3:31 is highly significant in that he demonstrates that he does not merely reject pagan religiosity for his own Jewish religious traditions. He argues that the Jewish claim to superiority, because only they had truly salvific religious beliefs and status, is no longer valid. Jews correctly claim (Rom 9:4-5) that they have God's law and thus a special relationship with God as his covenant people, evidenced in circumcision, in God's promises, and in the worship in the temple in which God reveals his glory (Rom 2:17-20, 25; 9:4). But due to the reality of the Jews' sinful behavior (Rom 2:21-23, 25-28) and due to the reality of God's new revelation "now" (*nyn*) in Jesus the crucified Messiah, forgiveness of sins, atonement of trespasses, and thus salvation and righteousness are granted only through faith in Jesus Christ (Rom 3:21-26).

The fact that Paul does not distinguish between pagans who sin and Jews who sin demonstrates that his analysis and evaluation of the pagan religions and the Jewish religion are not traditional or partisan but theological and salvation-historical. Pagan "secular" religions have no solution for the *condition humaine*, and the Jewish "revelatory" religion can no longer provide atonement for sins because Jesus the messianic Savior has come. God has put forward Jesus Christ as *hilastērion*, replacing the *kapporet* in the Holy of Holies as the place of his atoning presence (Rom 3:25). It is as the result of Jesus' death on the cross that people—whether foolish and ignorant pagans or observant and obedient Jews—are now "justified by

---

[68]Cf. Pesch, *Apostelgeschichte*, 2:140.
[69]Cf. Klaus Haacker, "Urchristliche Mission und kulturelle Identität. Beobachtungen zu Strategie und Homiletik des Apostels Paulus," *Theologische Beiträge* 19 (1988): 61-72. On beliefs about an afterlife, cf. Klauck, *Religious Context*, pp. 68-80; N. T. Wright, *The Resurrection of the Son of God*, Christian Origins and the Question of God, vol. 3 (London/Minneapolis: SPCK/Fortress, 2003), pp. 32-84.

his grace as a gift, through the redemption that is in Christ Jesus" (Rom 3:24). Neither pagan sacrifices in the countless temples through the Mediterranean regions, nor Jewish sacrifices in the temple in Jerusalem effect liberation from sins and their consequences. Forgiveness of sins, justification in God's court on Judgment Day, peace with God, access to God's grace, and the hope of sharing the glory of God are possible only "through our Lord Jesus Christ" (Rom 5:1-2).[70]

The logic of Paul's exposition of God's new revelation and of the significance of the death and resurrection of Jesus Christ reveals that he was convinced of the exclusive nature of God's revelation in and through Jesus Christ: There is nobody else and nothing else that can save from sins. This is the same conviction that Peter and John expressed in a speech before the Council of the Sanhedrin: "There is salvation in no one else, for there is no other name under heaven given among mortals by which we must be saved" (Acts 4:12). The gospel message of salvation in Jesus Christ is as exclusive as Jesus' understanding of his mission, according to John 14:6: "I am the way, and the truth, and the life. No one comes to the Father except through me."

1 Corinthians 1:18—2:5. In the context of a discussion about the role of contemporary Greco-Roman rhetoric for the proclamation of the message of Jesus Christ, Paul asserts that while Greeks are champions of wisdom *(sophia)*[71] and Jews demand signs *(sēmeia),* he proclaims, "Christ crucified, a stumbling block to Jews and foolishness to Gentiles" (1 Cor 1:22-23). For Jews, the message of a crucified Messiah-Savior is a *skandalon,* a belief "which causes offense or revulsion and results in opposition, disapproval, or hostility,"[72] since the messiah was expected to be a victorious redeemer (Pss. Sol. 17:21-45).[73] For Greeks, the message of a Jewish savior of the world who was executed on a cross is *mōria,* i.e., foolish nonsense, an absurd incongruity for human logic, an ugly contradiction to the beauty of human wisdom, a tasteless violation of acceptable topics of civilized conversation. In other words, neither Jews nor Greeks find the gospel

---

[70]See the helpful summary of I. Howard Marshall, *New Testament Theology: Many Witnesses, One Gospel* (Downers Grove, Ill.: InterVarsity Press, 2004), pp. 309-15.

[71]Aelius Aristides, a philosopher of the second century A.D., describes the Athenians as being preeminent in all matters of wisdom (1.330).

[72]BDAG, p. 926 s.v. *skandalon* 3.

[73]Cf. Martin Hengel, *Crucifixion in the Ancient World and the Folly of the Message of the Cross* (Philadelphia: Fortress, 1978), pp. 84-90; on messianic expectations in second temple Judaism, see recently Timo Laato, *A Star Is Rising. The Historical Development of the Old Testament Royal Ideology and the Rise of the Jewish Messianic Expectations* (Atlanta: Scholars Press, 1997); J. H. Charlesworth et al., *Qumran-Messianism. Studies on the Messianic Expectations in the Dead Sea Scrolls* (Tübingen: Mohr-Siebeck, 1998); Ed Condra, *Salvation for the Righteous Revealed: Jesus Amid Covenantal and Messianic Expectations in Second Temple Judaism,* Arbeiten zur Geschichte des antiken Judentums und des Urchristentums 51 (Leiden: Brill, 2002).

message appealing or convincing. The fact that Paul—a trained rabbi, an educated Roman citizen, and an experienced and widely-traveled orator, certainly
no fool—insists on proclaiming the message about Jesus' death on the cross as
the saving power of God (1 Cor 1:18, 23-24; 2:2, 4-5) despite these obstacles,
demonstrates that for him Jesus' death and resurrection is the critical center of
the good news about God's intervention in history which aims at extending salvation to sinners.

The saving action of God who extends his mercy to sinners is bound up with
Jesus Christ "who became for us wisdom from God, and righteousness and sanctification and redemption" (1 Cor 1:30). Jesus, the crucified and risen Messiah-
Savior, is the power of God and the wisdom of God (1 Cor 1:24). Jesus Christ is
the power of God, because it is through Jesus, and only through him, that God
declares felons to be righteous, sinners to be holy, and convicts to be redeemed.
Jesus Christ is the wisdom of God, since it is through Jesus' death and resurrection
that God creates life where people had been dead in their sins.[74] If salvation can
be found in the cults of secular religions or in the Temple in Jerusalem, the proclamation of Jesus' death on the cross as the event in and through which God forgives the sins of sinners is not only foolish and provocative, but entirely unnecessary. Paul's insistence that the Christian gospel and thus Christian identity is
bound up with Jesus' death on the cross underlines his conviction that salvation
can be found only through faith in Jesus Christ, a faith that is prepared to abandon
traditional human ways of thinking—whether they be secular, religious, or spiritual—and to accept God's saving revelation in Jesus the Messiah who died on a
cross and rose from the dead on the third day (cf. 1 Cor 15:3-5).

CONCLUSION

The document "Ecumenical considerations for dialogue and relations with people
of other religions," which was received by the Central Committee of the World
Council of Churches in 2002,[75] contains the following paragraph:

> In dialogue and relationships with people of other faiths, we have come to recognize
> that the mystery of God's salvation is not exhausted by our theological affirmations.
> *Salvation belongs to God.* We therefore dare not stand in judgment of others. While
> witnessing to our own faith, we seek to understand the ways in which God intends
> to bring God's purposes to their fulfillment. *Salvation belongs to God.* We therefore

---

[74]On Paul's emphasis on the cross in 1 Corinthians, cf. Florian Voss, *Das Wort vom Kreuz und die men-
schliche Vernunft. Eine Untersuchung zur Soteriologie des 1. Korintherbriefes.* FRLANT 199 (Göttingen:
Vandenhoeck & Ruprecht, 2002); Eckhard J. Schnabel, *Der erste Brief des Paulus an die Korinther.*
Historisch-Theologie Auslegung (Wuppertal: R. Brockhaus, 2006), pp. 111-59.
[75]Available at <http://www.oikoumene.org/index.php?id=3445>.

feel able to assure our partners in dialogue that we are sincere and open in our wish to walk together towards the fullness of truth. *Salvation belongs to God.* We therefore claim this hope with confidence, always prepared to give reason for it, as we struggle and work together with others in a world torn apart by rivalries and wars, social disparities and economic injustices.

While the apostle Paul would not have wanted to justify or promote injustice and conflict, and while he certainly did not believe that he had "exhausted" the depths of the riches and wisdom and knowledge of God (Rom 11:33-35; cf. Phil 3:12), he was convinced of the truth of his theological affirmations, of the deception of secular religions, of the fact that God now provides salvation only on account of the death and resurrection of Jesus Christ, and of the reality of God's judgment. Paul was a missionary, not a religionist involved in a dialogue that proceeds from the assumption that God is present in all religions, that salvation is possible through all faiths and ideologies, and that God's Spirit is at work in all religions, faiths, and ideologies.[76] Paul did not suggest that Athenians who worship Zeus, or Isis, or the emperor, "walk together" with him "towards the fullness of truth." Paul was convinced that pagan religiosity and spirituality constitute a deliberate rebellion against God. Paul did not hesitate to call idol worshipers fools whose religious activities demonstrate futile ignorance that is devoid of salvation. Paul never abandons his conviction that the sole criterion for valid religious knowledge and for relevant spiritual truth is God's revelation in Jesus, the crucified and risen Messiah (Rom 3:21-26; 1 Cor 1:23-24; 2:2). I. Howard Marshall perceptively comments that "the problem of transmitting the message [of the gospel] is a problem of *communication* or translation, in which the message must be put in such a way as to be intelligible and applicable to the receptor. It is not a problem of *discovery* in which the evangelist hopes that the 'receptor' will help him by means of dialogue to discover what the gospel is."[77]

The proclamation of Paul and of the other early Christian missionaries focused on Jesus—his person, his life and ministry in Galilee and Jerusalem, his messianic dignity, his prophetic teaching, his death and resurrection, his exaltation at God's right hand as Kyrios, his gift of the Holy Spirit, and his return as Judge.[78] They called on Jews and Gentiles to repent, turn to the living God, and accept his saving

---

[76]Cf. Stanley J. Samartha, *One Christ, Many Religions: Toward a Revised Christology* (Maryknoll, N.Y.: Orbis Books, 1991); idem, *Between Two Cultures: Ecumenical Ministry in a Pluralist World* (Geneva: WCC Publications, 1996). S. J. Samartha (1920-2001) was for many years the director of the program unit "Dialogue with People of Living Faiths and Ideologies" of the World Council of Churches.
[77]I. Howard Marshall, "Dialogue with Non-Christians in the New Testament," *European Review of Theology* 16 (1992): 28-47.
[78]Cf. Acts 2:36; 5:30-31; 10:34-43; 13:25-41; 17:30; 1 Cor 15:3-5; 2 Cor 5:21; Rom 4:25.

revelation in Jesus, the crucified and risen Messiah and Lord. They challenged their Jewish listeners to abandon their ignorance that caused the rejection, condemnation and crucifixion of Jesus, and they invited them to accept Jesus as the promised Messiah who, through his atoning death, forgives sins. They exhorted their pagan listeners to turn away from their temples, altars, and idols, to worship the one true and living God, and to accept Jesus as the Son of God and the Lord who alone can forgive sins and achieve reconciliation with the almighty, holy and merciful God.

6

Holy Pagans

Reality or Myth?

WALTER C. KAISER JR.

INCLUSIVISTS OFTEN ARGUE THAT THE Old and New Testaments contain examples of what they call "holy pagans,"[1] or believing Gentiles, who are said to have come to a saving faith with a minimal understanding of the Christian gospel; but especially without knowing or believing on the coming Man of Promise, the Messiah, our Lord Jesus Christ. Included in this list are such Old Testament worthies as Melchizedek, Job, Jethro, Balaam, Naaman[2] and the prominent New Testament example, the Roman centurion Cornelius.

A distinction is thereby introduced between Christian believers and non-Christian believers, who are saved, inclusivists affirm, by a different kind of faith than that directly connected with the object of biblical faith, viz., the Messiah, than that directly attached to a gospel that is described in Genesis 12:3 or Galatians 3:8. In this case, the object of faith, for these who are considered exceptions to the normal scriptural pattern, is no longer Christ, for faith now has meager cognitive content.

Some would argue that the goal of creating this new category of believers is to join these biblical examples of so-called holy pagans with possible contemporary believers who have had no witness at all to the gospel of Jesus Christ. Thus, our central question is: Can these occasional biblical references to Gentile worshipers of Yahweh in the Old and New Testaments serve as models in our modern world as well?

---

[1]Helpful bibliography includes Daniel Berrigan, "Holy Pagans in the Old Testament," *Worship* 33 (1959): 96-99; Jacob Milgrom, "The Alien in Your Midst," *Bible Review* 11 (1995): 18, 45; Elmer A. Martens, "The Particular and the Universal in the Old Testament," *Direction* 17 (1988): 60-66; Bruce V. Malchow, "Causes of Tolerance and Intolerance towards Gentiles in the First Testament," *Biblical Theology Bulletin* 20 (1990): 3-9; Wayne W. Allen, "God's Plan for the Nations: Healing. Part 2, The Service of the Prophets: Isaiah," *Caribbean Journal of Evangelical Theology* 5 (2001): 1-15; J. I. Packer, "'Good Pagans' and God's Kingdom," *Christianity Today*, January 17, 1986, pp. 22-25.

[2]Other lists include: Abel, Enoch, Noah, Lot, Ruth, Bathsheba, Ebed-melech and the Ninevites.

Interestingly enough, the example of Abraham becomes the key witness for the whole argument, for it would seem from a *prima facie* examination of Genesis 15:6, Abraham "merely" placed his faith in God in general and that act alone was sufficient for him to be justified before God by the Lord himself! We must first turn our attention, therefore, to this patriarch in Genesis 15.

ABRAHAM

In popular ways of describing the salvation offered in the Old Testament, many are of the opinion that men and women were saved either on the basis of works or alternatively on that of a syncretistic faith—a form of accommodationism that combined divergent religious elements (various beliefs, rites, and forms). The result is a religious mixture that exceeds all of the contributing parts.

The former position can be seen in the much quoted *Scofield Reference Bible* that declares, "The point of testing is no longer [in New Testament times] legal obedience as the condition of salvation, but acceptance or rejection of Christ."[3] Despite what this seems to be teaching, pre-modified dispensationalists who quoted this principle steadfastly maintained that there was always only one way of salvation in the Bible, not two ways, even if the object of faith in the two testaments was different. Yet the view that in the Old Testament salvation was obtained by works still finds deep roots in the popular American evangelical mind. But Galatians 3:21 seems to belie that thought (which is by now thoroughly disavowed by almost all dispensationalists). Paul teaches in verse 21b: "For if a law had been given that could impart life, then righteousness would have come by the law." Indeed, he argues earlier in the same verse, such would have "opposed the promises of God."

It is generally agreed that the most important passage on saving faith in the patriarchal narrative is Genesis 15:6—"Abram believed the LORD, and he credited it to him as righteousness."[4] The *hiphil* form of the verb "believed" (Hebrew *'aman*) is rather unusual since it uses the perfect Hebrew tense with the prefix Hebrew letter *waw*, and not, as one would expect to see here, a Hebrew imperfect tense with a *waw* conversive for a past occurrence. Apparently the writer wanted to indicate more than a mere happening in the past; he wanted to show Abraham's faith had a permanence and constancy (of a completed action with effects enduring into the future), rather than seeing it as an isolated past act. He also wanted to state that verse 6 came as a result of verses 1-5 in that Abraham's faith rested in the promised

[3] *The Scofield Reference Bible* (New York: Oxford University Press, 1909), p. 1115 n 2.
[4] The argument here follows a path similar to the one I laid out in my book *Toward Rediscovering the Old Testament* (Grand Rapids: Zondervan, 1987), pp. 121-28.

"Seed" that would come through his line.

T. V. Farris disagreed with this analysis and concluded:

> Verse 6, following immediately [vv. 2-5], would suggest that Abraham's faith was in response to the preceding promise [about God's provision of a "Seed"]. The syntactical form of the verb "believed," however, precludes that interpretation. The precise nuance of the syntax formula used in this instance, the conjunctive *vav* plus a perfect form of the verb, is a matter of dispute among Hebrew grammarians.[5]

Allen P. Ross came to the same conclusion, for he too wished to separate verse 6 from its context in Genesis 15:2-5. His reason was that the NIV left the conjunction untranslated in verse 6 "to avoid the implication that verse 6 resulted from or followed chronologically verse 5."[6] He then made the same grammatical point that Farris has made.

But surely both these analyses are incorrect, for the context of Genesis 15:1-5 is left dangling in the air, not to mention that the Hebrew grammarians are not at all agreed on the significance of the perfect tense in this type of construction. Moreover, like the NIV, these scholars must omit translating the conjunction in verse 6, lest it appear that verses 2-5 are connected to verse 6! This creates one problem to solve another, which is hardly making progress.

But important as this contextual discussion is, it is not the key issue here. Instead, the key is: Was Abraham's faith merely a general act of believing (a special deed on one occasion that is made a matter of public record)[7] or was it a particular faith associated with his salvation? True, Hebrews 11:8-9 indicated that Abraham had left his home city of Ur of the Chaldeans some twenty-five years earlier (Gen 12:1) also as an act of faith (we might also say as an act of "fearing God"); however, Genesis 15:6 is the first time Scripture explicitly spoke of his personal faith. It was also the first time in Scripture that faith and justification are bound together.[8] Moreover, had the faith Abraham exercised when he left Ur of the Chaldeans been

---

[5] T. V. Farris, *Mighty to Save: A Study in Old Testament Soteriology* (Nashville: Broadman, 1993), pp. 76-77. Also see Walter C. Kaiser Jr., "Salvation in the Old Testament: With Special Emphasis on the Object and Content of Personal Belief," *Jian Dio* 2 (1994):1-18.

[6] Allen P. Ross, "The Biblical Method of Salvation: A Case for Discontinuity," in *Continuity and Discontinuity*, ed. John S. Feinberg (Westchester, Ill.: Crossway Books, 1988), p. 168.

[7] This was the opinion of the great nineteenth century commentator George Bush, *Notes, Critical and Practical, on the Book of Genesis*, 2 vols. (New York: E. French, 1838-1839) 1:244.

[8] The subsequent linking of this root *ts-d-q* ("to justify") with salvation in later texts in the Bible forces us to conclude that the apostle Paul was on good grounds when he argued in Romans 4:1-16 that Abraham's salvation from sin was not "by works" but "by grace." Note that in Gen 12—22, every time Abram/Abraham decided to extricate himself by his own works, he dug himself more deeply into the hole from which he was trying to escape. Only God's gracious gift of crediting to Abram righteousness was effective; all else was a waste of his time and effort.

effective to the saving of his soul, why did God delay crediting it to him as righteousness until so many years later? Surely obeying God's commands even to the
point of "fearing" him (in that biblical sense) is not tantamount to saving faith!

Even though the promise-plan of God announced in Genesis 12:2-3 included
the three main elements in the promise doctrine of God (viz., the messianic
"Seed", the "land," and the good news/gospel that "all peoples on earth will be
blessed through you"), the biblical narrative focuses on the "land" promise in the
rest of chapter 12 (v. 7), and chapters 13 and 14. That divine promise of land was
put to the test, first in a famine that took the patriarch to Egypt (Gen 12:10-20),
then in the offer of the choicest real estate to Lot and his herdsmen (Gen 13), and
finally in the capture of Lot, who had to be rescued by Abraham in an overwhelming victory against four Mesopotamian kings (see Gen 14).

Genesis 15 shifts its attention from the promise of the land to the promise of
the "Seed," a male descendant in Abram's line—the same "Seed" that had been
promised to Eve (Gen 3:15). Abram's call to believe was signaled already in God's
opening words of the divine vision: "Do not be afraid" (Gen 15:1). It is important
to note how frequently faith, or believing God, is preceded and then coupled in
the Bible with fearing the Lord. For example, in Exodus 14:31, "The people feared
the LORD and believed in the LORD." When Israel did not fear God (e.g., in Deut
1:29, 32), it was because she "did not trust in the LORD" (Deut 1:32; Num 14:9).[9]

Abram had complained that he still was "childless" despite a divine promise
made twenty-five years ago back in Ur of the Chaldeans. He decided he would
help the Almighty fulfill that longstanding promise by legally adopting Eliezer of
Damascus (Gen 15:2). But God's response was a definite "No," and explained,
"This man will not be your heir, but a son coming from your own body will be your
heir" (Gen 15:4)—all this despite the advanced age of Abraham (100) and Sarah
(90)!

Here is the crucial text for our discussion: "Abram believed the LORD, and he
credited to him as righteousness" (Gen 15:6). Does this mean, then, that Abram
became a mere monotheist (or even a henotheist, one who believes in one god
while not denying the existence of other gods) who suddenly concluded that there

---

[9]I am indebted to Gordon Wenham for this discussion in his 1975-1976 lecture in the Theological
Students' Fellowship at Queen's University, Belfast, Ireland, and later printed in *Faith in the Old Testament* (Leicester, U.K.: Theological Students' Fellowship, n.d.), pp. 1-24, esp. p. 5. Wenham discusses the two types of expressions: "believing that" *(he'emin + lamedh)* and "believing in" *(he'emin +
beth)*. The first is an act of believing what a person says and accepting his or her statements as true and
trustworthy (e.g., Jacob believing that Joseph was still alive, Gen 45:26), while the second is more of
an endorsement of another person's character (e.g., the king of Gath believing in David's character,
1 Sam 27:12).

must be a supreme being, after staring at the starry heavens and being told that his "seed" would be as numerous as the stars of the heavens (Gen 15:5)? Is there no more to Abraham's belief than that small admission? This is the central question: What, then, was the object of Abram's faith?[10]

One of the most revered evangelical commentators of the nineteenth century, Franz Delitzsch, answered, "The promise . . . has truly Christ for its object; . . . the faith in which he [Abram] receives it, is faith in the promised seed."[11] No less certain was the twentieth century Lutheran commentator, H. C. Leupold, who boldly asserted, "Now the question arises, 'Is Abram's faith different from the justifying faith of the New Testament believer?' We answer unhesitatingly and emphatically, No. The very issue in this chapter has been Abram's seed."[12] Leupold, Delitzsch, and I do not hold that Abram or any other Old Testament character possessed a full understanding of the future name and redeeming work of Jesus the Savior. Instead, we argue here that the principle object of faith for Old Testament believers was none other than that Man of Promise, the Messiah, who was to come, and who was later revealed to be our Lord Jesus.

Traditionally, evangelicalism has not been happy to let this thesis stand. Many tended to lean heavily on the type of argumentation that Charles Ryrie stated so clearly:

> Did the Old Testament revelation include Christ as the conscious object of faith? From the inductive study already made [allegedly showing that God was the *sole* object of faith, but which affirmation is modified by saying that "this God was a Saviour"] it would seem that it did not. Furthermore, the two summary statements in the New Testament, which deal with forgiveness in Old Testament times, indicate the same. Both Acts 17:30 and Romans 3:25 teach that Christ's relationship to forgiveness was unknown in the Old Testament. In addition, there are several specific statements which show the ignorance of Old Testament saints regarding salvation through Christ—John 1:21; 7:40; 1 Peter 1:11.[13]

No less definite in his opposition to what is contended for here was Lewis Sperry Chafer. After quoting Matthew 19:17, he observed:

---

[10]This issue reminds us once again that the Old Testament is the "master problem" in theology, for any deviation from the norm in the Old Testament leads to error trickling down into the New Testament or into our theology. See Walter C. Kaiser Jr. *Toward Rediscovering the Old Testament* (Grand Rapids: Zondervan, 1987), pp. 13-32.

[11]Franz Delitzsch, *A New Commentary on Genesis*, trans. Sophia Taylor (1888; reprint, Minneapolis: Klock and Klock, 1978), 2:7.

[12]H. C. Leupold, *Exposition of Genesis* (Grand Rapids: Baker, 1953), 1:478.

[13]Charles Ryrie, *The Grace of God* (Chicago: Moody Press, 1970), p. 49.

True to the Jewish dispensation, He said with reference to the law of Moses: "This do and thou shalt live": but when contemplating the cross and Himself as the bread come down from heaven to give His life for the world, He said: "This is the work of God, that ye believe on him whom He [God] hath sent" (John 6:29). These opposing principles are not to be reconciled. They indicate that fundamental distinction which must exist between those principles that obtain in an age of law, on the one hand, and an age of grace, on the other hand.[14]

But these texts support other conclusions than the ones they are asked to bear in regard to the question before us. The "times of ignorance" (Acts 17:30) refers to the Athenian Gentiles rather than of a pre-Christian Israelite understanding in Old Testament times. More appropriate for Israel was the rebuke Jesus gave to the two disciples on the road to Emmaus on that first Easter morning: "O fools and slow of heart to believe all that the prophets have spoken" (Luke 24:25 KJV). In Jesus' estimation, these disciples and their contemporaries could and should have understood the events of that weekend at Calvary based on what had been taught in the Old Testament.

Likewise, the tolerance shown in the "forbearance" of God for the sins that had been committed "beforehand" (Rom 3:25) referred to the final work of satisfaction of the justice of God in the death of Christ, and not to a reduced level of culpability for sins committed during the Old Testament period—an impossibility from a biblical point of view! Surely, there were many in Israel and the nations who were just as ignorant of the Messiah and his work (John 1:21; 7:40) as were those two disciples on the road to Emmaus (Luke 24:25), but that did not absolve them any more than it did the two disciples whom Jesus roundly rebuked!

Moreover, 1 Peter 1:10-12 affirms just the opposite of what it is used here to say; namely, that there were five things the prophets of the Old Testament *did* know about the coming Man of Promise: (1) he was the Messiah, (2) he would suffer, (3) he would triumph over suffering in his glory, (4) he would suffer first and then he would be glorified and, (5) that what they were writing was not only for their day and age, but that God had "revealed" (Greek aorist indicative; an act done in the past) this truth about the Messiah also for those in the church, including those to whom Peter wrote. Indeed, they were ignorant of one thing: The time and full circumstances of that first advent, just as we are uninformed about the timing and details of the second advent.[15]

Nevertheless the question persists: Was Genesis 15:6, when Abraham was ap-

---

[14]Lewis Sperry Chafer, *Grace* (Findlay, Ohio: Dunham, 1922), p. 92.

[15]I have repeatedly used this argument in my writing and speaking. For example, see Walter C. Kaiser Jr., *The Uses of the Old Testament in the New* (Chicago: Moody Press, 1985), pp. 18-23, 209, for the grammatical and exegetical basis for the position taken here.

proaching 100 years of age, the first time that Abraham believed to the saving of his soul? If it was not, all we can say is that it was the first time that Scripture expressly mentions his faith as leading to his justification. What makes this text so prominent is that it gives the promise of the seed—a promise first made to Eve (Gen 3:15). Accordingly, Genesis 15:6 identifies the Seed (whom we now know is Jesus the Messiah) as the real object of Abraham's faith. Martin Luther commented on Genesis 15:6:

> Here the Holy Spirit states emphatically [that Abram believed in God who promised] so that we should learn from this passage that all who (*after Abraham's example*) believe in Christ are justified. . . . Our righteousness before God is simply this, that we trust in the divine promises (*of Christ*).[16]

To support syncretism,[17] the theory mentioned earlier, or some form of accommodationism, some have noted that the Lord himself was worshiped and believed on during patriarchal times under a series of divine names that were common to other cultures of that day. Does this fact prove that the faith of Israel was syncretistic in its origins—that the people of the time related to the one true God under names of some of the "local" deities since they did not know of Jesus' name and saving work? In order to prove this case, one would need to show how beliefs at first associated with these "local" deities ultimately merged in the biblical record with a new God named Yahweh.

This view, however, misunderstands Exodus 6:3 to mean that the patriarchs did not know Yahweh's name prior to the time of the exodus. Thus, the more than 150 references to Yahweh's name beginning as early as Genesis 2 are later harmonizations, since his name was not previously known, according to this theory.[18] However, Jewish and Christian scholars have rightly insisted that it was the character, nature, and meaning of the name Yahweh that was not previously recognized, even though the name was used frequently.[19] Moreover, nothing was more routine in the ancient Near East than to use a plurality of divine names to avoid the repetitious use of a single divine name in the text.

Joshua 24:14-15 only shows how Abram and his ancestors worshiped east of the Euphrates River before God called him or how some worshiped the gods of

---

[16]Martin Luther, *Luther's Commentary on Genesis*, trans. J. Theodore Mueller, 2 vols. (Grand Rapids: Zondervan, 1958) 1:265. See also Seth Erlandson, "Faith in the Old and New Testaments: Harmony or Disagreement?" *Concordia Theological Quarterly* 47 (1983): 1-14.

[17]For a definition and review of syncretism, see W. A. Visser't Hooft, *No Other Name: The Choice Between Syncretism and Christian Universalism* (London: SCM Press, 1963), p. 48.

[18]This is the view preferred by the evangelical Christopher J. H. Wright, "The Christian and Other Religions: The Biblical Evidence," *Themelios* 9 (1984): 6.

[19]See e.g., J. A. Motyer, *The Revelation of the Divine Name* (London: Tyndale Press, 1959).

Egypt and of Canaan. Nothing there endorses a view of God accommodating to
the earlier usages of the divine titles by gradually rolling them into an orthodox
doctrine of God. From Ur of the Chaldeans onward, Abram's relationship to God
exhibits a particularity that does not set a precedent for the claim that contemporary world religions come to God by means other than through Christ. The patriarchal age is not to be isolated from the historical rule of faith found in the first
commandment: "No other gods beside me." It is not as if the patriarchal days were
more ecumenically tolerant, only later to become mono-Yahwistic and unambiguously exclusivist. Israel's status was not a matter of chauvinism or favoritism—
something to be flaunted—but was that of the servant-bearers of blessing to all the
nations so they too could receive the same invitation to enjoy an intimate relationship with Yahweh.

But other alleged examples are cited, besides the parade example of Abraham,
to argue that the means of coming to faith was different in the Old Testament than
in the New Testament. Some claim that this offers a route to faith alternative to
that of believing in the Messiah. Melchizedek is presented as another such figure.

MELCHIZEDEK

The case of Melchizedek is most challenging, for he is described as being a "king
of Salem" and a "priest of God Most High" (*El Elyon;*[20] Gen 14:18). This Canaanite priestly king blessed Abram (usually done by the greater personage to the
lesser) in the name of "God Most High, Creator of heaven and earth" (Gen
14:19). To this priest/king, Abram then gave a tithe, a tenth of all he had taken as
booty, in his rescue of Lot. Now if Melchizedek was not a genuine believer, why
would Abram take the tithe that was usually set apart for the One true God who
had just given him an unprecedented victory and hand it over to one who could
otherwise be viewed as a pagan priest of a Canaanite deity? That hardly makes any
sense. Surely the story is too abbreviated to answer all of our questions, since its
main purpose was to tell how God had intervened to help Abram attain a great
victory.

The question, then, is where, when, and how this priest and king, in the midst
of an admittedly pagan culture, had become a believer in the Man of Promise,
whom he seems to recognize in principle in his high praise for the God of heaven
and earth? The text does not offer the slightest hint in answer to this question,
which is subsidiary to the primary interests of the text. However, we are told in no
uncertain terms that the God he served was "God, the Most High, Creator of

---

[20]It is true that *El Elyon,* "Most High God," was used of the head Canaanite deity, but Gen 14:22 iden-
    tifies the use of that divine title in this context with Yahweh himself.

heaven and earth." He did not use the personal name Yahweh, however.

But Abram *did* use the name Yahweh in this context, joining it to *El Elyon* and the title of Creator as he spoke to the King of Sodom: "I have raised my hand to the LORD [i.e., to Yahweh himself], God Most High, Creator of heaven and earth" (Gen 14:22). It appears that Abram deliberately joined the titles given to God by Melchizedek with the name Yahweh to help us as listeners and readers understand that the same Lord was being referred to and not two separate deities.

Melchizedek is another one of the many hints in the Old Testament that God was calling many Gentile believers to himself, even though the text does not elaborate further, since it is not the focus of the story.[21] God's purpose was for all the nations of the world to be blessed and retain the knowledge of God that had been imparted to all who had descended from Adam and Eve. It was the Gentiles' failure to retain God in their knowledge base and give him glory (Rom 1:21) that led them far away from One who provided for them all. Was Melchizedek one of those who had remained faithful to that ancient heritage and thus had retained the knowledge taught about the coming Messiah since the days of Eve (Gen 3:15) and Shem (Gen 9:27)? We do not know for certain.

Don Richardson, in *Eternity in Their Hearts*,[22] used Melchizedek to represent general revelation, labeling it the "Melchizedek factor," as opposed to the "Abraham factor," which signified special revelation. And since Hebrews 7:1-7 argued that Melchizedek was greater than Abraham, Richardson incorrectly judged God's general revelation, which goes out to all people, to be greater than inscripturated special revelation, which only comes to a lesser number.

One major problem with Richardson's thesis is his claim that Melchizedek came to know Yahweh, Creator of heaven and earth, only by general revelation and not through any special revelation. But this is an assumption, is it not?[23] Moreover, while Romans 1 and 2, along with texts like Psalm 19, show that there is a general revelation of God that has gone out to all peoples on earth, the supremacy of receiving God's special revelation is not to be denied.

A better suggestion was endorsed by Jonathan Edwards, who thought that Melchizedek "could have been saved through the traces of original revelation that

---

[21]See our fuller study on this issue in Walter C. Kaiser Jr., *Mission in the Old Testament: Israel as a Light to the Nations* (Grand Rapids: Baker, 2000).

[22]Don Richardson, *Eternity in Their Hearts*, 2nd ed. (Ventura, Calif.: Regal, 1984).

[23]See the fair critique by Tite Tiénou, "Eternity in their Hearts?" in *Through No Fault of Their Own? The Fate of Those Who Have Never Heard*, ed. James Sigountos and William Crockett (Grand Rapids: Baker, 1991), pp. 209-15.

still remained among his people,"[24] for all persons descended from Adam and that line, who at first knew God intimately and for some time, no doubt passed it on to their descendants.

Let us turn to another alleged example of an alternate kind of faith in the Old Testament.

JETHRO

God's servant Moses bumped into Jethro, "a priest in Midian" (Ex 18:1), as he fled Pharaoh of Egypt. Moses later married Jethro's daughter Zipporah, and so Jethro became his father-in-law. Interestingly enough, when Moses returned from Egypt and his father-in-law had heard all that "the LORD had done to Pharaoh and the Egyptians for Israel's sake . . . and how the LORD had saved them" (Ex 18:8), Jethro broke out into praise for Yahweh: "Now I know that the LORD [Yahweh] is greater than all the gods, for he did this to those who treated Israel arrogantly" (Ex 18:11). Then Jethro brought a burned offering and other sacrifices for the Lord and he broke bread with all the elders of Israel.

When, where, and how was it that Jethro first believed, for his sacrifices appear to be accepted by God and shared as part of the community of faith? Again, we are given no definitive information, except that the Lord accepted his sacrifices.

Was Jethro's family one that had remembered the meeting their fathers had had with Abraham some six hundred years ago? And had Jethro's line, as a result of this meeting, continued to believe and refused to give up the knowledge of God? This would be the reverse of Romans 1:21, for when they knew God as God, Jethro and his clan glorified him as God. Or had Moses witnessed to Jethro during those forty years of shepherding in the desert-like conditions of Midian and introduced him to Yahweh as his Lord and Sovereign?

One thing we do know is that Jethro's house went on believing, for his son Hobab led Israel in her wilderness wanderings, even though Israel also had the advantage of the pillars of cloud by day and of fire by night for divine guidance. Human wisdom, in this case, was not viewed as irreconcilable with divine guidance (Num 10:29-32). Six hundred years later, King Jehu exterminated the Baal worshipers in northern Israel with the help of Jehonadab, son of Rechab, also one of Jethro's later descendants (2 Kings 10:15-25). Three hundred years after that date, in Jeremiah 35, the Rechabites are depicted as still adhering not only to God's

---

[24]Jonathan Edwards, "History of Redemption," in *The Works of Jonathan Edwards*, ed. Harry S. Stout (New Haven, Conn.: Yale University Press, 1989), 9:179, as cited by Terrance L. Tiessen, *Who Can Be Saved? Reassessing Salvation in Christ and World Religions* (Downers Grove, Ill.: InterVarsity Press, 2004), p. 171.

word as they gather in the temple of Yahweh with the prophet Jeremiah but also to the human word of that distant relative in their clan. God used the Rechabites as an object lesson to teach Jeremiah that human obedience to his commands was possible, even though Israel seemed to show that any obedience, especially to God, was extremely difficult.

Jethro is also used, with what appears to be divine approval, as an efficiency expert for Moses. As Jethro himself cautioned, his advice was to be followed only if Yahweh also approved. He recommended that Moses conduct a leadership camp to teach the laws, show leaders how to live, and guide them in how to do their jobs. These selected leaders, advised Jethro, must have: (1) some natural ability, (2) the fear of God, (3) integrity and (4) a contempt for lust or personal gain.

Some might call Jethro a holy pagan because he was a Gentile and not a Jew, but he appears in every respect to be a believer in full fellowship with the people of God.

BALAAM, SON OF BEOR

If Melchizedek puzzled us a bit, Balaam the son of Beor is an even more difficult problem.[25] Was he a saint or a soothsayer?

Balaam's home, according to Numbers 22:5 was in "Pethor, which is near the River, in his native land." Traditionally, Pethor is located on the west bank of the Euphrates River about twelve miles south of Carchemish, listed as Pedru in the topographical lists of Thutmose III (fifteenth century B.C.), or as Pitru, a city captured by the Assyrian King Shalmaneser III in 857 B.C. Balaam was summoned from his home by Balak, king of Moab, to put a curse on Israel, which was encamped outside his territory toward the end of Israel's forty years of wilderness wanderings (Num 22:2-5).

A most exciting fragmentary inscription (known as the Deir 'Alla inscription), found on March 17, 1967, some twenty-five miles north of where Israel had camped in the Plains of Moab, is written in black and red ink on a plaster wall and dated to somewhere around 850 B.C.[26] Apparently it was used as a writing exercise for pupils many years after the time of Balaam.

---

[25]"Few traditions in the Hebrew Bible," opined Michael Moore, "manifest so great a degree of internal conflict as do the Balaam traditions. The simple task of assigning who Balaam was and what he did in Israelite history appears to have been one of the most delicate and complex issues Israelite students ever had to face." Michael S. Moore, *The Balaam Traditions: Their Character and Development*, Society of Biblical Literature Dissertation Series 113 (Atlanta: Scholars Press, 1990), p. 116.

[26]See Walter C. Kaiser Jr., "Balaam, Son of Beor, in Light of Deir 'Alla and Scripture: Saint or Soothsayer?" in *Go to the Land I Will Show You: Dwight Young Festschrift*, ed. Joseph Coleson and Victor Matthews (Winona Lake, Ind.: Eisenbrauns, 1996), pp. 95-106.

Both Scripture and the Deir 'Alla inscription agree: (1) that Balaam was called a "Seer" (*ḥōzeh;* an older name for a "prophet" in the Old Testament), (2) that he received divine communications at night, and (3) that the people of Moab received a curse rather than the expected blessing; and this was instead of a curse on their enemy Israel.

So was Balaam a believer or a man dependent on magical and evil arts to gain his reputation? He has left quite a trail over the pages of Scripture (Num 31:8-16; Deut 23:5-6; Josh 13:22; 24:9-10; Mic 6:5; 2 Pet 2:15; Jude 11; Rev 2:14). Despite his horrible end (Num 31:8-16), he was used of God to function in a remarkable way in the oracles he gave in Numbers 22—24. In this role, he is directed solely by Yahweh; and when God says he must bless Israel, he does just that.

The explanation that seems to fit the data best is the one given by William Foxwell Albright many years ago. He decided that Balaam must have become "a convert to Yahwehism, and that he later abandoned Israel to join the Midianites in fighting against the Yahwists."[27] Forbidden by Yahweh to curse Israel, he advised Moab and Midian to entice Israel to sin in the form of religious prostitution and the worship of dead ancestors (Ps 106:28-29; Hos 9:10). Apparently Baal Peor (Deut 3:29) is a Hebrew or Phoenician spelling for the Hurrian word *pahura*, which does appear in hieroglyphic Luwian and is also the Hurrian word for "fire," that seems to underlie the Greek *pyr*, "fire," hence "Baal of the fire." Now that Israel had indulged in religious prostitution and dead ancestor worship, God would act against Israel and do what Balaam's magical curses were prevented from doing.

So then, who was Balaam? Somewhere along the line he had come into contact with Yahwehism, for his prayers and protestations have a genuine ring about them. His oracles are treated as a true revelation of the Messiah who is to come, but his reputation seems to have been gained by divination and soothsaying. Balaam's life ended awkwardly as he died among the Midianites and the Moabites (Num 31:8).

Ultimately, only God knows whether he was converted or not, but the way he concluded his days casts him in a negative light. In fact, Scripture uses his name as a household word for falling away from the faith (2 Pet 2:15; Jude 11; Rev 2:14).[28]

RAHAB

Another alleged candidate for the dubious status of "holy pagan" is Rahab, "a prostitute" (Josh 2:1). Not only did she hide the spies, but she confessed her

---

[27]William Foxwell Albright, "The Oracles of Balaam," *Journal of Biblical Literature* 63 (1944): 233.
[28]See Walter C. Kaiser Jr. et al., *Hard Sayings of the Bible* (Downers Grove, Ill.: InterVarsity Press, 1996), pp. 166-68, for related issues in the Balaam case.

allegiance to Yahweh. Her testimony was:

> I know that the LORD has given this land to you and that a great fear of you has fallen
> on us, so that all who live in this country are melting in fear because of you. We have
> heard how the LORD dried up the water of the Red Sea . . . and what you did to Si-
> hon and Og, the two kings of the Amorites east of the Jordan, whom you completely
> destroyed, . . . for the LORD your God is God in heaven above and on the earth be-
> low. (Josh 2:9-11)

But how did Rahab know that the Lord had given the land of Canaan to Israel?
The God who had promised the land to Israel was the same God who had promised the Seed to Eve, Shem, and the patriarchs, along with the good news that in
Abram's seed, all the earth would be blessed (Gen 12:2-3). To believe in one part
of the promise was to affirm the whole promise, for how could anyone segment, divide, or extricate some parts as temporal and others as eternal and enduring? Therefore, it is probable that somewhere Rahab had heard about God's complete promise-
plan, the tripartite core of the promise: the Seed, the land, and the gospel.

This helps explain why Rahab makes it into the Hall of Faith in Hebrews
11:31. But even more convincing is the word from James 2:25: "In the same way
[that Abraham was justified by faith in the story just alluded to and originally told
in Gen 22 and 15:1-6; James had quoted Gen 15:6 in Jas 2:23], was not even Rahab the prostitute considered righteous for what she did when she gave lodging to
the spies and sent them off in a different direction?" Her confession that "Yahweh
is God" is shown to be genuine by the way she provided for the spies. That confession also included an acknowledgement that Yahweh had provided the land as
a gift to Israel, a fact only known from the famous threefold provision of Genesis
12:2-3.

Some may wonder if it is fitting and appropriate for a woman of such unsavory
character to be dealt with so mercifully and later to become the wife of a prince in
Judah. Nahshon, a great prince in Judah had a son named Salmon, who did indeed
marry Rahab, and thus was one through whom the promised line of the Messiah
came (cf. Mt 1:4-6; Ruth 4:18-22; and especially Num 7:12). We conclude that it
is fitting and appropriate, in the same way that it is fitting and appropriate for all
sinners who have received mercy and grace from our heavenly Father, including us.

Once again we see that it is critically important to understand what the object
of Abraham's faith was in Genesis 15:6, for the epistle of James links Rahab's faith
with that of Abraham. If we err in exegeting Genesis 15:6, the trickle down effect
can be seen all the way into the New Testament, as well as in the inferences many
inclusivists draw today when they incorrectly posit a more modest understanding
of Abraham's faith.

RUTH

An identical case can be made for Ruth the Gentile Moabitess woman, who left her homeland, family, and friends to follow her mother-in-law Naomi, who also had lost her husband. Later Ruth met Boaz, a relative of Naomi's late husband. He was greatly impressed that Ruth had left all to accompany her bereaved mother-in-law back to Israel: "May Yahweh repay you for what you have done. May you be richly rewarded by Yahweh, the God of Israel, under whose wings[29] you have come to take refuge" (Ruth 2:12). Subsequently Ruth and Boaz were married and she later bore him a son, who became the grandfather of king David, who was in the line of Messiah. To be sure, the abbreviated idiom of coming under the wings of the God of Israel is at first enigmatic, but in the context of the book of Ruth and the metanarrative, we can assume a faith fixed in the Lord who had promised that Seed who was to come.

NAAMAN, THE SYRIAN GENERAL

In one of the most celebrated Old Testament cases of a Gentile conversion, God used the witness of a captured Jewish maiden to point a commander of the foreign army of Syria, who had repeatedly trounced Israel, to the prophet in Samaria who could heal his leprosy.[30] This incident took place around 852-841 B.C. when Joram (also known as Jehoram of Northern Israel) and the Syrian King Ben Hadad II were experiencing a brief reprieve from the constant hostilities between Syria/Aram and Northern Israel.

Naaman, the commander of the army of Syria was both "highly regarded" and a "valiant soldier" (2 Kings 5:1). Even more startling is the fact that through Naaman, "the LORD had given victory to Aram/Syria" (2 Kings 5:1), a fact that surely was not politically correct from a Hebrew point of view, but most accurate from a theological one. Nothing seemed to have troubled Naaman except a case of leprosy, a word that covered a number of diseases in antiquity—similar to our word cancer today. But Naaman's situation looked more like Hanson's disease, our English elephantiasis, and this was a real disability for a man of his social standing and rank.

---

[29]The image of wings was used frequently to describe the activity of the gods of the ancient Near East. For example, in Egyptian art, the image of the winged gods hovered over the king. Ruth, who is depicted here as a defenseless young bird, is given shelter and protection under the wings of Yahweh himself, just as Ps 91:1, 4 affirmed: "He who dwells in the shelter of the Most High will rest in the shadow of the Almighty. . . . He will cover you with his feathers and under his wings you will find refuge."

[30]2 Kings 5:1-27. See the fine article by Walter A. Maier III, "The Healing of Naaman in Missiological Perspective," *Concordia Theological Journal* 61 (1997): 177-96.

But then he heard the words of a captive Jewish girl: "If only my master would see the prophet who is in Samaria; he would cure him of his leprosy" (2 Kings 5:3). Who was this girl? Who told her the prophet could cure leprosy? Would the God of Israel heal Gentile pagans as well—even if they were Israel's enemies? And why must Naaman go to Samaria to be healed? Moreover, how could she think Yahweh would do all of this when he had not chosen to deliver her from her captivity? Would not her problem with evil and suffering be an impediment to her faith, giving her reasons why her God would not intervene so miraculously for others? We have many questions but too few answers.

But Naaman took the girl seriously and went to Samaria with a letter of introduction from Ben Hadad II to Jehoram (though neither king is specifically identified by name in the text).

After objecting at first, Naaman decides he must at least try to dip in the muddy Jordan River seven times as the prophet Elisha commanded. When to his surprise he rose the seventh time with his flesh "clean like that of a young boy" (2 Kings 5:14), he made three requests of the prophet: (1) to take back two mule loads of Israelite soil so he could stand on good ground when he worshiped Yahweh, (2) to use the dirt for a foundation for offering burnt offerings and sacrifices to Yahweh, and (3) to be forgiven when he accompanied his king into the temple of Rimmon (the pagan god also known as Hadad or Baal), the chief god of Syria.

Elisha made no direct response to any of these three requests except, "Go in peace" (2 Kings 5:19). Apparently Naaman was changed. While he apparently still held the common ancient Near Eastern belief that local deities were intimately connected with their worshipers and the land in which they were worshiped, there is no doubt that he had true faith in Yahweh and worshiped him. But Naaman seems to represent something more, for his expression of faith has the ring of authenticity to it, anticipating a time when the fences of the ceremonial law would break and the good news would spread to every people regardless of the place where they worshiped Yahweh.

As for the odd requests he made, F. W. Krummacher, the great expositor of Elijah and Elisha, years ago observed:

> Should we suppose that Naaman associated with it any *superstitious* notion, such a surmise would only show our inability to estimate and comprehend some of the more refined and nobler natural feelings of the human soul. . . . What is there in a mere leaf . . . from a tree . . . on the Mount of Olives . . . [or] a few wild flowers . . . [from] the Garden of Gethsemane? . . . So . . . a few bushels of earth . . . could not, in physical properties, be at all superior to that of Damascus, yet *with him* it was earth from the land which the Lord had distinguished above all lands; it was earth from a memorable place where this delighted stranger had experienced inestimable benefit,

where he had found the living God and in Him eternal life.

He continued:

> Suppose that Namaan found pleasure in the thought of possessing some of this
> earth in his own distant heathen country, and sweet recollections, in praying and
> sacrificing upon it; what if he imagined, that stepping upon this earth would sub-
> serve, by mental association, to promote and animate his own feelings of broth-
> erhood towards the servants of Jehovah in distant Canaan? . . . Let innocent
> natural feelings have *their* privilege. . . . We have our treasure in *earthen* vessels;
> we cannot seize, all at once, the spirituality of angels . . . we remain mortals, and
> feel as mortals.[31]

Here, then, was another Gentile who came to faith in the living God who had revealed himself through his prophets and through the witness of a faithful maiden
who refused to let circumstances dictate her theology or her hope for the future
and even for hostile Gentiles. Naaman does not exhibit an alternate route to divine
forgiveness. His confession, worship, and witness evidence a marvelous work of
God and are included, therefore, in Scripture to show the outreach of God's blessing to all the nations.

CORNELIUS

The apostle Peter viewed the Roman centurion at Caesarea as a good example of
the fact that "God does not show favoritism, but accepts men [and women] from
every nation who fear him and do what is right" (Acts 10:34-35).

It is clear that Cornelius was a "God fearing" man (Acts 10:2). He donated
generously to those who were in need and prayed regularly to God (Acts 10:2).
One day an angel of God came to him in a vision about three in the afternoon
(Acts 10:3) and told him to seek out Peter who was down the coast in Joppa. In
the meantime, God prepared Peter by giving him a vision of a great sheet being
let down from heaven with all sorts of nonkosher animals and reptiles in it for
him to eat. Repeatedly he refused to imbibe, but God warned him not to call
unclean or impure what he had made pure. With that came the summons for
him to go to Caesarea with Roman soldiers to talk to their commander of a
brigade.

When Peter arrived, he found a large gathering of people. He noted that up
until a day or two ago, his theology had prevented him from speaking to such
Gentiles, but God had instructed him not to call any person unclean or impure.

---

[31]F. W. Krummacher, *Elisha*, trans. R. F. Walter (1839; reprint, Grand Rapids: Zondervan, 1956), pp.
205-6, italics original.

So Peter preached about who Jesus was and what he had accomplished on the cross and in his resurrection. While he was still speaking, the Holy Spirit fell on all who were listening to his message, leaving Peter with the conclusion that they had received the Holy Spirit just as the Jews had at Pentecost, so why not baptize everyone who believed?

The principle illustrated by Cornelius seems to be that where people live up to the light they possess, God will send a messenger to tell them the gospel of our Lord Jesus Christ. However, many inclusivists would go much further than this. John Sanders taught:

> Inclusivists do not claim that people are saved by their righteousness; they contend that people like Cornelius are saved because they have the "habit of faith," which involves penitence. But inclusivists do claim that it is not necessary to understand the work of Christ in order to be saved. G. Campbell Morgan wrote, "No man is to be saved because he understands the doctrine of the Atonement. He is saved, not by his understanding it, but because he fears God and works righteousness."[32]

Sanders went on to explain:

> Inclusivists use the story of Cornelius and other biblical references about Gentiles of faith . . . as evidence for their contention that God gave saving faith to the Gentiles long before the church arrived on the scene and that the unevangelized may be saved by Christ without knowing about Christ.[33]

Of course God saved Gentiles long before the arrival of the church at Pentecost, as we have strenuously contended in *Mission in the Old Testament*.[34] Abraham had been told that in his seed all the nations/Gentiles of the earth would be blessed (Gen 12:3).

But what is in contention here is whether or not the Messiah, or the Man of Promise, who was to come, was not (nor did he need to be) the focus of faith[35] in the pre-Christian era. It is an overstatement to claim that a certain quantity of doctrine must be understood and believed before one can be saved. After all, the thief on the cross focused his faith on the Lord who was crucified with him, but I doubt he could have passed many more theological tests than that!

To affirm that the object of faith must be the Seed who was to come (also referred to by other names, such as Messiah, Servant of the Lord, etc.) is not to fall

---

[32]John Sanders, *No Other Name: An Investigation into the Destiny of the Unevangelized* (Grand Rapids: Eerdmans, 1992), p. 223.

[33]Ibid., p. 224.

[34]Kaiser, *Mission in the Old Testament*.

[35]This is the claim made in John Sanders, ed., *What About Those Who Have Never Heard? Three Views on the Destiny of the Unevangelized* (Downers Grove, Ill.: InterVarsity Press, 1995), p. 38.

into what Terrance L. Tiessen calls "ecclesiocentric presuppositions."[36] Rather
than referring to the church or even centering our argument on the church as the
basis of argumentation, it is Scripture that demands that the object of faith must
be Christ, regardless of how little or how much one understands of his unique life
and work.

Our contention with David Wells is that Cornelius's "salvation occurred during
Peter's preaching [as] is expressly declared by the centurion himself (Acts
11:14)."[37] Since Scripture affirms this, we are not persuaded by those who argue
that Cornelius was a believer before Peter preached in his house. Had that been
true, why trouble Peter to make that arduous trip from Joppa to Caesarea? Fearing
God, as Cornelius obviously did, was a good step in the right direction, but the
"fear of God" is never equated in Scripture with receiving salvation.[38]

CONCLUSION

Upon detailed examination, the case for including holy pagans (or even "pagan
saints") among the believing on the basis of their adopting a theism or showing
enormous respect and fear for God, appears to collapse. Critical to the whole argument is the *object of belief*, in the case of Abraham in Genesis 15:6. If Abraham
is alluding to what God had just told him about the promised "Seed" coming
through him as the object of his faith (and thus, he believed in the Lord and what
he had just said), then Acts 4:12 is still normative. "Salvation is found in no one
else, for there is no other name under heaven given to men by which we must be
saved."

The other alternative, which we have opposed, is to claim that there are two
methods of salvation approved of in Scripture: the way of faith in Jesus Christ

---

[36] Tiessen, *Who Can Be Saved?* pp. 172-74, 176-78. Tiessen assumes that I use the following syllogism:
"Melchizedek, Jethro, Rahab, Ruth, and Naaman were saved [apparently, my major premise]. People
cannot be saved without faith in the promised Seed [apparently, my minor premise]. Therefore, they
must have had knowledge of and faith in the Seed" (p. 174). My argument is based on the biblical
text. It is not artificially "keeping the bar high on what one must know in order to have saving faith,
but still be[ing] optimistic about widespread salvation" (pp. 174-75). Inclusivists, to the contrary, do
have an unrecognized syllogism that goes something like this: Abraham put his trust in God. Old
Testament "holy pagans," and some around the world today who have never heard about Christ, seem
to show at times that they fear(ed) God and act(ed) justly. Therefore, they must have been saved just
as Abraham was, apart from any faith in Christ.

[37] David F. Wells, *God the Evangelist: How the Holy Spirit Works to Bring Men and Women to Faith*
(Grand Rapids: Eerdmans, 1987), p. 23.

[38] Bryan Widbin, "Salvation for People Outside Israel's Covenant?" in *Through No Fault of Their Own?*
p. 82, found that "never [is there] a hint that Israel saw 'the fear of God' among the nations as something less than a redemptive experience. She accepted it on both practical and theological grounds.
Israel's exclusive calling was to be a testimony to the nations. What happened apart from that was
Yahweh's business." But this equation must be defended exegetically to be sustained.

taught in the New Testament and that of a diminished faith, presumably allowed for in the Old Testament. Inclusivists claim that this diminished faith is hinted at in the examples of the people we have discussed in this chapter. But, based upon our examination of those figures, we respectfully disagree. Furthermore, such a conclusion runs counter to the clear insistence of the Old Testament that the method and means of salvation for everyone (in both testaments) are the same.

D. A. Carson succinctly summarizes the thesis of this chapter:

> Most of the pre-Christ [pre-New Testament] believers are those who enter into a covenantal, faith-based relationship with the God who had disclosed himself to them in the terms and to the extent recorded up to that time. . . . Inclusivists who draw a parallel between modern non-Christians who have never heard of Christ and such Old Testament believers overlook the fact that these believers on the Old Testament side were responding in faith to special revelation, and were not simply exercising some sort of general "faith" in an undefined "God."[39]

---

[39]D. A. Carson, *The Gagging of God: Christianity Confronts Pluralism* (Grand Rapids: Zondervan, 1996), p. 298.

7

Saving Faith
Implicit or Explicit?

STEPHEN J. WELLUM

MUST PEOPLE BELIEVE THE GOSPEL in order to be saved? It would seem that the obvious answer from Scripture is "yes." Here are three key texts which seem to say just that.

> For God so loved the world that he gave his one and only Son, *that whoever believes in him* shall not perish but have eternal life. For God did not send his Son into the world to condemn the world, but to save the world through him. Whoever *believes in him* is not condemned, but *whoever does not believe stands condemned already* because *he has not believed in the name of God's one and only Son*. (John 3:16-18)
>
> Salvation is found in no one else, *for there is no other name* under heaven given to men by which we must be saved. (Acts 4:12)
>
> That *if you confess with your mouth*, "Jesus is Lord," and *believe in your heart* that God raised him from the dead, you will be saved. For it is with your heart that *you believe and are justified*, and it is with *your mouth that you confess and are saved*. As the Scripture says, "Anyone who trusts in him will never be put to shame." For there is no difference between Jew and Gentile—the same Lord is Lord of all and richly blesses all who call on him, for, "*Everyone who calls on the name of the Lord will be saved*." How, then, can they call on the one they have not believed in? And how can they believe in the one whom they have not heard? And how can they hear without someone preaching to them? And how can they preach unless they are sent? As it is written, "How beautiful are the feet of those who bring good news!" . . . Consequently, faith comes from hearing the message, and the message is heard through the word of Christ. (Rom 10:9-15, 17)[1]

However, what seems obvious to some is not at all obvious to others, especially

---

[1] All Scripture quotations in this essay, unless otherwise noted, are from the NIV. In the texts quoted above, the italics are added.

when it comes to the thorny question of the status of those who have never heard the gospel, and whether such persons may experience the saving grace of God apart from hearing the gospel message and believing in the Lord Jesus Christ.[2] In recent years, within evangelical theology, there has arisen a spectrum of responses to this question, which may be labeled broadly under the headings of "exclusivism" and "inclusivism."[3] No doubt, both positions include within them a range of view-points. However, for our purposes, I will briefly describe the two views in the broadest of terms, not noting all the nuances of each position, but highlighting where they stand on the question before us.[4]

Exclusivism, which is being argued for in this book, has long been the position of most evangelicals. It contends that not only are the central claims and doctrines of Christianity universally true, but also that in order to receive salvation, people must repent of their sin and believe in the promises of God, now centered in the

---

[2]There is a huge debate over who the "unevangelized" are. For a discussion of this issue, see Daniel Strange, *The Possibility of Salvation Among the Unevangelised: An Analysis of Inclusivism in Recent Evangelical Theology* (Carlisle, U.K.: Paternoster, 2002), pp. 32-35. I will use Strange's understanding of the unevangelized as my working definition: "any person in history who has lived and died without hearing and understanding the Gospel of Jesus Christ from a human messenger" (p. 35).

[3]These are not the only names given to these positions. Sometimes "exclusivism" is also called "partic-ularism" and even "restrictivism"; "inclusivism" is also called "wider-hope" and "accessibilism." In this chapter I will be limiting my discussion to evangelical theology. Outside of evangelicalism, there are not only varieties of inclusivisms, but there is also the viewpoint of "pluralism," which relativizes all religious claims to superiority over any other religion. "Pluralism" entails a denial of the claims of his-toric Christianity and in particular the uniqueness and finality of Jesus Christ as Lord and Savior. If there is any "salvation" at all (which is variously conceived), pluralism teaches that people may be "saved" through a number of different religious traditions and communities. See for example, John Hick, *God and the Universe of Faiths* (London: Fount, 1977); idem, "The Non-Absoluteness of Chris-tianity," in *The Myth of Christian Uniqueness: Toward a Pluralistic Theology of Religions*, ed. John Hick and Paul F. Knitter (Maryknoll, N.Y.: Orbis, 1987); idem, "A Pluralist View," in *More Than One Way? Four Views on Salvation in a Pluralistic World*, ed. Dennis L. Okholm and Timothy R. Phillips (Grand Rapids: Zondervan, 1995), pp. 29-59. For a helpful critique of pluralism see D. A. Carson, *The Gag-ging of God: Christianity Confronts Pluralism* (Grand Rapids: Zondervan, 1996).

[4]For more detail in regard to the varieties of inclusivism see chapter two of this book. Helpful treat-ments of the various views may be found in the following works: John Sanders, *No Other Name: An Investigation into the Destiny of the Unevangelized* (Grand Rapids: Eerdmans, 1992); Clark H. Pin-nock, *A Wideness in God's Mercy: The Finality of Jesus Christ in a World of Religions* (Grand Rapids: Zondervan, 1992); idem, "The Finality of Jesus Christ in a World of Religions," in *Christian Faith and Practice in the Modern World*, ed. Mark A. Noll and David F. Wells (Grand Rapids: Eerdmans, 1988), pp. 152-68; Terrance L. Tiessen, *Who Can Be Saved? Reassessing Salvation in Christ and World Religions* (Downers Grove, Ill.: InterVarsity Press, 2004); William J. Crockett and James G. Sigoun-tos, eds., *Through No Fault of Their Own? The Fate of Those Who Have Never Heard* (Grand Rapids: Baker, 1991); Ronald H. Nash, *Is Jesus the Only Savior?* (Grand Rapids: Zondervan, 1994); Millard J. Erickson, *How Shall They Be Saved? The Destiny of Those Who Do Not Hear of Jesus* (Grand Rapids: Baker, 1996); Harold Netland, *Encountering Religious Pluralism: The Challenge to Christian Faith and Mission* (Downers Grove, Ill.: InterVarsity Press, 2001); as well as, Okholm and Phillips, *More Than One Way?* and Carson, *The Gagging of God.*

person and work of the Lord Jesus Christ.[5] In other words, one must believe the gospel in order to be saved. Furthermore, in relation to non-Christian religions, exclusivism contends that salvation is *not* found in the structures of those religions even though, it is admitted, non-Christian religions are not always wrong in what they believe, but where their teachings conflict with the teaching of Scripture, they are necessarily wrong.[6]

Inclusivism, on the other hand, is the view that it is *not necessary* for all people to believe the gospel in order to be saved. In agreement with exclusivism, inclusivism affirms that Christianity is true and that Jesus Christ is the only Savior and Lord; no human being will be saved apart from him. However, it differs from exclusivism in its affirmation that it is possible for someone who has never heard the gospel to receive salvation apart from faith in Christ. In order to clarify their view and to set it over against exclusivism, inclusivists often make a few important distinctions.

First, inclusivists distinguish between the *ontological* and *epistemological* grounds of salvation. Christ alone is the basis of salvation, even for a person who has never heard of him (hence an affirmation that Christ is the ontological basis of salvation). However, just because Christ alone is the ground of salvation, it does not necessarily follow that one must believe in him in order to receive the benefits of his saving work, at least in this life (hence a denial of the epistemological necessity of faith in Christ for salvation). Following on the heels of this distinction is a second: the distinction between *believers* and *Christians*. "Believers" are defined as "all those who are saved because they have faith in God," while a "Christian" is a "believer who knows about and participates in the work of Jesus Christ."[7] In this way, inclusivists argue that the unevangelized may be saved "by grace through *faith*," but the faith in question is more of a general, uninformed, genuine-seeker faith in God. It is not a faith that necessarily rests in the specific promises of God tied to special revelation, or, in light of the coming of Christ, has him as its object. Eventually humble seekers after God, who have thrown themselves on God's mercy due to the gracious work of the Spirit in them, will discover, either imme-

---

[5]The only exceptions that most exclusivists would allow for are infants before and after birth, the mentally handicapped, and those incapable of faith. They argue that one must be careful not to equate infants and unevangelized adults—something which inclusivists often do—since there is a great difference between infants and the mentally disabled and adults who are in the normal possession of their faculties. Tiessen, for example, as an inclusivist, draws a tight connection between infants and the unevangelized (see *Who Can Be Saved?* pp. 204-29). Ronald Nash, on the other hand, argues that this is an example of inclusivists committing a category mistake (see *Is Jesus the Only Savior?* pp. 135-36).

[6]For example, see Carson, *Gagging of God*; Netland, *Encountering Religious Pluralism*; Nash, *Is Jesus the Only Savior?*; R. Douglas Geivett and W. Gary Phillips, "A Particularist View: An Evidentialist Approach," in Okholm and Phillips, *More Than One Way?* pp. 213-45.

[7]Sanders, *No Other Name*, pp. 224-25. For the same distinctions, see also Pinnock, *A Wideness in God's Mercy*, pp. 161-66; Tiessen, *Who Can Be Saved?* pp. 165-203.

diately at death or thereafter, that the one who saved them was none other than the Lord Jesus. However, in this life, they were not aware of this fact.[8]

Inevitably, these distinctions raise some important questions for inclusivism: How exactly do people receive the benefits of Christ's work if they do not believe in him? What is the content of their faith if it is not linked to God's special, covenantal revelation? Is not saving faith in both Testaments of Scripture that which rests in the promises of God, and now, given our place in redemptive history, is centered in Jesus Christ? Does the Holy Spirit now manifest his saving presence in the world apart from hearing the gospel and faith in Christ? What is the *biblical* warrant for such a view? How are we to make *theological* sense of it?

Depending upon their overall theology, the answers given vary among inclusivists, even though the basic viewpoint is agreed upon by most, if not all of them. But it is important to stress: the answers given to these questions are not minor issues for evangelical inclusivism since they take us to the very heart of their position. For inclusivism to be credible as a *biblical* position it must explain how Jesus Christ can be utterly unique and the only basis for salvation, while simultaneously denying that knowledge of and faith *in Christ* is necessary for receiving the benefits of his saving work.

The purpose of this chapter is to evaluate critically how inclusivists argue both biblically and theologically that specific knowledge about Christ is not necessary for saving faith vis-à-vis the unevangelized. Given the vast nature of this topic, I propose to go about the task in two steps. First, I want to outline both the theological rationale and biblical arguments for inclusivism on this issue of the nature of saving faith.[9] However, given the diversity of overall theological viewpoints within inclusivism, specifically in regard to the complex issues surrounding the God-world relationship, I will discuss two inclusivist viewpoints: synergistic inclusivism and monergistic accessibilism.[10] As we shall discover, even though these views are quite different in their overall theology, they have much in common in regard to their un-

---

[8]Inclusivists do argue that eventually the unevangelized will have explicit faith in Christ. However, since they have never heard the gospel in this life, they will not know Christ has saved them until either an encounter with Christ at death or a post-mortem one. Tiessen argues for an encounter at the moment of death (see *Who Can Be Saved?* pp. 216-29), while Pinnock contends for the post-mortem option (see *A Wideness in God's Mercy*, pp. 168-72).

[9]Since theological viewpoints are organically related, it is important to note the theological rationale which lies behind the use and interpretation of specific texts of Scripture. The position of inclusivism touches so many areas of Christian doctrine that assumptions in one area directly affect conclusions that are reached in other areas.

[10]Synergism refers to the theological positions which range from classic Arminian theology to open theism. Monergism refers to the views which identify with Reformed theology, including modified Calvinism. For a helpful description and summary of these positions within evangelicalism, see Daniel Strange, *Possibility of Salvation*, pp. 3-16.

derstanding of saving faith and the unevangelized. Second, I want to give a biblical-
theological critique of the positions outlined, arguing that the inclusivist distinctions
noted above cannot be biblically and theologically sustained and furthermore, that
in order for one to benefit from the saving work of Christ, Scripture teaches that one
must exercise explicit faith in the covenant promises of God, now, given our place in
redemptive history, centered in Jesus Christ.

INCLUSIVISM'S ARGUMENT FOR SALVATION BY GRACE THROUGH
IMPLICIT FAITH

Synergistic inclusivism. Under this heading there are a number of examples which
could be chosen. I will focus primarily on the work of Clark Pinnock, given the
fact that he is probably the most well-known and influential exemplar of this approach.[11] In fact, in his book *Flame of Love*[12] he provides, in my view, the best
theological rationale as to how inclusivists attempt to reconcile the difficult challenge of affirming the uniqueness of Christ while denying that faith in Christ is
necessary for salvation on the part of the unevangelized. He does so by developing
what he calls the "pneumatological proposal." In fact, his pneumatological approach has been a catalyst for other inclusivists to think through these important
matters and to adopt it as part of their overall argument.[13] Let us now briefly outline and describe his basic argument.

Clark Pinnock, as well as many other inclusivists, begins his argument by highlighting the tension between two biblical axioms: universality and particularity.[14]
The "universality axiom" is related to expressions of God's universal salvific will
(e.g., 1 Tim 2:4; 2 Pet 3:9) grounded in God's universal presence in the world.
Pinnock, in contrast to much of historic evangelical theology (particularly Reformed theology), views God's will solely in terms of God's universal salvific
stance toward the world. He is not fond of making distinctions such as God's "decretive" and "perceptive" will, which have allowed theologians to speak of God
genuinely valuing many states of affairs that are not compatible with his chosen

---

[11]For other basic exemplars of this approach see Sanders, *No Other Name,* and Amos Yong, *Beyond the
    Impasse: Toward a Pneumatological Theology of Religions* (Grand Rapids: Baker, 2003).
[12]Clark H. Pinnock, *The Flame of Love: A Theology of the Holy Spirit* (Downers Grove, Ill.: InterVarsity,
    1996).
[13]See, for example, Amos Yong, "Discerning the Spirit(s) in the World of Religions: Toward a Pneu-
    matological Theology of Religions" in *No Other Gods Before Me? Evangelicals and the Challenge of
    World Religions,* ed. John G. Stackhouse Jr. (Grand Rapids: Baker, 2001), pp. 37-61; idem, *Beyond
    the Impasse;* and Stanley J. Grenz, "Toward an Evangelical Theology of the Religions" *Journal of Ec-
    umenical Studies* 31, nos. 1-2 (1994): 49-65.
[14]For others who begin this way, see Sanders, *No Other Name,* pp. 215-24, and Yong, *Beyond the Im-
    passe,* pp. 109-15.

plan for the world.[15] Nor is he fond of making distinctions between "common" and "saving" grace, which have allowed theologians to speak of God's relations to people in different ways, since, as he argues, "if the Triune God is present, grace must be present too."[16] That is why, for Pinnock, to speak of the "universality axiom" entails that God's grace *must* be available to all people. He states: "If God really loves the whole world and desires everyone to be saved, it follows logically that everyone must have access to salvation."[17]

But this creates a tension with the "particularity axiom," namely, "the belief that Jesus is the only way to God."[18] Why the tension? Because, as Pinnock notes, "if hearing the gospel clearly is required for salvation, it would seem that God does not want all to be saved."[19] He then asks: "Does God love the whole world or not? God may desire all to be saved, but it is hard to see how they possibly can be. How can a large number meet the requirement of believing in the gospel? It would seem that they cannot."[20]

So how do we resolve this tension? Pinnock entertains the possibility that general revelation, including non-Christian religions, may play a role in the salvation of the human race, a role preparatory to the gospel of Christ. In contrast to much of historic evangelical theology, but endemic to most, if not all, inclusivist approaches, Pinnock affirms that general revelation is salvific.[21] Since God meets us everywhere, including the natural world which includes non-Christian religions, "no nook or cranny is untouched by the finger of God" and "God is always reaching out to sinners. . . . There is no general revelation or natural knowledge of God that is not at the same time gracious revelation and a potentially saving knowledge."[22] This is not to say, as Pinnock clearly states, that there are not "depths of darkness, deception, and bondage in them [world religions]" nor is it to affirm that "religions themselves as such are vehicles of salvation." But it is to affirm that "God *may* use religion as a way of gracing people's lives and that it is *one* of God's options for evoking faith and communicating grace."[23]

But how is one to make *theological* sense of this? This is where his pneumatological approach enters in. How are we to conceptualize the universality of God's

---

[15]On this distinction, see John M. Frame, *No Other God: A Response to Open Theism* (Phillipsburg, N.J.: Presbyterian & Reformed, 2001), pp. 105-18.

[16]Pinnock, "An Inclusivist View," in *More Than One Way?* p. 98.

[17]Pinnock, *A Wideness in God's Mercy*, p. 157.

[18]Pinnock, *Flame of Love*, p. 192.

[19]Ibid.

[20]Ibid. For a similar statement of the tension, see Sanders, *No Other Name*, p. 25.

[21]For more on inclusivism and general revelation, see Daniel Strange's chapter in this book.

[22]Pinnock, *Flame of Love*, p. 187.

[23]Pinnock, "An Inclusivist View," pp. 99-100.

grace? How are we to conceive of access to God's grace given the "scandal of historical particularity"? Pinnock's proposal is that we see the universality of God's
grace in relation to the universal work of the Holy Spirit. In fact, as he states it,
we must conceive of it in relation to the "twin, interdependent missions of the Son
and Spirit."[24] Here is his proposal in summary:

> Christ, the only mediator, sustains particularity, while Spirit, the presence of God
> everywhere, safeguards universality. Christ represents particularity by being the only
> mediator between God and humanity (1 Tim 2:5-6), while Spirit upholds universal-
> ity because no soul is beyond the sphere of the Spirit's operations. Spirit is not con-
> fined to the church but is present everywhere, giving life and creating community.
> Hovering over the waters of creation, Spirit is present also in the search for meaning
> and the struggle against sin and death. Because inspiration is ubiquitous and works
> everywhere in unseen ways, Spirit is in a position to offer grace to every person. Be-
> cause Spirit works everywhere in advance of the church's mission, preparing the way
> for Christ, God's will can be truly and credibly universal.[25]

Once again, it is important to stress that Pinnock's proposal is a move away
from historic evangelical theology in how he conceives of the Son-Spirit relationship. Historically, as Pinnock admits, evangelical thought has viewed the work of
the Spirit in relation to Christ. However, Pinnock believes that that approach has
had the effect of exalting Christ above the Spirit and subordinating the Spirit to
the Son.[26] Instead, he suggests, we should try a new idea. After all, he states, "It
lies within the freedom of theology to experiment with ideas."[27] What is this new
idea? It is that we view "Christ as an aspect of the Spirit's mission, instead of (as
is more usual) viewing Spirit as a function of Christ's."[28]

What advantage does this new approach offer us? Pinnock is convinced that it
will help reduce the tension between universality and particularity as well as allow
us to consider "particularity in the context of universality."[29] Thus, prior to and
geographically larger than the Son's mission, is the universal and gracious work of
God's Spirit in the world.[30] Pinnock conceives of history as a stage play with the

---

[24]Pinnock, *Flame of Love*, p. 192.
[25]Ibid.
[26]See ibid., pp. 79-82.
[27]Ibid., p. 80.
[28]Ibid.
[29]Ibid., p. 197.
[30]See ibid., p. 193, where Pinnock also links the work of the Spirit with the Wisdom of God (Prov 8:1-
4) and then concludes that "God's wisdom is present in creation, and God calls out to all people
everywhere by means of it. Beyond Torah and special revelation, wisdom speaks within human experience itself.... God speaks even where Christ is not yet named—God does not leave himself without witness (Acts 14:17)."

Spirit as its director. Wherever the Spirit touches, which is everywhere, God's good gifts are spread generously and graciously, even to people outside of the church. By the Spirit, God reaches out to sinners in general and special revelation, so working in them that they may ultimately become obedient to the Son, even though in this present life they may never know him. That is why, Pinnock argues, we should *not* say there is no salvation outside the church, but simply that there is no salvation outside of grace.[31]

With this proposal, Pinnock believes that he has accomplished a number of things. First, he has supplied the necessary theological warrant for seeing "the offer of grace as something as broad as history itself."[32] Creation and redemption are continuous, not discontinuous. They are both works of grace, thus grounding the possibility that God's salvific intent is both universal and found in creation itself. Second, and what is crucial for our purposes, Pinnock also believes that he has provided the necessary theological rationale for thinking that the unevangelized may be saved by "grace through faith"—tied to the universal work of the Spirit—even though their "faith" is not explicitly Christian faith.[33] In truth, it is Pinnock's pneumatological approach which lies at the heart of his entire inclusivist position, as well as many other inclusivist approaches as well.[34]

Biblical warrant for Pinnock's synergistic inclusivism. What biblical texts does Pinnock appeal to in order to warrant his proposal and hence his inclusivism?

---

[31]See ibid., p. 194.

[32]Ibid., p. 198.

[33]Pinnock states: "The truth of the incarnation does not eclipse truth about the Spirit, who was at work in the world before Christ and is present now where Christ is not named. The mission of the Son is not a threat to the mission of the Spirit, or vice versa. On the one hand, the Son's mission presupposes the Spirit's—Jesus was conceived and empowered by the Spirit. On the other hand, the mission of the Spirit is oriented to the goals of incarnation. The Spirit's mission is to bring history to completion and fulfillment in Christ. Thus the double mission of Son and Spirit can provide the perspective we need to handle the tension of universality and particularity" (*Flame of Love*, p. 194).

[34]Amos Yong in *Beyond the Impasse*, pp. 105-28, stresses this precise point in regard to Pinnock, arguing that it was in Pinnock's turn to pneumatology that we see his most fully-developed inclusivism. Yong states: "it is possible to read *Flame of Love* [Pinnock's pneumatology] as an extended and systematic argument for inclusivism. . . . Because of the systematic coherence by which all the doctrines are unified around the pneumatological theme, there is much greater depth to the assertion of the ubiquitous presence and activity of the Spirit than before. . . . Though Jesus is not named in other faiths, Spirit is present and may be experienced" (p. 119). In fact, all inclusivist views, to some extent, have to argue something similar to Pinnock. Why? Because it is the only way to make theological sense of how salvation is by "grace through implicit faith" apart from hearing the gospel message. Even Tiessen, who approaches inclusivism from a Reformed view, has to agree with Yong that "pneumatology is the key to overcoming the dualism between Christological particularity and the cosmic Christ. The Spirit who is at work outside the church is the Spirit of Jesus, just as he is the Spirit of God. People who have responded to elementary forms of God's self-revelation and who later hear and understand the gospel will welcome and accept it as the Spirit of God illumines their minds concerning this more specific truth" (*Who Can Be Saved?* p. 183).

There are four kinds of texts to which he refers, which I will briefly state.

1. As noted above, Pinnock appeals to texts such as 1 Timothy 2:4 and Hosea 11:8-10 to argue that God's stance toward the world is that of grace, and not wrath, which seems to entail, at least for him, that God *must* make his grace available to all without exception.

2. Texts such as Acts 17:27 are referenced in order to justify that God's presence, by his Spirit, is everywhere, and as such, given (1), God's grace must then be viewed as universally accessible through general and special revelation. At this juncture, Pinnock also correlates texts that speak about the wisdom of God and the Spirit of God (Prov 8:1-4, 24, 30-31) to buttress his point.

3. Texts such as Romans 5:18 imply that the mission and work of Christ our representative not only have universal implications, but that this in some sense must be applied to all people everywhere, short of universalism, which can only take place by the universal work of the Spirit. He states: "Christ's work is complete and for all—'one man's act of righteousness leads to justification and life for all' (Rom 5:18). There is no way around it—we must hope that God's gift of salvation is being applied to people everywhere. If so, how else than by the universal presence and activity of Spirit?"[35] Christ's universal work, then, *requires* the universal work of the Spirit in all people, even in those who have never heard the gospel.[36]

4. Texts that speak of God's salvific will extending beyond Jews and Christians imply that the Spirit is at work outside of the covenant community, bringing them to faith—what Pinnock calls "the faith principle"—a principle which, he thinks,

---

[35]Pinnock, *Flame of Love*, p. 188.
[36]It is impossible to unpack all of Pinnock's thought, given the constraints of this chapter. However, it is important to stress that Pinnock's understanding of the cross work of Christ is not in terms of substitution, but *Christus Victor* and the governmental theory of the atonement (see Clark H. Pinnock, "From Augustine to Arminius: A Pilgrimage in Theology" in *The Grace of God, The Will of Man: A Case for Arminianism*, ed. Clark Pinnock [Grand Rapids: Zondervan, 1989], pp. 15-30; Clark H. Pinnock and Robert C. Brow, *Unbounded Love* [Downers Grove, Ill.: InterVarsity Press, 1994], pp. 99-110). In Pinnock's view, Jesus acted as the representative of all humanity, so that in his act of representation, not substitution, creation is restored. As Pinnock states in *Flame of Love*, pp. 95-96, "God effected the conversion of humanity in Jesus, who represented the race and thereby altered the human situation. In his death and resurrection, humanity *de jure* passed from death to life, because God has included it in the event. Its destiny has been objectively realized in Christ—what remains to be done is a human response and salvation *de facto*. The possibility of newness must be laid hold of by faith." Importantly, Pinnock draws out some of the theological implications of this understanding of Christ's cross work—implications which underlie his inclusivism—namely, that in Christ, God reconciled the world by including everyone in it. Furthermore, "the effectiveness of this reconciliation is not so much opting in as not opting out. In faith we add our yes to God's prior yes" (*Flame of Love*, p. 109). For a more detailed description and critical interaction with these points of Pinnock's theology as they relate to inclusivism, see the helpful work of Daniel Strange, *The Possibility of Salvation*.

is enshrined in Hebrews 11:6, a kind of general faith in God.[37] Proof of this is found in such figures as Cornelius (Acts 10:34-35), and in such OT "holy pagans" as Enoch and Melchizedek. All of these individuals, Pinnock insists, were saved by the gracious work of the Spirit in them apart from explicit faith in Jesus. As he states: "The fact that different kinds of believers are accepted by God proves that the issue for God is not the content of theology but the reality of faith.... [T]heological content differs from age to age in the unfolding of redemption, but the faith principle remains in place."[38] Or, as he asserts, "Since God has not left anyone without witness, people are judged on the basis of the light they have received and how they have responded to that light. Faith in God is what saves, not possessing certain minimum information.... The Bible does not teach that one must confess the name of Jesus to be saved.... The issue God cares about is the direction of the heart, not the content of theology."[39]

Theological warrant for Pinnock's synergistic inclusivism. In addition to the above biblical reasons, Pinnock gives at least three theological reasons to warrant his pneumatological grounding of his synergistic inclusivism.

1. Pinnock appeals to his social view of the Trinity—a relational ontology—as the ground of his proposal and a further justification of his view that God's stance toward the world is always that of love and grace. In the triune identity, he argues, we discover a God who is relational, nonstatic, open—a God of love.[40] Since God is a loving relationality, he concludes that grace is primary, which for him, grounds his understanding of God's universal salvific will.[41]

2. He appeals, as most synergists do, to the theological doctrine of "prevenient grace" to account for the universal, gracious operations of the Spirit in the world, even in the sphere of non-Christian religions. Pinnock writes: "God wants a rela-

---

[37]See, for example, Pinnock, *A Wideness in God's Mercy*, pp. 105-6, 157-68, and John Sanders, "Inclusivism," in *What About Those Who Have Never Heard? Three Views on the Destiny of the Unevangelized*, ed. John Sanders (Downers Grove, Ill.: InterVarsity Press, 1995), pp. 36-42.

[38]Pinnock, *A Wideness in God's Mercy*, pp. 105-6.

[39]Ibid., pp. 157-58. See also the same statement in Sanders, *No Other Name*, p. 225: "If knowledge of Christ is necessary for salvation, then how are we to explain the salvation of the Old Testament believers, whose knowledge was quite limited concerning the Messiah but who were justified by faith in God's Word?"

[40]See Pinnock, *Flame of Love*, pp. 21-48; idem, "An Inclusivist View," pp. 102-6. When Pinnock states that God is "open," he is referring to his view that God, in creating creatures with libertarian freedom, has limited himself in terms of his sovereign power and knowledge in the world. For a more detailed treatment of his open view of God, see Clark Pinnock, ed., *The Openness of God* (Downers Grove, Ill.: InterVarsity Press, 1994); idem, *Most Moved Mover* (Downers Grove, Ill.: InterVarsity Press, 2001); cf. Gregory Boyd, *The God of the Possible* (Grand Rapids: Baker, 2000).

[41]See Pinnock, *Flame of Love*, p. 23, where he argues that God is fundamentally love, and as such, when it comes to grace and salvation, he has "the whole human race in view in his desire to save, and the Spirit everywhere draws sinners from the far country to the Father's love."

tionship with sinners, and if we accept the category of prevenient grace, we acknowledge that God offers himself to creatures. The Spirit speaks to everyone in the depths of their being, urging them not to close themselves off from God but to open themselves up. Because of the Spirit, everyone has the possibility of encountering him—even those who have not heard of Christ may establish a relationship with God through prevenient grace."[42] Interestingly, Pinnock's view of prevenient grace is not viewed merely in the context of soteriology, where it is normally placed by Arminian theologians. Rather, it is viewed in the context of the doctrine of creation. This is evident in Pinnock's rejection of the Reformed distinction between "common" and "saving" grace:

> God's presence fills the world and touches every heart. Spirit should not be restricted to one segment of history or one sphere of reality. The Spirit flourishes everywhere, beyond the boundaries of church. The Spirit's ministry is global, not only domestic, and ontic, not only noetic. The Spirit can be encountered in the entire range of experience, having always been present in the whole world, even in the groaning creation, preparing it for new birth (Rom 8:23).[43]

In this regard, as some have noted, Pinnock's view of prevenient grace has more in common with Karl Rahner than John Wesley.[44]

3. Pinnock employs the Eastern church's rejection of the Western church's insertion of the *filioque* clause into the Nicene Creed.[45] Not only does Pinnock think

---

[42]Ibid., p. 199.

[43]Ibid., p. 200.

[44]See this observation in Strange, *The Possibility of Salvation*, pp. 85-107, and idem, "Presence, Prevenience, or Providence? Deciphering the Conundrum of Pinnock's Pneumatological Inclusivism," in *Reconstructing Theology: A Critical Assessment of the Theology of Clark Pinnock*, ed. Tony Gray and Christopher Sinkinson (Carlisle, U.K.: Paternoster, 2000), pp. 220-58; cf. Kevin J. Vanhoozer, *First Theology: God, Scripture, and Hermeneutics* (Downers Grove, Ill.: InterVarsity Press, 2002). In this regard, Vanhoozer astutely observes that for certain theologians (which would include Pinnock), the category of prevenient grace has shifted from soteriology to the doctrine of creation, where it has now become a matter of ontology. Vanhoozer states: "For these theologians, there is only one kind of grace, one kind of call, one kind of way in which God is related to the world. God exerts a constant attractive force on the soul—a kind of divine gravity. This universal call comes through a variety of media: the creation itself, conscience, as well as the proclamation about Christ. Grace is therefore 'prevenient': that which 'comes before' a person's ability to repent and believe. . . . For much of modern theology, then, prevenient grace has become a matter of *ontology*" (pp. 103-4).

[45]I will outline this debate. In John 15:26, we are told that the Holy Spirit proceeds from the Father, but at the same time Jesus sends the Spirit. Which is it? Does the Spirit proceed from the Father or from the Father *and the Son*? This question sparked a major debate in the history of the church which eventually led to the Western church adopting the *filioque* clause—"and from the Son." The adoption of this clause was one of the theological factors that led to the first major division within the church, known as the Great Schism in 1054 A.D. The question of debate was whether the Son sends the Spirit as well as the Father or whether the Father alone sends the Spirit. The West added the *filioque* clause to the Nicene Creed thus endorsing the view that the Spirit was sent by the Father *and the Son*.

that this insertion represented a misuse of power; his main problem with the clause is how the Western church has viewed the Son-Spirit relationship as a result. Historically, as represented by the *filioque*, the work of the Spirit has been viewed in light of the Son and of gospel realities. Thus, when the Spirit operates savingly in the world, it is always in relationship to the Son and bringing people to faith in the Son. This is something Pinnock wants to reverse:

> The idea of adding *filioque* was not perverse theologically. The risen Lord did and does pour out the Spirit on the church. But the phrase in the creed can lead to a possible misunderstanding. It can threaten our understanding of the Spirit's universality. It might suggest to the worshiper that Spirit is not the gift of the Father to creation universally but a gift confined to the sphere of the Son and even the sphere of the church. It could give the impression that the Spirit is not present in the whole world but limited to Christian territories. Though it need not, the *filioque* might threaten the principle of universality—the truth that the Spirit is universally present, implementing the universal salvific will of Father and Son. One could say that the *filioque* promotes Christomonism.
>
> In my view the phrase diminishes the role of the Spirit and gives the impression that he has no mission of his own. It does not encourage us to contemplate the broad range of his operations in the universe. It tends to restrict Spirit to the churchly domain and deny his presence among people outside. It does not encourage us to view the divine mission as being prior to and geographically larger than the Son's. It could seem to limit Spirit to having a noetic function in relation to Christ, as if the Spirit fostered faith in him and nothing more. It undercuts the idea that Spirit can be active where the Son is not named and supports the restrictive reading of the axiom 'Outside the church, no salvation.' . . . The creed [Nicene] was better before this term was added to it, because it recognized Spirit as the power permeating the cosmos and energizing all of history. The mission of the Spirit is not subordinate to the Son's but equal and complementary. The *filioque* was introduced into the creed in an irregular way and adversely affects our understanding of salvation.[46]

Based upon these kinds of biblical texts and theological arguments, Pinnock believes he has warranted his synergistic inclusivism and its specific understanding of the Spirit's universal, salvific work in the world, even in other religions, thus al-

---

The East argued that only the Father sent the Spirit. What is the importance of this debate? At least two points historically. First, the issue of order and role relations within the Godhead. Second, by not viewing the Spirit as sent from both the Father *and the Son*, there was a tendency in the East to separate the work of the Spirit from the Son, and the objective realities of the gospel. This is the point that Pinnock picks up even though his view is quite out of step with Eastern theologians. For a succinct summary of the debate and description of positions see Robert Letham, *The Holy Trinity* (Phillipsburg, N.J.: Presbyterian & Reformed, 2004), pp. 201-51.

[46]Pinnock, *Flame of Love*, pp. 196-97.

lowing the unevangelized access to salvation. For, after all, asks Pinnock, "If the
Spirit gives life to creation and offers grace to every creature, one would expect
him to be present and make himself felt (at least occasionally) in the religious dimension of cultural life. Why would the Spirit be working everywhere else but not
here?"[47] This is not to say that Pinnock thinks everything in non-Christian religions is equally valid. But he is convinced that since over the centuries the majority
of humanity has existed without hearing the gospel, it is important to affirm that
the Spirit is at work in the world, even in other religions, bringing people to faith.
In fact, we should view other religions in a similar situation to the history of Israel.
Just as the history of Israel led to the coming of Jesus and God was at work apart
from explicit faith in Christ but leading up to him, Pinnock believes that we may
"watch for anticipations in other faiths to be fulfilled in Christ."[48]

But, it may be legitimately asked, by what criterion does one discern whether
the Spirit is at work in other religions? If the Spirit is at work in the unevangelized
to bring them to "faith," then what does this faith look like? After all, as Pinnock
acknowledges, "there are things in the world that cannot be attributed to God."[49]
For Pinnock, the answer is found in the double mission of the Son and Spirit and
the link between them. He states:

> Truth incarnate is the criterion for testing spirits. The question to ask is christolog-
> ical (1 Jn 4:2-3). Spirit is in agreement with the Son and agrees with what he said
> and did. . . . What the Spirit says and does cannot be opposed to revelation in Christ,
> because Spirit is bound to the Word of God. . . . To identify prevenience, we look for
> the fruit of the Spirit and for the way of Jesus Christ.[50]

Now that sounds fine, but what exactly does it mean? Historically, the work of the
Spirit has been linked to the work of the Son. When we ask the question: How do
we discern whether the Spirit is at work in the world?, the answer is found in terms
of the gospel. Is there repentance of sin and faith in the Lord Jesus Christ? Is there
a turning to God by believing the gospel message? Obviously Pinnock cannot affirm this since it would entail that there can be no saving faith apart from explicit
faith in Christ. Instead, for him, the "Christological criterion" is not noetic but
ethical, that is, the Spirit at work producing *the way of Jesus in the world*. This is
"faith" that is exhibited in a changed life, as Pinnock insists: "So wherever we see
traces of Jesus in the world and people opening up to his ideals, we know we are
in the presence of Spirit. Wherever, for example, we find self-sacrificing love, care

---

[47]Ibid., pp. 200-201.
[48]Ibid., p. 202.
[49]Ibid.
[50]Ibid., p. 209.

about community, longings for justice, wherever people love one another, care for the sick, make peace not war, wherever there is beauty and concord, generosity and forgiveness, the cup of cold water, we know the Spirit of Jesus is present."[51] For proof of this assertion, Pinnock appeals to Matthew 25:31-46, contending that this is Jesus' own criterion for recognizing his sheep. Pinnock asks: "Why does he [Jesus] consider these his sheep? Because they are just like the children of the merciful Father. Obviously they belong to the kingdom, *because their faith is manifest in their actions*. They are doing the works of the kingdom by the grace of God."[52] That is why, for Pinnock, "saving faith" is not merely cognitive or belief in specific promises since this is impossible in the case of the unevangelized. Rather, "saving faith" is *implicit*; it must be viewed in relation to the "fruit of the Spirit" created in one's life. This does not entail a "salvation by works." Rather, it is evidence that signals a response to God's grace at work in the individual.[53]

Here, then, is Pinnock's argument for his pneumatological, synergistic inclusivism. By this argument, he believes he has provided the necessary biblical and theological warrant for inclusivism's belief that God's saving grace is extended to all, that Christ alone is Savior, and that salvation is "by grace through *faith*" but not necessarily explicit faith in Christ.

Monergistic accessibilism. Not all inclusivists are of the synergistic variety, however. For example, Terrance Tiessen represents a monergistic inclusivism which he labels "accessibilism." He clearly distinguishes his position from its synergistic cousin on such issues as: the nature of sin, human freedom, divine sovereignty, unconditional election, particular atonement and so on.[54] However, even though his overall theology is different, "accessibilism" also exhibits much in common with synergistic inclusivism on such issues as: God's mercy leads him to give all people equal access to salvation; all of God's revelation (general and special) is potentially salvific; the same status exists for infants, mentally incompetent and competent unevangelized adults; a similar kind of universal work of grace occurs in everyone, enabling all people, including the nonelect, to respond to God's revelation in faith in a way that leaves them accountable for their response; and, for our purposes in this chapter, the important "believer" vs.

---

[51]Ibid., pp. 209-10.

[52]Ibid., p. 210, italics added.

[53]See ibid., pp. 210-11, where Pinnock clearly attempts to distinguish his view from a works salvation view: "Good works do not merit grace, but they may signal a response to grace. . . . Jesus is the criterion of salvation even for those who never knew him or his message. Participation in salvation is not impossible for people outside the church. The factors are behavioral as well as cognitive."

[54]See Tiessen, *Who Can Be Saved?* pp. 17-20. For a more detailed discussion of his overall modified Calvinistic theology, see Terrance L. Tiessen, *Providence and Prayer: How Does God Work in the World?* (Downers Grove, Ill.: InterVarsity Press, 2000).

"Christian" distinction.[55] Let us now describe his basic approach in eight steps, with specific focus on his argument that salvation is "by grace through implicit faith" for the unevangelized, at least in this life.

1. By God's appointment, all human beings were represented in Adam and thus when he sinned, we all sinned. The consequence of original sin is as follows:

> Everyone is born a sinner, alienated from God, guilty of enmity toward God and certain to commit acts of personal disobedience as soon as we are capable of moral judgments. Thus, there are no innocent people, whether they are unborn, infant, disabled, or competent adults. Every human being, therefore, needs to be saved from the guilt of sin and its terrible consequences.[56]

2. There is only one means by which salvation of sinners can be accomplished, namely the finished work of Jesus Christ. He is the ontological ground for the salvation of anyone.

3. God has chosen to save a people for himself (unconditional election) and Christ's death on the cross secures that salvation for them (particular redemption). The elect include not only those who have believed the gospel but also all those who have never heard but who have responded in a faith appropriate to the revelation they have received.[57]

4. How does God bring about a faith response in the elect? Tiessen argues that the Holy Spirit effectually works in the lives of the elect, changing their hearts so that they willingly believe. Today, the normal means of doing so is by the preaching of the gospel. But for those who existed before the time of Christ, or for those who have never heard, the Spirit works effectively in them so that they respond with appropriate "faith" to the revelation at their disposal. The Spirit's work is *not* limited to the covenant people of God, to those who have received special revelation alone.

5. In terms of revelation, Tiessen argues that God has not left himself without witness, but not everyone has an equally full revelation. Everyone has received general revelation, and the covenant people of God have received a greater, special revelation. But these two categories do not exhaust all the categories, since there is a third kind of "special revelation" which takes place outside of the covenant community (e.g., dreams and visions). Tiessen labels it a "particular non-univer-

---

[55]See the development of these points in *Who Can Be Saved?* pp. 123-216, 230-58. On this last point, namely, that there is "a kind of universal work of grace" in everyone, synergistic and accessibilistic inclusivism view it differently; but, I would contend, this grace functions similarly in their arguments.

[56]See Tiessen, *Who Can Be Saved?* p. 22. Also see pp 73-82 for development of this point.

[57]For Tiessen, the elect also includes infants and the mentally incompetent (ibid., pp. 204-16).

sally normative revelation,"[58] that he believes God may utilize today to speak to the unevangelized, independent of gospel proclamation. Furthermore, Tiessen insists, not only are people held accountable for the kind of revelation they have received, but if they respond to it in a "faith-appropriate" way, they will be saved.

6. What, then, is the nature of this saving faith tied to the revelation that people have received? In the case of general revelation, a "faith-appropriate response" is one of thanks to God as the Creator and Provider. If people respond in this way, they will be saved.[59] At this point, Tiessen rejects the standard evangelical interpretation of Romans 1:18-32, namely, that general revelation is nonsalvific. He agrees that Paul clearly states that those who suppress the truth of general revelation and do not give God thanks are without excuse. However, he disagrees that Paul even addresses the issue "that *everyone* ultimately and *finally* does this."[60] From this observation, Tiessen concludes that *if* there is a positive response to general revelation then it is a result of the work of the Spirit in people's lives, and as such, it is an example of true, saving faith.[61]

Additionally, also tied to general revelation, Tiessen believes that the "faith-appropriate response" to the revelation of *God's moral demands* upon the human conscience is nothing less than "obedience to this law, which is possessed by those who do not have Scripture, as the righteousness that pleases God."[62] At this point, it seems that Tiessen is very close to Pinnock's understanding of an appropriate "faith response" to general revelation, which is demonstrated in a person's *ethical* behavior. What biblical warrant does Tiessen give? First, he appeals to Romans 2:13-16 which emphasizes the "law written upon people's hearts." Second, he "assumes"[63] that since the work of Christ was effective for OT believers who did not know of Christ but who threw themselves on God's mercy, in the same way, "people with guilty consciences who are under conviction by the Holy Spirit would be led to stop depending on themselves and would entrust themselves to the mercy of the Creator and Judge whom they encounter in creation and in the voice of their conscience."[64] Tiessen, like other inclusivists, draws an analogy between the function of the Mosaic covenant in the life of Israel and the law written upon the heart

---

[58]See Tiessen, *Who Can Be Saved?* pp. 120-22. Tiessen speculates that this third kind of revelation was the kind of revelation that Abimelech, Cyrus, and the Magi might have received.

[59]Ibid., p. 144. Tiessen states: "The faith response to God's revelation of his eternal power and divine nature through his work of creation would, therefore, include a worship of the Creator God and a spirit of thankfulness for what he has made and provided for us."

[60]Ibid., p. 141.

[61]See ibid., p. 142.

[62]Ibid., p. 144-45.

[63]This is the way Tiessen states it. Ibid., p. 143.

[64]Ibid.

among the Gentiles. He suggests, quoting Millard Erickson, that "the law written within, could serve the same function as the Mosaic or written law."[65] How? By bringing an awareness of the need of divine grace which might also "cause one to cast oneself upon the mercy of God."[66]

Interestingly, even though Tiessen admits that there are no biblical examples of individuals who have responded appropriately to general revelation, he still insists that God *could* have acted in this way.[67] He then goes on to argue that, in actuality, it is not probable that general revelation exists solely by itself. After listing eight factors that make it unlikely that there are any people who are completely ignorant of any form of special revelation,[68] he concludes: "We need not assume that their salvation comes about only through means of general revelation."[69] But even with this important caveat, Tiessen is convinced that we must "begin with the assumption that the Spirit of God works in a saving way with all people, although the means and content of his self-revelation vary."[70]

What about other kinds of revelation? What is the appropriate faith response to them? With regard to the nature of saving faith vis-à-vis OT believers both within and outside of Israel, Tiessen's argument is almost identical to Pinnock's and typical of inclusivism. OT "believers" were saved by grace through faith, but not explicitly "Christian" faith, and as such their situation is parallel to the unevangelized today. For most inclusivists this is probably the strongest biblical support of their implicit faith position. As Tiessen asserts: "The biblical instances cited above [OT believers] do demonstrate that one *can* be saved *by* Christ without knowing *about* him, at least not by means of a human messenger, *and this provides ground for our hopefulness about God's work of grace outside the church now.*"[71] In addition, Tiessen unpacks the nature of saving faith in old covenant believers in the following three ways.[72]

---

[65]Ibid. Tiessen's citation of Millard Erickson is from *How Shall They Be Saved?* p. 152.

[66]Tiessen, *Who Can Be Saved?* p. 143.

[67]See ibid., p. 149.

[68]See ibid., pp. 150-51. The eight factors are (1) the remnants of special revelation that have been passed on in the cultural and religious traditions of the nations; (2) the long period of time between the Fall and a written revelation, during which it seems highly implausible that God made no special contact with people; (3) the contact of the nations with the Scriptures; (4) the fact that God still encounters people directly in dreams and visions as he did in the OT; (5) the fact that the Son operates throughout the world, just as he did before and during the incarnation; (6) the work of the Holy Spirit who operates universally in the world; (7) God's promise that those who sincerely seek him with all their hearts will find him; and (8) the possibility of universal at-death encounters with Christ that will elicit from all a response consistent with their prior response to God's revelation to them.

[69]Ibid., p. 164.

[70]Ibid., p. 155.

[71]Ibid., p. 180, italics added.

[72]For a full development of his argument, see ibid., pp. 165-203.

First, the saving faith of "OT believers within Israel" was nothing less than "an utter abandonment of reliance on one's own strength, righteousness, effort, or that of anyone other than God himself. It was also a belief in the gracious, merciful provision of that holy, loving God."[73] Even though Tiessen admits that Israel's faith was not a general faith in an undefined God, it was still *not* explicit faith in Christ. Tiessen thinks the situation of "old covenant believers" is analogous to that of Jewish people today. He argues that just "because they [Jewish people today] are ignorant concerning Jesus or concerning his true identity, they can hardly be deemed to be 'rejecting' him."[74] I assume from this statement that Tiessen holds out the possibility that unevangelized Jews today who exhibit an OT Abrahamic faith, but not a faith in Christ, may still have "saving faith." In fact, he seems to go one step further, implying that *evangelized* Jews may still exhibit saving faith, even if they reject the proclamation about Jesus, because of their misunderstanding of Jesus due to centuries of anti-Semitism at the hands of nominal Christians.[75]

Second, in regard to the saving faith of "OT believers outside Israel," Tiessen rightly admits that "we are told little about it" in Scripture.[76] Unlike Clark Pinnock, Tiessen does not approve of the label "pagan saints" to people such as Abel, Enoch, Noah, Job and so on. Instead he prefers to call them "God-fearers," given the fact that they probably had some contact with special revelation tied to their identification with Israel. However, he thinks Melchizedek and Jethro are probably the best examples of OT believers outside of Israel. In the case of Melchizedek, Tiessen argues that he was a worshipper of *El Elyon*, a Canaanite deity, whose identity "is curiously merged with Abraham's God."[77] He then goes on to hypothesize that since the book of Hebrews gives anticipatory significance to the old covenant sacrifices, this could open the door to think that other sacrifices offered by devout people outside the Mosaic covenant may point to Jesus and find their efficacy in him. Obviously, Tiessen admits, we have no data on this, but then he incredibly states: "If we *were* eventually to grant that God might accept the sacrifices of some non-Christians because the Spirit works faith in their lives, then those sacrifices would also derive their efficacy from Christ's sacrifice."[78]

Third, Tiessen also finds in "NT examples of old covenant believers" further proof for his implicit faith position. For example, Cornelius is an illustration of

---

[73]Ibid., p. 166. Tiessen's quotation involves a citation of Millard Erickson, *How Shall They Be Saved?* pp. 191-92.

[74]Tiessen, *Who Can Be Saved?* p. 168.

[75]Ibid., p. 200.

[76]Ibid., p. 169.

[77]Ibid., p. 171.

[78]Ibid., p. 172, italics original.

one who was saved "through his obedience to the light he had, but he needed 'the fuller light' so that he could become 'all he might be.'"[79] Furthermore, the disciples, the apostle Paul, and the disciples of John in Ephesus (Acts 19:1-7) are examples of people who had saving faith in the old covenant sense, but then, given more revelation, became Christians. In their case, God's work of salvation was a gradual process in their lives and it was almost impossible to say the precise moment they were saved.

In light of these biblical examples, it is important to note at least two major assumptions at work for Tiessen (and many inclusivists). First, Tiessen assumes that even though significant redemptive-historical shifts took place with the coming of Christ, he does not think that the old covenant era is completely over. He states:

> In terms of the history of God's saving work, the new covenant has clearly been inaugurated, and the Spirit is now being given to all who believe in Jesus. I am arguing, however, that precisely because the unevangelized are, by definition, ignorant of Jesus, they live in a different 'spiritual economy' and await the fuller revelation of God in Christ, as believers did prior to the Word's taking on flesh.[80]

In fact, Tiessen thinks that there are some people, particularly Jews, who today "still live under the revelational terms of the old covenant, even though they are historically living in the new covenant."[81] And second, Tiessen assumes that in regard to salvation, even though Scripture indicates a precise moment when a person moves from darkness to light, "the experience of the first disciples of Jesus illustrates for us, however, just how difficult it is to identify that moment."[82] For him, this entails that "we need not assume that the unevangelized are not saved, simply because they are not (yet!) Christians."[83] Instead, we need to view their salvation as an illustration of the fact that salvation is past, present, and future. Just as Christians were, are being, and shall be saved, in a similar way we may speak of the unevangelized in this process as well.[84]

7. In order to minimize the idea of implicit faith, Tiessen proposes that everyone who is saved will eventually believe in Jesus, at least in a "universal at-death moment encounter" with Christ. "Admittedly," Tiessen confesses, "the proposal that we all meet Christ at death moves us beyond Scripture's explicit teaching into

---

[79]Ibid., p. 177.
[80]Ibid., p. 227.
[81]Ibid., p. 198. See also this same idea in Pinnock, *A Wideness in God's Mercy*, pp. 159-66; Sanders, *No Other Name*, pp. 224-32.
[82]Tiessen, *Who Can Be Saved?* p. 194.
[83]Ibid., p. 202
[84]For a discussion of this point, see ibid., pp. 184-203, 225-27.

the speculative,"[85] but this does not stop him from holding it tentatively. Tiessen clearly distinguishes his approach from a second chance and post-mortem salvation, explaining that his approach has the great advantage of making faith in Christ still necessary, even though information about him is not necessary before death.[86] Ultimately what this "at-death encounter" confirms, is that persons who have already responded in faith to the form of revelation they have received, will "then respond with faith and joy to the Son who had been at work in their lives, though they were ignorant of much about him."[87]

8. In a similar way to synergistic inclusivism, Tiessen argues that God provides a "universally sufficient enabling grace." Given the effects of sin, asks Tiessen, how is it fair that God can hold the nonelect responsible for their failure to believe if they do not have the ability to do so? It is best to believe that at least once in every person's life, the Spirit of God enables them to respond to the specific revelation that they have with a saving faith response. However, it is only the elect whom the Spirit of God effectively draws and persuades.[88] Even though Tiessen distinguishes his view from the prevenient grace of synergism, it seems to function in a similar fashion, namely, to preserve the universality axiom. As with other points of Tiessen's view, he admits that there are no explicit biblical texts that teach a universally sufficient grace: "By way of specific explicit biblical teaching, one is hard put to cite texts specifically indicating a universal distribution of grace to all people that enables them to respond to divine revelation in a responsible way."[89] Nonetheless, he thinks it is a plausible notion as both a legitimate deduction from biblical texts, as well as a view which does not negate any specific biblical text.

Here, then, in summary fashion, is Tiessen's argument for monergistic accessibilism. Obviously much more could be said, but in my description of monergistic accessibilism and synergistic inclusivism, I have sought to highlight the main biblical and theological warrants underlying each viewpoint, especially as it relates to the issue of the nature of saving faith. Let us now turn to a biblical-theological critique of inclusivism's view of implicit faith.

A BIBLICAL-THEOLOGICAL CRITIQUE OF INCLUSIVISM'S VIEW OF IMPLICIT FAITH

This is a huge area and my comments will only begin to scratch the surface of such an important topic. However, my critique will focus on two areas: the theological

---

[85]Ibid., p. 218.
[86]See ibid., pp. 217-18.
[87]Ibid., p. 223.
[88]See ibid., pp. 230-58.
[89]Ibid., p. 494.

rationale for and the biblical grounding of inclusivism's defense of salvation by
grace through implicit faith.

The theological rationale: The pneumatological underpinning of inclusivism. In
the discussion of Clark Pinnock's synergistic inclusivism, I noted how his pneumatological approach served to provide the necessary theological rationale for
thinking that the unevangelized may be saved by grace through *faith*, even though
that faith is not explicitly Christian faith. The following critique will primarily
pertain to Pinnock's proposal; however, I also think that it relates to Tiessen's
monergistic view as well. Let me explain why this is the case.

Even though Tiessen's development of his view, given his overall theology, does
not follow the same path as Pinnock and other inclusivists,[90] he has a similar understanding of the universal work of the Spirit among the unevangelized which
serves as the theological rationale for how salvation is by "grace through implicit
faith." Like Pinnock, Tiessen affirms that we must view the particularity of Christ
in the context of the universality of the Spirit. For example, he appeals to Acts 2:17
to argue that the work of the Holy Spirit, who was poured out on "all flesh," entails
that the Spirit operates within the church, but he also infers that the Spirit's "work
is not restricted to the church."[91] I interpret Tiessen to mean that the Spirit's work
is not only tied to gospel proclamation, but is also a universal work in the world,
working independently of that proclamation. This point is further confirmed
when Tiessen approvingly appeals to Amos Yong's understanding that "pneumatology is the key to overcoming the dualism between christological particularity
and the cosmic Christ," an understanding agreeing with Pinnock's view.[92]

Furthermore, there is a sense in which Tiessen's appeal to "universally sufficient
grace"—even though, admittedly, it is theoretically different than Pinnock's synergistic approach—functions in his accessibilism in a similar way as Pinnock's
pneumatological approach functions in his view. How so? As noted above, inclusivists wrestle with the tension between the universality and particularity axioms.
Given the fact that God desires all to be saved, if hearing the gospel is required for
salvation, then it would seem that God does not want all to be saved. The solution
to this tension is to argue that general revelation is potentially salvific and that the
Spirit is universally at work enabling sinners to turn to God and respond in faith,
apart from gospel revelation. Pinnock makes theological sense of this by appeal to
the universal, prevenient work of the Spirit in the world. Tiessen makes sense of
it, not by appeal to a prevenient grace, but by appeal to another kind of universal

[90]For example, I have found no place in Tiessen's writings where he denies the *filioque* clause.
[91]*Who Can Be Saved?* p. 151.
[92]Ibid., p. 183.

grace, i.e., a "universally sufficient grace." Even though the two positions differ in their explanations, both affirm the universal work of the Spirit *prior to and geographically beyond* the covenantal revelation, now centered in Jesus Christ. In this way, Tiessen believes, like Pinnock, albeit for different reasons, that he has provided the theological rationale for linking a salvifically sufficient revelation and a sufficient enabling grace for all people so that, in the end, the unevangelized *could* believe if they *would* do so. In this way, he believes he has preserved the universality axiom and upheld the justice of God in holding the nonelect responsible for their actions.[93]

All of this is to say that in my critique of the pneumatological approach of inclusivism, my comments specifically pertain to Pinnock (and those who follow his approach), but they also pertain to other inclusivists as well. In fact, in the end, all inclusivists have to make theological sense of how God is universally at work in the world giving all people equal access to the means of salvation, removing people's inability to respond, and all of this apart from God's special, covenantal revelation.

What, then, is my problem with the pneumatological underpinning of inclusivism? The crux of the matter is posed in a question: Is it legitimate, biblically speaking, to view the particular work of the Son in relation to the universal work of the Spirit, as the pneumatological approach attempts to do? I find no biblical warrant for it. It is my contention that, in attempting to understand the Son's work as an aspect of the Spirit's universal work, the pneumatological proposal fails to do justice to an overall biblical theology. Specifically, its attempt to view Christ as an

---

[93] A critique of Tiessen's understanding of "universally sufficient grace" is outside the purview of this chapter, but two points may be mentioned. First, regardless of his attempt to show how this is truly a *sufficient* grace within monergism and that it is different than a synergistic prevenient grace (see pp. 241-42), I am unconvinced and find his proposal incoherent. Tiessen argues that this universally sufficient grace to the nonelect gives them the ability to respond, but it is only by the efficacious work of the Spirit in the elect that they will respond. How, then, is this grace truly *sufficient*? If it truly enables the nonelect to respond, then why argue for an additional efficacious grace? One only needs an efficacious grace if there is no such thing as a universally sufficient grace. In the end, Tiessen's view looks much more like a "prevenient grace" after all. In many ways what drives his approach is the attempt to make sense of the culpability of the nonelect for their unbelief. As Tiessen notes, unless God gives a universally sufficient grace "it seems patently unjust that those who are not given the ability to believe are condemned for not doing so" (p. 232). In many ways, it is this last statement which drives much of the inclusivists' argument and leads them to affirm that all people must have access to salvation through means other than God's specific, covenantal means. The issue of justice and fairness is an important one. We must be careful, however, that we do not accept the false assumption that in order for God to be just, every individual on earth must have equal access to his saving grace. We must also be careful that we do not propose speculative schemes to explain how God is just in holding all people responsible for their actions and for the revelation at their disposal. Second, and more importantly, I find no biblical grounding for his argument.

aspect of the Spirit's mission is *not* biblical. I will first make a preliminary observation regarding theological method before I sketch out what I believe is a more biblical understanding of the Son-Spirit relation across the canon of Scripture.

A preliminary observation regarding theological method. Inclusivists, like Pinnock, who argue for the pneumatological proposal force us to ask some basic methodological questions: How does one *do* a theology of the Holy Spirit? How does one move from biblical text to theological formulation? Specifically, how does one resolve the question that is at stake here: What is the Son-Spirit relation in Scripture? My reflections here on this big subject are only to make clear how I approach the task, especially in my critique of the pneumatological approach.[94]

In terms of theological method, it is crucial that our reading of Scripture reflect what it is and claims to be. What, then, is Scripture? What does it claim to be? Scripture is nothing less than God's self-revelation through human authors— God's Word written—that comes to us *progressively* and with a *christological* focus. Since Scripture is *God's* self-revelation, there is a unity to it—a unified divine communicative act[95]—declaring God's unfailing purposes and plan. Furthermore, God's self-revelation, in Word and Act, involves historical progression, along a redemptive-historical story line, meaning that the task of a biblical theology[96] is to trace this historical unfolding of redemptive history, which presses on toward its consummation in Jesus Christ (cf. Heb 1:1-2). In light of this, it is helpful to think of reading Scripture according to three horizons: textual, epochal, and canonical.[97] Thus, in reading any text we not only exegete it in terms of its syntax, context, and genre, but we also place that text in light of where it is in redemptive history, and even, in the final analysis, where it is in light of the entire canon of Scripture. It is only when we do the latter that we read Scripture according to its truest, fullest, *divine* intention. In fact, to read the Bible as unified Scripture is not just one interpretative interest among others, but the interpretative strategy that best corresponds to the nature of the text itself, given its divine inspiration.

What does all of this have to do with my critique of the pneumatological ap-

---

[94]For an in-depth treatment of these issues, see Richard Lints, *The Fabric of Theology* (Grand Rapids: Eerdmans, 1993); Michael S. Horton, *Covenant and Eschatology* (Louisville: Westminster John Knox, 2002); T. Desmond Alexander and Brian S. Rosner, eds., *New Dictionary of Biblical Theology* (Downers Grove, Ill.: InterVarsity Press, 2000); Kevin J. Vanhoozer, *The Drama of Doctrine* (Louisville: Westminster John Knox, 2005). In application to the issues of inclusivism, see Strange, *Possibility of Salvation*, pp. 139-290.

[95]On this see Vanhoozer, *First Theology*; idem, *Is There a Meaning in This Text?* (Grand Rapids: Zondervan, 1998).

[96]"Biblical theology" is being used in a technical sense. For a definition and explanation of biblical theology, see Alexander and Rosner, *New Dictionary of Biblical Theology*, pp. 3-11; Graeme Goldsworthy, *According to Plan* (Downers Grove, Ill.: InterVarsity Press, 2001).

[97]The three horizons are taken from Richard Lints, *Fabric of Theology*.

proach of inclusivism? Everything. As we seek to understand the Son-Spirit relation, it is best to do so along the redemptive-historical story line, in light of the
whole canon, discovering how the Spirit of God is presented, both in the OT and
in light of the coming of Jesus Christ. And when we do so, what we discover is the
opposite of the pneumatological proposal. Instead, we discover what much of
evangelical theology has always claimed, namely that the Spirit is the Spirit of the
crucified and exalted Christ and, in the words of Kevin Vanhoozer is "the deputy
of Christ rather than an independent itinerant evangelist."[98] In other words, we
discover that Scripture presents the work of the Spirit always in relation to the
Son, entailing that when the Spirit is at work in people, his unique work *is to bring
people to faith in Christ* which must always be viewed in a covenantally defined way.

   Toward a biblical theology of the Son-Spirit relationship. This section uses the
word "toward" for the simple reason that all I can do here is sketch, as I see it, the
main structures of thought in regard to the Son-Spirit relation as it is progressively
revealed in the canon.

   The work of the Spirit in the OT era and his relationship to the Son. There are
just under 100 explicit references to the "Spirit *(ruach)* of God" in the OT, starting
from Genesis 1:2.[99] None of these references unambiguously demand that we
think of the "Spirit of God" as one with God yet differentiable from him (except
possibly Is 63:7-14). The Spirit's distinct "personal" nature will become clearer in
the NT, in light of the coming of the Christ, since there we must think of the
Spirit not merely as the "power" of God, nor merely the "manifest presence" of
God, but as the third person of the triune Godhead. With that said, when it comes
to describing the work of the "Spirit of God" in the OT, it is important to distinguish between general and more specific works. Let us look at these in turn.

   First, we may think of the work of God's Spirit in a general way, active as creator, sustainer, revealer, quickener, and enabler. We may even summarize the
Spirit's work in terms of seven main functions.[100] (1) In creation, we see the Spirit's
work in the way God created and sustains the universe and all animate beings
(Gen 1:2; 2:7; cf. Ps 33:6; Job 26:13; 33:4; 34:14-15). (2) The Spirit of God is active
in the control of nature and history (Ps 104:29-30; Is 34:16; 40:7). (3) God's Spirit

---

[98]Vanhoozer, "Does the Trinity Belong in a Theology of Religions?" p. 66.
[99]Max Turner, "Holy Spirit," in *New Dictionary of Biblical Theology*, pp. 551-58; cf. David F. Wells,
   God the Evangelist (Grand Rapids: Eerdmans, 1987), pp. 1-4; Gordon D. Fee, *Paul, the Spirit, and
   the People of God* (Peabody, Mass.: Hendrickson, 1996), pp. 9-15; Sinclair B. Ferguson, *The Holy
   Spirit* (Downers Grove, Ill.: InterVarsity Press, 1996), pp. 15-33; J. I. Packer, *Keep in Step with the
   Spirit* (Old Tappan, N.J.: Revell, 1984), pp. 55-63.
[100]See Wells, *God the Evangelist*, pp. 3-4, for these seven main ways the Spirit's work is described in the
   OT.

is active in revelation as he makes known what was not known (Num 24:2; 2 Sam 23:2; 1 Chron 12:18; 15:1; Neh 9:30; Job 32:8; Is 61:1-4; Ezek 2:2; 11:24; 37:1; Mic 3:8; Zech 7:12). (4) By these revelations the Spirit of God teaches the people of God the way to be faithful and obedient to the Lord (Neh 9:20; Ps 143:10; Is 48:16; 63:10-14). (5) The Spirit's power elicits personal responses to God in terms of faith, repentance, obedience, willingness to listen to God's instructions, as well as fellowship with the Lord through praise and prayer (Ps 51:10-12; Is 11:2; 44:3; Ezek 11:19; 36:25-27; 37:14; 39:29; Joel 2:28-29; Zech 12:10). (6) The Spirit of God is instrumental in equipping people for leadership, particularly those leaders in Israel—prophets, priests and kings (Gen 41:38; Num 11:16-29; 27:16,18; Deut 34:9; Judg 3:10; 6:34; 11:29; 13:25; 14:19; 15:14; 1 Sam 10:10; 11:6). (7) God's Spirit equips people with skill and strength for creative work, such as in the construction of the tabernacle and temple (Ex 28:3; 31:1-11; cf. 1 Kings 7:14; Hag 2:5; Zech 4:6).

At this point, contra Pinnock and others, it is important to stress that this general work in the OT does *not* entail that the Spirit's presence is always a saving or transforming presence (e.g., Balaam, Saul).[101] Nor should we hastily conclude that what is true of a particular individual in Scripture is true of the whole of humanity. As Sinclair Ferguson wisely reminds us, we cannot assume from the fact that the Spirit endowed Bezalel with gifts of design and craftsmanship (Ex 31:1-15) that all artistic gifts, however used, are general endowments of the Spirit,[102] let alone evidence of God's saving presence. Yes, the Spirit is described as the one who works in relation to the created order, but it is clear, in both the OT and NT, that this general ministry of the Spirit should not always be identified with the Spirit's

---

[101]In Pinnock and many other inclusivists (Tiessen excepted), there is an incipient reductionism in understanding God's presence in the world. Why is all presence a *saving* presence? Evangelical theology has believed that it is important to distinguish different ways God is present in creation. Hear what Louis Berkhof, *Systematic Theology* ([1941; reprint, Grand Rapids: Eerdmans, 1982], p. 61) has to say: "Though God is distinct from the world and may not be identified with it, He is yet present in every part of his creation, not only *per potentiam* but also *per essentiam*. This does not mean, however, that He is equally present and present in the same sense in all his creatures. The nature of His indwelling is in harmony with that of his creatures. He does not dwell on earth as He does in heaven, in animals as He does in man, in the inorganic as He does in the organic creation, in the wicked as He does in the pious, nor in the Church as He does in Christ. There is an endless variety in the manner in which He is immanent in His creatures, and in the measure in which they reveal God to those who have eyes to see." See also the important discussion in Daniel Strange, "Deciphering the Conundrum of Pneumatological Inclusivism," pp. 242-47. Thus, one need not conclude that God's presence is necessarily a "redemptive" presence. Strange states: "I think that in his desire to prove universal accessibility, Pinnock has blurred and confused the general and universal operations of the Spirit in creation, the specific and particular operations of the Spirit in salvation, and mistaken saving presence with divine providence" (ibid., p. 246).
[102]Ferguson, *The Holy Spirit*, p. 246.

work in saving grace. It is possible for the former to be present when the latter is not.[103]

Second, as we read through the OT, the Spirit's work is not only viewed in these general terms, but it is also narrowed and focused in a more direct way as it is linked with a future, eschatological age tied to the Messiah's coming and the new covenant, Messianic age. This is the point that Pinnock and those who follow his approach fail to do justice to. Let us think of this more specific work of the Spirit in at least two ways.[104]

1. The OT predicts that when Messiah, David's greater Son, comes, he will have the Spirit in full measure (Is 11:1-5; 42:1-8; 61:1-3; cf. Lk 4:17ff. and Mt 12:28). This taps into a whole stream of thought in the OT, where leaders (primarily prophets, priests, and kings) were anointed by the Spirit (see 1 Sam 16:13-14), but they often failed in their representative tasks before the Lord and the people of God. But, as the prophets announce, when the Messiah comes, the promised seed from Abraham's line, David's greater Son, he will have the Spirit in full measure. And, most importantly, he will not fail in his saving work, for in his coming he will literally usher in the "age to come," which is precisely what is picked up in the NT as the Spirit is linked with the conception, birth, growth, baptism, temptations, ministry, and cross work of Christ (Mt 4:1; Mk 1:10; Lk 1:31, 35; 2:47; 4:14-21; Jn 1:33-34; Rom 1:4; 1 Cor 15:45; 2 Cor 3:17-18; 1 Tim 3:16; 1 Pet 3:18). This portrait of Jesus and the Spirit functions primarily, as Max Turner reminds us, "to confirm to readers that Jesus is indeed the Messiah anticipated by the OT,"[105] that the eschatological era predicted in the OT has finally dawned in him. But it is also more than this. As Jesus himself reminds us in John 13—16, the primary significance of the Spirit's coming is announced in programmatic terms: "When the Counselor comes, whom I will send to you from the Father, the Spirit of truth who goes out from the Father, he will testify about me. And you also must testify, for you have been with me from the beginning" (Jn 15:26-27). In other words, the linkage of the Spirit with Christ is to bear witness to him in a very specific way. As Ferguson reminds us, "From womb to tomb to throne, the Spirit was the constant companion of the Son."[106] As a result, his work is that of chief witness for Christ, to bear witness of him, indeed to bring people to him in saving faith—

---

[103]See Carson, *Gagging of God*, pp. 291-96, who makes this same point.

[104]See, for a development of these points, Anthony A. Hoekema, *The Bible and the Future* (Grand Rapids: Eerdmans, 1979), pp. 55-67; cf. Geerhardus Vos, "The Eschatological Aspect of the Pauline Conception of the Spirit" in *Redemptive History and Biblical Interpretation*, ed. Richard B. Gaffin Jr. (Phillipsburg, N.J.: Presbyterian & Reformed, 1980), pp. 91-125.

[105]Turner, "Holy Spirit," p. 552.

[106]Ferguson, *The Holy Spirit*, p. 37.

indeed explicit faith. After all, the Spirit is the Spirit *of Christ.*

2. The OT predicts that the coming of the Holy Spirit will signify nothing less than the dawning of the new covenant age (Is 32:15-17; 44:3-4; 59:20-21; Ezek 36:25-27; 37:14; 39:29; Joel 2:28-32 [cf. Jer 31:29-34]; Zech 12:10). OT prophets often presented the time of the Lord's visitation of his people as, "the time of the anticipated new covenant, as the time when the Spirit will be poured out upon men and women, young and old, without the distinctions implicit in the essentially tribal nature of the old covenant."[107] Peter, in Acts 2, quotes Joel 2 as proof that the work of Jesus the Christ, is complete, and as a result, the Spirit, anticipated and promised in the OT, has now come. D. A. Carson reminds us, "When in Acts the prophetic Spirit falls upon the church, mediating God's presence, enabling believers to speak with tongues and to perform deeds of power, forging the early links among Jewish, Samaritan, and Gentile believers, and gently nudging the church into an expanding vision of Gentile mission, this is understood to be nothing other than what God himself had promised in Scripture."[108] That is why it is best to interpret Pentecost as a unique, redemptive-historical event, rooted and grounded in OT prophetic expectation; it must be viewed as part and parcel of Jesus' saving work. In fact it is the *culmination* of his earthly work (cf. Jn 7:39) by which he has inaugurated the new covenant age, thus giving the Spirit *to all Christians* so that they may not only come to know him but also be gifted and empowered for service.[109]

Interestingly, those who adopt the pneumatological approach often fail to note this point. Instead of understanding Pentecost in the covenantal, redemptive-historical categories of Scripture, they use passages such as Acts 2:17—"I will pour out my Spirit on all people"—to refer to the universal work of the Spirit in all people apart from the proclamation of the gospel. Amos Yong, for example, says of Acts 2:17 that it "should caution us against reading the 'all' of Acts 2:17 in an exclusively ecclesiological sense."[110] Tiessen agrees.[111] But both fail to acknowledge that the words "all people" in Acts 2:17 are defined in terms of the new covenant, not as a reference to the universal work of the Spirit in people where the gospel has not gone. Under the old covenant, the structure of the covenant community meant that the Spirit was uniquely poured out on leaders. But what the prophets anticipate is a crucial change: the coming of the new covenant era would witness

---

[107]Carson, *Gagging of God*, p. 265.
[108]Ibid.
[109]For a more detailed treatment of this data, see Christopher J. H. Wright, *Knowing the Holy Spirit Through the Old Testament* (Downers Grove, Ill.: InterVarsity Press, 2006).
[110]Yong, *Beyond the Impasse*, p. 40.
[111]See Tiessen, *Who Can Be Saved?* p. 151.

a *universal* distribution of the Spirit, but universal in the sense of *all those within the covenant community.* Thus, *all* those under the new covenant enjoy the promised gift of the eschatological Holy Spirit, but this can hardly be used as a text to support the universality axiom of inclusivism.[112] In fact, as we go through the book of Acts, specifically chapters 8 and 10, we see the expansion of the covenant community to include both Jews and Gentiles. But there is never a suggestion that the Spirit is also poured out upon people all over the world apart from gospel proclamation. As many have observed, the Samaritans in Acts 8 and the Gentiles in Acts 10 do not receive the promised Spirit until *after* the gospel is proclaimed to them, thus linking the Spirit's outpouring to Christ and the entire new covenant era.

The work of the Spirit in the NT era in relation to the Son. In describing the work of the Holy Spirit in the OT, I have already made specific application to the Spirit's work in the NT. Probably the best way to capture that work is in terms of "inaugurated eschatology" and the famous "already-not yet" tension. The OT perspective and expectation is picked up in that the Spirit's work in the NT, in a direct and specific way, is linked to the coming of Messiah and the new covenant age. The eschatological, future age that the OT prophets anticipated has now arrived even though it still awaits final consummation. And the proof of all of this is not only found in the coming of the Messiah—his life, death, resurrection and exaltation—but also in the gift that the risen and exalted Lord has now poured out at Pentecost, even the promised Holy Spirit (Acts 2; cf. Jn 14—16; Eph 1:13-14).[113]

This is why, especially in Paul, the Holy Spirit "not only prompts us to look backward to God's earlier promises about his coming and work, but forward as well, for in Pauline thought the Spirit is the *arrabōn,* the deposit and hence the guarantee, of the promised inheritance awaiting us in the consummation."[114] Thus, for Paul and the rest of the NT, the reception of the Spirit means that one has become a participant in the new mode of existence associated with the future age, and now partakes of the powers of the "age to come." Yet, Paul equally insists that what the Spirit gives is only a foretaste of far greater blessings to come. This understanding is borne out in five ways in which Paul relates the Holy Spirit to the believer in the NT. First, the Spirit testifies of our "sonship" (Rom 8:14-27;

---

[112]For a further development of the relationship between the biblical covenants and the nature of the new covenant, see my "Baptism and the Relationship between the Covenants," in *Believer's Baptism: Sign of the New Covenant in Christ,* ed. Thomas R. Schreiner and Shawn D. Wright, NAC Studies in Bible and Theology (Nashville: Broadman & Holman, 2006), pp. 127-53.

[113]For a more detailed and excellent treatment of the work of the Holy Spirit across redemptive history, see James M. Hamilton Jr., *God's Indwelling Presence: A Study of the Ministry of the Holy Spirit in the Old and New Testaments,* NAC Studies in Bible and Theology (Nashville: Broadman & Holman, 2006).

[114]Ibid., pp. 265-66.

Gal 4:4-5). The Spirit bears witness that we are the children of God now, even though we still await our full rights associated with sonship. Second, the role of the Spirit is that of "firstfruits" (*aparchē*—Rom 8:23; 1 Cor 15:20, 23), which speaks both of what we have now, yet await in the future. Third, the Spirit is the "pledge" or "deposit" (*arrabōn*—2 Cor 1:22; 5:5; Eph 1:14) guaranteeing our future inheritance. Fourth, the Holy Spirit is also called a "seal" (2 Cor 1:22; Eph 4:30; 1:13), which signifies that believers are nothing less than God's possession. Fifth, the Spirit is related to the resurrection of our bodies (Rom 1:3-4; 8:11; 1 Cor 15:42-44). The Spirit is not only active in relation to Christ's resurrection but ours as well, which signifies that some day our bodies shall be raised from the dead, just as Christ, the Last Adam, was raised from the dead so that we may share in the glorious existence of the final, consummated state. Anthony Hoekema nicely summarizes: "In conclusion we may say that in the possession of the Spirit we who are in Christ have a foretaste of the blessings of the age to come, and a pledge and guarantee of the resurrection of the body. Yet we have only the firstfruits. We look forward to the final consummation of the kingdom of God, when we shall enjoy these blessings to the full."[115]

In seeking to understand the work of the Spirit (and the Son), this framework of inaugurated eschatology is significant. David Wells captures its importance when he asserts:

> When Paul speaks of the God-sent Holy Spirit, his perspective is always eschatological, looking forward to the end, of which our present experience of redemption and life in the Spirit is the beginning. The Spirit is the gift of the new age, the guarantee and foretaste, the pledge and first installment of what is to come when the fullness of salvation is revealed at Christ's return (Eph 1:13-14; Rom 8:23). It is this teaching on the relation between the old and the new, the flesh and the Spirit, the historical and the eschatological that forms the whole context within which Paul expounds his doctrines of the church and of salvation. It is in this context that he elaborates on his doctrine of the Spirit.[116]

What, then, are we to conclude from this redemptive-historical look at Scripture in terms of the Son-Spirit relation? Does it yield the same conclusions as the pneumatological approach? Does it give biblical grounds to think that the Spirit is salvifically at work in the world, bringing people to salvation apart from explicit faith in Christ? My answer is "no." In fact, as we examine the Son-Spirit relation progressively across redemptive history, what we discover is the opposite of the

---

[115]Hoekema, *Bible and the Future*, p. 67.
[116]Wells, *God the Evangelist*, pp. 9-10. I would also add to Wells's statement: It is the framework of inaugurated eschatology that expounds NT Christology as well.

pneumatological approach. In the canon, the work of the Spirit, as it is progressively disclosed, is never divorced from the work of the Son and bringing people to faith in him. In other words, the Spirit's work is always tied to gospel realities.[117] Thus, in light of the coming of Christ, it is the Spirit's role to bear witness *of him;* to convict the world of sin, righteousness and judgment so that they may believe *in him* (Jn 16:7-11).[118] In truth, the Spirit's work, now in redemptive history, is to apply the work of Christ to us so that we may be brought to saving faith *in Christ* and increasingly conformed to his image. There is no indication in the Bible that the Spirit ever operates in a saving way apart from the gospel. Even though the Spirit's work as the third person of the Godhead is not fully disclosed in the OT, we are never led to think that God is salvifically at work in people's lives apart from bringing people into a covenantally defined relationship centered in the promises of God, now fulfilled in Christ.

What, then, is the main problem with the pneumatological approach? It is simply this: The work of the Spirit is stripped of its redemptive-historical connections, and then made to buttress the theological underpinning of the inclusivist's understanding of the "universality axiom." Or, as Daniel Strange rightly contends, "Rather than being Christocentric in his inclusivism, which I believe he would claim to be, Pinnock's position is pneumatocentric and as a result the particularity of Christ is compromised. . . . Pinnock's desire to universalize the particular has meant a separation of the epistemological from the ontological."[119] And I would add: Pinnock's desire to universalize the particular has further compromised the whole plot line of Scripture and its presentation of the Son-Spirit relation in redemptive history.[120]

---

[117]Pinnock's dismissal of the *filioque* clause is disappointing. For an excellent discussion of the historical and theological issues surrounding the clause, see Gerald Bray, "The *Filioque* Clause in History and Theology," *Tyndale Bulletin* 34 (1983): 91-144; cf. Letham, *Holy Trinity*, pp. 201-51.

[118]J. I. Packer, *Keep in Step with the Spirit*, pp. 65-66, likens the Spirit's work to a floodlight ministry: "The Spirit's message to us is never, 'Look at me; listen to me; come to me; get to know me,' but always, 'Look at *him*, and see his glory; listen to *him*, and hear his word; go to *him*, and have life; get to know *him*, and taste his gift of joy and peace.' The Spirit, we might say, is the matchmaker, the celestial marriage broker, whose role it is to bring us and Christ together and ensure that we stay together. As the second Paraclete, the Spirit leads us constantly to the original Paraclete, who himself draws near, as we saw above, through the second Parclete's coming to us (Jn 14:18). Thus, by enabling us to discern the first Paraclete, and by moving us to stretch out our hands to him as he comes from his throne to meet us, the Holy Spirit glorifies Christ, according to Christ's own word." See also the helpful discussion of Carson in the same direction, *Gagging of God*, pp. 264-68.

[119]Strange, "Deciphering the Conundrum," p. 250. Also see idem, *The Possibility of Salvation*, pp. 226-64.

[120]See Bruce A. Ware, "How Shall We Think about the Trinity?" in *God Under Fire*, ed. Douglas S. Huffman and Eric L. Johnson (Grand Rapids: Zondervan, 2002), pp. 260-64, who makes a similar point.

If I am correct in my rejection of the pneumatological approach, then the crucial theological rationale for the inclusivist separation of the epistemological from the ontological has been removed. The Spirit's work is to bring people to Christ so that they may know and believe in him. To affirm that the Spirit may work in us graciously so that we "believe" in God, but not in Jesus Christ as the object of our faith, is foreign to the entire work of the Spirit as described in the NT. In fact, when the NT speaks of faith, it is never faith in the abstract or divorced from the proper object of saving faith. Nor is it the Spirit so working in people that they exhibit "Christ-like" qualities and a mere faith in "God." Appeal to Matthew 25:31-46, as Pinnock does, is hardly conclusive. In fact, it is best to interpret this text as referring not to people in general, but, in context, to Jesus' disciples.[121] No, the Spirit's work, as it is disclosed across the canon of Scripture, is to bear witness *to him* so that people, by grace, may be brought to saving faith in Christ and Christ alone. I cannot help but concur with the late Ronald Nash when he asserts: "I believe it is reckless, dangerous, and unbiblical to lead people to think that the preaching of the gospel (which I insist must contain specifics about the person and work of Christ) and personal faith in Jesus are not necessary for salvation."[122]

But inclusivists object: What about OT "believers"? Are they not proof that it is possible to be saved by grace through *faith*, but not explicit faith in Christ? Let us now turn to this point, which seems to be the strongest biblical support for the inclusivist position.

The biblical grounding. The nature of saving faith: Evidence from OT "believers." As noted above, one of the crucial distinctions for inclusivism is the distinction between "believers" and "Christians" (which is then tied to the ontological/epistemological distinction).[123] The biblical warrant for this distinction is primarily found in OT "believers" within and outside of Israel, who exhibit faith, but not explicitly Christian faith. Since this is so, inclusivists argue, by analogy, that it is legitimate to think of other "believers" who are not Christians, namely, unevangelized "believers" in other religions, in whom the Spirit has been at work bringing about a faith-response to the revelation at their disposal. Even though this line of argument is common within the entire range of inclusivism, it is not as strong as it first appears. Let me begin with an overall evaluation of the argument before turning to some specific examples and categories of "believers" that inclusivists appeal to.

---

[121]See D. A. Carson, *Matthew,* Expositor's Bible Commentary (Grand Rapids: Zondervan, 1984), pp. 518-23. See also Carson's discussion of this related to Clark Pinnock in *Gagging of God*, pp. 300-301.

[122]Nash, *Is Jesus the Only Savior?* p. 126.

[123]For more on the OT data, see Walter Kaiser's chapter in this book.

First, my overall response follows a similar path to my response to the pneuma-tological proposal, namely, we must heed the progress of biblical revelation and place these "believers" correctly in the overall plot-line of Scripture. When we do so, we discover that the categories "believers" and "Christians" do *not* derive from distinctions between people who receive only general revelation instead of special revelation. Rather, they originate from God's providential placement of individual believers along the redemptive-historical time line in relation to Christ's redemptive work. That is why D. A. Carson is right when he notes: "Most of the pre-Christ believers are those who enter into a covenantal, faith-based relationship with the God who had disclosed himself to them in the terms and the extent recorded up to that time."[124] Furthermore, it is important not to overlook "the fact that these believers on the Old Testament side were responding in faith to special revelation, and were not simply exercising some sort of general 'faith' in an undefined 'God.'"[125] The implication, then, is this: We must be careful in drawing a parallel between today's unevangelized and OT believers, a strategy that is at the heart of the inclusivist argument.

For example, let us think of Abraham, who certainly serves as the key paradigm of faith in both Testaments (see Gen 15:6; Rom 4:9-12, 16-17; Gal 3:6-29; Heb 11:8-19). The important role Abraham and the Abrahamic covenant play in Scripture is beyond question. Not only does the Abrahamic covenant serve as the basis for all God's dealings with the human race and the backbone for understanding the biblical covenants, but its location in the storyline of Scripture also shows that it must be understood in view of the unfolding drama of Genesis 3—11, especially the promise given in Genesis 3:15. As a result of the disobedience of Adam, sin and death have entered God's good world. Unless God acts in grace and power, the original creation will stand completely under divine judgment. But, thankfully, God chooses to act in grace. He promises that his purposes for creation and the human race will continue through his provision of a Redeemer, the seed of the woman, to reverse the disastrous effects of the Fall. This promise continues in the Noahic covenant (Gen 8—9), but as with Adam, Noah fails. By the time we reach Genesis 11, we have Genesis 3 all over again in the rebellious human attempt to make a name apart from God at the Tower of Babel. But unlike the times of Noah, when God destroyed everyone except Noah and his family with the flood, God does not destroy the human race. Instead, God allows the nations to exist and then graciously calls and elects Abraham out of the nations. Ultimately, God's intent is to work through the covenant mediator, Abraham, and his seed to

[124]Carson, *Gagging of God*, p. 298.
[125]Ibid.

bring blessing to the nations. In this context, one must view the Abrahamic covenant as the means by which God will fulfill his promises for humanity. In Abraham and his seed, all God's promises for the human race will be realized—promises that God takes upon himself to accomplish in the inauguration of the covenant in Genesis 15.

In light of this, when we begin to ask about the nature of Abraham's saving faith, Genesis 15:6 becomes the key text—"Abram believed the LORD, and he credited it to him as righteousness." Not only does the text stress that Abraham's faith is God-centered, but in its context, it must also be viewed as covenantally-defined and informed. In this important way, Abraham's faith must be viewed as an explicit faith, because he believes the promises of God—promises centered in God's provision of a Redeemer (Gen 3:15), centered in the God who provides (Gen 22:14). Did he have Jesus Christ as the object of his faith? The best answer to that question is yes and no. No, in that he did not know it was Jesus who was the seed of the woman; but yes, in that his faith was in the promise of God, centered in the promised seed, which eventually, as the plan of God unfolds, leads us directly to Christ. At the minimum, we have to affirm that Abraham's faith was a specific, covenantally defined faith (see Rom 4:13-25).[126]

So then, how does this fit with the inclusivist argument that those, like Abraham, who were saved, yet did not know Jesus explicitly, serve as examples of saving faith among the unevangelized today? Not well, because faith in the OT, as in the case of Abraham, is always tied to the promises of God, rooted in the initial *protoevangelium* in Genesis 3:15. No OT saint, not even Adam, was ever saved apart from explicit trust in these promises. As we move through redemptive history, the content of the promise is more defined and informed, but one cannot say that faith in the OT is ever of a generalized sort.[127] Now let us turn more specifically to the various categories of OT "believers" that inclusivists appeal to, and evaluate the strength of their argument.

OT believers within Israel. What kind of faith did they have? Most agree that

---

[126]For a further discussion of Romans 4 and the nature of Abraham's faith, see Thomas R. Schreiner, *Romans*, Baker Exegetical Commentary on the New Testament (Grand Rapids: Baker, 1998), pp. 222-44. See also the statement of S. S. Taylor about the content of the faith of Abraham in, "Faith, faithfulness," in *New Dictionary of Biblical Theology*, p. 489: "Abraham took God at his word, responding in the only fitting manner to the word of Yahweh. Yahweh conferred upon Abraham the status of being rightly related to him, not on the basis of a righteous deed, but solely on the basis of Abraham's trust in the divine promise. In its starkness, this verse is unique among OT statements concerning faith."

[127]For a development of this, see Stephen G. Dempster, *Dominion and Dynasty: A Theology of the Hebrew Bible*, New Studies in Biblical Theology (Downers Grove, Ill.: InterVarsity Press, 2003). Cf. also Paul R. House, *Old Testament Theology* (Downers Grove, Ill.: InterVarsity Press, 1998).

their faith is parallel with Abraham's faith, i.e., they exhibited a covenantal, faith-based relationship with God centered in his redemptive promises. D. A. Carson correctly observes:

> From the perspective of the biblical plot-line, there is some genuine continuity be-
> tween such Old Testament saints and the New Testament saints (e.g., Rom. 1:1-2;
> 11:1-36; Phil. 3:3, 7, 9). Under the old covenant, institutions, sacrificial systems, and
> entire priestly orders were to be adhered to as part of obedient faith on the part of
> the people, but such institutions and systems also pointed forward, as we have seen,
> to Jesus Christ—to his sacrifice, his priesthood, the heavenly tabernacle, and so
> forth.[128]

Thus, their faith, like Abraham, was rooted in the God of Scripture and his covenant promises.

For this reason the analogy often drawn by inclusivists between pre-messianic believers and the unevangelized today is false.[129] Daniel Strange is correct in noting that if an analogy is to be drawn it is "not between the unevangelised and Pre-messianic believers, but between Pre-messianic believers and those who explicitly confess Christ today. There is a continuity of special revelation to Israel that progresses and develops the truth of God's promises."[130]

At this point, something must be said regarding Hebrews 11, the great chapter of faith. Inclusivists commonly argue that this establishes the minimum content of saving faith, namely, that "without faith it is impossible to please God, because anyone who comes to him must believe that he exists and that he rewards those who earnestly seek him" (Heb 11:6). From this inclusivists conclude that saving faith is not explicitly Christian; rather it is a more "general" faith "in God" depending upon the revelation that is at the hearers' disposal. But there are serious problems with this interpretation of the text. In the first instance, if one pushes this text to the wall, it would minimally require that saving faith only be found in people who affirm a theism, which would eliminate all nontheistic religious "be-

---

[128]Carson, *Gagging of God*, p. 298.

[129]So Sanders, *No Other Name*, pp. 225-30, and Pinnock, *A Wideness in God's Mercy*, p. 161. Carson, *Gagging of God*, p. 298 n. 86, cites other inclusivists who argue in this way.

[130]Strange, *Possibility of Salvation*, p. 165. I add that the analogy drawn by Tiessen between the function of the Mosaic covenant as a tutor leading people to see their need for God's grace, and the role of the "law written on the heart" in the unevangelized is false. The Mosaic covenant as a covenant was much more than a moral guide. It was an entire package which included within it God's means of forgiveness through the sacrificial system, which pointed forward to Christ. Faith under the old covenant was expressed not only in terms of obedience to the covenant, but also in taking God at his Word, believing that he alone provides what is necessary for the forgiveness of sin. But, the "law written on the heart" has no promise attached to it, let alone a provision of forgiveness.

lievers," something many inclusivists are not willing to do.[131] But second, and more important, the immediate context of the text cannot sustain the inclusivist interpretation of it. That immediate context—in fact the entire argument of Hebrews—is that the OT, in all of its figures, priestly institutions, covenants and so on, was not an end in itself but a means to an end, i.e., that which anticipated and looked forward to the coming of Christ. In fact, the entire letter is an extended *a fortiori* argument, i.e., of the lesser (OT types and shadows which foreshadow the coming of Christ) to the greater (what Christ has now brought to pass in the new covenant era). The Hebrew Christians, to whom this book was written, were in danger of going back to the OT types and shadows and forgetting that to which they pointed in Christ. Thus, by exposition of OT text after text, the author encourages his readers to believe what God has promised, which has now been fulfilled in Christ, while simultaneously warning them not to spurn their new covenant privileges. If they do, he warns, there is no hope for them. Why? Because in Jesus Christ the end of the ages has dawned and, as a result, there is no going back.

In light of this, Hebrews 11 serves as both encouragement and warning for these Christians to persevere in their walk with the Lord. The argument goes something like this: If OT saints persevered by faith, longing for the promises of God to be brought to fulfillment, then how much more should we persevere as those who live in light of what the OT could only anticipate. In other words, the entire context of Hebrews 11 describes a "faith" which is rooted in God's covenant promises, now brought to fulfillment in Christ. To use this text to prove a minimalist, generalized notion of saving faith from the OT is illegitimate.[132]

OT believers outside of Israel. Perhaps we have better examples here of those who are "believers" but not in a covenantally defined way. But is this really the case? I begin with two observations. First, as Tiessen rightly acknowledges, we have little data to go on.[133] That, in and of itself, should give us pause. Second, it is crucial *not* to think of these individuals as "old covenant" believers, something, for example, Tiessen consistently does.[134] To be a member of the "old covenant" (i.e., Mosaic covenant) meant that one was either an ethnic Jew or that one had aligned himself with the people of God (e.g., Rahab, Ruth, etc.). In both in-

---

[131]See, for example, Pinnock, *A Wideness in God's Mercy*, pp. 100-101. Pinnock thinks that God will even accept people whose beliefs fall short of the truth, even in regard to theism, such as in Buddhism. He states: "Of course, Buddhism is not Christianity and it does not try to be. But how does one come away after encountering Buddhism and deny that it is in touch with God in its way" (p. 100). For a critique of this, see Geivett and Phillips, "A Particularist View," p. 240.

[132]For a development of this, see George H. Guthrie, *Hebrews*, NIV Application Commentary (Grand Rapids: Zondervan, 1998), pp. 371-85.

[133]See Tiessen, *Who Can Be Saved?* p. 169.

[134]Ibid., pp. 169-84.

stances, the faith of these "believers" was a special, covenant-defined faith, not merely a hazy, faith-response to general revelation or an undefined "God."[135] In fact, when one goes through the list of these "believers" (e.g., Abel, Enoch, Noah, Job, Melchizedek, Lot, Jethro, Naaman, Rahab, Ruth, etc.), in almost every instance, as Tiessen admits, they "had special revelation about which we know."[136] The only two people that Tiessen believes may offer us insights into God's work of grace outside Israel are Melchizedek and Jethro.[137]

Let me make two brief points in regard to Melchizedek since he has been treated elsewhere in this book. First, in contrast to Pinnock (and many others), it is not at all necessary to think that Melchizedek worshiped a Canaanite deity and thus serves as an example of a "pagan" who exhibits "faith" independent of special revelation.[138] This is borne out when we think of how Melchizedek is presented in the Genesis narrative. In this regard, Carson is right to insist that "when the Melchizedek passage is placed within the developing narrative within the book of Genesis, one can no longer think of monotheism emerging after endless struggles with pagan polytheism. It is far more natural in reading the account to suppose that there were still people who believed in the one true God, people who preserved some memory of God's gracious self-disclosure to Noah, people who revered the memory of the severe lesson of Babel."[139] Second, it is without biblical warrant for Tiessen to speculate that because Melchizedek, a priest outside of Israel, is a type of Christ (see Heb 7), and that in the old covenant sacrifices pointed forward to Christ, that God may accept sacrifices offered by devout people outside the Mosaic covenant who come in "faith."[140] That conclusion certainly is not drawn anywhere in the OT, and more importantly, it is not drawn in the book of Hebrews. In fact, the opposite is the case. As Hebrews unpacks the typological nature of the priests of the OT vis-à-vis Christ, it does so in a twofold manner: first,

---

[135]In this regard note how Paul understands Jew and Gentile relations in the OT. In Eph 2:12, he views the Gentiles of the OT era as "separate from Christ, excluded from citizenship in Israel and foreigners to the covenants of promise, without hope and without God in the world." What needed to be accomplished in the work of Christ was the payment of sin under the first covenant so that a new covenant could be inaugurated—a new covenant which would bring both Jew and Gentile together with equal access and privileges (see Eph 2:14-18; Col 2:13-15).

[136]Tiessen, *Who Can Be Saved?* p. 170. Tiessen goes on to say: "Either God made himself specially known to them in a personal way (e.g., Abel, Enoch, Noah, Job, Abimelech), or they had contact with Jews (e.g., Lot, Ruth, Naaman), or they at least had knowledge of the Israelites' faith or of God's activity among them (e.g., Rahab, Naaman, the foreigners whom Solomon anticipated would come to pray toward the temple)" (pp. 170-71).

[137]For a further discussion of these figures, see Walt Kaiser's chapter in this volume.

[138]For a more detailed defense of this point, see Strange, *The Possibility of Salvation*, pp. 179-89.

[139]Carson, *Gagging of God*, p. 250.

[140]See Tiessen, *Who Can Be Saved?* p. 172.

Christ eclipses the Levitical priesthood regulated by the old covenant in a new order foreshadowed and typified by Melchizedek (Heb 7), and secondly, Christ ful-
fills all that the Levitical priests foreshadowed and typified, including the sacrifices
they offered (see Heb 5:1-10; 8:1-6; 9:1-10:18). But in regard to sacrifices offered
by Melchizedek, nothing is developed in this way since nothing is said of it in the
Genesis 14 text. In fact, when Hebrews thinks of the fulfillment of the sacrificial
system, it is never in light of Melchizedek, but always in terms of the Levites and
the OT sacrificial system. Thus, Tiessen's conclusion is speculation. But speculation leaves us in a biblically unwarranted situation, and thus leads to poor theological conclusions.

At this point, the NT example of Cornelius is often appealed to as well. Here
is a man, so the argument goes, who is both a Gentile and a person with saving
faith, i.e., a "believer." Once again, a lot of discussion has taken place on whether
Cornelius warrants the inclusivist case.[141] Is he saved before Peter preaches the
gospel, or after? Does he fit into the category of a "believer" who is "informationally B.C." or not? Regardless of whether or not he fits into the pre-messianic
believer category, it is important to observe that his faith, as a God-fearer, is covenantally defined. Thus, the analogy between him and the present-day unevangelized is weak.

Furthermore, it is crucial to establish the purpose of the entire Cornelius narrative. The point in Acts 10—11 is not so much to pass judgment on whether or
not Cornelius was saved (I do not think the text says he was saved prior to faith in
Christ), but "to conclude that in principle people from outside the Jewish race are
acceptable to God"[142] now as a result of the triumphant work of Christ. And, as
the text notes, it is not until Peter preaches the gospel and insists that "everyone
who believes in him receives forgiveness of sins through his name" (Acts 10:43)
that the promised, eschatological Holy Spirit falls on Cornelius and his conversion
is recognized in baptism.

Two observations need to be made in passing. First, the Cornelius narrative
demonstrates beyond question the incredible redemptive-historical and ephochal
changes that are now taking place in light of the coming of Christ. Now that
Christ has come the only way to receive forgiveness of sins is through faith in him
(cf. Jn 5:23). This is borne out by the fact that it is after faith in Christ is exercised

---

[141]Within inclusivist literature, see Pinnock, *A Wideness in God's Mercy*, pp. 165-66; Sanders, "Inclusivism," pp. 38-40; Tiessen, *Who Can Be Saved?* pp. 175-78. For critiques of the inclusivist use of Cornelius, see Nash, *Is Jesus the Only Savior?* pp. 137-40; Strange, *The Possibility of Salvation*, pp. 194-
97; Carson, *Gagging of God*, pp. 306-7.

[142]Carson, *Gagging of God*, p. 307. Also cf. John R. W. Stott, *The Spirit, the Church and the World: The
Message of Acts* (Downers Grove, Ill.: InterVarsity Press, 1990), pp. 181-99.

that we witness the reception of the Spirit—evidence that the new covenant era anticipated by the prophets has now arrived, in fulfillment of the promises of the Abrahamic covenant. Furthermore, in light of what I have argued above, it is illegitimate to appeal to this narrative, taken out of its redemptive-historical context, and argue that it is evidence that the Spirit is now operating in people apart from bringing them to explicit faith in Christ. Cornelius does not prove this at all. And secondly, as Ramesh Richard observes, instead of seeing here a universal salvific will that extends to "believers outside of a covenant-defined relationship," we see a "universal salvific welcome to anyone from any nation" within the confines of particularity, namely, faith in Jesus Christ.[143] This latter observation, as Strange insists, entails that it is very difficult biblically to separate ontology and epistemology. In other words, we must affirm that, "confession of Christ is necessary for salvation."[144]

Believers who respond to general revelation alone. Since inclusivists believe that it is possible for people to respond appropriately by grace to general revelation, it is legitimate to ask about the nature of this "saving faith." Interestingly, Tiessen admits that he finds "no biblical examples of people who were saved through general revelation alone,"[145] but thinks it is possible to identify the sort of faith that God *would* require *if* people responded to it appropriately. What, then, is the nature of this "faith"?

In terms of the created order, Tiessen believes that a saving faith response would be demonstrated in a "spirit of thankfulness for what he [God] has made and provided for us."[146] In regard to the moral conscience, a proper faith response would be a "faith" demonstrated in a person's ethical behavior. Biblical proof of this latter point is found in Romans 2:13-16, which Tiessen believes describes the Gentiles whose lives were commendable before God, prior to their believing the gospel.[147] There are a number of problems with this proposal; I will mention two.

First, where in Scripture do we see this kind of "faith" as saving faith? There is no specific content to it; it is foreign to biblical faith which has as its object the God of Scripture and his redemptive promises. Second, Tiessen's (as well as other inclusivists') reading of Romans 1—2 cannot be sustained. For example, it is doubtless true—when stressing in Romans 1:18-32 that those who suppress the

---

[143]Ramesh Richard, *The Population of Heaven* (Chicago: Moody Press, 1994), p. 64.

[144]Strange, *Possibility of Salvation*, p. 198.

[145]Tiessen, *Who Can Be Saved?* p. 149.

[146]Ibid., p. 144.

[147]Ibid., pp. 144-45. Remember Pinnock described it in the same way in terms of a faith manifest in actions. Like Pinnock, Tiessen argues that this is not a works salvation, but a faith which shows itself in obedience to God's law.

truth are justly condemned—that Paul never says that everyone actually suppresses the truth. At the level of logical possibility, this must be admitted. However, when we investigate how the text functions in Romans, this logical possibility is something that Paul does not sanction nor defend. In a parallel fashion, it is possible to imagine some pagan, afflicted by conscience, who cries out to God for mercy. But once again, this is *not* what the text says. In fact, the best interpretations of Romans 2:13-16 do not even allow for this latter possibility. Either the text refers to a hypothetical situation, which no one achieves, or it refers to Gentile *Christians*, not those who have never heard the gospel.[148] Either way, what inclusivists have done is take logical possibilities and uncertainties and made them actualities, even when the entire argument of Romans 1—3 explicitly says that no one has responded positively to general revelation, that no one is righteous, there is no one who seeks after God, and that the only hope for the unevangelized is the work of Jesus Christ and faith in him.

The nature of saving faith in Scripture. Although I have found the proposed biblical ground for implicit saving faith in OT "believers" wanting, the question remains: What, then, is the nature of "saving faith"? Is it merely a faith which desires God in some sense, meaning that God is more concerned about the direction of people's heart than the content of their theology? Is it a faith which expresses itself solely in a lifestyle of obedience to the moral conscience within? Can it be defined apart from its proper object?

In answering these questions, I agree with Carson that one must be careful to avoid false antitheses, which too often show up in the literature.[149] Obviously it is wrong to define faith merely in terms of content and devoid of the direction of one's heart and life. On the other hand, it is just as improper to ignore that saving faith also involves specific content, regardless of where one is in redemptive history. It is hard to avoid the conclusion that Scripture is concerned that one's theology is correct, which necessarily involves some kind of content. As D. A. Carson wisely asks: "Does Paul sound as if he does not care about the content of theology

---

[148]For a detailed exegesis of this text, see Schreiner, *Romans*, pp. 116-26; cf. Carson, *Gagging of God*, pp. 310-12. See also the excellent article by Douglas J. Moo, "Romans 2: Saved Apart from the Gospel?" in *Through No Fault of Their Own? The Fate of Those Who Have Never Heard*, ed. William V. Crockett and James G. Sigountos (Grand Rapids: Baker, 1991), pp. 137-45. Moo lays out the various options and argues for the hypothetical interpretation over the Gentile Christian view. However, whatever view one adopts, Moo is emphatic that "Paul never says that Gentiles apart from the gospel can be saved by meeting the demands of the law, or by doing good works. The texts could mean this only if they are ripped out of context. Once the context is recognized, Paul's purposes understood, and his theology of justification taken into account, we quickly see that Gentiles cannot be saved apart from the gospel" (p. 145).

[149]See Carson's helpful discussion in, *Gagging of God*, pp. 296-97.

in Galatians 1:8-9? Does John, in 1 John 4:1-6? Far from resorting to antitheses, John purposely links sound doctrine, transparent obedience, and love for the brothers and sisters in Christ, as being joint marks of the true believer (and thus of true faith!)."[150]

Having said that, with regard to saving faith in Scripture, probably the most important point to stress is that it must always be viewed in relation to its proper object. What distinguishes *biblical* faith from other "faiths" is this: Who is its object? I have argued that there is no reason to think that the object of biblical saving faith is any other than the covenant Lord of Scripture as revealed in its promises (see Gen 15:6; Rom 4:20-25; Gal 3:16; Heb 7:6; 11:8-9).[151]

Historically, theologians have sought to capture the essence of saving faith with the following three Latin words: *notitia* ("knowledge," faith involves a knowing of certain truths); *assensus* ("assent," faith involves a believing that those truths are true); and *fiducia* ("trust," faith trusts and rests in God and his promises). In inclusivism discussions, most of the debate over saving faith involves the content element. Is the object of faith explicitly Christ? What about OT believers? As noted above, even though God has progressively revealed himself to us in history and the content of biblical faith increases with greater revelation, there is no evidence that the object of saving faith, whether in the OT or NT, is any other than God himself in the mediator, Jesus Christ (see, e.g., Jn 14:1; Acts 10:43; 16:31; Rom 10:12-13).

How is this possible in the OT? Because the promises of God, in seed or embryonic form, are still centered in Christ. He was the one *promised* to the patriarchs (Gen 3:15; 12:1-2; 2 Sam 7), and predicted by the prophets (Is 7:14; 9:1-12; 52:13-53:12; Ps 2; 110). Indeed all of Scripture bears witness to him (Lk 24:27; Rom 1:3-4). Yes, saving faith in the OT was directed to "God," but it was never an undefined God. Rather, it was the God who enters into covenant relation with his people, the one who binds himself to his promises, and the one who demands that they take him at his Word.

In this regard Jesus' words in John 5:23 (cf. 1 Jn 2:23; 4:2-3) are crucial—"that all may honor the Son just as they honor the Father. He who does not honor the Son does not honor the Father, who sent him." Such a statement only makes sense if both the Father and Son are the proper objects of saving faith, which is understood in light of the progress of revelation. Jesus is not saying that OT covenant believers (e.g., Abraham, Moses, David) were not truly honoring the Father be-

---

[150]Ibid., p. 297.

[151]See the following works for a more detailed development of the nature of saving faith in Scripture: Anthony A. Hoekema, *Saved by Grace* (Grand Rapids: Eerdmans, 1989), pp. 132-51; Bruce Demarest, *The Cross and Salvation* (Wheaton: Crossway, 1997), pp. 256-63; Robert D. Culver, *Systematic Theology: Biblical and Historical* (Fearn, U.K.: Christian Focus, 2005), pp. 714-32, 780-90.

cause they failed to know and honor the Son. Rather, as D. A. Carson rightly notes:

> He [Jesus] is focusing on the latest development in the history of redemption: the incarnation of the Word, the sending of the Son. Just as there were many who did not listen to the prophets of old, leaving but a remnant who faithfully obeyed Yahweh's gracious disclosures, so now with the coming of the Son there will be some who think they honour God while disowning God's Word, his gracious Self-Expression, his own Son. But they are deluded. Now that the Son has come, the person who withholds the honour due the Son similarly dishonours the Father (cf. Jn 14:6; Acts 4:12).[152]

This is why it is impossible to speak of saving faith in Scripture apart from Christ. Robert Culver, in quoting Charles Hodge, nicely summarizes this point:

> In view of the doctrine of Romans 10:13, 14, 17, Hodge is surely correct when he asserts that calling upon Christ "implies faith; faith implies knowledge: knowledge implies objective teaching. 'Faith cometh by hearing, and hearing by the word of God.' . . . There is no faith, therefore, where the gospel is not heard; and where there is no faith, there is no salvation."[153]

CONCLUDING REFLECTIONS

Must people believe the gospel in order to be saved? My answer is yes. Surely the status of those who have never heard the gospel is not an easy subject. Hopefully, reading the chapters in this book, one will better realize the complexity of theological positions and arguments, and the need to think through the issues with great care. However, after evaluating critically how inclusivists argue theologically and biblically for their view, I have found their argument lacking in biblical support. I offer two concluding reflections.

---

[152]D. A. Carson, *The Gospel According to John* (Grand Rapids: Eerdmans, 1991), p. 255. The issue of one's location in redemptive history is crucial in the inclusivist/exclusivist debate. Repeatedly, inclusivists argue that the unevangelized are in the same "informationally B.C." place as those in the OT era. In my view this is fundamentally mistaken. Not only does the analogy break down between pre-Messianic believers and the unevangelized due to the OT believers having the special, covenantal revelation of God, but it flies in the face of how God's plan is worked out on the stage of human history. As epoch after epoch unfolds, Scripture does not give us any evidence of persons going back to that previous era, especially now that Christ has come. That is why Tiessen's argument that Jews today who have not heard the gospel can still be saved in an old covenant sense is disturbing. But what is more disturbing is his belief that even if Jews today hear the gospel and reject it they still may be saved due to the bad history between Gentile Christians and Jews. Where in the NT do we find evidence of this? For a helpful treatment of the importance of the epochal shifts in redemptive history, see John Piper, *Let the Nations be Glad: The Supremacy of God in Missions* (Grand Rapids: Baker, 1993), pp. 115-66; cf. Carson, *Gagging of God*, pp. 308-10.
[153]Culver, *Systematic Theology*, pp. 726-27.

First, in a difficult subject such as this, biblical scholars and theologians must be careful to avoid speculation. It is easy to hypothesize and ask questions about many issues that Scripture does not specifically address, but we must be careful that we first let Scripture address us with its own categories and presentation. As noted above, there are a number of places where inclusivists draw conclusions with little or no biblical warrant. So, for example, when inclusivists argue that Romans 1—2 does not deny the logical possibility that the Spirit can work in the conscience of the unevangelized to produce saving faith, their argument cuts across the grain of the text. Or, they argue that John 14:6 or Acts 4:12 does not necessarily address the case of the unevangelized, so we cannot conclude that faith in Jesus is necessary for salvation, when the whole tenor of John's gospel and of Acts is to lead people to the conclusion that *faith in Jesus* is the condition of salvation. In the end, we must remember that logical possibilities are not necessarily *biblical* possibilities. And theologizing must be carefully tied to the biblical text. Unless Scripture explicitly sanctions and warrants it, we must be careful in drawing hypotheses that rise to the level of settled conclusions.[154]

Second, a major entailment of my conclusion is the urgent need for missions and evangelism. We must take seriously the fact that God has ordained both the way of salvation through our Lord Jesus Christ and the means by which the gospel takes effect in people's lives, namely by its proclamation. Even though there are a lot of questions to think through, we must never compromise this point: Apart from the preaching, hearing, and believing of the gospel, there is no salvation. May the Lord of the church, by his Spirit, ever work in us so that we may faithfully take the glorious gospel of God's sovereign grace to the nations for his glory and honor, and supremely for the honor and glory of the Lord Jesus Christ.[155]

---

[154]In Tiessen's work *Who Can Be Saved?* he says he does not have explicit biblical support for a certain position, and then argues it anyway. In my view, this is a questionable theological method. For example, note the following quotes: (1) "I find no biblical examples of people who were saved through general revelation alone" (p. 149); (2) "Admittedly, however, the proposal that we all meet Christ at death moves us beyond Scripture's explicit teaching into the speculative. Consequently, such a hypothesis can only be held tentatively, but it is consistent with everything that we do know from Scripture" (p. 218); (3) "By way of specific explicit biblical teaching, one is hard put to cite texts specifically indicating a universal distribution of grace to all people." (p. 494). In my view, instead of relying upon speculative arguments, I would rather move in the agnostic direction on matters that Scripture does not explicitly address.

[155]In regard to the missionary mandate a great place to begin is with John Piper, *Let the Nations be Glad!* (Grand Rapids; Baker, 2003). Also cf. Christopher J. H. Wright, *The Mission of God: Unlocking the Bible's Grand Narrative* (Downers Grove, Ill.: InterVarsity Press, 2006), and Andreas J. Köstenberger and Peter T. O'Brien, *Salvation to the Ends of the Earth: A Biblical Theology of Mission,* New Studies in Biblical Theology (Downers Grove, Ill.: InterVarsity Press, 2001).

8

Inclusivism versus Exclusivism
on Key Biblical Texts

ROBERT A. PETERSON

WHEN DEBATING THE MERITS of their respective positions, inclusivists and exclusivists disagree over how to interpret many biblical texts. Throughout this volume the contributors have dealt with many disputed passages. Here revisiting only the most important texts, we will seek to demonstrate the superiority of exclusivist exegesis by contrasting it with inclusivist exegesis.

GENESIS 14:18-20: MELCHIZEDEK
Although Clark Pinnock makes stronger claims,[1] Terrance Tiessen frankly admits that most attempts to find so-called pagan saints or "holy pagans" (terms that he and we find unhelpful) in Scripture fall short of the mark. After listing twelve Old Testament figures saved outside of Israel, he reduces that number to two because "most of these had special revelation about which we know."[2] The two are Melchizedek and Jethro. Because Tiessen does not develop an argument based on Jethro, and because he is treated elsewhere in this volume,[3] we will contrast inclusivist and exclusivist handling of the Scriptures treating Melchizedek.

Inclusivist exegesis. Melchizedek, king of Salem and priest of God Most High, mysteriously appears in the biblical narrative in Genesis 14:18-20, where he meets

---

[1]Clark H. Pinnock, *A Wideness in God's Mercy: The Finality of Jesus Christ in a World of Religions* (Grand Rapids: Zondervan, 1992), pp. 26, 94, 179.
[2]Terrance L. Tiessen, *Who Can Be Saved? Reassessing Salvation in Christ and World Religions* (Downers Grove, Ill.: InterVarsity Press, 2004), pp. 170-71; see Steve Wellum's, essay, p. 177 n. 136.
[3]See Walter Kaiser's essay, pp. 123-41. See also his treatment of Melchizedek on pp. 130-32.

Abram after his defeat of the kings, blesses him, and collects a tithe from him. He reappears only in Psalm 110:4, a prophecy that Christ would be a priest forever in Melchizedek's order, and then in Hebrews 7, where the Melchizedek/Christ typology is developed. Tiessen admits that the Bible does not tell us how Melchizedek came to know God and explores three options.[4] He rejects the option that Melchizedek came to faith through general revelation alone because the Bible does not teach this. The second option, that Melchizedek was saved through remnants of original supernatural revelation, is possible, but Tiessen prefers a third option—that he was saved through special revelation.[5]

Exclusivist exegesis. Tiessen's exploring of these three options is fair and helpful. We agree that because Scripture says nothing about it, it is unwise to speculate that Melchizedek was saved through general revelation. We do not oppose the idea of God's using remnants of original divine revelation to save people because this would fit the Bible's storyline,[6] but are cautious in this case, due to Scripture's silence. We agree with Tiessen that Melchizedek was probably saved through special revelation of God about which we are not told. But we do not see how this furthers the case of general revelation inclusivism because Melchizedek was not saved through general revelation but special revelation. It is best to simply admit that Scripture does not say how God saved Melchizedek and leave it at that. Daniel Strange wisely concludes, "Because of [Melchizedek's story's] enigmatic nature, it is unlikely by itself to persuade one to commit to either . . . inclusivism or an opposing exclusivism."[7] We do not insist upon church exclusivism but only gospel exclusivism or special revelation exclusivism.[8]

JOHN 14:6

In support of their position, exclusivists have long pointed to Jesus' saying in John 14:6—"I am the way, and the truth, and the life. No one comes to the Father except through me"—to argue their case.[9]

Inclusivist exegesis. But inclusivists raise questions about this. They say that John 14:6 portrays Jesus as the world's only Savior and shows that he wants people

---

[4]Tiessen, *Who Can Be Saved?* pp. 171-72.
[5]Ibid.
[6]D. A. Carson, *The Gagging of God: Christianity Confronts Pluralism* (Grand Rapids: Zondervan, 1996), p. 250.
[7]Daniel Strange, *The Possibility of Salvation Among the Unevangelised: An Analysis of Inclusivism in Recent Evangelical Theology*, Paternoster Biblical and Theological Monographs (Waynesboro, Ga.: Paternoster, 2002), pp. 188-89. See his whole treatment of Melchizedek, pp. 179-89.
[8]For an explanation of this terminology, see pp. 27-30.
[9]Scripture quotations in this essay are from the ESV.

to come to know him, but says nothing about the unevangelized.[10] Tiessen urges us to note that Jesus spoke John 14:6 to hearers to whom he was revealing himself. "It is important that we do not overextend such statements to the unevangelized, who are, by definition, without such revelation."[11]

Exclusivist exegesis. How do exclusivists respond to these arguments? They place John 14:6 squarely within the contexts of the whole Bible and of the Gospel of John. The inclusivist exegetical comments above are not technically wrong, but they miss the main point of the fourth Gospel. It is true that John 14:6 does not mention the unevangelized, and that Jesus was not speaking directly to them. These points are strictly correct, but theologically flawed.

The four Gospels portray Jesus—the unique fulfillment of Old Testament hope—as the promised Messiah, the Son of God and the Savior of the world. Each Gospel ends with Jesus' death, resurrection, and an expression of the urgency of the church taking the gospel to the whole world: Matthew 28:18-20; Mark 16:15-16; Luke 24:46-47; John 20:22-23, 30-31. And within the larger biblical story John's Gospel occupies a special place, as D. A. Carson underscores:

> On the face of it, in a book that constantly presents faith in Jesus as the only solution to the curse and wrath under which we operate (e.g., John 1:12; 3:15, 16, 36), John 14:6 is of a piece with this Johannine demand for faith in Jesus, and can be side-stepped by the inclusivists . . . only with the greatest implausibility.[12]

This is correct as an exposition of John 14:6 in the context of the fourth Gospel demonstrates. In the preceding verses, Jesus pictures heaven as the Father's house with many rooms (Jn 14:1-5). When he, then, declares, "I am the way. . . . No one comes to the Father except through me," he means that he is the only road (Greek *hodos*) to the Father's heavenly house. He is the only Savior of the world. But inclusivists protest that faith is not mentioned in this verse. That is true, but faith is mentioned in the preceding (Jn 14:1) and following (Jn 14:10-12) context of the verse.

Furthermore, faith is implied in the two other parts of this "I am" saying. "I am . . . the truth." Jesus means that he is the incarnate revealer of the Father and as such the proper object of saving faith. We see this in other places where John presents Jesus as revealer and object of faith: John 5:22-24; 8:38, 42-43, 45-47, including places where he portrays Jesus as "the light": John 1:9, 12; 3:16-21; 8:12, 24, 28; 12:35-36, 44-50. In addition, when Jesus says, "I am . . . the life," he means

---

[10]Pinnock, *A Wideness in God's Mercy*, pp. 79, 101; John Sanders, *No Other Name: An Investigation into the Destiny of the Unevangelized* (Grand Rapids: Eerdmans, 1992), p. 64.
[11]Tiessen, *Who Can Be Saved?* pp. 84-85.
[12]Carson, *Gagging of God*, p. 304.

that he gives eternal life to everyone who believes in him. Other places where John presents Jesus as life-giver and object of faith include John 5:21-24; 10:24-28; 11:25-27.

From beginning to end, John's gospel emphasizes the need for explicit faith in Jesus if people are to be saved:

> Whoever believes in him is not condemned, but whoever does not believe is condemned already, because he has not believed in the name of the only Son of God. (Jn 3:18)

> Whoever believes in the Son has eternal life; whoever does not obey the Son shall not see life, but the wrath of God remains on him. (Jn 3:36)

> Now Jesus did many other signs in the presence of the disciples, which are not written in this book; but these are written so that you may believe that Jesus is the Christ, the Son of God, and that by believing you may have life in his name. (Jn 20:30-31)

We conclude that inclusivist exegesis misses the forest for the trees in John 14:6, thereby unintentionally taking the verse out of the context of the fourth Gospel.

ACTS 4:12

Along with John 14:6, exclusivists frequently appeal to Peter's words in Acts 4:12: "And there is salvation in no one else, for there is no other name under heaven given among men by which we must be saved."

Inclusivist exegesis. The inclusivist case for Acts 4:12 is similar to that for John 14:6. According to Pinnock, Acts 4:12 teaches three things: Jesus has brought the salvation predicted in the Old Testament; this salvation restores bodies as well as souls; and this salvation "is available only through faith in the name of Jesus."[13] But the text says nothing about the fate of the unevangelized or about the role other religions play in salvation.[14] Hence exclusivists who appeal to this text are revealing their presuppositions and forcing it to perform a task for which it was not designed.[15]

Exclusivist exegesis. The exclusivist response is much the same as it was for John 14:6—inclusivists are technically correct in their comments on Acts 4:12, but they inadvertently ignore its context in Acts. It is true that "the destiny of the unevangelized per se is not at issue here."[16] But, given this text's location in Acts, and the whole message of Acts, it has important implications for inclusivism and exclusivism.

---

[13]Clark Pinnock, "Acts 4:12: No Other Name under Heaven," in *Through No Fault of Their Own?* ed. William V. Crockett and James G. Sigountos (Grand Rapids: Baker, 1991), pp. 108-9.
[14]Ibid, pp. 109-11.
[15]Ibid., pp. 111-14. See also Sanders, *No Other Name*, pp. 62-64; Tiessen, *Who Can Be Saved?* p. 85.
[16]Sanders, *No Other Name*, p. 62.

Before ascending, Jesus promised the disciples: "But you will receive power when the Holy Spirit has come upon you, and you will be my witnesses in Jerusalem and in all Judea and Samaria, and to the end of the earth" (Acts 1:8). In Acts 4 the disciples are realizing the first part of Jesus' promise—they are in Jerusalem—but Peter's words also pertain to their taking the gospel to Judea and Samaria, and "to the end of the earth."

Peter, before the Sanhedrin, reminds them that a lame man was healed in Jesus' name, confesses Jesus as crucified and risen, blames them for spurning Jesus and says: "And there is salvation in no one else, for there is no other name under heaven given among men by which we must be saved" (Acts 4:12). Carson sounds the correct note:

> When to these Jews, many of them doubtless sincere and devout, Peter responds with an exclusive formulation, he quite clearly cannot mean that although salvation, including the final resurrection, is brought about by Jesus and Jesus alone, it is not necessary for devout Jews to recognize that name in order to participate in the resurrection. Clearly this does not *directly* address the fate of those who have never heard. But if Peter can speak in such exclusivistic terms to people whose heritage was steeped in the biblical revelation, would he have been somewhat more flexible for those whose religious heritage, from the vantage point of the Bible, is steeped in idolatry?[17]

Eckhard Schnabel in this volume says the loud amen to this rhetorical question:

> The fact that Paul does not distinguish between pagans who sin and Jews who sin demonstrates that his analysis and evaluation of the pagan religions and the Jewish religion is not traditional or partisan but theological and salvation-historical. Pagan "secular" religions have no solution for the *condition humaine*, and the Jewish "revelatory" religion can no longer provide atonement for sins because Jesus the messianic Savior has come. God has put forward Jesus Christ as *hilastērion* replacing the *kapporet* in the Holy of Holies as the place of his atoning presence (Rom 3:25). It is as the result of Jesus' death on the cross that people—whether foolish and ignorant pagans or observant and obedient Jews—are now "justified by his grace as a gift, through the redemption that is in Christ Jesus" (Rom 3:24). Neither pagan sacrifices in the countless temples through the Mediterranean regions, nor Jewish sacrifices in the temple in Jerusalem effect liberation from sins and their consequences. Forgiveness of sins, justification in God's court on Judgment Day, peace with God, access to God's grace, and the hope of sharing the glory of God are possible only "through our Lord Jesus Christ" (Rom 5:1-2).[18]

---

[17]Carson, *Gagging of God*, p. 305, italics original.
[18]Pages 118-19.

The chapters following Acts 4:12 also fit an exclusivist paradigm better than an inclusivist one. Darrell Bock, based on study of the apostles' speeches in Acts 13 and 17, rejects Pinnock's implications for Acts 4:12. "I am more confident than Pinnock that Acts 10:35, 14:17, and 17:23 answer the 'salvation-in-Christ' question in an exclusivist direction, and that as a result the implication of Acts 4:12 falls into a similar category."[19]

I conclude by pointing to a challenge made by Ron Nash to read Acts wearing inclusivist lenses. After citing Acts 2:38; 16:30-31; 13:46; 20:26-27; and 26:18, he concludes: "This survey through the book of Acts makes it clear that Peter and Paul did not speak and act like inclusivists. Acts 26:18 helps us see that *God* does not speak or act like an inclusivist either."[20] There God told Paul: "I am sending you to open their eyes and turn them from darkness to light, and from the power of Satan to God, so that they may receive forgiveness of sins and a place among those who are sanctified by faith in me."

ACTS 10: CORNELIUS

Tiessen speaks for most inclusivists, "Cornelius is probably the most important individual in the New Testament for the focus of this inquiry."[21] Why? Because a case can be made that he was saved before he trusted in Christ. And an analogy can then be made between Cornelius and the unevangelized today.

Inclusivist exegesis. Luke says many good things about Cornelius before he became a Christian. He was "a devout man who feared God with all his household, gave alms generously to the people, and prayed continually to God" (Acts 10:2). An angel told him, "Your prayers and your alms have ascended as a memorial before God" (Acts 10:4). Do these words indicate: "Before he heard the Gospel, Cornelius was a God-fearing believer . . . in a good and acceptable relationship with God"?[22]

Furthermore, God uses Peter's encounter with Cornelius to teach him that "in every nation anyone who fears him and does what is right is acceptable to him" (Acts 10:35). Does Pinnock accurately interpret the lesson that Peter learned? "Peter is saying that those like Cornelius who have faith in God, wherever they may live in the whole world, are accepted by God in the way Abraham was accepted, on the basis of faith."[23]

---

[19]Darrell L. Bock, "Athenians Who Have Never Heard," in *Through No Fault of Their Own?* p. 124 n. 8.
[20]Ronald H. Nash, *Is Jesus the Only Savior?* (Grand Rapids: Zondervan, 1994), pp. 172-74; the quotation is from p. 174, italics original.
[21]Tiessen, *Who Can Be Saved?* p. 175. See also Sanders, *No Other Name*, pp. 222-24, 265-66; idem, *What About Those?*, pp. 39-40; Pinnock, *A Wideness in God's Mercy*, pp. 95-98.
[22]Pinnock, *A Wideness in God's Mercy*, p. 95.
[23]Ibid., p. 96.

Exclusivist exegesis. Pinnock overreaches the evidence. Tiessen correctly and modestly admits: "As Carson notes, the Greek term translated 'acceptable' *(dektos)* [in Acts 10:35] 'is never used in reference to whether or not a person is accepted by God in some saving sense.'"[24] Peter's lesson is spelled out at the beginning of the sentence that Acts 10:35 completes: "Truly I understand that God shows no partiality, but in every nation anyone who fears him and does what is right is acceptable to him." God taught Peter that the gospel belongs to the Gentiles as well as the Jews.[25] This is borne out by the fact that the next verse tells of "preaching good news of peace through Jesus Christ" (Acts 10:36). And Peter ends the same message thus: "To him all the prophets bear witness that everyone who believes in him receives forgiveness of sins through his name" (Acts 10:43).

We admit that exclusivists have treated the Cornelius episode variously[26] but hold that Cornelius was not forgiven until he believed in Christ. In fact, the angel, after instructing Cornelius to seek Peter, states: "He will declare to you a message by which you will be saved, you and all your household" (Acts 11:14).[27] Tiessen, following Sanders, argues that the words "will be saved" in this verse point to the future dimension of salvation: "The angel's statement to Cornelius was an indication that God wanted him to know of the work of Christ, on the basis of which he and his household would be saved in the last day" and to know full salvation in Christ.[28]

What are we to make of this appeal to future salvation? It looks like an inclusivist maneuver to try to get out of a hard spot. Of course salvation is past, present, and future. But the three tenses go together and the inclusivist attempt to separate them fails. Are we to believe that Cornelius was saved from his sins by fearing God and giving alms and that after believing the gospel he was promised salvation on the last day? From what was he already saved, then? How can people be saved now but not saved on the last day? This inclusivist argument is not convincing when it appeals to different tenses of salvation.

Even if Cornelius was saved before trusting Christ, a point we do not concede, still inclusivism would not be proved. As Strange perceptively notes, another question would still have to be answered affirmatively: "Is there a valid analogy to be drawn between the experience of Cornelius and unevangelized believers today?"[29]

---

[24]Tiessen, *Who Can Be Saved?* p. 175. He cites Carson, *Gagging of God*, p. 307.
[25]Ibid.
[26]Tiessen notes this in *Who Can Be Saved?* pp.176-78.
[27]A point made by David Wells, *God the Evangelist: How the Holy Spirit Works to Bring Men and Women to Faith* (Grand Rapids: Eerdmans, 1987), p. 23. We learned this from Tiessen, *Who Can Be Saved?* pp. 175-76, who also cites John Stott.
[28]Tiessen, *Who Can Be Saved?* p. 178.
[29]Strange, *Possibility of Salvation*, pp. 194-95.

We agree with Strange: "There is enough dissimilarity between Cornelius' experience and that of the 'faith principle' to make Pinnock's analogy tenuous. The main dissimilarity is that Cornelius was in contact in some degree with special revelation through the channel of the Jewish faith and an angelic visitation, and not merely in contact with general revelation."[30]

ROMANS 1:18-23

All agree that Paul in Romans 1:18—3:20 brings the world to its knees before a holy God in order to show Jew and Gentile alike their need of Christ. There is also general agreement that Romans 1:18-32 teaches that God has revealed his power and deity in creation, that sinners in general do not benefit from this revelation, and as a result are "without excuse" (Rom 1:20). But here inclusivists and exclusivists part ways because the former hold that "God uses general revelation to mediate his saving grace" and the latter deny this.[31]

Inclusivist exegesis. Inclusivists insist that their view takes sin seriously, denies saving efficacy to works, and ascribes it to faith.[32] They respond to the exclusivist protest that Romans 1:18-23 presents no positive response to general revelation, but only a negative one. Quoting Millard Erickson, Tiessen urges: "The most negative statement we could make from Romans 1, therefore, is that 'there may be those who respond positively, but Paul makes no mention of them.' This is different from hearing a positive *assertion* that no one does respond."[33]

When asked to describe the response to general revelation that saves, Tiessen gives a measured answer: "This faith response to God's revelation of his eternal power and divine nature through his work of creation, would, therefore, include a worship of the Creator God and a spirit of thankfulness for what he has made and provided for us."[34]

Exclusivist exegesis. How does exclusivism evaluate inclusivism's case for salvation by grace mediated through general revelation? In three ways. First, exclusivists point out that inclusivists base their view on what Romans 1:18-23 does *not*

---

[30]Ibid., 195.

[31]Sanders, *No Other Name*, p. 233. See also idem, *What about Those?* pp. 46-50; Pinnock, *A Wideness in God's Mercy,* p. 33. For a telling response to Sanders's claim (*What About Those?* pp. 46-48) that Rom 1—2 concern not works righteousness but a boundary marker dispute, see Douglas Moo, *The Epistle to the Romans* (Grand Rapids: Eerdmans, 1996), p. 92.

[32]Ibid., pp. 234-36.

[33]Tiessen, *Who Can Be Saved?* p. 141; italics original. He quotes Millard J. Erickson, *How Shall They Be Saved? The Destiny of Those Who Do Not Hear of Jesus* (Grand Rapids: Baker, 1996), p. 149. David K. Clark agrees: "Is Special Revelation Necessary for Salvation," in *Through No Fault of Their Own?* ed. William V. Crockett and James S. Sigountos (Grand Rapids: Baker, 1991), pp. 35-45.

[34]Tiessen, *Who Can Be Saved?* p. 144.

say. Tiessen's approval of Erickson's words reveals this weakness: "There may be those who respond positively, but Paul makes no mention of them."[35] Here the basis for inclusivism includes what is considered a possibility—"There *may* be those who respond positively" (italics added)—and what Paul does *not* say. Combining a possibility with silence constitutes a slim biblical basis for general revelation inclusivism.

Second, what Paul *does* say in Romans 1:18-23 cuts across the grain of inclusivism. He says that God discloses his holy hatred of sin committed by those who hold down the truth (Rom 1:18). They know the truth because God has plainly communicated it to them (Rom 1:19). This truth involves God's "eternal power and divine nature," which have been perceived by human beings ever since the creation of the world (Rom 1:20). How have they perceived God's attributes? "In the things that have been made" (Rom 1:20). What result obtains? "They are without excuse" (Rom 1:20). Paul explains that this knowledge of God gets through to sinners but instead of worshiping him, they thanklessly dishonor him, become futile in their thinking, and engage in idolatry and sexual sins (Rom 1:21-27). Paul teaches that since creation every human being is bombarded with general revelation from God. In that sense they "know God" (Rom 1:21). But no positive response to general revelation is even hinted at in these verses. Instead, because of their negative response sinners are deemed inexcusable (Rom 1:20).

Third, and this follows from the last point, the whole argument of Romans runs against inclusivism. Paul gives the purpose statement for his epistle in Romans 1:16-17, where he extols the gospel as the way of salvation for all who believe in Christ, Jew and Gentile. After showing the universal need for the gospel in Romans 1:18—3:20, he returns to the epistle's theme—the gospel—in Romans 3:21-31, where he speaks of faith in Christ's atonement as the way to salvation. Viewed in this light, Romans 1:18-23 functions as a part of Paul's strategy to show that all persons under heaven are in trouble with their Creator. "All, both Jews and Greeks, are under the power of sin, as it is written. 'None is righteous, no not one; no one understands, no one seeks for God. All have turned aside; together they have become worthless; no one does good, not even one'" (Rom 3:9-12).

This is the reason why Paul does not mention people responding savingly to general revelation in Romans 1:18-23—he does not believe that there are any. Thomas Schreiner deserves quotation:

> To posit that anyone could experience the saving righteousness of God through natural revelation would run roughshod over the intention of this text. The conclusion of this section (Rom 3:9-20) demonstrates that sin exercises universal power. The ar-

---

[35]Ibid., p. 141.

gument is not that most people are under the power of sin, but that all people, without exception, are under the dominion of sin. Faith becomes a reality only through the preached word (Rom 10:14-17).[36]

ROMANS 2:13-15

Inclusivists and exclusivists also contest the meaning of Paul's words in Romans 2:13-15: "For it is not the hearers of the law who are righteous before God, but the doers of the law who will be justified. For when Gentiles, who do not have the law, by nature do what the law requires, they are a law to themselves, even though they do not have the law. They show that the work of the law is written on their hearts, while their conscience also bears witness, and their conflicting thoughts accuse or even excuse them."

Inclusivist exegesis. Sanders favorably cites Bruce Lockerbie's description of the people in Romans 2:14-16 as "Gentiles who acknowledge God and do his will" and will be saved on judgment day.[37] Sanders then explains that such people will not be saved by their own moral efforts, but, quoting Lockerbie with approval: "These will be devout pagans, who, in the presence of sin, have been ashamed, have cried out in spiritual anguish, and confessed to whatever representation of the Holy Spirit they acknowledge."[38] Tiessen too understands Romans 2:14-16 as describing persons without Scripture who are saved by responding obediently to God's moral demands discerned through conscience. "Paul describes obedience to this law . . . as the righteousness that pleases God." He quickly adds a caveat: "These people are not justified by their works, but this righteousness gives evidence to the work of God in their lives."[39]

Exclusivist exegesis. Exclusivists respond with three arguments. First, they again claim that inclusivists base their conclusions on the Bible's silence. Concerning Lockerbie's devout pagans who cry out to the Deity in spiritual anguish and confess their sins, Nash concludes: "The problem is, Romans 2:14-16 says nothing about pagan Gentiles who seek salvation because of guilty consciences, and it certainly says nothing about their search being successful."[40] It looks to us as if inclusivism is being read into Romans 2 rather than out of it.

Second, inclusivists do not lay sufficient weight on what Romans 2:14-16 *says.*

---

[36]Thomas R. Schreiner, *Romans* (Grand Rapids: Baker, 1998), pp. 85-86.

[37]Sanders, *No Other Name*, p. 235.

[38]Ibid. Sanders quotes Bruce Lockerbie, *The Cosmic Center: The Supremacy of Christ in a Secular Wasteland* (Portland, Ore.: Multnomah, 1986), pp. 175-76.

[39]Tiessen, *Who Can Be Saved?* pp. 144-45. Tiessen draws a faulty parallel with John 3:20-21, faulty because "the light" spoken of in those verses is Christ, as the preceding verse shows; see D. A. Carson, *The Gospel according to John* (Grand Rapids, Eerdmans, 1991), pp. 207-8.

[40]Nash, *Is Jesus the Only Savior?* p. 121.

How do these verses function in their immediate context? Carson answers well:

> In Romans 2:14-16, Paul's point is that even people without the law show by their actions that distinctions between right and wrong are known to them. Like everyone else, they do experience crises of conscience. Sometimes their consciences actually defend them: no one, not even the pagan Gentile, is as bad as he or she might be. At other times, their consciences convict them. Paul's point, then, is that even those without the law must admit that distinctions between right and wrong are found everywhere, and everywhere people fall short and sometimes fail to live up to whatever light they have. That is very different from saying some pagans so live up to the light they have that they turn to God revealed in nature and call to him for mercy. The texts do not even hint as such a vision.[41]

Third, inclusivism suffers from theological myopia. Paul's whole point in Romans 1:18—3:20 is to charge "that all, both Jews and Greeks, are under the power of sin . . . so that every mouth may be stopped and the whole world may be held accountable to God" (Rom 3:9, 19). After exegeting Romans 2, Moo correctly concludes:

> Paul never says that Gentiles apart from the gospel can be saved by meeting the demands of the law, or by doing good works. The texts could mean this only if they are ripped out of context. Once the context is recognized, Paul's purposes understood, and his theology of justification taken into account, we quickly see that Gentiles cannot be saved apart from the gospel.[42]

ROMANS 10:17-18

It will surprise some to learn that this passage, so often used to spark missionary motivation, enters into the debate. What could be clearer than Paul's repeated affirmations that people must hear and believe the gospel to be saved?

> If you confess with your mouth that Jesus is Lord and believe in your heart that God raised him from the dead, you will be saved. For with the heart one believes and is justified, and with the mouth one confesses and is saved. For the Scripture says, "Everyone who believes in him will not be put to shame." . . . For "everyone who calls on the name of the Lord will be saved." But how are they to call on him in whom they have not believed? And how are they to believe in him of whom they have never heard? And how are they to hear without someone preaching? And how are they to preach unless they are sent? . . . So faith comes from hearing, and hearing through the word of Christ. (Rom 10:9-11, 13-15, 17)

---

[41]Carson, *Gagging of God*, p. 311.
[42]Douglas J. Moo, "Romans 2: Saved Apart from the Gospel?" in *Through No Fault of Their Own? The Fate of Those Who Have Never Heard*, ed. William V. Crockett and James G. Sigountos (Grand Rapids: Baker, 1991), p. 145.

Disagreement arises, however, because Paul quotes Psalm 19:4 in the very next verse: "But I ask, have they not heard? Indeed they have, for 'Their voice has gone out to all the earth, and their words to the ends of the world'" (Rom 10:18).

Inclusivist exegesis. Many inclusivists (Tiessen excepted) hold that Paul, true to the context of Psalm 19, here refers to general revelation. Pinnock argues: "Paul asks in Romans 10:18, 'Did they not hear? Of course they did.' Because of cosmic or general revelation, anyone can find God anywhere at anytime, because he has made himself and his revelation accessible to them."[43] Sanders agrees:

> Moreover, restrictivists commonly overlook Paul's appeal to the creation revelation in Romans 10:18. Quoting the great creation hymn Psalm 19, Paul says that the "gospel" has gone out to all the world. Inclusivists argue that what Paul is saying here is that all who respond to the revelation they have by calling out to God will be saved by Jesus Christ, since calling out to God is, in fact, calling upon the Lord Jesus.[44]

Exclusivist exegesis. Exclusivists offer three responses. First, contrary to inclusivist interpretation, Romans 10:18 refers in context to Jews not Gentiles, as Daniel Strange explains:

> We must consider the context of these verses and to whom Paul is referring. Sanders and Erickson's isolation of verse 18 (Paul's use of Psalm 19:4) to argue for a "gospel according to nature," whereby one can be ontologically saved by Christ while being epistemologically unaware of Christ, depends on the focus being on Gentiles (who have no access to special revelation). However, the major contemporary evangelical commentaries on Romans all argue that Paul is referring to either Israelites exclusively or primarily.[45]

Strange is correct, as Romans 10:19 shows. There Paul writes, "But I ask, did Israel not understand?" And the major Romans commentaries agree that verse 18 refers to Israel.[46]

Second, exclusivists maintain that the inclusivist understanding of Romans 10:18 is unnatural and disrupts Paul's flow of argument. When Paul cites Psalm 19:4, he is not speaking of general revelation, but of the gospel, as Romans commentaries attest:

> The implied object of the verb "heard" in Paul's question must be "the word of

---

[43]Pinnock, *A Wideness in God's Mercy*, p. 104.

[44]Sanders, *No Other Name*, p. 68; see also p. 234. Millard J. Erickson, "Hope for Those Who Haven't Heard? Yes, But . . . ," *Evangelical Missions Quarterly* 11 (August 1975): 124; R. Todd Mangum, "Is There a Reformed Way to Get the Benefits of the Atonement to 'Those Who Have Never Heard'?" *Journal of the Evangelical Theological Society* 47, no. 1 (March 2004): 129.

[45]Daniel Strange, "General Revelation: Sufficient or Insufficient?" in this volume, pp. 40-77.

[46]C. E. B. Cranfield, *The Epistle to the Romans*. 2 vols., International Critical Commentary (Edinburgh: T & T Clark, 1979), 2:537-38; Moo, *Epistle to the Romans*, p. 666; Schreiner, *Romans*, p. 572.

Christ"; "their voice" and "their words" in the Psalm verse must then refer to the voices and words of Christian preachers. . . . Paul is not, then, simply using the text according to its original meaning. His application probably rests on a general analogy: as God's word of general revelation has been proclaimed all over the earth, so God's word of special revelation in the gospel, has been spread all over the earth. His intention is not to interpret the verse of the Psalm, but to use its language, with the "echoes" of God's revelation that it awakes, to assert the universal preaching of the gospel.[47]

It is also possible that, if Paul has the rest of Psalm 19 in mind, he may have taken vv. 1-6, as well as vv. 7-11, as referring to Torah, in which case he could be celebrating the fact that the "word" of Deut. 30:14 was not freely available to all, as God always intended. This link between the occurrences of *rhēma* in Romans 10:8, 17-18 seems to point in this direction.[48]

Therefore, since Romans 10:18 does not speak of general revelation coming to the unevangelized but of the gospel being preached to Israel, it is a poor proof text for inclusivism.

Third, Romans 10:9-18 testifies loudly to sinners' need to hear and believe the gospel to be saved. But Sanders raises an objection based on logic:

> Some believe that Paul asserted the necessity of knowing about Christ for salvation when he said that "if you confess with your mouth Jesus as Lord, and believe in your heart that God raised Him from the dead, you shall be saved" (10:9). But logically this means nothing more than that confession of Christ is *one* sure way to experience salvation: Paul does not say anything about what will happen to those who do not confess Christ because they have never heard of Christ. The text is logically similar to the conditional statement "If it rains, the sidewalk will be wet." If the condition is fulfilled (if it rains), then the consequent will follow (the sidewalk will be wet). But we cannot with certainty say, "If it is not raining, the sidewalk will not be wet." Someone may turn on a sprinkler. . . . The argument is simply fallacious. . . . [W]e can be just as certain that the text is not explicitly telling us that all the unevangelized are damned.[49]

Carson effectively answers Sanders's appeal to logic:

> At the level of logic, Sanders's conclusion is normally justified. Statements of the sort "If A, then B" do not guarantee the truth of "If not A, then not B," and that is what exclusivism demands. But there is one important exception. If all members of class A are precisely identical to all the members of B, then if the conditional statement "If A, then B" holds, so also does the conditional statement "If not A, then not B."

---

[47]Moo, *Epistle to the Romans*, pp. 666-67.
[48]N. T. Wright, "Romans" in *The New Interpreter's Bible* (Nashville: Abingdon, 2002), 10:669.
[49]Sanders, *No Other Name*, p. 67, italics original.

In other words, if all those who confess with their mouth that Jesus is Lord . . . constitute class A, and all those who are saved constitute class B, then if the members of the two classes are the same, it is precisely true to say that if you do not confess Jesus as Lord, . . . you are not saved.

In other words, what Sanders has done is *assume* that the two classes do not precisely coincide—which is, of course, nothing other than assuming his conclusion. Of course, exclusivists . . . must not simply assume the opposite. But in fact, it can be shown that the perfect coincidence of the two classes is precisely what Paul presupposes. This is clear not only from Paul's treatment of the entire biblical story-line, but from this chapter of the epistle to the Romans. . . . For Paul, it is impossible to call on the true God without believing in Jesus.[50]

We agree. Romans 10:9-18, as strongly as any passage in Scripture, emphasizes the necessity of all sinners believing in Jesus to be saved. Confessing Jesus' lordship and believing that he (died and) lives again saves (Rom 10:9). This is God's way for persons to receive salvation (Rom 10:10). And this is consistent with Old Testament revelation (Rom 10:11). It is the same for both Jews and Greeks—there is one Lord Jesus Christ who blesses all who call on him for salvation (Rom 10:12). This too corresponds to Old Testament truth (Rom 10:13). For sinners to experience salvation, God must send a preacher, who must preach to them, they must hear of Jesus, must believe in him, even call on him for salvation. This too coincides with the Old Testament (Rom 10:14-15). In sum: "faith comes from hearing, and hearing through the word of Christ" (Rom 10:17). It is no wonder, then, that Romans 10:9-17, along with John 14:6, and Acts 4:12, have been the favorite passages of exclusivists.

HEBREWS 11:6

"And without faith it is impossible to please him, for whoever would draw near to God must believe that he exists and that he rewards those who seek him." What is the faith that saves? Inclusivists and exclusivists answer this question differently. The former define faith in broad terms, as a generic faith response, a seeking after God, while the latter insist on more biblical content to the object of faith, content culminating in the New Testament in Jesus Christ. Hebrews 11:6 is a favorite inclusivist text for the "faith principle."

Inclusivist exegesis. Pinnock first defined this principle:

In my judgment, the faith principle is the basis of universal accessibility. According to the Bible, people are saved by faith, not by the content of their theology. Since

---

[50]Carson, *Gagging of God*, pp. 312-13, italics original. See also Nash, *Is Jesus the Only Savior?* pp. 144-45.

God has not left anyone without witness, people are judged on the basis of the light they have received and how they have responded to that light. Faith in God is what saves, not possessing certain minimum information. Hebrews is clear: "And without faith it is impossible to please God, because anyone who comes to him must believe that he exists and that he rewards those who earnestly seek him." (Heb 11:6)[51]

Sanders develops the idea, showing inclusivism's theocentric rather than Christocentric focus of faith. After quoting Hebrews 11:6, he explains:

> Anyone who believes that God will respond benevolently to those who seek him thereby gives evidence of trusting God and thus possesses saving faith.... According to E. H. Plumptre, being saved through the sort of faith described in Hebrews 11:6 "is compatible with ignorance of any historical revelation through Moses or through Christ." Inclusivists contend that saving faith involves the process of moving from some truths about God's character to a degree of trust in the person of God that results in obedience to his will.[52]

Tiessen regards Hebrews 11 as key because it says so much about Old Testament believers' faith. Although this faith was exercised in response to God's special revelation, the content of this revelation—and hence of faith's object—varied greatly. But one aspect of this faith was constant—it always manifested itself in action.[53] In addition, it is important to note that: "Hebrews 11 tells us nothing about people who are ignorant even of old covenant special revelation."[54]

Exclusivist exegesis. Exclusivists take exception on three grounds. First, if a "faith principle" were to be extracted from Hebrews 11, it would be one based on God's covenant with his Old Testament people. This is underscored by references to God's promises to them (Heb 11:9, 11, 13, 17, 39), his commendations of them (Heb 11:2, 4, 5, 39), his warning them (Heb 11:7) and to his speaking (Heb 11:18). The object of such a faith is special revelation and does not fit inclusivism, as Carson explains:

> Inclusivists who draw a parallel between modern non-Christians who have never heard of Christ and such Old Testament believers overlook the fact that these believers on the Old Testament side were responding in faith to special revelation, and were not simply exercising some sort of general "faith" in an undefined "God."[55]

Second, although Hebrews 11:6 says important things about faith, including

[51]Pinnock, *A Wideness in God's Mercy*, pp. 157-58.
[52]Sanders, *No Other Name*, p. 228.
[53]Tiessen, *Who Can Be Saved?* pp. 166-68.
[54]Ibid, p. 169.
[55]Carson, *Gagging of God*, p. 298. Tiessen agrees, *Who Can Be Saved?* p. 168. So does Nash, *Is Jesus the Only Savior?* p. 127.

its necessity, it does not exhaust the Bible's teaching on the content of faith. It does not even exhaust the epistle to the Hebrews's teaching on the content of faith. In the chapters before and after the famous "faith chapter," faith is defined in Christocentric terms:

> Therefore, brothers, since we have confidence to enter the holy places by the blood of Jesus, . . . and since we have a great priest over the house of God, let us draw near with a true heart in full assurance of faith. . . . Let us hold fast the confession of our hope without wavering, for he who promised is faithful. (Heb 10:19, 21, 23)
>
> Therefore, . . . let us run with endurance the race that is set before us, looking to Jesus, the founder and perfecter of our faith, who for the joy that was set before him endured the cross, despising the shame, and is seated at the right hand of the throne of God. (Heb 12:1-2)

It is thus a dilution of Hebrews's depiction of faith to reduce it to mere belief in God's existence and his willingness to reward faith. Nash tells how unconverted Saul of Tarsus more than satisfied inclusivism's "faith principle," but that when converted to Christ Paul the apostle did not regard himself as previously saved.[56]

Third, "the faith principle" ignores the progress of biblical revelation. Douglas Geivett and Gary Phillips point this out: "Hebrews 1:1-2 states, as the thesis of the letter, that at a particular moment in history the focus of special revelation has narrowed to the incarnate Son. Thus chronology cannot be dismissed. The point is that now salvation is available only through an explicit faith in Jesus Christ."[57] And that means that it is a methodological mistake for inclusivism to appeal to texts describing the salvation of Old Testament saints to learn God's requirements for the unevangelized today. It is unwise to hope for the salvation of the unevangelized on the basis of the inclusivist "faith principle." What the unevangelized need instead is to hear and believe the gospel of Christ.

CONCLUSION

We respect our fellow Christians who take an inclusivist position and have tried to represent their views fairly and accurately. But our examination of their exegesis of eight key biblical passages contrasted with that of exclusivism has exposed the unstable biblical foundations of their position. In a word, their exegesis is weak. Out of frustration we ask a question. *What would it take to disprove inclusivism bib-*

---

[56]Nash, *Is Jesus the Only Savior?* pp. 174-75.
[57]R. Douglas Geivett and W. Gary Phillips, "A Particularist View: An Evidential Approach," in *More Than One Way? Four Views on Salvation in a Pluralistic World,* ed. Dennis L. Okholm and Timothy R. Phillips (Grand Rapids: Zondervan, 1995), p. 240.

lically to its proponents? The fact that it is difficult to answer this question does not work in inclusivism's favor.

If we point to passages that show that God requires for salvation faith in his Son Jesus, the world's only Savior—John 14:6; Acts 4:12; Romans 10:9-18—inclusivism offers two replies. First, these texts do not have the unevangelized in view. Second, they do not say that persons will be lost if they do not believe the gospel.

If we point to the primary biblical texts treating general revelation—Romans 1:18-23 and 2:13-15—and point out that they leave sinners "without excuse" (Rom 1:20) and say that they "will also perish" (Rom 2:12), inclusivism generates an answer: Although these texts mention no positive response of the unsaved to general revelation, they do not actually assert that no one positively responds to it.

If we show that the foremost "pagan saints"—Melchizedek and Cornelius—were not saved by general revelation but by believing God's special revelation, that does not prevent inclusivism from considering them models of the unevangelized today.

If we show that the text upon which inclusivism bases its "faith principle"—Hebrews 11:6—when considered in the contexts of its chapter, book, and testament, teaches a biblical "faith principle" that insists that saving faith is directed to special revelation, even Christ since his appearing, inclusivism is undeterred.

Frankly, given the way inclusivism handles Scripture, it seems impossible to refute it biblically. But this is not to commend inclusivism or to suggest that it really is based on scriptural teaching. Rather, the difficulty of refuting inclusivism biblically underscores its faulty treatment of Scripture. As this chapter demonstrates, a comparison of exclusivist and inclusivist exegesis shows that the latter repeatedly falls short. Although it appeals to the Bible, its appeals do not represent sound exegesis, but ways to get around clear biblical teaching, ways summarized in the four preceding paragraphs.

Good theology is not built on a combination of appeals to what the Bible does not say and theoretical possibilities. Rather, it is based on solid and clear exposition of Holy Scripture. And this is what exclusivism demonstrates and inclusivism lacks.

9

The Gospel for All Nations

ANDREAS J. KÖSTENBERGER

THE GOSPEL, THE GOOD NEWS of salvation in Jesus Christ, is one of the major pervasive themes in New Testament and biblical theology.[1] It is at the heart of the message of the four canonical Gospels and is central to Paul's, the apostles', and the early church's message and understanding of their mission.[2] According to the New Testament writers, the gospel is not a *human* message; it is the gospel *of God* (Mk 1:14; Rom 1:1; 15:16; 2 Cor 11:7; 1 Thess 2:2, 8, 9; 1 Pet 4:17). As Paul makes clear, the gospel was not a *novel* message, only devised in the days subsequent to Jesus' first coming; it was "promised beforehand" in both the Law and the Prophets (Rom 1:2-3; cf. Gen 15:6; Hab 2:4; see also 1 Cor 15:3-4).[3] For this reason, those who departed from the true gospel preached not only a different gospel but in fact no gospel at all (Gal 1:6), and Timothy was charged simply to "guard the good deposit" of the gospel (2 Tim 1:14) rather than to change it or improve upon it. Jesus, likewise, commissioned his followers, not to act as reincarnations of the Son, but as those representing the gospel message to others (Jn 20:21-22).[4]

The dual fact that the gospel is truly the gospel of God and that this gospel was promised beforehand long ago places the emphasis squarely on God's initiative, foreknowledge, provision, and sovereignty. As Paul contends over against his Judaizing opponents who elevated the Mosaic law above the Abrahamic promise,

---

[1]See Andreas J. Köstenberger, "Diversity and Unity in the New Testament," in *Biblical Theology: Retrospect & Prospect*, ed. Scott J. Hafemann (Downers Grove, Ill.: InterVarsity Press, 2002), pp. 156-57; G. Goldsworthy, "Gospel," in *New Dictionary of Biblical Theology*, ed. T. Desmond Alexander and Brian S. Rosner (Downers Grove, Ill.: InterVarsity Press, 2000), pp. 521-24.

[2]See C. C. Broyles, "Gospel (Good News)," in *Dictionary of Jesus and the Gospels*, ed. Joel B. Green, Scot McKnight and I. Howard Marshall (Downers Grove, Ill.: InterVarsity Press, 1992), pp. 283-86; A. B. Luter Jr., "Gospel," in *Dictionary of Paul and His Letters*, ed. Gerald F. Hawthorne, Ralph P. Martin and Daniel G. Reid (Downers Grove, Ill.: InterVarsity Press, 1993), pp. 369-72.

[3]All Scripture quotations in this essay are from the NIV.

[4]Cf. Andreas J. Köstenberger, *The Missions of Jesus and the Disciples According to the Fourth Gospel* (Grand Rapids: Eerdmans, 1998).

God's purposes are consistent over time; salvation has always been by grace through faith (Gal 3:6, citing Gen 15:6). God's promise to Abraham and the later-given Mosaic law are not in conflict. Yet it is the former, rather than the latter, that is foundational, diverting attention away from the law as a permanently relevant salvific structure and instead drawing attention to God's relationship with Abraham and Abraham's disposition and actions toward God. God's promise to Abraham, likewise, constitutes the focal point from which to understand how the gospel is in fact God's good news and saving message "for all the nations," not merely for the Jews (Mt 28:18-20; Acts 1:8; 28:23-31; Rom 4:17, citing Gen 17:5; Gal 3:8, citing Gen 12:3). Not only this, but the Abrahamic promise makes clear also that salvation is found only in Abraham's true "seed," the Lord Jesus Christ (Gal 3:16).

The following essay traces the "gospel" trajectory through the Gospels, the book of Acts, Paul's writings and the rest of the New Testament. Each one of the four Evangelists, as well as Paul and the other New Testament writers, give prominent coverage to the good news of God's saving message in Christ. It will be seen that the gospel is firmly grounded in the Hebrew Scriptures and that it is Christocentric in orientation and universal in application. It will also become clear that together with God and the Lord Jesus Christ, the gospel is the major theme uniting the entire Bible, serving as an integrating motif that sets forth God's definitive and final revelation and redemption in Christ, and in him alone. After a summary treatment of the gospel in biblical theology, the essay concludes with a discussion of the Christian gospel and the theology of inclusivism.

THE GOSPEL IN THE GOSPELS

The gospel is at the very heart of the first canonical Gospel. Matthew summarizes the thrust of Jesus' ministry thus: "Jesus went throughout Galilee, teaching in their synagogues, preaching the good news of the kingdom, and healing every disease and sickness among the people" (Mt 4:23; in virtually identical terms, Mt 9:35; similarly, Lk 8:1; Jesus' disciples, Lk 9:6). When asked by the disciples of John the Baptist about the nature of his ministry, Jesus describes it by saying that "the good news is preached to the poor" in keeping with Isaiah's words (Mt 11:5; cf. Is 61:1; see also Lk 4:18). In his end-time discourse, Jesus affirmed that "this gospel of the kingdom will be preached in the whole world as a testimony to all nations, and then the end will come" (Mt 24:14; par. Mk 13:30; cf. Mt 26:13; par. Mk 14:9).

Similarly, Mark, in his "gospel about Jesus Christ, the Son of God" (Mk 1:1), states that after John the Baptist was put in prison, Jesus went to Galilee proclaiming the good news of God, "The time has come. The kingdom of God is near. Repent and believe the good news!" (Mk 1:15; cf. Mt 4:17). In his call to discipleship in Mark 8:35, "For whoever wants to save his life will lose it, but whoever loses his life *for me and for the gospel* will save it" (cf. Mt 16:24-25, pars.), Jesus so closely identifies himself with the gospel as to use "me" and "the gospel" in parallelism (similarly, Mk 10:29). Hence, for Mark, Jesus and the gospel are so closely linked as to be virtually indistinguishable.

In Luke's Gospel, remarkably, angels are the bearers of good news, first to Zechariah the father of John the Baptist (Lk 1:19), and then to the shepherds: "I bring you good news of great joy that will be for all the people. Today in the town of David a Savior has been born to you; he is Christ the Lord" (Lk 2:10-11).[5] Later, John the Baptist is shown to "preach the good news" to the people (Lk 3:18; cf. Mt 3:2). In one of the most significant Christological passages in Luke's Gospel (unique to Luke), Jesus cites Isaiah 61:1-2: "The Spirit of the Lord is on me, because he has anointed me to preach good news to the poor" (Lk 4:18; cf. Lk 7:22; but see Mt 11:5). Jesus is the Servant of the Lord who, in fulfillment of Old Testament predictions, has come to proclaim good news, particularly to the poor, a repeated emphasis in Luke (cf., e.g., Lk 6:20; 7:22; 14:13, 21; 16:20, 22; 18:22; 19:8; 21:3). Why is salvation in Jesus good news for the poor? Because it elevates those who have no status in this world to favored status with God and puts them on equal footing with others. Later in Luke, Jesus emphatically states that the universal preaching of the good news of the kingdom of God is the very purpose of his mission (Lk 4:43; cf. 8:1; 16:16; 20:1; training the disciples, 9:6).

Interestingly, John, in his Gospel, does not feature the *euangelion* word group at all (though see Rev 10:7; 14:6). Instead, Jesus is presented as the Word (Gr. *logos*) who was in eternity with God and who took on humanity to reveal the Father (Jn 1:1, 14, 18). Throughout John's gospel, Jesus' preaching is simply called his "message" or "word" (*logos;* e.g., Jn 4:41; 8:31, 37, 43, 51-52; 12:48; 14:23-24), just as Jesus' deeds are called his "works" (*erga;* e.g., 5:20, 36). At the heart of this message is Jesus himself, the one-of-a-kind Son of God, the Messiah, and the Way, the Truth, and the Life, without whom no one can come to the Father (Jn 1:14, 18; 3:16, 18; 14:6; 20:30-31). And it is this message that Jesus entrusted to his followers to proclaim so that others might believe in him and be saved (Jn 17:20).

John underscores the authenticity of the gospel message particularly by his use

---

[5]Interestingly, Luke features only the verb, *euangelizō* ("to bring good news"), but not the noun, *euangelion*, in his gospel. The same pattern obtains in the book of Acts (though see Acts 15:7 [recording a statement by Peter] and 20:24 [Paul]).

of "witness" terminology.[6] Similar to Luke, the fourth Evangelist stresses the accuracy of the facts set forth in his Gospel (cf. Lk 1:1-4). The first of many witnesses featured in John's Gospel is John the Baptist (simply called "John" in this Gospel). Whereas the Synoptists portray John's ministry as more multifaceted, John depicts him as the paradigmatic, though by no means only, witness to Jesus (Jn 1:7-8, 15, 19, 32-34; 3:26; 5:33-36).[7] Other witnesses to Jesus enlisted by the fourth Evangelist include Jesus and his works (Jn 3:11, 32; 5:36; 8:14, 18; 10:25, 32, 37-38; 15:24; 18:37), Moses and the Scriptures (Jn 5:39, 46), the Father (Jn 5:32, 36-37; 8:18), the Spirit (Jn 14—16, esp. Jn 15:26), the disciples (e.g., Jn 15:27) and the fourth Evangelist himself (Jn 19:35; 21:24).[8]

The unmistakable implication of John's witness theme is that the gospel message is amply attested by a whole series of divinely commissioned eyewitnesses and is therefore worthy of full acceptance (see also John's purpose statement in Jn 20:30-31). In fact, John's "witness motif," in an ironic reversal of the world's version of the events surrounding Jesus' trial and crucifixion, turns the tables: In reality, it is not Jesus who is put on trial by the world and his Jewish opponents, but rather it is the world and the Jews who are on trial for their rejection of Jesus, the Messiah and Savior of the world. Jesus' trial is unmasked as a travesty of justice, while the numerous witnesses to Jesus prove his, and the church's, testimony to be true.[9]

Hence all four Gospels put the preaching of the message of Jesus (in the Synoptics, the good news of the kingdom of God and of salvation in Jesus Christ), faithfully witnessed to by the Evangelists, at the center of Jesus' mission. In Jesus, God's kingdom has come, for he is the King and both the messenger and the mes-

---

[6]The "witness" *(martyr-)* word group in John's Gospel comprises the verb *martureō* ("to bear witness"; 33 out of 76 New Testament occurrences are in John) and the noun *martyria* ("testimony"; 14 of 37 instances). To this should be added the following occurrences of these two words in the remaining Johannine writings: 1 Jn: 6 and 6; 3 Jn: 4 and 1; Rev: 4 and 9 (Revelation also features the additional words *martyrion* and *martys*). This means that 47 of 76 New Testament instances of *martyreō* and 30 of 37 instances of *martyria* are found in John's writings.

[7]As Andrew T. Lincoln, *Truth on Trial: The Lawsuit Motif in the Fourth Gospel* (Peabody, Mass.: Hendrickson, 2000), p. 21, notes, the lawsuit, witness, and trial motifs have major precedents in Old Testament literature, especially the book of Isaiah (cf. Is 40—55, esp. Is 42:18-25; 43:22-28; 50:1-3). Not only do these motifs occur in each of the five main sections of John's narrative (prologue; Jn 1:19—12:50; 13—17; 18—20; epilogue); they do so in highly significant ways, forming the narrative framework of the gospel (p. 141). According to Lincoln, just as there are seven signs and seven discourses in John's gospel, there are seven witnesses: John the Baptist, Jesus himself, Jesus' works, God the Father, the Scriptures, the Samaritan woman, and the crowd.

[8]Craig S. Keener, *The Gospel of John* (Peabody, Mass.: Hendrickson, 2003), p. 393, notes the possible literary inclusion in John's gospel which opens and closes with a witness to Jesus (the Baptist and the evangelist, respectively).

[9]See Andreas J. Köstenberger, "'What Is Truth?' Pilate's Question in Its Johannine and Larger Biblical Context," in *Whatever Happened to Truth?* gen. ed. Andreas J. Köstenberger (Wheaton, Ill.: Crossway, 2005), pp. 19-51.

sage of that kingdom. That gospel, which is rooted in the Old Testament depiction of the Servant of the Lord (e.g., Is 61:1-2), is preached first by the Baptist (Mt 3:1), and then by Jesus (Mt 4:17), who proclaims it to the Jews (cf. Acts 10:36) and envisions its universal proclamation to all the nations subsequent to his cross-death and exaltation but prior to his second coming (Mt 24:14; 26:13, pars.). Hence the gospel is both Christ-centered and universal in scope, and is "good news" precisely and only because it speaks of salvation and the forgiveness of sins in and through the Lord Jesus Christ.

All four Gospels also have as their culminating and indispensable component the passion of Jesus the Messiah. They are united in their depiction of the final days of Jesus' earthly ministry issuing in his rejection by the Jewish leaders, the pronouncement of his formal death sentence by the Roman authorities, his crucifixion, burial, and resurrection after three days. The Gospels thus are not primarily biographies of Jesus—"lives of Jesus"—but accounts of God's provision of salvation in and through his Messiah and Son, the Lord Jesus Christ, patterned after the recounting of God's saving acts (such as the exodus) in the Hebrew Scriptures.[10] Some have called the Gospels "passion narratives with extended introductions," which is only a small overstatement.[11] In fact, almost from the beginning do we find Jesus anticipating his rejection by the Jewish leadership and his violent, vicarious cross-death. All four Evangelists concur that Jesus repeatedly predicted his passion as his earthly ministry drew to a close (e.g., Mk 8:31; 9:31; 10:33-34, 45, pars.; John 6:51; 12:24, 32).

The gospel of the Gospels, therefore, is inextricably linked with Jesus' personal characteristics as the Messiah and Son of God and his saving work at the cross. Matthew's genealogy, for instance, makes clear that it is Jesus, as the son of Abraham and the son of David, who was born of the Virgin Mary and came as the God-sent Messiah. Mark introduces his gospel as "[t]he beginning of the gospel about Jesus Christ, the Son of God" (Mk 1:1). Jesus is the Son of Man who came "to give his life as a ransom for many" (Mk 10:45) and who came "to seek and to save what was lost" (Lk 19:10). John's purpose for writing his Gospel is that "you may believe that Jesus is the Christ, the Son of God, and that by believing you may have life in his name" (Jn 20:31). This Jesus is "the way and the truth and the life," and no one can come to the Father except through him (Jn 14:6).

It follows from the preceding remarks on the gospel in the Gospels that there

---

[10]Cf. Willard M. Swartley, *Israel's Scripture Traditions and the Synoptic Gospels: Story Shaping Story* (Peabody, Mass.: Hendrickson, 1994).

[11]Martin Kähler, *The So-Called Historical Jesus and the Historical Biblical Christ*, trans. Carl E. Braaten (1896; reprint, Philadelphia: Fortress, 1988), p. 80 n. 11.

is no gospel, no good news of salvation, apart from Jesus Christ. What is more, salvation is contingent upon personal faith in Jesus on the basis of his substitutionary cross-work. As John writes, "Yet to all who received him, to those who believed in his name, he gave the right to become children of God" (Jn 1:12). Peter confesses, representative of the Twelve, "We believe and know that you are the Holy One of God" (Jn 6:69); and, "You are the Christ, the Son of the living God" (Mt 16:16, pars.). The necessity of personal faith in Jesus is particularly pronounced in John's gospel, where the word "believe" (*pisteuō*) occurs close to one hundred times and the presence or absence of faith is made the sole distinguishing characteristic between followers of the Messiah and those who, as Jesus puts it, "are not my sheep" (Jn 10:26).

Conversely, John, in particular, makes clear that "those who do not believe [in Christ] stand condemned already because they have not believed in the name of God's one and only Son" (Jn 3:18). For people to "cross over from death to life" (Jn 5:24), they have to believe in Jesus and his word. The world without Christ is a dark place, and people are lost without him (Jn 3:19-21). For this reason, "Those who believe in the Son have eternal life, but those who reject the Son will not see life, for *God's wrath remains on them*" (Jn 3:36). Thus there is no "third way" for people: either they believe and are saved, or God's wrath remains on them. This is precisely why the gospel, and it alone, is such good news, because, without it, people are lost in their sin and doomed to hell.[12]

THE GOSPEL IN ACTS

The book of Acts presents the gospel in almost personified terms as being on an irresistible march forward in the then-known world from Jerusalem to Judea to Samaria and to the ends of the earth (Acts 1:8).[13] It is the "Word of God" that grew (Acts 6:7; 12:24; 19:20) as the apostles went everywhere and proclaimed that "[s]alvation is found in no one else, for there is no other name under heaven given to men by which we must be saved" (Acts 4:12).[14] At the heart of the apostolic proclamation was the message that "God has raised this Jesus to life" and that "God has made this Jesus, whom you crucified, both Lord and Christ" (Acts 2:32,

[12]For a helpful discussion of these and other New Testament passages, see R. Douglas Geivett and W. Gary Phillips, "A Particularist View: An Evidentialist Approach," in *More Than One Way? Four Views on Salvation in a Pluralistic World*, ed. Dennis L. Okholm and Timothy R. Phillips (Grand Rapids: Zondervan, 1995), pp. 230-39.

[13]Cf. Andreas J. Köstenberger and Peter T. O'Brien, *Salvation to the Ends of the Earth: A Biblical Theology of Mission*, New Studies in Biblical Theology 11 (Downers Grove, Ill.: InterVarsity Press, 2001), esp. pp. 127-57; see also pp. 192-93, "The Advance of the Gospel." See also Eckhard J. Schnabel, *Early Christian Mission*, 2 vols (Downers Grove, Ill.: InterVarsity, 2004).

[14]See Geivett and Phillips, "Particularist View," pp. 230-33.

36). The requirement for being accepted into the Christian community is solely repentance and faith in Jesus Christ for the forgiveness of sins (Acts 2:38). There is no record of anyone being saved apart from faith in Jesus Christ. To the contrary, Paul preaches the resurrected Jesus to the Athenian philosophers (Acts 17), and many new believers in Ephesus who had previously practiced magic publicly burned their scrolls to mark a decisive break with their sinful past (Acts 19:19).

Though persecuted by the Sanhedrin, the apostles, "day after day, in the temple courts and from house to house . . . never stopped teaching and proclaiming the good news that Jesus is the Christ" (Acts 5:42). Those who were scattered throughout Judea and Samaria by a great persecution against the church at Jerusalem preached the good news wherever they went (Acts 8:4). In Samaria, Philip "preached the good news of the kingdom of God and the name of Jesus Christ," and people responded (Acts 8:12). Later, he instructed the Ethiopian eunuch and told him the good news about Jesus (Acts 8:35; cf. 8:40). Peter and John, too, preached the gospel in Samaria (Acts 8:25).

Then, starting in Syrian Antioch, people went to tell the good news about the Lord Jesus "to Greeks also," and God blessed and many believed (Acts 11:19-20; cf. Acts 15:35). Paul's synagogue address in Pisidian Antioch preaches as "this message of salvation" that Jesus, in fulfillment of the words of the prophets, was crucified, buried, and raised from the dead, and appeared to many (Acts 13:26-31, elaborating in 13:32-41 by citing Ps 2:7; Is 55:3; Ps 16:10; and Hab 1:5). On their first missionary journey, Paul and Barnabas "continued to preach the good news" in Galatia (Acts 14:7, 15, 21), exhorting people "to turn from these worthless things to the living God, who made heaven and earth and sea and everything in them" (Acts 14:15). Subsequent to the Jerusalem Council, Paul and Barnabas "and many others" preached the gospel in Antioch (Acts 15:35). Later, Paul and his companions crossed over to Macedonia in Greece to preach the gospel there as well (Acts 16:10). On his second missionary journey, Paul preached "the good news about Jesus and the resurrection" in Athens (Acts 17:18).

As the gospel progresses in its victorious march from Jerusalem to Rome, one thing remains constant: the apostles and Paul preach one and the same gospel to Jews and Gentiles alike (see the resolution of a potential schism at the Jerusalem Council in Acts 15). With Jews and Gentiles representing humanity in its totality, this makes clear that there is no other message of salvation, nor is there salvation or access to God apart from Jesus. As Jews, Paul and the apostles were monotheists, believing only in God the Creator and God of Abraham, Isaac and Jacob as revealed in the Hebrew Scriptures (cf. Deut 6:4). Faith in, and worship of, Jesus were accommodated within this Jewish monotheistic framework, but all forms of polytheism or pagan worship were excluded. The book of Acts concludes with an emphatic demonstration of the early church's mission having been accomplished: Paul in Rome welcoming all who visited him, boldly and without hindrance preaching the kingdom of God and teaching about the Lord Jesus Christ (Acts 28:31).[15]

THE GOSPEL IN PAUL

The preaching of the gospel where it has not yet been made known (e.g., Rom 15:20; 2 Cor 10:16) and its preservation are Paul's pervasive and central concerns in his writings and ministry.[16] Paul received his commission in a dramatic encounter with the risen Christ on the road to Damascus (Acts 9; cf. Gal 1:11-12). Paul's conversion led to a "paradigm shift" in his thinking. He who had previously persecuted Christians in the conviction that Jesus' crucifixion signified that he was cursed by God now came to realize that Jesus was in fact at the center of God's saving purposes as Israel's Messiah, Son of God, and Lord of all. Over time, Paul came to understand his mission within the framework of God's larger purposes in Christ.[17]

In Galatians, Paul defends "the truth of the gospel" (Gal 2:5, 14)—which he received, not from men, but from God (Gal 1:1, 11-12)—against the Judaizing heresy, which claimed that "works of the law" such as circumcision must be required as part of a person's entrance into the covenant community.[18] According to Paul, anyone who teaches a gospel other than the one he had received (cf. Acts 14:7, 15, 21 and the discussion above) taught a "different gospel" (Gal 1:6; cf. 2 Cor 11:4), which in truth was "no gospel at all" (Gal 1:7; including Peter: Gal 2:14). Paul's primary problem with the message of the Judaizers was that "if righteousness could be gained through the law, Christ died for nothing" (Gal 2:21). For his part, Paul was committed to the centrality of "the cross of Christ" in salvation (Gal 6:12-14).

In his letters to the Thessalonian church which he had planted on his second missionary journey (cf. Acts 17:1-9), Paul discussed the circumstances and challenges of his gospel preaching. His proclamation occurred not only in word but in

---

[15]For a classic treatment of the subject, see Michael Green, *Evangelism in the Early Church* (Grand Rapids: Eerdmans, 1970); see also F. F. Bruce, *The Spreading Flame* (1958; reprint, Grand Rapids: Eerdmans, 1964).
[16]See esp. Köstenberger and O'Brien, *Salvation to the Ends of the Earth*, pp. 161-201; Peter T. O'Brien, *Gospel and Mission in the Writings of Paul: An Exegetical and Theological Analysis* (Grand Rapids: Baker, 1995); and *The Gospel to the Nations: Perspectives on Paul's Mission*, ed. Peter Bolt and Mark Thompson (Downers Grove, Ill.: InterVarsity Press, 2000).
[17]See Köstenberger and O'Brien, *Salvation to the Ends of the Earth*, pp. 161-72.
[18]On the phrase "truth of the gospel" in Galatians, see esp. Moisés Silva, in *The Gospel to the Nations*, pp. 51-61. On the background to Paul's use of *euangelion*, see O'Brien, *Gospel and Mission*, pp. 77-81.

demonstration of God's power, which enabled him to overcome intense opposition (1 Thess 1:5; 2:2). Paul's gospel preaching was also accompanied by acts of love, a caring attitude, sacrifice, and godly example (1 Thess 2:8-9). In his second letter, Paul makes the important point that the gospel is not merely to be considered, or entertained as a suggestion, but to be "obeyed" (2 Thess 1:8; cf. Rom 1:5; 10:16; 1 Pet 4:17).

In Paul's first epistle to the Corinthians, another church he had planted (1 Cor 4:15; cf. Acts 18:4-11), he emphatically states that the gospel does not reflect human wisdom but divine power owing to the cross of Christ (1 Cor 1:17). In a defense of his gospel ministry, Paul contends that he chose to forego his right to financial support and that he was committed to do whatever it takes to preach the gospel to all and to share in its blessings (1 Cor 9:1-23, esp. vv. 14-23; cf. 2 Cor 11:7). The epistle also contains a succinct summary of the gospel Paul proclaimed as he had received it: "that Christ died for our sins according to the Scriptures, that he was buried, that he was raised on the third day according to the Scriptures" (1 Cor 15:3-4). The bodily resurrection of Christ is an indispensable part of the gospel, for if Christ has not been raised, believers' faith is worthless; they are still in their sins (1 Cor 15:17).

In his second epistle to the Corinthians, Paul notes that "even if our gospel is veiled, it is veiled to those who are perishing. The god of this age has blinded the minds of unbelievers, so that they cannot see the light of the gospel of the glory of Christ" (2 Cor 4:3-4). In fact, Paul laments that "if someone comes to you and preaches a Jesus other than the Jesus we preached, or if you receive a different spirit from the one you received, or a different gospel from the one you accepted, you put up with it easily enough" (2 Cor 11:4; cf. Gal 1:6-7). Yet there is no gospel other than the one preached by Paul.

The most remarkable and extensive presentation of Paul's gospel is found in Romans, which is dominated by the topic from beginning to end. In the opening verse, Paul states that the gospel is *central to his own apostolic calling and mission*; he was set apart for "the gospel of God" (Rom 1:1; cf. 15:16, a literary *inclusio*). The phrase "gospel of God" focuses on God's initiative in providing salvation in and through Jesus Christ.[19] Paul also notes that the gospel is not a novel proposal but a message proclaimed already to God's people Israel in the Hebrew Scriptures, referring to "the gospel which God promised long ago through his prophets in the

---

[19]The expression "of God" in the phrase "the gospel of God" is a subjective genitive, indicating that God is the source and authority of the good news of salvation in Christ (a genitive of source; see Köstenberger and O'Brien, *Salvation to the Ends of the Earth*, p. 175). God has acted to bring about his salvific purposes in human history.

holy Scriptures." The *content* of this gospel is concerning God's Son, Jesus Christ our Lord, a descendant of David in his humanity but the powerful Son of God by the resurrection from the dead (Rom 1:2-4; cf. 2 Tim 2:8). This statement balances the twin truths of Jesus' humanity and deity.

Paul is not ashamed of the gospel, because it is the power of God for the salvation of everyone who believes (Rom 1:16). The notion of the gospel being powerful and effective is rooted in the Old Testament conception of "the word of the LORD" as a powerful, effective, and dynamic force (e.g., Gen 1:3, 6; Ps 147:15; Is 40:8; 55:10-11; Jer 23:29). The power of God, which manifests itself in his decisive salvific intervention in and through the death and resurrection of Jesus Christ results in the salvation of all those who believe, in keeping with the teaching of the Hebrew Scriptures in both the Law and the Prophets (cf. Rom. 1:2; 4:3).[20]

The prophet Paul specifically cites in his preface to the book of Romans Habakkuk, who wrote, "The righteous will live by faith" (Rom 1:17, citing Hab 2:4). Paul's gloss on the meaning of this verse is given immediately prior to the quote from the book of Habakkuk: "God's righteousness is revealed from faithfulness to faith" (*ek pisteōs eis pistin*).[21] In the Hebrew, the verse reads, "The righteous will live by *his* faith," whereby the suffix "his" is ambiguous and could refer either to God's faithfulness or to the person's faith. Paul, in his interpretation of the passage in Habakkuk, avers that both are in fact true: God's righteousness is revealed "from faithfulness to faith," that is, the gospel is rooted in God's covenant-keeping faithfulness and constitutes an offer of salvation to all those who believe.

As Paul elaborates later in the epistle, "But now a righteousness from God, apart from law, has been made known, to which the Law and the Prophets testify. This righteousness from God comes through the faithfulness of Jesus Christ [TNIV note] to all who believe. There is no difference, for all have sinned and fall short of the glory of God, and are justified freely by his grace through the redemption that came by Christ Jesus. God presented him as a sacrifice of atonement, through faith in his blood. He did this to demonstrate his justice . . . so as to be just and the one who justifies those who have faith in Jesus" (Rom 3:21-26).[22]

How can God be righteous *and* declare righteous—acquit the guilty!—those who have sinned? Paul's answer: God is able to do so "by his grace through the redemption that came by Christ Jesus." Humans are saved, not by seeking to con-

---

[20]Ibid., p. 176, cite 2 Sam 7:12-16; Is 11; Jer 23:5-6; 33:14-18; Ezek 34:23-31; 37:24-28.
[21]For the rendering of *pistis* with "faithfulness," see all major translations of Rom 3:3. See also the TNIV and HCSB footnotes at Rom 3:22: "the faithfulness of Jesus Christ." On the interpretation of Rom 1:17, see esp. James D. G. Dunn, *Romans 1-8*, Word Biblical Commentary 38A (Dallas: Word, 1988), pp. 43-46, 48-49.
[22]Cf. Köstenberger and O'Brien, *Salvation to the Ends of the Earth*, pp. 178-79.

form to a set of external regulations—the law—but by reentering into right rela-tionship with God—being reconciled to God—through the atoning sacrifice of Jesus Christ (Rom 5:6-11). Not that the law is bad, but all human efforts to please God are ultimately rendered ineffective by the indwelling sin nature (Rom 7:14-25); hence, "Those controlled by the sinful nature cannot please God" (Rom 8:8).

But the primary purpose of Paul's Roman epistle is not the justification of man (as the Reformers thought, in a vast improvement over Roman Catholicism), but the justification of God—that is, the demonstration of God's righteousness and faithfulness and the vindication of his salvation-historical purposes toward hu-manity, both Israel and the Gentiles. As Paul writes, "It is not as though God's word had failed" merely because the Jewish nation rejected Jesus their Messiah (Rom 9:6). God was not unjust as some alleged; there is no injustice with God (Rom 9:14). The problem was rather the Jewish disregard for the righteousness from God and their substitution of their own righteousness and failure to submit to God's righteousness (Rom 10:4). In God's sovereign purposes, he has impris-oned all in disobedience, so that he may have mercy on all (Rom 11:32).[23] This includes "the large-scale conversion of Jewish people at the end of this age" (the "all Israel" in Rom 11:26).[24] At the end of his letter to the Romans, Paul even calls the preaching of the gospel of God (cf. Rom 1:1) his "priestly duty" (Rom 15:16).

In the "prison epistles" Paul continues to uphold the centrality of the gospel and the preeminence of Christ. In the theme verse of Ephesians, he identifies God's overarching purpose as being "to bring all things in heaven and on earth together under one head, even Christ" (Eph 1:10). In Colossians, Paul affirms that "in Christ all the fullness of the Deity lives in bodily form" (Col 2:9; cf. Col 1:19) and that Christ is "the image of the invisible God" and "the head of the body, the church," in order that he might have supremacy in everything (Col 1:15-18). Paul emphatically states that "God was pleased to have all his fullness dwell *in him*, and *through him* to reconcile to himself all things . . . by making peace through his blood, shed on the cross" (Col 1:19-20). Paul's affirmation of Christ's preemi-nence came in the context of a decisive refutation of the Colossian heresy which insisted on ascetic practices and the worship of angels (Col 2:18). In Philippians, Paul says that for him "to live is Christ" (Phil 1:21) and to die means to "be with Christ" (Phil 1:23). His sole desire is for the Philippians to live their lives "in a manner worthy of the gospel of Christ" (Phil 1:27). Thus the gospel is not just a message to be proclaimed, but also a lifestyle to be lived.

---

[23]On Paul as the apostle to the Gentiles and Israel in God's plan, see ibid., pp. 185-91.

[24]Ibid., p. 190, citing Douglas J. Moo, *The Epistle to the Romans*. New International Commentary on the New Testament (Grand Rapids: Eerdmans, 1996), p. 774.

In his first letter to Timothy, Paul calls the gospel "the glorious gospel of the blessed God, which he entrusted to me" (1 Tim 1:11). The gospel is glorious; it is a gift of God; and it is a precious stewardship entrusted to the apostle and believers (cf. 1 Thess 2:4). In 2 Timothy, Paul calls his foremost disciple to join him in suffering for the gospel by the power of God (cf. 1 Thess 3:2). The grace of God was given before the beginning of time (cf. 2 Thess 2:13) but has now been revealed through the coming of our Savior, Jesus Christ, who has destroyed death and brought life and immortality to light through the gospel (2 Tim 1:8-10). The gospel is thus a matter of life and death—it is the message of Jesus' victory over death through the resurrection (cf. 2 Tim 2:8); the message of believers' salvation from death through Christ; and the message of life or death depending on one's acceptance or rejection of God's offer of salvation in Christ. Consequently, both Timothy and Titus are charged to "guard the good deposit," that is, the pure and unadulterated gospel message, over against the false teachers who are Satan's instruments trying to lead believers astray (e.g., 2 Tim 2:14). In 2 Corinthians 8:18, Titus is commended by Paul for his "service to the gospel."

Throughout his ministry and in all his writings, Paul held to the centrality of the gospel and to the preeminence of Christ as God's exclusive means of salvation.[25] God's provision is not for some esoteric group claiming secret knowledge or for the Jews only; it is for all those, Jew as well as non-Jew, who confess faith in Jesus Christ (Rom 10:17). Perhaps most memorably, Paul states this in Galatians, where he makes clear that all those who have faith are Abraham's true sons (Gal 3:7). By his faith and obedience, Abraham became the father of all believers, and those who inherit God's promise to Abraham are all who believe in Abraham's descendant, the Lord Jesus Christ (Gal 3:6-29; cf. Gen 12:3; 15:6). What is more, one day, at Christ's second coming, faith will turn to sight, and people will be held accountable for the way they spent their lives (2 Cor 5:7-8). Hence the hope and expectation of Jesus' return—and no one else's—are shown to be part and parcel of the gospel message. This further adds to the Christocentrism in which salvation is conceived in Scripture.

THE GOSPEL IN THE GENERAL EPISTLES AND REVELATION

The book of Hebrews stresses at the very outset the definitive nature of God's revelation in his Son (Heb 1:2). This rules out claims by others—be it Mohammad, Joseph Smith, or similar latter-day prophets—that God has appointed them to

---

[25]Cf. Robert L. Plummer, *Paul's Understanding of the Church's Mission: Did the Apostle Paul Expect the Early Christian Communities to Evangelize?* Biblical Monograph Series (Carlisle, U.K.: Paternoster, 2006).

supplant his revelation in and through Jesus Christ. Interestingly, the author of Hebrews notes that the Israelites in the wilderness also "had the gospel preached" to them, yet it "was of no value to them, because those who heard did not combine it with faith" (Heb 2:4; cf. Heb 2:6). Not only is God's revelation in Christ supreme, Christ, as the perfect, eternal high priest, has also brought the perfect, once-for-all sacrifice (Heb 9:1-18). According to the writer of Hebrews, the blood of Jesus has opened up for us a "new and living way" to God, so that now we can "draw near to God with a sincere heart in full assurance of faith" (Heb 10:19-22). Jesus is "the author and perfecter of our faith," who endured the cross and sat down at God's right hand (Heb 12:2).

Peter affirms the eternal and abiding nature of the gospel message (1 Pet 1:25, citing Is 40:6-8; cf. Is 40:12). He stresses the need for righteous suffering in keeping with Christ's example in light of the prospect of the second coming (1 Pet 1:6-7, etc.), the reality of which was denied by some (2 Pet 3:1-13). Rejection of the gospel message will result in certain judgment (1 Pet 4:17). John affirms that "Jesus Christ, the Righteous One" is "the atoning sacrifice for our sins, and not only for ours but also for the sins of the whole world" (1 Jn 2:2-2), over against those who deny human sinfulness, the need for substitutionary atonement, and even that Jesus came as a true human being. Jude exhorts his readers to "contend for the faith that was once for all entrusted to the saints" (Jude 3), since there were some who turned "the grace of our God into a license for immorality and deny Jesus Christ our only Sovereign and Lord" (Jude 4).

The book of Revelation, finally, culminates in the depiction of the returning Christ and exhorts the faithful to fearlessly confess his name in the face of intense persecution. Jesus is that Lamb of God and Lion of Judah who holds the key to the future and is able to break the seals of the scroll (Rev 5). One of John's visions features an angel flying in mid-air, who had "the eternal gospel to proclaim to those who live on the earth—to every nation, tribe, language and people" (Rev 14:6). The angel exhorts his listeners, "Fear God and give him glory, because the hour of his judgment has come. Worship him who made the heavens, the earth, the sea and the springs of water" (Rev 14:7). Two reasons for worship of God are cited here: the imminence of his judgment, and the fact that he is the Creator of heaven and earth. Jesus is also God's sole authorized agent of judgment and ruler of the millennial kingdom (Rev 20). For this reason believers ought to pray with the seer, "Amen. Come, Lord Jesus" (Rev 22:20).

As Revelation makes clear, God is the Creator of all, and Jesus is the Savior of all who respond to his offer of salvation in faith. The truth of the gospel does not depend on human assent; the gospel is eternal. People's eternal destiny is not up to human negotiation, nor is God open to alternative suggestions regarding the way of salvation. He has chosen to provide one, and only one, way of salvation, by grace and through faith in the Lord Jesus Christ, with eternal bliss in heaven or eternal punishment in hell as the results of people's acceptance or rejection of God's provision.[26] God's salvation must be appropriated on God's terms and in God's way.

THE GOSPEL IN BIBLICAL THEOLOGY

The gospel of Jesus Christ is one of the most central themes in all of Scripture.[27] The term "to declare the good news" is already found in the Old Testament (e.g., Is 40:9; 52:7 cited in Rom 10:15; Is 61:1 cited in Mt 11:5; Lk 4:18), and the author of Hebrews states the Israelites in the wilderness "had the gospel preached" to them (Heb 2:4, 6). Jesus started out his ministry by calling people to repentance and faith in the "good news" (Mk 1:15, pars.). Paul discovered in the gospel the power for salvation of all who accept it by faith, Jews as well as Greeks (Rom 1:16; 2:9-10; 10:12; 1 Cor 1:22, 24; Gal 3:28; Col 3:11; cf. Lk 2:32; Acts 13:46-48; 28:25-28).

Not only did the gospel indicate that the historical Jesus was to be identified with the resurrected, exalted Lord and Christ who had been predicted in the Old Testament, it was also a message of forgiveness for sins on account of the substitutionary death of Christ at the cross. As Paul and his apostolic colleagues read the Hebrew Scriptures in light of Jesus as the Christ (cf. Acts 17:2-3; Rom 1:2, 17; 1 Cor 15:3-5), they realized that already there the Messiah is cast as a suffering and resurrected Messiah, whose plight is to take the place of others (e.g., Is 53). The gospel of the first Christians, which in turn is rooted in Jesus' messianic consciousness, thus has as its content the crucified and risen Messiah and Lord—in conscious application of Old Testament passages to the person and work of Jesus.

This conviction repeatedly surfaces in all four Gospels (e.g., Mk 8:31; 9:31; 10:33-34, 45, pars.), in Paul (e.g., Rom 3:25; 2 Cor 5:21), as well as in Peter (1 Pet 1:2, 10-12, 18-20), in Hebrews (Heb 1:3, etc.) and in the other New Testament writings (e.g., 1 Jn 2:2; Rev 5:5-6). Finally, in the book of Acts, the gospel is frequently personified, so that it is not Paul and the first Christians who pursue their mission but the gospel itself that marches irresistibly and victoriously to the ends of the earth (cf. Acts 6:7; 12:24; 19:20).

THE GOSPEL AND MISSIONS

The good news of a coming Savior pervades the Old Testament, and the New Tes-

---

[26]On hell, see especially Christopher W. Morgan and Robert A. Peterson, eds., *Hell Under Fire: Modern Scholarship Reinvents Eternal Punishment* (Grand Rapids: Zondervan, 2004).

[27]The following summary is partially taken from Köstenberger, "Diversity and Unity in the New Testament," pp. 156-57.

tament is all about proclaiming the good news that in Jesus Christ this Savior has now come.[28] Shortly after the Fall, we see the first glimmer of a gospel in Gen 3:15. God, in his faithfulness to his creation, enters into covenants with Noah (Gen 9:9-13) and Abraham (Gen 12:1-3; cf. Gen 15:1-8; 17:1-27). Significantly, God's plan for and through Abraham extends not merely to his physical descendants Israel but ultimately to all who are his children through faith (Gal 3:6-9, 26-29; Rom 4:16-17). This Abrahamic covenant, then, provides the framework for God's dealings with humanity for the rest of biblical history, culminating in the new covenant established by Abraham's "seed," Jesus Christ (Gal 3:16).

In a crucial further development, David is assured by God that his kingdom will be established forever (2 Sam 7:13). The establishment of the Davidic kingship is critical for an understanding of Yahweh's rule over the nations and the fulfillment of his covenant promises to Abraham. In yet another crucial development, Isaiah speaks of the Servant of Yahweh, whose ministry pertains to both Israel and the nations (Is 42:1-4; 49:1-6; 50:4-9; 52:13—53:12; cf. 61:1-3). The Servant's death will be followed by his resurrection and exaltation by Yahweh (Is 52:13—53:12), and he will bring many into a right relationship with God (Is 53:11). Neither the Second Temple period nor first-century Judaism evidence a missionary thrust to the surrounding nations.[29] It is not until the period subsequent to Jesus' ascension that the church engages in intentional outreach beyond the confines of ethnic Israel.

All four Evangelists make clear that Jesus' mission is first and foremost to Israel (e.g., Mt 10:5-6; 15:24). Though Jesus does minister to individual Gentiles at their initiative, he does not embark on a Gentile mission, more broadly conceived. At the same time, Jesus clearly envisions a mission to the Gentiles subsequent to his cross-death and exaltation (e.g., Jn 10:16; 12:32). What is more, the risen Jesus commands his followers to go and disciple the nations (Mt 28:16-20). As the book of Acts and the New Testament epistles make clear, the gospel embarked on an irresistible victory march throughout the Greco-Roman empire to the ends of the earth (Acts 1:8); neither internal problems nor external persecution could stop its advance.

What do we learn from this brief survey of the gospel in biblical history in relation to our present topic? Some of the major lessons are:

---

[28]For a monograph-length treatment of the mission motif in Scripture, see Köstenberger and O'Brien, *Salvation to the Ends of the Earth*.

[29]See especially Scot McKnight, *A Light Among the Gentiles: Jewish Missionary Activity in the Second Temple Period* (Minneapolis: Fortress, 1991). See also Martin Goodman, *Mission and Conversion: Proselytizing in the Religious History of the Roman Empire* (Oxford: Clarendon, 1994); and chapter 3 in Köstenberger and O'Brien, *Salvation to the Ends of the Earth*.

1. The gospel is part of the very fabric of biblical revelation, reaching back all the way to the beginnings of humanity, encompassing God's promises to Noah, Abraham, and David, and fulfilling prophetic predictions regarding the Servant of Yahweh who was to come for Jews and Gentiles alike. As Luke makes clear, Jesus accomplished the role of Yahweh's Servant (Lk 2:32; 4:18-19; cf. Is 42:6; 49:6-9; 61:1-2). Yet the story does not end there. Paul and Barnabas continue the ministry of Servant, for they are now the "light for the Gentiles" (Acts 13:47, citing Is 49:6), and while proclamation still begins with the Jews (Acts 3:26; 13:46; 18:5; 28:25-28), no distinction is now made between them and Gentiles as far as salvation and inclusion into God's people is concerned: faith in Jesus as Lord is all that is required (e.g., Acts 4:12; 16:31).

2. The God of Noah, Abraham and David, the God of the messianic promise and of the biblical covenants, is also the God of the gospel of the Lord Jesus Christ. No wedge must be driven between God on the one hand and Jesus Christ on the other. God has no other plan than to save through Jesus Christ, and he has given humanity no other way to re-enter into fellowship with God than through repentance and faith in Jesus Christ. There is nothing in Scripture about "anonymous Christians," enlightened pagans, morally upright people being saved on the basis of good works, Jews being saved on the basis of their adherence to the Mosaic law in the interim between Christ's first and second coming, the ultimate salvation of all people on the basis of God's love and mercy, or other alternative paths of salvation. Scripture clearly points to Jesus Christ as the exclusive center of God's saving purposes.

3. The New Testament church is obliged to obey her Lord's "Great Commission" of going and discipling the nations. If there were other avenues of salvation, this would weaken Christ's missionary mandate, if not make it redundant. If people can be saved apart from faith in Christ, it could be argued that it would be better if the church were not to proclaim the Christian gospel, because such proclamation renders people guilty for rejecting the gospel while if the gospel had never been preached in the first place, people would have been free to respond to whatever "light" they might have been given. But Scripture does not mitigate Christ's call to the church to evangelize in this way, nor did the early church, occasional setbacks notwithstanding, doubt the urgency and compelling necessity of this call. To paraphrase Paul's words in 1 Corinthians 15:12-19, if there are other ways of salvation, why still preach the gospel? But as Paul wrote, he did all things for the sake of the gospel, and became all things to all people so as to by all means save as many as possible (1 Cor 9:22-23). For this reason Paul was "compelled to preach" and wrote: "Woe to me if I do not preach the gospel" (1 Cor 9:16). The church today must do no less.

THE GOSPEL, MISSIONS, AND INCLUSIVISM

Daniel Strange, in his important monograph *The Possibility of Salvation Among the Unevangelised*, defines the "unevangelized" as "any person in history who has lived and died without hearing and understanding the gospel of Jesus Christ from a human messenger."[30] As Strange notes, this would seem to include at least four groups of people: (1) children who died in infancy and those mentally unable to respond to the gospel; (2) those who lived prior to the time of Christ and thus before the formulation known as "the gospel"; (3) those who have been presented with a less-than-adequate version of the gospel; and (4) those who have not received a presentation of the gospel, such as because they lived in a geographically remote area.[31]

It is not the purpose of the present chapter to deal with the first question (although important), which is not directly addressed in Scripture. Regarding individuals in the other three categories, we may draw the following conclusions from our study of the gospel in the Old Testament, the Gospels, the book of Acts, Paul, and the rest of the New Testament.

1. The gospel is God's saving message to a world living in darkness and a humanity lost in its sin. The gospel is not a human message, nor was its conception a function of human initiative, but its origin and its impetus derive solely from God. For this reason our role with regard to the gospel is not that of evaluation, criticism or reformulation, but that of grateful acceptance and obedience. As humans we are not equal partners with God as far as the gospel message is concerned; we are rather his commissioned representatives, charged with proclaiming the gospel in the exact form in which we received it (e.g., Jn 17:20; 20:21; 1 Cor 15:3-4).

2. Acceptance of the gospel is not optional for salvation but rather required, owing to pervasive human sinfulness. As the book of Hebrews states, "people are destined to die once, and after that to face judgment. . . . Christ was sacrificed once to take away the sins of many; and he will appear a second time . . . to bring salvation *to those who are waiting for him*" (Heb 9:27-28). Apart from believing in Jesus Christ, "God's wrath remains" on people (Jn 3:36), and they are spiritually dead (Jn 5:24; Eph 2:1). People must be "born of God" (Jn 1:12; 3:3, 5; 1 Jn 3:9; 4:7; 5:1, 4, 18), that is, be spiritually regenerated (Tit 3:5; 1 Pet 1:3). As Paul

---

[30]Daniel Strange, *The Possibility of Salvation Among the Unevangelised: An Analysis of Inclusivism in Recent Evangelical Theology* (Carlisle, U.K.: Paternoster, 2002), p. 35. For another recent treatment of this issue, see chapter 2, "Restrictivism and Inclusivism: 'Is This Missions Trip Really Necessary?'" in David J. Hesselgrave, *Paradigms in Conflict: 10 Key Questions in Christian Missions Today* (Grand Rapids: Kregel, 2005), pp. 53-80.

[31]Ibid., pp. 33-34.

writes in his epistle to the Ephesians, "[a]nd you also were *included in Christ when you heard the word of truth, the gospel of your salvation. Having believed,* you were marked in him with a seal, the promised Holy Spirit" (Eph 1:13). Inclusion in Christ comes only by hearing and believing the gospel.

3. The gospel is not vaguely theological, as if it were amenable to various ways of salvation depending on a person's belief in a particular kind of god, or depending on the degree to which people were able to hear the gospel presented in a clear way; it is decidedly and concretely Christological, that is, centered on the salvation provided through the vicarious cross-death of the Lord Jesus Christ.[32] Hence Paul is able to speak of "the gospel . . . regarding his [God's] Son . . . Jesus Christ our Lord" (Rom 1:2-4). Significantly, this gospel is not a New Testament novelty but was "promised beforehand through his [God's] prophets [such as Habakkuk, Rom 1:17 citing Hab 2:4] in the Holy Scriptures" (Rom 1:2). Abraham already had resurrection faith (Rom 4; Gal 3; Heb 11:8-12).

4. The messianic motif pervading all of Scripture and centering in the Lord Jesus Christ coupled with the risen Jesus' "Great Commission" for his followers to go and disciple the nations inextricably link an understanding of the gospel as the exclusive message of salvation in Jesus Christ with the church's mandate to engage in missionary outreach. This is clear especially from the gospels of Matthew, Luke, John, the book of Acts and several of Paul's writings. Conversely, any messages proclaimed in the name of Christ that feature a "different gospel" or a different Christ (such as compromising his simultaneous full humanity and deity, e.g., 1 Jn 4:2-3) are rejected.[33] The church must engage in missions, because "faith comes from hearing the message, and the message is heard through the word of Christ" (Rom 10:17). If anyone confesses with his mouth, "Jesus is Lord," and believes in his heart that God raised him from the dead, he will be saved (Rom 10:9; see also Rom 10:10-13).

5. In light of the clear biblical passages examined above, and in light of the strong and pervasive trajectory of references to the gospel throughout Scripture, there seems no proper biblical foundation on which to argue for the salvation of anyone on a basis other than explicit faith in Jesus Christ. Scripture makes clear that humanity is universally sinful, and that God's wrath remains on every individual who has not placed his or her trust in Jesus Christ on the basis of his substitutionary death on the cross and his subsequent resurrection. While there may be philosophical or larger theological objections to such a notion (such as the dif-

---

[32]Cf. Geivett and Phillips, "Particularist View," p. 241, with reference to the depiction of Jesus as the Word in John's prologue.

[33]See Köstenberger and O'Brien, *Salvation to the Ends of the Earth,* pp. 227-32.

ficulty experienced by some of reconciling this notion with the love of God), and while there may be commonsense concerns on the basis of human conceptions of "fairness" or other similar considerations, there can be little doubt that Scripture nowhere teaches, or easily allows the implication, that there is a way to salvation other than through explicit faith in Jesus Christ during a person's lifetime (e.g., Heb 9:27-28). In fact, this is not an obscure topic; it is the central contention of the biblical message concerning the gospel, that "Salvation is found in no one else, for there is no other name under heaven given to people by which we must be saved" (Acts 4:12).

10

God's Zeal for His World

J. NELSON JENNINGS

GOD HAS FULLY COMMITTED HIMSELF to re-create his good but sin-infected world. By coming into the world as the unique God-Man, Jesus of Nazareth, God kept his early promise to send a redeeming seed of Eve (Gen 3:15).[1] This human being who was crucified and raised from the dead now reigns in the heavens, and one day he will come back to earth to complete his redemptive mission. Upon Jesus' return, the entire world finally and clearly will see the glorious new heaven and earth, toward which God beckoned the apostle John and all of creation to gaze and wonder: "Behold, I am making all things new" (Rev 21:5).

Throughout the historical outworking of his redemption of the world through Jesus Christ, God's zeal clearly has been the driving force. While he was creating the world, God joyfully expressed his pleasure at the goodness of what he had made. However, when Satan led Adam and Eve into disobedience, God displayed his zealous wrath in pronouncing his promised curses against the garden tempter, the human race, and the rest of creation. Later in Noah's day, being "sorry that he had made man on the earth, and it grieved him to his heart" (Gen 6:6), God in his angry judgment destroyed his world that had spiraled downward into full rebellion. Yet God's passionate grace and mercy has always shone through these and other instances of his just punishment of wrong and wrongdoers. He saved Noah and his family (and thus their descendants) from the raging flood waters. Centuries later through the prophet Isaiah, God foretold a coming "child" and "son" who would be called "Wonderful Counselor, Mighty God, Everlasting Father, Prince of Peace." How could people be assured God would in fact send such an everlasting and righteous ruler? "The zeal of the LORD of hosts will do this" was the re-

---

[1]Scripture quotations in this essay are from the ESV.

vealed guarantee (Is 9:6-7). God's zealous wrath and grace ultimately were displayed in Jesus' sacrificial atonement on the cross and will be magnified in his future reappearance. From beginning to end, then, it has been God's zeal that accomplishes his mission of judging and saving the world.

The central questions taken up by this book, namely those of who will be saved and through what type of faith, obviously are matters of crucial concern. But as indicated by the book's title—*Faith Comes by Hearing*—such questions need to be seen within the larger and more primary framework of God's mission of saving his world through the multinational gospel of Jesus Christ. God's passion is to re-create his world. Such divine zeal fuels his redemption of the world in Christ, a redemption that is described and revealed to us in the Bible and is still being played out in the world today. God's zealous mission for his world is the central burden of the Scriptures. The recently articulated issue that this book has discussed in terms of "exclusivism" and "inclusivism" (terms which, as we shall explain, can easily become misnomers above and beyond their aforementioned nuances) is a subplot within the larger drama of the world's redemption in Jesus.

This chapter will focus on various aspects of God's zealous mission, all the while locating the smaller discussion of exclusivism versus inclusivism within that larger picture. I hope thereby to shed fresh light on why the book's commitment to an exclusivist position makes good biblical, missiological and pastoral sense.

GOD'S ZEAL

God's commitment to his world is relentless, wholehearted, and passionate. He has always cared deeply about the world he made. He has thus been deeply hurt by his creatures' sin and rebellion. Even so, our brokenhearted God has acted out of the depths of his loving heart to save people and the sin-cursed created order over which we human beings have stewardship responsibilities. In other words, instead of being some detached concept simply to be acknowledged, the God of the Bible is this rebellious world's personal and gracious ruler who has a zealous commitment to be trusted, and who wants to richly bless his obedient creatures.

It is therefore not an irrelevant, erudite analysis to say that the Bible's main storyline is that of creation-fall-redemption-consummation. God's passion and zeal shine brightly through these four main acts of the biblical drama. We see his delight in the world he made; his righteous anger in pronouncing curses after Adam and Eve's Fall into sin; his long-suffering, compassionate grace in sending his Son to die a sacrificial death and then rise in triumph; finally, his glorious display of splendor and majesty in the new heaven and earth. We know that God is personal and passionate through Scripture's record and revelation of his overarching interactions with his world.

God's redemption of the world is by far the longest act of the biblical drama. At the same time, the other acts are necessary for redemption to make sense or even to occur at all: God saves his created world from sin and to final glorification. Moreover, God's creation, the world's Fall, and the future consummation all affect the nature of redemption. To adjust our theatrical imagery, creation, Fall and consummation together form the backdrop for God's center-stage work of saving the world through Christ.

Ontological salvation. Of special importance for the discussion of exclusivism and inclusivism is God's commitment to redeem the world in actual history, or *ontologically,* through Jesus of Nazareth. Right after the Fall, God declares to the serpent in Genesis 3:15 that he "will put enmity between you and the woman, and between your offspring and her offspring; he shall bruise your head, and you shall bruise his heel." Notwithstanding some interpreters' claims of metaphorical or mythical language, traditionally evangelicals (and their predecessors) have taken this *protoevangelion* to refer to the actual atoning work of Jesus Christ on the cross. The unfolding Old Testament then amplified this foretelling of Jesus' person and work through the sacrificial system, the Davidic kings and messianic psalms, direct prophecies, and otherwise. The historical figure Jesus of Nazareth achieved salvation through a historical act for all those who are saved, namely whoever believes (actually in history, one wants to add for consistency's sake) in him.

The apostle Paul picked up on the imagery of the *protoevangelion* of Genesis 3:15 in Romans 16:20: "The God of peace will soon crush Satan under your feet. The grace of our Lord Jesus Christ be with you." The second half of the verse is important for linking those who share in Christ's victory over Satan—i.e., those who experience salvation—with those who receive God's grace in Jesus Christ. While such a link by itself does not prove an exclusivist notion of salvation, Paul's conscious addressing of his letter to those in Rome who exhibited "the obedience of faith for the sake of his name among all the nations, including you who are called to belong to Jesus Christ" (Rom 1:5-6) indicates an understanding of those who consciously believed in Jesus Christ and not others, an understanding that leans toward an exclusivist view. Paul's letter to the Romans was written to believers in Jesus who are among those who love God and are called according to his purpose—those who are foreknown, predestined, called, justified and glorified (Rom 8:28-30).

Paul thus linked what was happening in his own day—particularly the movement of Gentiles, "the nations," to faith in Jesus Christ—to the macro-historical

gospel of God, which he promised beforehand through his prophets in the holy Scriptures, concerning his Son, who was descended from David according to the flesh and was declared to be the Son of God in power according to the Spirit of holiness by his resurrection from the dead, Jesus Christ our Lord. (Rom 1:1-4)

Accordingly, Paul aspired "to preach the gospel, not where Christ has already been named, lest I build on someone else's foundation, but as it is written, 'Those who have never been told of him will see, and those who have never heard will understand'" (Rom 15:20-21). Paul's citation here of Isaiah 52:15 clearly was not an argument for people somehow seeing and understanding God's grace without having heard of the gospel of Jesus Christ. Rather, the reference to Isaiah 52—53 refers to the extension of God's mercy to "many nations" (Is 52:15a) through the person and work of the Suffering Servant (of whom in previous eras those nations had not been told or heard), the one so movingly set forth in Isaiah 52:13—53:12.

Epistemological reception. Paul's ambition was to preach the gospel to the end of the earth, even to the western extremity of his known world, namely Spain. Paul had this ambition because he knew from the Scriptures God's commitment to save the world not only ontologically through Jesus the Son of David but also *epistemologically* with regard to people's reception of God's gracious redemption. The nations, all people, needed to hear and believe the good news of what God had done in Jesus. Isaiah 52:15 would thus be fulfilled as people came to see and understand God's love and mercy in the gospel.

Along with Isaiah foretelling how all nations would come to hear and believe in God's salvation, the Torah records how God chose Abraham and his children to be the unique channel of blessing to the entire world. Paul notes that Abraham himself was the model of salvation by faith for all people:

Abraham "believed God, and it was counted to him as righteousness." Know then that it is those of faith who are the sons of Abraham. And the Scripture, foreseeing that God would justify the Gentiles by faith, preached the gospel beforehand to Abraham, saying "In you shall all the nations be blessed." So then, those who are of faith are blessed along with Abraham, the man of faith. (Gal 3:6-9)

That is, Abraham believed God's specific word, in which he promised that Abraham's descendants would outnumber the stars (Gen 15:1-6). Moreover, besides Abraham being the model of faith, his descendants would produce the world's Savior, Jesus the Christ (Gal 3:16). Thus "in Christ Jesus the blessing of Abraham [has] come to the Gentiles, so that we might receive the promised Spirit through faith" (Gal 3:14).

Responsible declaration. Paul also understood that he, along with the entire Christian church, was heir to Old Covenant Israel's role of communication channel to the nations regarding who God is, how he has acted mightily on Israel's behalf, and how all peoples are responsible to him. It would not have been lost on

Paul how God had explained to Abraham that the delay in giving the land of Canaan to his descendants was the need to deal further with (and eventually judge) the current inhabitants (Gen 15:16). This incident was indication of God's ongoing dealings with all peoples of the earth, regardless of their contact with Israel.

At the same time, Paul knew that Pharaoh and the Egyptians were especially held accountable for hardening their hearts against the explicit and special encounter they had with God while Israel was among them. After all, one of God's central purposes in delivering Israel from Egypt was that Pharaoh and the Egyptians would "know that I am the LORD" (Ex 14:18). That particular accountability did not mean that Pharaoh and the Egyptians would not have been held accountable otherwise: God's eventual judgment on the Canaanites for their long-time sin demonstrated how he holds all people fully accountable for their response to him as their Creator-King. Rather, God's special demonstration of his power and patience through Moses and Israel to Pharaoh and the Egyptians points to how, as the Sri Lankan theologian Vinoth Ramachandra has succinctly put it, "While Yahweh works in all nations, in no nation other than Israel did he act *for the sake of* all nations."[2] Israel's sociopolitical life was to serve as a testimony to the surrounding nations, and the coming of Israel's Messiah as the Savior of the world was Old Covenant Israel's greatest and most particular contribution to God's mission to redeem his people from among all nations.

Paul, therefore, was also well schooled in Israel's ongoing responsibility for God's, not to mention its own, reputation among surrounding nations (Deut 29:24-28; Jer 22:8). God had made Israel to be "a light to the nations, that my salvation may reach to the end of the earth" (Is 49:6). God's calling of Jonah to Nineveh was thus in perfect keeping with his passion to be merciful to people throughout the earth—people he created and with whom he had continually dealt as their Creator and King—by using his people to bring the particular message of his love and grace.

Of course, God's redemptive work climaxed in Jesus. Paul announced to a small slice of the nations in Athens, "The times of ignorance God overlooked, but now he commands all people everywhere to repent, because he has fixed a day on which he will judge the world in righteousness by a man whom he has appointed; and of this he has given assurance to all by raising him from the dead" (Acts 17:30-31). All peoples had always been responsible to God their Creator-King; God through general revelation had been showing "his eternal power and divine nature" to peo-

---

[2]Vinoth Ramachandra, *The Recovery of Mission: Beyond the Pluralist Paradigm* (Grand Rapids: Eerdmans, 1996), p. 231, emphasis original.

ple throughout the earth (Rom 1:20). "*But now*" Jesus *ontologically* has lived, died, risen, ascended—and is set to return in judgment. "Now he commands all people everywhere to repent," i.e., *epistemologically* people must respond to God's *declaration* of the gospel through Paul and other followers of Jesus. In light of Jesus' culminating work, Paul's request to the Colossian Christians to pray for him and to be alert to "declare the mystery of Christ" and "answer each person" (Col 4:2-6) flowed out of the burden and calling on God's New Covenant people to inherit Old Covenant Israel's unique role to be communication channels of God's gospel-declaration to all people.

GOD'S COLABORERS

> If anyone is in Christ, he is a new creation. The old has passed away; behold, the new has come. All this is from God, who through Christ reconciled us to himself and gave us the ministry of reconciliation; that is, in Christ God was reconciling the world to himself, not counting their trespasses against them, and entrusting to us the message of reconciliation. Therefore, we are ambassadors for Christ, God making his appeal through us. We implore you on behalf of Christ, be reconciled to God. (2 Cor 5:17-20)

God in his zeal has decisively accomplished the world's redemption in Christ. People who come to faith in him are now part of the new order that will be fully manifest in the new heaven and new earth. God promised his redemption, God fulfilled his prediction in Jesus, and God now appeals to people everywhere to repent and trust in Jesus. God's mission to reclaim the world is *his* mission indeed; Christians' calling to be ambassadors for Christ—Christian missions—rests on God's plan, action and passionate appeal to his created people throughout the world.

Missions motivation and this book. As discussed earlier, one argument made against inclusivism is that it "cuts the nerve cord" of Christian missions and evangelism. Insofar as an exclusivist view of salvation—the view that, epistemologically speaking, people before they die must repent and believe in the good news about Jesus—includes God's commitment, starting with Abraham, to use his people as communication channels to the world's peoples, that argument against inclusivism carries significant weight. Since this chapter's discussion to this point leans strongly in the direction of God having made the commitment to use his people primarily, and perhaps even exclusively,[3] as his ambassadors, the exclusivist

---

[3]Angelic messengers, so often noted in testimonies in our day by Muslim converts to Christ, are a caveat in the claim that Christians are God's *exclusive* gospel messengers. For accounts and analyses of some of these testimonies, see J. Dudley Woodberry and Russell G. Shubin, "Muslims tell . . . 'Why I Chose Jesus'," in *Mission Frontiers*. March, 2001. Available online at http://www.missionfrontiers .org/2001/01/200101.htm.

bent of the presentation of the progressive unfolding of God's redemption in Christ and the communication of the news about that redemption should be felt.

There is, then, a legitimate push of the exclusivist argument that, more than by inclusivist beliefs that see additional means of obtaining salvation, the motivation and urgency for Christian missions and evangelism are strengthened by the conviction that people before they die must repent and believe in the gospel news about Jesus. At the same time, the Bible's overarching thrust in appealing for the need to communicate the gospel to all people comes more from God's zealous initiative to redeem his world than from people's need to hear and believe. In no sense do I want falsely to dichotomize or prioritize. Even so, as already summarized both Testaments focus on the big picture of God's passionate Christocentric salvation to a glorious future of the rebellious world he initially created as good. Christians' zeal for the gospel thus stems most fundamentally from God's zeal for his world. Part of God's zealous initiative is to enlist his people as gospel ambassadors, so because of divine zeal we who are Jesus' followers share that same zeal for the gospel to be spread to all the world's people.

Ironically, inclusivists can draw equal encouragement for their position from the Bible's macro emphasis on God's redemption of the world in Christ (at least from an incomplete description of that emphasis, as we will see). For example, Terrance Tiessen, aforementioned spokesman for the inclusivist view of salvation he terms "accessibilism," could effectively add this chapter's emphasis on God's zeal to his argument for missions motivation. He explains that Christians "engage zealously in evangelism out of obedience to the example and request of our Lord and out of our love for Christ and for our neighbor. Above all, we do Christian mission for the glory of God whose name will be magnified by those who come to know him as Father."[4] I believe (and no doubt so does Tiessen) that having the wellspring of Christian mission rest in God's passionate heart, a zeal that Christians share through the power of the indwelling Holy Spirit, is what sustains missions efforts done out of Christian obedience and love.

The discussion here is nuanced, so we must take care not to misunderstand. On the one hand, insofar as our focus is on people's need to believe the gospel before they die, an exclusivist position does provide a stronger motivation for missions and evangelism than does inclusivism. Tiessen argues in various ways that his accessibilist view leads to just as vigorous a motivation for missions and evangelism as does exclusivism. Stressing first that Christian evangelism is "God's normal or ordinary means of salvation," Tiessen concludes that "there is plenty of motivation

[4]Terrance L. Tiessen, *Who Can Be Saved? Reassessing Salvation in Christ and World Religions* (Downers Grove, Ill.: InterVarsity Press, 2004), p. 259.

for missionary service, even if we abandon an ecclesiocentric [exclusivist] under-standing of the means God uses for salvation." He also notes "that the situation with regard to motivation [for evangelistic mission] is more complex than has sometimes been assumed by ecclesiocentrists who are concerned that accessibilism will undermine the church's passion for evangelization of the world."[5] Even so, Millard Erickson states the obvious, while appreciating Tiessen's and others' gen-uine attempts at explaining their positions' motivational bases for missions and evangelism: "The strongest motivation for evangelism is attached logically to the exclusivist view, since without hearing the gospel explicitly, people are eternally lost. At the same time, it simply is not true that no other view supplies a motive for evangelism and missions."[6]

On the other hand, more so than in discussions about which position better supports missions *motivation* per se, where the exclusivist-inclusivist divide be-comes clear is in the Bible's teaching on how *God* has committed himself to carry out *his* mission in the world. As outlined earlier, part of God's determined method of executing *his* mission is *his* enlistment of *his* people as *his* ambassadors of the good news of *his* saving acts. To state the matter with an emphasis on the *particu-larity* of how God has been carrying out his mission, from his calling of Abraham (and before him Noah and even Adam and Eve's son Seth) God has committed himself to accomplish his salvation of particular people through the life, death, and resurrection of the particular God-Man, Jesus Christ. Furthermore, the good news of Jesus' person and work is to be conveyed by his particular people to other particular people, many of whom also will believe, be saved, and become full par-ticipants in the life of God's people as his colaborers.

God's particular mission. It is here at the particularity of God's determined method not only of accomplishing but also of communicating his gospel to the nations of the world that some of the inconsistencies and loopholes within an in-clusivist view of salvation become evident. The exclusivist understanding is that people must hear the gospel by the particular means that God has determined—through his special revelation conveyed by Jesus' own followers. Before Jesus appeared, during the Old Covenant, God's followers were Abraham and his chil-dren. Now that Jesus has come, the apostles and those who have believed their message continue on as God's particular communication channels.

It is puzzling how Terrance Tiessen seems to set aside his firm commitment to the *particularity* of God's work of salvation precisely at this point. He stands

---

[5]Ibid., pp. 262, 279, 288.
[6]Millard J. Erickson, *How Shall They Be Saved? The Destiny of Those Who Do Not Hear of Jesus* (Grand Rapids: Baker, 1996), p. 268.

clearly for the particularity and uniqueness of Jesus Christ as the world's only Savior. He also stands clearly for God's particular intention to save his particular elect people in Christ.[7] But when it comes to standing for the means of communicating the message of Jesus as Savior to God's particular elect people, the exclusivist, Pauline *particular* means of Jesus' followers is abandoned for the accessibilist "normal or ordinary" means. As noted above, Tiessen stresses that Christian evangelism is "God's normal or ordinary means of salvation." However, such a claim is categorically different from believing that Christians are God's unique and *particular* communication channels of the gospel—the hearing and believing of which is necessary and central for the elect's salvation.

Tiessen's shift here is hard to explain aside from accepting his claim that he genuinely believes that God saves people beyond the reach of the church's gospel proclamation. He offers various reasons for this belief. One is that because there are varying standards by which people will be judged, dependent on the revelation given them, "God may graciously save some who do not believe in Jesus as Savior if they are ignorant of him through no fault of their own."[8] We already touched on this matter of alleged various standards of judgment in our brief discussion of the Canaanites and the Egyptians.

Another of Tiessen's reasons is the related interpretation of John 3:18-20 ("Whoever believes in him is not condemned, but whoever does not believe is condemned already"), namely that this passage "says nothing at all . . . about those who are not rejecting Jesus or failing to believe in him because they have never heard of him."[9] As we shall see below, the incredible generosity of John 3:16-18 lies in the all-inclusive salvation of "whoever" believes in the particular Son of God (through the particular means of communicating that message, Jesus' followers), just as God was gracious toward any Israelite who looked to the bronze serpent prescribed by God to Moses and then displayed by him (in particular) to the people (Jn 3:14-15). Apparently for his own stated reasons (if not simply out of personal preference), Tiessen believes that the exclusive particularity of God's generous salvation—exclusively of his particular elect people and exclusively through the particular Son of God—does not include God's exclusive and particular means of conveying the gospel of his salvation in Christ.

There is no need here to repeat a detailed litany of how God has committed himself to a particular communication channel of the news of his salvation, namely Jesus' followers. Simply to review, God called and used Abraham, Old

---

[7]Tiessen, *Who Can Be Saved?* pp. 83-99.
[8]Ibid., p. 123.
[9]Ibid., p. 264.

Covenant Israel, Jesus himself, the apostles, and since then all believers as Jesus' "witnesses in Jerusalem and in all Judea and Samaria, and to the end of the earth" (Acts 1:8). God's Spirit has come upon Christ's church since Pentecost, empowering us for witness throughout the world. This particular mission, including a particular communication channel, is how God has determined to redeem his world.

As stated at this chapter's outset, following the Bible's lead in its theocentric thrust helps us to consider the exclusivist-inclusivist issue in its properly subservient place. In this chapter as a whole, we are working out our theocentric consideration of the exclusivist-inclusivist issue in relation to Christian missions. At this particular juncture, we are stressing the particularity of how God has been working out his mission as a compelling thrust for an exclusivist view and zeal for missions. God's passion to redeem his world has been channeled through his sending a particular Savior for the salvation of his particular people (= all who believe), the good news of which is to be conveyed in particular by Jesus' followers.

Missions motivation and humility. Christians thus have a zeal for missions because we share God's zealous passion to redeem his world in the particular fashion that he has determined. But in sharing God's zeal, Christians must be careful to share as well Jesus' humble approach and posture in carrying out God's mission in the world. Jesus did not ride a white horse into Jerusalem as a brazen politico-military leader. He was constantly interrupted, he asked questions, he served among his society's most poor and broken people. Ultimately he achieved the world's redemption from the curse of sin by allowing Satan and evil to "bruise his heel" on the cross—only to crush Satan through his atoning death and victorious resurrection. After Jesus' humble example, then, his followers are to listen, learn, and serve in their role as gospel ambassadors.

This point about humble service is important for all Christians, but it is particularly important for an exclusivist mentality. The human heart, including that of people redeemed in Christ, is desperately wicked and quick to become proud. If the Bible indeed teaches that people must repent and believe in the gospel of Jesus Christ, and if the exclusive human messengers of that gospel are indeed Jesus' followers,[10] history has demonstrated how Christians can easily become triumphalistic conquistadors, particularly when crosscultural ministry is involved. As this chapter continues to explore various facets of the wider framework of God's zeal for his world, we will seek to bolster the case for an exclusivist notion of how peo-

---

[10]Once again, allowing for the possibility of gospel messengers beyond Christians, specifically angels, does not disprove the exclusivist view that people who are saved are those who repent and believe the gospel in this life.

ple are saved. Throughout we must remember that, just as Jesus our master was humble in his dealings with people, so must his followers be, including in how the good news of salvation is communicated.

THE WHOLE WORLD

The God of the Bible is concerned for the whole world, for all peoples. As Jesus himself affirmed, "Repentance and forgiveness of sins should be proclaimed in his name to all nations" (Lk 24:47). God is not simply a tribal god who deals only with a particular group, defending them against all others. Nor is he a monolingual deity who reveals himself exclusively in one special or esoteric religious language. The Bible was originally given over a millennium and a half within multiple cultural and linguistic contexts. Moreover, God's Word is "infinitely translatable"[11] into all human languages, demonstrating God's concern to relate directly to all types of people in their mother tongues.

God's commitment to all peoples is eminently evident today: Jesus' followers are now in actuality more worldwide and multinational than ever before. Many North American Christians are familiar with the news about the significant growth of the church throughout the Southern Hemisphere, including Latin America and sub-Saharan Africa. The majority of Christians now live outside the West, and there is no single geographic center of the worldwide Christian movement. God compassionately continues to bring the gospel of Jesus Christ to people all over the earth.

Inclusive exclusivism. God's loving commitment to his world is thus inclusive of all tribes, tongues, and nations. No ethnicity is excluded from God's gracious invitation, and clear command, to repent and trust in Jesus Christ. It is precisely here where the label "exclusivism" gets exposed as a misleading misnomer. The unwarranted image many people have of exclusivism, in comparison to inclusivism (and especially pluralism), is that of closed-minded stinginess. Exclusivists can falsely be represented as scowling and hard-nosed, stressing God's justice and his acceptance of only the tiny minority of the human race that is both fortunate enough to hear the gospel and small-minded enough to believe it to be necessary for its and anyone else's salvation. To be fair, not all inclusivists see exclusivists in such an unflattering way, especially those inclusivists engaged in honestly and carefully searching the Scriptures together with others to determine what the Bible teaches. Nevertheless, the image of an exclusivist position (and the corresponding image of God) can be that of narrowness and meanness—including at a

---

[11]Andrew F. Walls, *The Cross-Cultural Process in Christian History* (Maryknoll, N.Y.: Orbis, 2002), p. 29.

subconscious level within those of us who are exclusivists.

Nothing could be farther from the truth, however. The God of exclusivism, to use that phrase, is one who has always been zealously committed to save a fascinating, colorful, and multinational people for himself. Such an exhaustive array of ethnic representatives will inhabit a glorious new creation that will be more robustly magnificent than can be conjured up by human imagination. Such a God is not stingy with his love, but is overwhelming with grace and mercy toward his wayward creation.

It is crucial to note the inclusive trajectory of redemptive history. It is not as though God evolved from being Israel's tribal deity to a universal God who gradually became interested in all peoples. As noted above, God from the beginning has had his sights set on all people he has made. His initial command to Adam and Eve was to "Be fruitful and multiply and fill the earth and subdue it" (Gen 1:28). God repeated that same covenantal mandate to Noah and his sons after the flood waters subsided (Gen 9:1). God later "dispersed [people] over the face of all the earth" (Gen 11:9), all the while dealing with and living close to all people (Acts 17:26-28). God's interest in all people did not begin with the incarnation of Jesus but with his eternal plan for creation and redemption.

It was in order to set the stage for the world's Savior, and subsequently to command "all people everywhere to repent" and trust in that risen Savior and coming Judge, Jesus Christ (Acts 17:30-31), that God chose Abraham and his descendants to be a communication channel to all nations of the *protoevangelion*. Moreover, Old Covenant Israel was the one nation from whom Jesus was to emerge. Prior to Jesus' coming, Israel was exiled for its disobedience, then graciously brought back (at least partially) from being scattered among the surrounding nations. That return of Old Covenant Israel from exile was a foreshadowing of the greater return from exile of all of God's people scattered throughout the nations of earth (Jer 32:37-38; cf. 16:14-15; 23:3, 8). It has been through the preaching of the gospel and "the obedience of faith for the sake of his name among all the nations" (Rom 1:5b) that God has been calling his people back to be "a chosen race, a royal priesthood, a holy nation, a people for his own possession" (1 Pet 2:9). In other words, the trajectory of redemptive history—including, as we will see, within an exclusivist understanding of how God saves particular people through their entrance into his covenant people by faith in Jesus Christ—is gracious and inclusive of all peoples and nations.

At the same time, God's inclusive grace has an exclusivist specificity to it. As perhaps the most beloved words of the English Bible put it, "For God so loved the world, that he gave his only Son, that whoever believes in him should not perish but have eternal life" (Jn 3:16). God *loved* the world, despite its rebellion against him, and he graciously *gave* his unique Son, Jesus Christ. Moreover, *whoever*—regardless of nationality, language, gender, socioeconomic status, ethnicity, or any other defining characteristic—believes in the gospel will be saved. While all of these points stress God's inclusive grace, there are specific recipients of that grace, namely those who *believe* in God's Son.

Exclusivism's inclusion of all believers. There seems to be a Christian consensus that those people whose personal faculties render them incapable of believing the gospel will in fact be saved. Such categories of people would include those who die before birth, infants who die before being able to understand the gospel, and the mentally handicapped.[12] King David's assurance that he would one day join his deceased infant son (2 Sam 12:23) is one oft-cited piece of the biblical evidence for such a consensus. At the same time, God's love and grace will not save, in a totally indiscriminate manner, just anyone having the faculties to believe. God saves those who out of their own humility and unworthiness trust in God's grace and love in Christ.

Some might feel that various types of inclusivism convey more of a magnanimity or generosity of spirit than do forms of exclusivism. After all, inclusivists at least appear to be striving to include more people within salvation by stretching the boundaries and requirements. What needs to be understood, however, is that exclusivists gladly affirm the biblical thrust that God's gracious and loving salvation in Christ is for *all* people who believe: Again, "*whoever* believes in him should not perish but have eternal life." There is no loss of magnanimity or generosity in John 3:16. The heart of God's covenant love calls forth the humble faith of the great host of undeserving people that he is saving from among all peoples and nations of the earth.

THE OUTRAGEOUS GOSPEL

The gospel of Jesus Christ is outrageously magnanimous and generous in its scope. So, therefore, is the appeal of Christian missions and evangelism.

To the end of the earth. Jesus predicted to his postresurrection disciples that they (and by extension the rest of us who would come into the church) would "receive power when the Holy Spirit has come upon you, and you will be my witnesses in

---

[12]Terrance Tiessen includes these three categories of people, along with "everyone who lived before the incarnation of the Son of God" and "those living after Jesus' resurrection who are never told this good news in a comprehensible manner," among the "unevangelized." However, labeling all such groups as "unevangelized" can be misleading, since those not possessing the faculties of believing can more precisely be called "unevangelizable." The distinction, of course, lies in whether the emphasis is on the fact that some are "never told this good news" in a comprehensible way ("unevangelized") or on the (lack of) capacity to comprehend. See Tiessen, *Who Can Be Saved?* p. 13.

Jerusalem and in all Judea and Samaria, and to the end of the earth" (Acts 1:8). Soon thereafter, at Pentecost, "those who received [Peter's] word were baptized, and there were added that day about three thousand souls" (Acts 2:41). God then through persecution scattered Christians "throughout the regions of Judea and Samaria," and those fleeing but Spirit-empowered followers of Jesus "went about preaching the word" (Acts 8:1, 4). Cultural barriers were crossed in Antioch when some Christians "spoke to the Hellenists [Greek-speaking Jews] also, preaching the Lord Jesus. And the hand of the Lord was with them, and a great number who believed turned to the Lord" (Acts 11:20-21). The book of Acts then ends in upbeat, open-ended fashion, recording how Paul under house arrest in Rome "welcomed all who came to him, proclaiming the kingdom of God and teaching about the Lord Jesus Christ with all boldness and without hindrance" (Acts 28:30-31). Christian history continues the account of the gospel's spread "to the end of the earth" up to our own day and beyond.

Repent and believe. What the book of Acts and Christian history thus tell us is the worldwide, inclusive trajectory of the preaching and believing (and rejection) of the good news about King Jesus. Jesus' followers fanned out in all directions— into northeast Africa, across Syria and into India (and before too long into China), and northwesterly into Europe. The gospel's spread has not always been smooth or uniform. Some people have heard about Jesus later than others, and some throughout the earth have yet to hear about him. The call to all people, however, has continued to be to repent and believe in Jesus. Moreover, there is no indication that God has changed in his commitment to use Jesus' followers as his communication channel of the good news of Jesus' reign and achievement of salvation for all who believe in him.

Church maturity. God's appeal through his people is for all, indiscriminately, to believe in Jesus and be saved. As Christians make this gospel appeal, God's mission to grow and mature his church is also evident. Observable, numerical church growth clearly is part of God's mission concern. At the same time, so is the church's maturation in terms of spiritual character. As noted earlier, it takes great humility to share the Christian gospel, especially across cultural barriers. And as any experienced crosscultural emissary knows, the gospel communicator grows tremendously through crosscultural interaction, usually in ways unforeseen and beyond one's control. Like all other human beings, Christians tend to link the universal, transcendent gospel with their own cultural particularities, for example language, music style and dress. How else, then, could Western Christians break free from believing that Latin, pipe organs and certain vestments were central and necessary apart from encountering other cultural frameworks within which such particularities do not fit? The modern Western missions movement enabled such revealing encounters. Christian missions efforts are thus one of God's central means of working out his mission to mature his people.

Put differently, the scope of God's mission grows even greater for us when we realize not only that the Christian church communicates the gospel to outsiders for their acceptance, but that the Christian church also never ceases to be an object of God's mission to bring us to maturity.

Glimpses of shalom. On top of all that, the gospel of God's kingdom includes the good news that Jesus reigns on high and that he grants foretastes of the coming heavenly city. That is, God's mission grows even greater for us when we realize his commitment thoroughly to re-create his rebellious world. God is at work in public, socio-economic-political arenas as part of his mission to make the world right again. God's mission and Christians' corresponding missions efforts thus are not confined to crosscultural evangelization of lost people. God's comprehensive, gracious mission is to grant, among the world's peoples, faith in Jesus Christ, maturing of the church, and glimpses of the new heaven and new earth.

Christian missions are to be stretched by knowing that "God does not only want to save individuals; he wants to build churches as communities that give the world a small foretaste of the shalom of God that is produced when the kingdom of God breaks into our history."[13] The relevant point for this chapter is this: An exclusivist understanding of the gospel wholeheartedly affirms that the good news of who Jesus is and what he has accomplished is outrageously gracious and comprehensive in its scope.

CONTEXTUAL QUESTIONS

He shall bruise your head, and you shall bruise his heel;
Whoever believes in him should not perish but have eternal life;
Behold, I am making all things new;
The zeal of the Lord of hosts will do this.

Against the backdrop of a fallen creation, the biblical drama is that of God's zealous mission to redeem his world into a magnificent new heaven and new earth.

"Exclusivism-Inclusivism." In his letter to the Christians in Rome, the apostle Paul writes of the comprehensive nature of God's mission, which focuses on calling people to believe in Jesus: "The creation itself will be set free from its bondage to decay and obtain the freedom of the glory of the children of God. For we know that the whole creation has been groaning together in the pains of childbirth until now." All of creation "groans" during the present "already-but-

---

[13]Ibid., p. 283.

not-yet" phase of God's salvation of the world. "And not only the creation, but we ourselves, who have the firstfruits of the Spirit, groan inwardly as we wait eagerly for adoption as sons, the redemption of our bodies. For in this hope we were saved." We who have been saved still wait and hope for the completion of our and the creation's salvation. And who are "we"? "If you confess with your mouth that Jesus is Lord and believe in your heart that God raised him from the dead, you will be saved. For with the heart one believes and is justified, and with the mouth one confesses and is saved." And in Paul's mind the *exclusive* identification of those who are saved with those who believe *includes* all kinds of people without distinction: "For 'everyone who calls on the name of the Lord will be saved'" (Rom 8:21-24; 10:9-13).

The trajectory of the biblical drama of redemption *includes* the whole creation, *including* God's people gathered from sin's exile among *all* the nations. As actors now cast into the unfolding redemptive drama, Christians join in God's call to *all* people *everywhere* to repent and believe *exclusively* in the risen and reigning Jesus. The *exclusive* character of those who are saved—those who believe and confess Jesus as the risen Savior—is inexorably intertwined with the *inclusive* character of God's people as believers from *all* kinds of people.

I suggest that, at least in relation to God's mission and Christian missions, the concepts of "exclusivism" and "inclusivism" are best understood in the ways just described.

This book, however, is addressing the "exclusivism-inclusivism" issue as it has arisen and taken shape in recent decades. As earlier chapters have described, related questions and answers have been formulated in specific and nuanced ways. That is because issues like this one of "exclusivism-inclusivism" arise in contexts that are genuinely new and different from the contexts within which the Scriptures, our rule of faith and practice, were originally given. The Bible thus may or may not speak directly to the questions that are raised, and we must think and discuss together carefully how best to understand matters that are often difficult and unclear.

To unpack the matter in an oversimplified way, the general context that has given rise to the present "exclusivism-inclusivism" (and "pluralism") discussions is that of various twentieth-century attempts to explain Christianity's relationships with different religious traditions throughout the world. Western Christianity did not have to wrestle very much with such questions prior to World War I. After all, Western powers and the intertwined Christian religion obviously were spreading across the world, and it was assumed that other traditions would soon be swept away. However, Hindu, Confucian, Buddhist, Islamic, primal and other religions did not in fact go away (quite the opposite), and West-

erners living among these various religious traditions often were hard-pressed to
account for their adherents' admirable points. Moreover, World War I, in which
"Christian nations" were killing each other, raised all sorts of doubts about
Christianity's assumed superiority. Rising liberal theological influence contributed to an erosion of Christian self-assurance in many quarters. Politically, the
post-World War II breakup of European empires, combined with national independence movements throughout Africa and Asia in the late 1950s and
1960s, caused many Christians in both the West and non-West to search for answers to new questions that people were asking in relation to the assumed Christian frameworks that previous generations of Western missionaries had so con-
fidently preached.

For example, were all non-Christian religions in fact dark, morally bankrupt,
and satanic? After all, did not Mahatma Gandhi, for example, draw inspiration
from Jainism and Hinduism in leading a just, nonviolent independence movement
in India? Did classifying sincere and morally upright adherents of other religions
as totally blinded by sin and Satan square with the admirable lives they were leading and the intriguing teachings they were advocating? Another prominent example involved pre-Christian ancestors: Were they all de facto consigned to an eternity in hell? Claiming that they were might have been easy for Western
missionaries to assert, since Westerners had little to no sense of the living reality
of ancestors. But for most of the world, ancestors were very much present and active in people's lives and communities, and they were worthy of people's respect
and close attention.

Such questions are still with us today. The challenge of facing them biblically
is compounded by the air of a strident, politically correct tolerance that we breathe
in most contemporary societies.

In my judgment, the relative newness and challenge of questions like these call
especially for the worldwide input of Christians who will honestly discuss and
search the Scriptures together. On the one hand, the Bible is clear in how it speaks.
On the other hand, though, the Bible speaks in the languages and thought-forms
of individual linguistic cultural contexts. Particular nuances and insights come out
in some contexts better than they do in others. Such a reality is no one's fault but
by God's design, since God committed himself to display his "manifold [multi-
multifaceted] wisdom" through the inherently international church.

World religions. How then should Christians theologically understand other
religious traditions throughout the world? First, articulating any theological position on this topic must be informed by personal interaction with various kinds of
people. Abstract, distant theorizing will inevitably be contextually confined, missiologically irrelevant and pastorally out of touch. To avoid such pitfalls, we are to

be what one author has termed "engaged evangelicals."[14] Furthermore, Christians' personal interaction with others should include evangelism; even interreligious dialogue should include attempts to persuade as well as to listen and learn.[15]

Based on my own interaction to this point with both other religious adherents and Christians from other parts of the world, my theological understanding of other religious traditions can perhaps best be described as a three-legged stool: sin, searching and Satan are always present. Sin and rebellion contribute to people hiding from God. Searching—genuine, honest, and at least to certain degrees true searching—for God is also present due to the ongoing image of God in all people, preserved and nurtured by God's common grace. Satan also is at work, deceiving and blinding people to the truth of God's nature and work in the world. All three areas, while present in varying degrees depending on the tradition and occasion, must be acknowledged to avoid a misleading reductionist viewpoint.[16]

Ancestors. What about pre-Christian ancestors? As already noted, the salvific state of those who have lived in earlier generations and died without hearing the Christian gospel is a very poignant concern for many people around the world; often it is one of the first questions asked by those beginning to consider the Christian faith. Many of us exclusivists do not existentially feel the same degree of poignancy, especially those of us who are native to Western cultures. Most of us in the West are several generations removed from the time when the Christian gospel first entered our heritage. Furthermore, our post-Enlightenment, scientific worldview has explained away the ancestors' reality that so deeply affects the lives of many people around the world. Whatever the case, those of us who do not sense the presence of ancestors must be careful about making quick pronouncements based on conclusions we draw strictly from what appears to be clear, logical consistency. International evangelical discussions on this issue should develop further to enable us to articulate our position in a way that is most biblically, missiologically, and pastorally informed and nuanced.[17]

Saying as much is not at all the same as assuming an agnostic position. An ag-

[14]Timothy C. Tennent, *Christianity at the Religious Roundtable: Evangelicalism in Conversation with Hinduism, Buddhism, and Islam* (Grand Rapids: Baker, 2002), p. 26.

[15]Paul J. Griffiths, *An Apology for Apologetics: A Study in the Logic of Interreligious Dialogue*, Faith Meets Faith Series, gen. ed., Paul F. Knitter (Maryknoll, N.Y.: Orbis, 1991), p. 3.

[16]For a similar viewpoint, see Harold A. Netland, *Encountering Religious Pluralism: The Challenge to Christian Faith and Mission* (Downers Grove, Ill.: InterVarsity Press , 2001), pp. 308-10.

[17]For example, it could be that living with the ancestors' reality is closer to the world of Old Covenant Israel, as connoted for example by the biblical accounts of how Solomon (and other kings) "slept with his fathers" (2 Chron 9:31), than a scientific worldview. Having a sense of the ancestors' reality could affect at least an articulation of the Bible's teaching concerning the ancestors' eternal state.

nostic view asserts that we cannot know and therefore must not pronounce (one way or another) what has happened after death to ancestors who did not hear about Jesus Christ. Furthermore, neither is expressing the desire for further discussion the same as the stated position that people universally have an "at-death encounter with Christ," whereby those who had never heard the gospel will respond to their at-death meeting with Jesus in a manner consistent with their responses to revelation they had been given during their lifetimes. Such a position enables an assurance—at best potentially false and misleading—to people that their ancestors "to whom [God] gave repentance and faith (however basic) during their lives will have met Jesus at the moment of death and rejoiced to know their Savior."[18]

Nor does wanting further discussion mean that we should not hold to a definite position in light of the Bible's clear teaching. Claiming to have no position at all not only is disingenuous but also disqualifies one from making much of any contribution to the discussion—and most importantly denies what the Bible unavoidably says about the matter. While thus wanting to learn better how best to articulate my position, along with that of other exclusivists (of various nuanced types), I believe that God graciously and inclusively saves all those who hear and believe the good news of Jesus Christ, and in his wisdom and justice he judges all those who die in their sin and rebellion outside of belief in Jesus Christ. As Jesus himself distinguished between those who do not bear the fruit of trusting in him during their lives and those who do, "These will go away into eternal punishment, but the righteous into eternal life" (Mt 25:46). Apart from ancestors or anyone else having heard, believed, and (time permitting between believing and dying) born fruit of their saving faith, we should hold no false hope of the salvation which is so graciously but exclusively found in Christ.

As we strive best to understand and articulate these matters, part of our ongoing discussions should also be to allow the Bible to shape our questions as well as our answers, whether concerning ancestors or any other issue, no matter how poignant or inscrutable the matter might seem. For example, it could be that more central than the direct question about the eternal state of pre-Christian ancestors would be the question (alluded to earlier) about the extent to which Christians should or should not be aware of their ancestors' ongoing reality.[19] What does re-

---

[18]Tiessen, *Who Can Be Saved?* pp. 223-24.

[19]Of the increasing number of non-Western contributors available to Western readers, one author-mentor I have found particularly helpful for both shaping how we frame issues and offering biblical answers to them is Kwame Bediako of Ghana. Regarding the whole matter of ancestors, for example, see his "Jesus in African Culture: A Ghanaian Perspective," in *Jesus in Africa: The Christian Gospel in African History and Experience*. Theological Reflections from the South Series (Yaoundé, Ghana: Regnum Africa, 2000), pp. 20-33, esp. pp. 29-32.

main central for Christians in terms of our focused zeal and action is that God is zealously committed to redeem his world through Jesus Christ, that for the glory of his justice God will punish all those who die without believing in Jesus, and that the gospel must therefore be believed and conveyed to others by God's people.

THE ZEAL OF THE LORD OF HOSTS

God's zeal guarantees the success of his mission and of Christian missions. By his love, grace, and mercy the church of Jesus Christ is now more worldwide, multi-national and multidirectional in its missions activities than ever before. God's passionate redemption of his world is taking place through his people, weak though we are, as we communicate, verbally and through our lives in maturing Christian communities, glimpses of the ultimate shalom to come when Jesus returns.[20]

God *includes all* types of people within his redemptive scope. Jesus has died and risen for the salvation of *all* kinds of people. Such an *inclusive* embrace by God in Christ of *all* sorts of people is what undergirded Paul's encouragement to the diverse Christians in Rome "to live in such harmony with one another, in accord with Christ Jesus, that together you may with one voice glorify the God and Father of our Lord Jesus Christ. Therefore welcome one another as Christ has welcomed you, for the glory of God" (Rom 15:5-7). God's zealous gospel welcome of *whoever* believes in Christ drove Paul's passionate gospel instruction to the Galatian Christians that "in Christ Jesus you are all sons of God, through faith. For as many of you as were baptized into Christ have put on Christ. There is neither Jew nor Greek, there is neither slave nor free, there is neither male nor female, for you are all one in Christ Jesus" (Gal 3:26-28). God's passionate redemption in Christ fueled Paul's zealous "ambition to preach the gospel, not where Christ has already been named," so that "Those who have never been told of him will see, and those who have never heard will understand" (Rom 15:20-21). God's zeal for people all over the world fed Paul's zeal to preach salvation *exclusively* in Christ Jesus, *inclusive* of anyone who would believe.

Christians' zeal for missions and evangelism is strengthened by knowing that people outside of Christ must hear and believe the gospel or face God's righteous judgment. But the taproot of our zeal is God's passionate commitment to have us in particular join him in his mission of gathering, maturing, and using his people

---

[20]Concerning how Christian congregations witness in the concrete to surrounding societies through loving service, one helpful and available contribution by a non-Western evangelical is Ramachandra, pp. 265-84. As the book's title *(The Recovery of Mission: Beyond the Pluralist Paradigm)* indicates, Ramachandra's valuable contribution moves forward as well the general exclusivism-inclusivism-pluralism discussion (particularly in answering popular pluralist notions) with which this book is concerned.

to redeem his sinful world toward the glorious re-creation he has promised that he will bring about in Christ. May God's zeal so nourish Christians' zeal today to *include all* people throughout the whole world among those who hear and believe the wonderfully *exclusive* good news of salvation in Christ Jesus.

II

Answers to Notable Questions

CHRISTOPHER W. MORGAN
AND ROBERT A. PETERSON

1. IS IT JUST FOR GOD TO SEND PEOPLE TO HELL WHO NEVER HEARD THE GOSPEL?

Inclusivists such as John Sanders charge exclusivism with unfairness and injustice: How could it be fair and just for those who have never even had a chance to hear the gospel, which is necessary for salvation, to be condemned to hell?[1] The question sounds powerful, but behind it lie faulty assumptions. The first mistaken assumption is that our condemnation is based on a rejection of the gospel. Scripture teaches that our condemnation is based on the fact that we are sinners, not because at some point in time we rejected the gospel. We are condemned in Adam's sin, Paul asserts in Romans 5:18: "the result of one man's trespass was condemnation for all men." Other Scriptures do the same.[2] Furthermore, God's wrath is revealed against everyone who suppresses his truth revealed through creation, as Paul declares in Romans 1:18-25. God communicates clearly who he is in and through creation, but all—Jews and Gentiles alike—refuse him, are under sin and therefore justly deserve his divine displeasure (Rom 3:9-23).[3]

Strictly speaking, the Bible denies that there are persons who have never heard of God. As Romans argues, and as the sermons in the book of Acts confirm, everyone knows of God's existence, power, goodness, and patience (Rom 2:4; Acts

---

[1]John Sanders, *No Other Name: An Investigation into the Destiny of the Unevangelized* (Grand Rapids: Eerdmans, 1992), pp. 60-69.

[2]Ephesians 2:3 declares, "Like the rest, we were by nature objects of wrath" (NIV). John's gospel instructs similarly: people are spiritually dead, in need of new birth, already condemned, and presently under the wrath of God (Jn 3:3, 16-18, 36).

[3]Tiessen acknowledges this point. See Terrance L. Tiessen, *Who Can Be Saved? Reassessing Salvation in Christ and World Religions* (Downers Grove, Ill.: InterVarsity Press, 2004), pp. 73-82, 134-37.

14:15-17; 17:30). In that sense, all know God. But they rebel against him; they refuse him and his claims on their lives. This rebellion is universal and is the basis of our guilt.[4] William Edgar is right: Our condemnation is not based on hearing the *gospel* and refusing it, but on knowing God and refusing him. So, biblically speaking, when we ask, "What about people who have never heard of God, especially the Christian God?," we are framing a faulty question.

A second mistake lying behind this question is a confusion of justice and mercy. It is just and fair for God to send to hell those who are guilty, because of their union with Adam and their rejection of their Creator. It is merciful and gracious—and not necessary—for God to provide salvation for guilty sinners. Nevertheless, because of his grace and mercy (in a way consistent with his justice), God made atonement for our sins through Christ's death and resurrection. And in grace and mercy, God sends the good news to the guilty so they can repent and trust Christ.

Here is where the question of fairness appropriately comes to the fore. Is it fair that God punishes the guilty in hell? Yes, of course. Is it fair that millions will never hear the gospel? No, it is not. But how God's love for sinners and sovereignty in salvation converge has puzzled and will continue to puzzle the best Christian minds, just as the question of why some suffer more than others.[5] There is a problem of fairness that concerns the extent of God's mercy, but there is not a problem of justice that concerns God's punishment of the guilty. In other words, the question of fairness is appropriate but is misplaced by most inclusivists.[6] That God punishes the guilty is fair; that God's mercy is not shown universally does not seem fair, but that question centers on the doctrine of election, not exclusivism and inclusivism.[7]

William Edgar helpfully concludes:

All of us, then, are lost before a righteous God, stand guilty before him, and deserve

---

[4]See William Edgar's chapter.

[5]Jonathan Edwards made a similar point when he criticized annihilationists and their confusion of mercy and justice: "There are innumerable calamities that come to pass in this world through the permission of Divine Providence, against which (were it not that they are what we see with our eyes, and which are universally known and incontestable facts) this caviling, unbelieving spirit would strongly object; and which, if they were only proposed in theory as matters of faith, would be opposed as exceedingly inconsistent with the moral perfections of God." See his "Concerning the Endless Punishment of Those Who Die Impenitent," in *The Wrath of Almighty God: Jonathan Edwards on God's Judgment Against Sinners*, ed. Don Kistler (Morgan, Penn.: Soli Deo Gloria, 1996), pp. 335-36.

[6]See Clark H. Pinnock, "An Inclusivist View," in *More Than One Way? Four Views on Salvation in a Pluralistic World*, ed. Dennis L. Okholm and Timothy R. Phillips (Grand Rapids: Zondervan, 1995), p. 97.

[7]Evangelical Calvinists and evangelical Arminians differ on the nature of election but the great majority of them join hands in affirming exclusivism.

his anger. It is *fair* for God to be angry with the world because we have transgressed his covenant and committed cosmic treason. . . . Certainly we should not be judged based on something we never knew. But we do know, and according to Romans, we know a great deal. Now, it may be that some hear the gospel itself and refuse it. It seems their condemnation is greater. Perhaps also there is greater condemnation for those who live in countries with a long Christian history and with access to the Bible than for those in relatively unevangelized places. . . . But it is clear that to whom much has been given, much will be required (Lk 12:47-48). "Human beings are judged in God's sight for the response they make to whatever light they have—and no human being is without light."[8]

2. SHOULD INFANTS AND THE SEVERELY MENTALLY CHALLENGED BE COMPARED TO THE UNEVANGELIZED?

Inclusivists often insist that the destiny of those who have never heard the gospel parallels that of infants and persons with severe mental disability. They reason that judgment is according to knowledge and that all of these cases involve insufficient knowledge. They also charge exclusivists with inconsistency, because most hold to the salvation of infants and mentally challenged apart from a knowledgeable faith in Christ.[9]

How are we to evaluate this argument? First, inclusivists are right to point out that everyone is judged according to knowledge. They are also perceptive in finding some inconsistency in some exclusivist arguments for infant salvation.

But inclusivists also err in drawing this analogy—claiming that infants and the mentally handicapped are parallel to those who have never heard the gospel. At first glance this analogy seems sound, but upon careful reflection it unravels. As we explained in question one, the unevangelized do know about God. God has revealed himself and his truth to them through the creation and their consciences (Rom 1:18-25; 2:14-15). But although they know the truth, they suppress it (Rom 1:18, 21) and exchange it for idolatry and error (Rom 1:23, 25). They are therefore judged based on their knowledge and their rejection of God and his truth. By contrast, infants and persons who are severely mentally challenged do not have such knowledge and are incapable of rejecting anything. Consequently, the inclusivist comparison does not stand.

What are we to conclude concerning the eternal destiny of infants who die? Although their reasons differ depending on other theological commitments, and al-

---

[8]See Edgar, p. 88. In his last sentence, he quotes Carl F. H. Henry, "Is It Fair?" in *Through No Fault of Their Own? The Fate of Those Who Have Never Heard*, ed. William V. Crocket and James G. Sigountos (Grand Rapids: Baker Books, 1991), p. 247.
[9]See Sanders, *No Other Name*, pp. 231-32; Tiessen, *Who Can Be Saved?* pp. 204-29.

though some of their reasons are better than others, evangelicals generally agree that such persons will be in heaven.[10]

3. HOW ARE WE TO VIEW NON-CHRISTIAN RELIGIONS?

Today, when globalization and pluralism are realities, we all face the important question: How are we to view non-Christian religions? Though this question is massive and lies outside the focus of this book, we will set forth several foundational principles for an evangelical theology of religions.[11] First, we err when we caricature other religions, only showing them in the worst light. This is irresponsible and damaging to our mission. We must apply Jesus' Golden Rule here and convey other religions in a way that is fair and accurate. Second, we should not assume that non-Christian religions are completely false. A Christian understanding of the goodness of creation, the reality of general revelation, the permanence of the image of God in all humans, and the gift of God's common grace leads us to expect that non-Christian religions contain some elements of truth and add some value to their cultures.[12]

Third, we should recognize that since the Fall human beings are radically sinful and distort everything they touch—including religion, even especially religion. In arguably the best evangelical theology of religions to date, Harold Netland proposes an important balance: "Just as human cultures, as the product both of God's creative activity and of human sin, reflect a mixture of good and evil, so too we should expect that in the religious dimensions of human experience there exist elements of both good and evil, truth and falsity."[13] Human beings are not as sinful as they could be but their sin is pervasive—it affects their minds, wills, emotions, longings and, therefore, their religion. Apart from reception of special revelation and submission to God, people will not think correctly about the true God, will not desire to worship him properly, and they will not love him. Instead, they will prefer themselves, their own agenda, and their own idolatrous religion (Rom 1:18-32). John Stott observed, "Even his religiosity is a subtle escape from the God he is afraid of and ashamed to meet."[14] Fourth, some—although not all—of the the-

---

[10]For treatments on this issue, see Ronald H. Nash, *Is Jesus the Only Savior?* (Grand Rapids: Zondervan, 1993), pp. 135-36; idem, *When a Baby Dies: Answers to Comfort Grieving Parents* (Grand Rapids: Zondervan, 1999); Millard J. Erickson, *How Shall They Be Saved? The Destiny of Those Who Do Not Hear of Jesus* (Grand Rapids: Baker, 1996), pp. 235-53.

[11]For sound and careful evangelical interaction with the particulars associated with a theology of religions, see Harold Netland, *Encountering Religious Pluralism* (Downers Grove, Ill.: InterVarsity Press, 2001). He elaborates most of the points we make.

[12]Ibid., pp. 330-37.

[13]Ibid., p. 328.

[14]John R. W. Stott, *Christian Mission in the Modern World* (London: Falcon, 1975), p. 69.

ology and activity of non-Christian religions is rooted in the demonic and satanic (1 Cor 10:20; 2 Cor 4:4; Eph 4:17-18).

Fifth, it is also crucial that we affirm the uniqueness of Yahweh and the Lord Jesus Christ. The Bible stresses this, and so must we. The Christian God is unique, incomparable and allows no rivals (e.g., Ex 20; Is 45). Eckhard Schnabel correctly stresses:

> Both Israel and the early Christians were convinced that God had indeed provided a path to salvation, a path that is inextricably linked with the divine revelation of the perspectives, the principles, and the promises of faith and worship that please God. Both Israel and the early Christians were convinced that such a divine revelation had taken place in Israel. Jews were convinced that such a saving revelation had occurred in the history of the descendants of Abraham. And the early Christians were convinced that the climax of God's saving revelation had taken place in the person and history of Jesus of Nazareth, the messianic Son of man. Both Israel and the early Christians held that other systems of faith and worship were human—grounded in human concerns, framed by human beings, and controlled by human ideas about deities and sacrifices.[15]

Sixth, we should likewise affirm that salvation can be found only in Christ, and therefore, other religions cannot save. Jesus himself asserted, "I am the way, truth, and life. No one comes to the Father except through me" (Jn 14:6). Peter declared that there are no other avenues of salvation (Acts 4:12). Paul maintained that every knee will bow and every tongue will confess Jesus Christ as Lord (Phil 2:5-11). Schnabel insightfully concludes:

> The proclamation of Paul and of the other early Christian missionaries focused on Jesus—his person, his life and ministry in Galilee and Jerusalem, his messianic dignity, his prophetic teaching, his death and resurrection, his exaltation at God's right hand as Kyrios, his gift of the Holy Spirit, and his return as Judge (Cf. Acts 2:36; 5:30-31; 10:34-43; 13:25-41; 17:30; 1 Cor 15:3-5; 2 Cor 5:21; Rom 4:25). They called on Jews and Gentiles to repent, turn to the living God, and accept his saving revelation in Jesus, the crucified and risen Messiah and Lord. They challenged their Jewish listeners to abandon their ignorance that caused the rejection, condemnation and crucifixion of Jesus, and they invited them to accept Jesus as the promised Messiah who, through his atoning death, forgives sins. They exhorted their pagan listeners to turn away from their temples, altars, and idols, to worship the one true and living God, and to accept Jesus as the Son of God and the Lord who alone can forgive sins and achieve reconciliation with the almighty, holy, and merciful God.[16]

---

[15]Eckhard Schnabel, pp. 98-99.
[16]Schnabel, pp. 121-22.

Seventh, we should seek to dialogue with members of other religions. Exclusivists and general revelation inclusivists like Terrance Tiessen share common ground here. Tiessen helpfully maintains: "Dialogue with members of other religions is valuable. It is not a substitute for evangelism, but it is also not simply a means of evangelism."[17] Exclusivists and general revelation inclusivists agree that such dialogue can serve to build relationships, express friendship, display respect, clarify the distinct theological positions, grow in mutual understanding, uncover weaknesses in our own faith and practice, advance the sanctity of human life, and promote civil peace.[18]

Finally, since we believe in the uniqueness of Christ and the necessity of faith in him for salvation, we also ultimately seek the salvation of all people, including members of other religions. Recognizing this missional aspect of Christianity, we should also engage in the proclamation of the gospel to them. Such witness is not "arrogant" or "hate speech" as some in our pluralistic society claim, but loving and necessary. Schnabel states it well:

> While the apostle Paul would not have wanted to justify or promote injustice and conflict, and while he certainly did not believe that he had "exhausted" the depth of the riches and wisdom and knowledge of God (Rom 11:33-35; cf. Phil 3:12), he was convinced of the truth of his theological affirmations, of the deception of secular religions, of the fact that God now provides salvation only on account of the death and resurrection of Jesus Christ, and of the reality of God's judgment. Paul was a missionary, not a religionist involved in a dialogue that proceeds from the assumption that God is present in all religions, that salvation is possible through all faiths and ideologies, and that God's Spirit is at work in all religions, faiths, and ideologies. Paul did not suggest that Athenians who worship Zeus, or Isis, or the emperor, "walk together" with him "towards the fullness of truth." Paul was convinced that pagan religiosity and spirituality constitute a deliberate rebellion against God. Paul did not hesitate to call idol worshippers fools whose religious activities demonstrate futile ignorance that is devoid of salvation. Paul never abandons his conviction that the sole criterion for valid religious knowledge and for relevant spiritual truth is God's revelation in Jesus, the crucified and risen Messiah (Rom 3:21-26; 1 Cor 1:23-24; 2:2).[19]

---

[17]Tiessen, *Who Can Be Saved?* p. 424.

[18]See Netland, *Encountering Religious Pluralism*, pp. 323-48; Tiessen, *Who Can Be Saved?* pp. 424-76. It is important to note a major difference between exclusivists and general revelation inclusivists like Tiessen, whose claim we reject: "Given the perspective that I have put forward, I grant that the member of another religion *may* be personally in saving relationship with God, in spite of the fact that their religion, as such, is erroneous and, as a system, is counterproductive for people seeking God" (ibid., p. 441; emphasis original). Cf. also ibid., p. 393.

[19]See Schnabel, p. 121

4. WHAT ARE THE PURPOSES OF GENERAL REVELATION?

Inclusivists maintain that God's communication through general revelation is a sufficient means for saving faith. Exclusivists disagree and hold that special revelation is necessary. This suggests an important question: "If general revelation is insufficient to save, what is its purpose?"

General revelation is God's communication of himself to all people at all times in all places through his creation, the human conscience, and providence (Ps 19:1-6; Acts 14:15-17; 17:22-31; Rom 1:18-25; 2:14-16). Psalm 19:1-6 teaches that God's creation constantly displays his glory and handiwork to everyone everywhere, while the rest of that psalm teaches that the law of YHWH is central to covenant relationship with him (Ps 19:7-14). In Acts 14:15-17, Paul tells that God has borne witness of himself through creation, showing his goodness by providing rain and food. Paul uses these truths as an entry point for sharing the gospel. In Acts 17:22-31, he again points to God as the Creator of all and as sovereign over history. D. A. Carson captures the meaning of Acts 17:27: "God's purpose in his ordering of history is to incite human beings to pursue him."[20]

In Romans 1:18-25, the classical text on general revelation, Paul states that God clearly reveals his "invisible attributes, namely his eternal power and divine nature" through creation, but that people suppress this truth in rebellion against God. They prefer idolatry to genuine worship of the true God. This rebellion is universal—Jews and Gentiles alike are guilty before God (Rom 3:9-20). In Romans 2:14-16, Paul argues that "even people without the law show by their actions that distinctions between right and wrong are known to them."[21] Carson perceptively asserts, "To go no farther than Romans 2, Paul makes it clear that people are judged according to the light they have received, and no other—and that such light is sufficient to ensure universal condemnation."[22]

So, general revelation communicates truth about God to everyone. This revelation should lead all of us to seek and worship God, yet the Bible gives no evidence of anyone actually seeking him solely because of it. What is the problem? Is something wrong with general revelation? No, it is genuine, good, clear and effectively communicates many truths about God.[23] The problem lies neither in the Giver of general revelation nor in the revelation itself. Rather, the problem lies in the receivers of that revelation—fallen human beings. Since the Fall, we are corrupt and revolt against God's absolute authority over us. We follow our own ways,

---

[20]Carson, *Gagging of God*, p. 500.
[21]Ibid., p. 311.
[22]Ibid., p. 312.
[23]This is not to say that special revelation would ever be unnecessary. On the contrary, it has always been the platform for God's saving action. See Strange, pp. 54-77.

or the ways of the gods we create and domesticate, rather than submit to God. Our minds, wills, and emotions are stained by sin (Rom 1:18-32; 3:9-20; Eph 4:17-19). As such, we suppress and distort God's truth.

While Romans 1 shows that humans should respond to God positively through general revelation, it and Romans 3 both underscore that all are guilty precisely because no one responds to this revelation as he or she ought. God demands that all humans be righteous (Rom 1:18), but "none is righteous, no not one" (Rom 3:10). Through the creation, all know God and his truth (Rom 1:19-21), but "no one understands" (Rom 3:11). God gave a witness so that humans would seek after him (Acts 17:27; Rom 1:18-21), but apart from grace no one does (Rom 3:11). Humans should turn to God (Rom 1:22-25), but "all have turned aside" (Rom 3:12). Humans should fear, love, thank, and worship the Creator (Rom 1:21-25), but have traded him in for idols resembling the creation and ultimately possess "no fear of God before their eyes" (Rom 1:23-25; 3:18). This rebellion and its ensuing guilt are universal.

The problem, then, does not reside in God or his general revelation; the problem is found in universal human sinfulness that rejects God and his revelation. More than anyone else, the apostle Paul makes this plain. Yet interestingly, he also appeals to general revelation in his evangelism. When preaching about Jesus to fellow Jews, Paul often points to Jesus as fulfillment of the Law and Prophets and therefore cites the Old Testament (cf. Acts 13:13-52). But when preaching to pagans, Paul often places the gospel within a larger framework. In Acts 14:8-18, he points first to God as Creator and to his witness through general revelation. In Acts 17:16-31, Paul likewise highlights God as Creator, his true nature, and his witness through creation and providence.[24] For Paul, therefore, general revelation was insufficient for salvation, but it was an important starting point for the proclamation of the gospel.

Before the missionary ever arrives on the scene, God has been at work, communicating himself to unbelievers. And while it is true that these unbelievers suppress God's truth, it is also true that the missionary repeats, clarifies and expands this previous communication by sharing the gospel.[25] Missionaries do not start from scratch, but build on the point of contact God has already made with the unbelievers through general revelation as they urge them to turn to Christ in faith.

5. WHAT IS SAVING FAITH?

Inclusivists and exclusivists answer this question differently. The latter insist that saving faith must be placed in God's special revelation, culminating in the gospel

---

[24]For a helpful examination of Paul's method of evangelism and approach to contextualization, see Carson, *Gagging of God*, pp. 491-514.
[25]See Strange, pp. 72-77.

of Christ. The former have a wider conception of faith, maintaining that the unevangelized today, like Old Testament saints and "holy pagans," can be saved without faith in Christ.

But Old Testament saints were not saved by generic faith in God based on general revelation but on faith in the God of Israel based on special revelation.[26] New Testament passages abundantly testify to this truth: Romans 4:1-8; Galatians 3:7-9; Hebrews 11.

Moreover, our examination of Melchizedek and Cornelius, the two most famous "pagan saints," showed that they too were recipients of special revelation.[27] We agree with Tiessen, the foremost inclusivist, when he favors the view that Melchizedek was saved through special revelation.[28] We maintain that Cornelius was not forgiven until he believed in Christ. This best accords with the angel's instructions to Cornelius before he met Peter: "He will declare to you a message by which you will be saved, you and all your household" (Acts 11:14).[29]

Our prior examination of the inclusivist notion of the generic "faith principle" based on Hebrews 11:6 did not sustain inclusivist claims.[30] On the contrary, a consideration of Hebrews 11:6 in the context of its chapter, book, and testament led us to conclude that it did not intend to define saving faith comprehensively. Instead, such a faith must be placed in divine special revelation, and based on Hebrews 1:1-2, that revelation culminated in the Son through whom God spoke "in these last days." Consequently, it is a mistake to regard the unevangelized today as "informationally B.C." or as similar to the so-called holy pagans. The unevangelized need "confidence to enter the holy places by the blood of Jesus" to "draw near with a true heart in full assurance of faith," and to look "to Jesus, the founder and perfecter of our faith" (Heb 10:19, 22; 12:2).

It is imperative that saving faith be defined by the Bible itself and that means paying attention to the Bible's story line.[31] And that means that since the first coming of Christ the only way of salvation, as expressed by Jesus himself and his apostles is explicit faith in him.

> Jesus said to him, "I am the way, and the truth, and the life. No one comes to the Father except through me." (Jn 14:6)

---

[26]See Walter Kaiser's chapter in this book, pp. 123-41

[27]See Robert Peterson's treatment in this book, pp. 184-85.

[28]Tiessen, *Who Can Be Saved?* pp. 171-72. For our agreement, see pp. 189-91 of this book.

[29]A point made by David Wells, *God the Evangelist: How the Holy Spirit Works to Bring Men and Women to Faith* (Grand Rapids: Eerdmans, 1987), p. 23. John Stott agrees with Wells according to Tiessen, *Who Can Be Saved?* pp. 175-76.

[30]See Peterson's examination on pp. 197-99 of this book.

[31]Steve Wellum elaborated on this point in his chapter.

Then Peter, filled with the Holy Spirit, said to them, . . . "And there is salvation in no one else, for there is no other name under heaven given among men by which we must be saved." (Acts 4:8, 12)

If you confess with your mouth that Jesus is Lord and believe in your heart that God raised him from the dead, you will be saved. For with the heart one believes and is justified, and with the mouth one confesses and is saved. For the Scripture says, "Everyone who believes in him will not be put to shame." . . . For "everyone who calls on the name of the Lord will be saved." But how are they to call on him in whom they have not believed? And how are they to believe in him of whom they have never heard? And how are they to hear without someone preaching? And how are they to preach unless they are sent? . . . So faith comes from hearing, and hearing through the word of Christ. (Rom 10:9-11, 13-15, 17)

6. HOW DOES INCLUSIVISM SQUARE WITH EVANGELICAL THEOLOGY?

This is difficult to estimate. On the one hand, some go too far when they assert that inclusivists are not evangelicals. Many are evangelicals and it is unfair to consider them otherwise. On the other hand, we consider inclusivism a serious error that can damage the church's theology and mission.

While differing with those who want to take away the label "evangelical" from inclusivists, we note that inclusivists redefine some of the key tenets of evangelicalism. Take, for example, the four emphases that constitute Alister McGrath's definition of evangelicalism:

1. A focus, both devotional and theological, on the person of Jesus Christ, especially his death on the cross;
2. The identification of Scripture as the ultimate authority in matters of spirituality, doctrine, and ethics;
3. An emphasis upon conversion or a "new birth" as a life-changing religious experience;
4. A concern for sharing the faith, especially through evangelism.[32]

The teachings of world religions inclusivists run contrary to the first tenet, the uniqueness of Christ, because they hold that other religions are valid means of salvation. General revelation inclusivists confess Christ's uniqueness, although they do not require that faith have him as its object in this life. Evangelical inclusivists

---

[32] Alister E. McGrath, *A Passion for Truth: The Intellectual Coherence of Evangelicalism* (Downers Grove, Ill.: InterVarsity Press, 1996), p. 22. We recognize that attempts to define evangelicalism chart a course through murky and slippery terrain. We are merely using McGrath's overview as typical. Marsden's is similar to McGrath's with one addition: a "spiritually transformed life." See George M. Marsden, *Evangelicalism and Modern America* (Grand Rapids: Eerdmans, 1984), pp. ix-x.

typically have a high view of Scripture. Although we sometimes disagree with how they use Scripture to do theology, we do not dispute that they hold McGrath's second tenet.

In our estimation, McGrath's third and fourth tenets are the ones most significantly redefined by evangelical inclusivists. Tenet three, the necessity of personal conversion, is compromised because inclusivism separates conversion from faith in Christ.[33] It holds that persons can be saved without ever hearing the gospel of Christ.

The fourth tenet, a concern for evangelism, is also affected. Although the emphasis on sharing the gospel is still maintained by most evangelical inclusivists, the character and necessity of the church's mission is altered.[34] The historic urgency of proclaiming the gospel to those who will be lost without believing it in this life is diminished. It is replaced in part by preaching the gospel so that some who have already been saved by their general faith may realize their full joy and potential in Christ. We agree with the response of Hudson Taylor, when asked if the heathen would be lost if he did not go to China: "I think the heathen *are lost*. That's why I go to China."[35]

Even in the best case scenario, inclusivism affects several important doctrines. For example, even many of the most orthodox inclusivists rework some elements of historic Christology by cutting the cord between ontology and epistemology in relation to the person of Christ, separating a knowledge of his work from that of the Holy Spirit. They alter the doctrine of salvation by maintaining that people can be saved apart from hearing the gospel and putting explicit faith in Christ. They also fail to address how sanctification occurs apart from the revealed means God employs—the church, the Scriptures, etc. They broaden the composition of the church—as they see it, it also includes people who may belong to other religions—and they redefine the church's mission.

7. WHAT DO WE SAY TO PEOPLE WHO ARE TROUBLED BY EXCLUSIVISM?

This is another thorny but practical question. It comes in various contexts. It might be raised by our next door neighbor who practices Buddhism, or by our pluralistic sister who rebels against the church, or by a devout Christian who is trou-

---

[33]See Wellum's chapter devoted to this issue, pp. 142-83.
[34]See Jennings's chapter devoted to this issue, pp. 220-40.
[35]Walter B. Knight, *Knight's Master Book of New Illustrations* (Grand Rapids: Eerdmans, 1956), p. 381, italics original.

bled by the biblical teachings concerning hell. How do we respond to such a question? It might be helpful to consider how we would respond to a related difficult question, with which most of us have more experience. What do we say to someone who is undergoing intense suffering? That all sin and death result from the Fall? That death is "natural" and human life is fleeting? That she should trust in the sovereign God who knows what he is doing? That God and his people love her and are there to strengthen her?

Although we may have some biblical convictions about the matter of suffering, it seems that our response will be shaped by multiple contextual factors. For example, when was the tragedy—did it happen one hour ago, one month ago or twenty years ago? What is the spiritual background of those needing comfort—are they Christians, what is their theological foundation, have they suffered intensely before, are they responding to this occasion appropriately? What is the nature of the suffering—is this person eighty years old and dying of cancer, is it a parent whose child died in a freak accident, is it a police officer injured in the line of duty? What is our relationship to the persons suffering—did we meet them five minutes ago, are we their pastor, are they close friends, are they aware of examples of suffering in our own lives?

Obviously what we say to someone suffering depends in large measure on the circumstances. For example, though we believe that God is sovereign, in most cases this will not be the time to bring that up, or we might minister to the sufferer as well as Job's friends did to him! Plainly, it is not always appropriate or wise to tell everyone everything we believe that the Bible teaches about certain matters in such times.

Similarly, what we say to someone troubled by the uniqueness of Christ and the necessity of faith in him for salvation is also shaped by the situation. Who is this person and what leads them to raise this question? Is she a philosophical pluralist who is dismissive of our view of truth? Is he a Japanese currently being evangelized and objecting to Christianity because it seems to destroy family traditions? Is she a former Muslim recently converted to Christianity and worried about her mother's spiritual status? Is he a former Buddhist, mature in Christ, knowledgeable about the Bible, and in pain because he does not want to believe that his family members are eternally condemned? Is she a missionary candidate who just wants to be sure that she is giving her life to a true and meaningful cause?

8. IS THERE ANY HOPE FOR THOSE WHO HAVE NEVER HEARD THE GOSPEL?

So, we must finally ask: Is there any hope for those who have not heard the gospel? Yes, but not in the way that inclusivists suppose. The hope of those who have never heard is found in God who sent his Son to be the Savior of the world. And God has also sent us—we are participants in his mission of reconciliation. The best way to help the unevangelized is not to become more optimistic about their eternal destiny apart from the gospel. Rather, it is to allow our understanding of God and his Word to generate a greater burden for the unevangelized and to pray, give and go to make sure that they hear the gospel.

Like the apostle Paul, we need to act on our theology. It is not enough to believe as Paul believed; we also need to feel what he felt so we can witness to the lost as he did. Paul was a theologian *and* a practitioner—a missionary, church planter and pastor. In Romans 9, Paul writes one of his most complex theological pieces, addressing the relationship between the sovereignty of God and human responsibility, the nature of Israel, and the outworking of salvation history. Yet he begins and ends his section with an emphasis on his burden for the salvation of the people of Israel. Paul tells of his "great sorrow and unceasing anguish in his heart" for the lost (Rom 9:2). So intense is his burden that he even wished that he himself could be accursed and cut off from Christ instead of them (Rom 9:3). Indeed his "heart's desire and prayer" for them is "that they may be saved" (Rom 10:1). Paul's commitment to the truth led him to clarify and defend it, but even more, his commitment to the truth thrust upon him a burden for the lost so great that he was willing to spend and be spent so that the unreached might know, love and worship Christ.

It is the prayer of the contributors to *Faith Comes by Hearing: A Response to Inclusivism* that this generation will mirror Paul's dedication and be so committed to the Great Commission that the question, "What about those who have never heard?" becomes obsolete. We pray that there will be so much time, energy, money, prayer and personnel invested in reaching the unreached that the question becomes, "How can we, the worldwide body of Jesus' followers, most faithfully and strategically share the gospel and plant new churches among unreached peoples and their cultures?" Indeed, there is hope for those who have never heard. The hope is found in the good news of our Lord Jesus Christ. Let us be exclusivists not only in our theology, but also in our practice as we proclaim this good news among all peoples of the earth!

Our affirmation, confession, rejoicing, and dedication mirror those of the framers of the Lausanne Committee for World Evangelization (1974):

> We affirm our belief in one-eternal God, Creator and Lord of the world, Father, Son and Holy Spirit, who governs all things according to the purpose of his will. He has been calling out from the world a people for himself, and sending his people back into the world to be his servants and witnesses, for the extension of his kingdom, the building up of Christ's body, and the glory of his name. We confess with shame that

we have often denied our calling and failed in our mission by becoming conformed to the world or by withdrawing from it. Yet we rejoice that even when borne by earthen vessels the gospel is still a precious treasure. To the task of making that treasure known in the power of the Holy Spirit we desire to dedicate ourselves anew.[36]

God is passionately engaged in gathering people to know, love, and worship him from every tribe, language, people, and nation. And he has called us to join him on this mission. May we faithfully and enthusiastically participate in his eternal, global purpose as we long to hear and sing the songs of Revelation 5:

> You are worthy to take the scroll and to open its seals, because you were slain, and with your blood you purchased men for God from every tribe and language and people and nation. You have made them to be a kingdom and priests to serve our God, and they will reign on the earth. (Rev 5:9-10)

> Worthy is the Lamb, who was slain, to receive power and wealth and wisdom and strength and honor and glory and praise! (Rev 5:12)

> To him who sits on the throne and to the Lamb be praise and honor and glory and power, for ever and ever! (Rev 5:13)

---

[36]Edward R. Dayton and Samuel Wilson, eds., *The Future of World Evangelization* (Monrovia, Calif.: MARC, 1984), p. 59.

Selected Bibliography

Anderson, Gerald H., and Thomas F. Stransky, eds. *Christ's Lordship and Religious Pluralism*. Maryknoll, N.Y.: Orbis, 1981.

Anderson, J. Norman D. *Christianity and World Religions*. Downers Grove, Ill.: InterVarsity Press, 1984.

Bavinck, J. H. *An Introduction to the Science of Missions*. Grand Rapids: Baker, 1960.

———. *Prolegomena*. Vol. 1, *Reformed Dogmatics*. Grand Rapids: Baker, 2003.

———. *The Church Between Temple and Mosque*. Grand Rapids: Eerdmans, 1966.

Berkouwer, G. C. *General Revelation*. Grand Rapids: Eerdmans, 1955.

Bloesch, Donald. *Essentials of Evangelical Theology*. 2 vols. New York: Harper & Row, 1982.

Bonda, Jan. *The One Purpose of God: An Answer to the Doctrine of Eternal Punishment*, translated by Reinder Bruinsma. Grand Rapids: Eerdmans, 1993.

Borland, James A. "A Theologian Looks at the Gospel and World Religions." *Journal of the Evangelical Theological Society* 33 (March 1990): 3-11.

Braaten, Carl E. *No Other Gospel! Christianity Among the World's Religions*. Minneapolis: Fortress, 1992.

Bray, Gerald. "The *Filioque* Clause in History and Theology." *Tyndale Bulletin* 34 (1983): 91-145.

Burkert, Walter. *Greek Religion: Archaic and Classical*. Oxford: Blackwell, 1985.

Carson, D. A. *The Gagging of God: Christianity Confronts Pluralism*. Grand Rapids: Zondervan, 1996.

Craig, William Lane. "No Other Name: A Middle Knowledge Perspective on the Exclusivity of Salvation through Christ." *Faith and Philosophy* 6 (April 1989): 172-88.

Crockett, William J., and James G. Sigountos, eds. *Through No Fault of Their Own? The Fate of Those Who Have Never Heard*. Grand Rapids: Baker, 1991.

D'Costa, Gavin, ed. *Christian Uniqueness Reconsidered: The Myth of a Pluralistic Theology of Religions*. Maryknoll, N.Y.: Orbis, 1990.

———. *The Meeting of Religions and the Trinity*. Maryknoll, N.Y.: Orbis, 2000.

———. *Theology and Religious Pluralism: The Challenge of Other Religions*. New York: Oxford, 1986.

Demarest, Bruce A. *General Revelation: Historical Views and Contemporary Issues*. Grand Rapids: Zondervan, 1982.

Edwards, David L., and John R. W. Stott. *Evangelical Essentials: A Liberal-Evangelical Dialogue*. Downers Grove, Ill.: InterVarsity Press, 1988.

Erickson, Millard J. "Hope for Those Who Haven't Heard? Yes, But . . ." *Evangelical Missions Quarterly* 11 (April 1975): 122-26.

———. *How Shall They Be Saved? The Destiny of Those Who Do Not Hear of Jesus*. Grand Rapids: Baker, 1996.

Fackre, Gabriel. *The Christian Story: A Narrative Interpretation of Basic Christian Doctrine.* Grand Rapids: Eerdmans, 1984.

Flemming, Dean E. *Contextualization in the New Testament: Patterns for Theology and Mission.* Downers Grove, Ill.: InterVarsity Press, 2005.

Garland, Robert. *Introducing New Gods: The Politics of Athenian Religion.* Ithaca, N.Y.: Cornell University Press, 1992.

Gärtner, Bertil. *The Areopagus Speech and Natural Revelation.* Lund: Gleerup, 1955.

George, Timothy. "Forum Discussion on Inclusivism." In *Who Will Be Saved? Defending the Biblical Understanding of God, Salvation, and Evangelism,* edited by Paul R. House and Gregory A. Thornbury, pp. 145-62. Wheaton, Ill.: Crossway, 2000.

Goldingay, John E., and Christoper J. H. Wright. "'Yahweh Our God Yahweh One': The Old Testament and Religious Pluralism." In *One God, One Lord in a World of Religious Pluralism,* edited by Andrew D. Clarke and Bruce W. Winter, pp. 43-62. 2nd ed. Cambridge: Tyndale House, 1991.

Goodman, Martin. *Mission and Conversion: Proselytizing in the Religious History of the Roman Empire.* Oxford: Clarendon, 1994.

Gradel, Ittai. *Emperor Worship and Roman Religion.* Oxford Classical Monographs. Oxford: Clarendon, 2002.

Green, Michael. *"But Don't All Religions Lead to God?" Navigating the Multi-Faith Maze.* Grand Rapids: Baker, 2002.

———. *Evangelism in the Early Church.* Grand Rapids: Eerdmans, 1970.

Grenz, Stanley J. *Renewing the Center: Evangelical Theology in a Post-Theological Era.* Grand Rapids: Baker, 2000.

———. "Toward an Evangelical Theology of the Religions." *Journal of Ecumenical Studies* 31 (Spring 1995): 49-65.

Heim, S. Mark. *The Depth of the Riches: A Trinitarian Theology of Religious Ends.* Grand Rapids: Eerdmans, 2001.

———. *Is Christ the Only Way?* Valley Forge, Penn.: Judson, 1985.

———. *Salvations: Truth and Difference in Religion.* Maryknoll, N.Y.: Orbis, 1995.

Hesselgrave, David J. *Paradigms in Conflict: Ten Key Questions in Christian Missions Today.* Grand Rapids: Kregel, 2005.

Hick, John. *An Interpretation of Religion.* New Haven, Conn.: Yale University Press, 1989.

———. *God Has Many Names.* Philadelphia: Westminster Press, 1980.

Kaiser, Walter C., Jr. *Mission in the Old Testament: Israel as a Light to the Nations.* Grand Rapids: Baker, 2000.

Kärkkäinen, Veli-Matti. *An Introduction to the Theology of the Religions: Biblical, Historical and Contemporary Perspectives.* Downers Grove, Ill.: InterVarsity Press, 2003.

Klauck, Hans-Josef. *The Religious Context of Early Christianity: A Guide to Graeco-Roman Religions.* Studies of the New Testament and Its World. Edinburgh: T & T Clark, 2000.

Köstenberger, Andreas J., and Peter T. O'Brien. *Salvation to the Ends of the Earth: A Biblical Theology of Mission.* New Studies in Biblical Theology. Downers Grove, Ill.: InterVarsity Press, 2001.

Köstenberger, Andreas J. *The Missions of Jesus and the Disciples According to the Fourth Gospel.* Grand Rapids: Eerdmans, 1998.

Küng, Hans. "The World Religions in God's Plan of Salvation." In *Christian Revelation and World Religions,* edited by Josef Neuner, pp. 25-66. London: Burns & Oates, 1965.

Little, Christopher R. *The Revelation of God Among the Unevangelized.* Pasadena, Calif.: William Carey Library, 2000.

MacMullen, Ramsay. *Paganism in the Roman Empire.* New Haven, Conn.: Yale University Press, 1981.

Mangum, R. Todd. "Is There a Reformed Way to Get the Benefits of the Atonement to 'Those Who Have Never Heard'?" *Journal of the Evangelical Theological Society* 47, no. 1 (March 2004): 121-36.

McDermott, Gerald R. *Can Evangelicals Learn from World Religions? Jesus, Revelation and Religious Traditions.* Downers Grove, Ill.: InterVarsity Press, 2000.

————. *Jonathan Edwards Confronts the Gods.* New York: Oxford University Press, 2000.

McQuilkin, Robertson. *The Great Omission.* Grand Rapids: Baker, 1984.

Morgan, Christopher W., and Robert A. Peterson, eds. *Hell Under Fire: Modern Scholarship Reinvents Eternal Punishment.* Grand Rapids: Zondervan, 2004.

Nash, Ronald H. *Is Jesus the Only Savior?* Grand Rapids: Zondervan, 1994.

Netland, Harold A. *Dissonant Voices: Religious Pluralism and the Question of Truth.* Grand Rapids: Eerdmans, 1991.

————. *Encountering Religious Pluralism: The Challenge to Christian Faith and Mission.* Downers Grove, Ill.: InterVarsity Press, 2001.

O'Brien, Peter T. *Gospel and Mission in the Writings of Paul: An Exegetical and Theological Analysis.* Grand Rapids: Baker, 1995.

Okholm, Dennis L., and Timothy R. Phillips, eds. *Four Views on Salvation in a Pluralistic World.* Grand Rapids: Zondervan, 1995.

Packer, J. I. "Good Pagans and God's Kingdom." *Christianity Today,* January 17, 1986, pp. 22-25.

Pinnock, Clark H. *A Wideness in God's Mercy. The Finality of Jesus Christ in a World of Religions.* Grand Rapids: Zondervan, 1992.

Piper, John. *Let the Nations Be Glad! The Supremacy of God in Missions.* Grand Rapids: Baker, 1993.

Plummer, Robert L. *Paul's Understanding of the Church's Mission: Did the Apostle Paul Expect the Early Christian Communities to Evangelize?* Paternoster Biblical Monographs. Carlisle, U.K.: Paternoster, 2007.

Race, Alan. *Christians and Religious Pluralism: Patterns in the Christian Theology of Religions.* Maryknoll, N.Y.: Orbis, 1982.

Rahner, Karl. *Theological Investigations,* translated by Karl and Boniface Kruger. Baltimore: Helicon, 1969.

Ramachandra, Vinoth. *The Recovery of Mission: Beyond the Pluralist Paradigm.* Grand Rapids: Eerdmans, 1996.

Richard, Ramesh. *The Population of Heaven.* Chicago: Moody Press, 1994.

Richardson, Don. *Eternity in Their Hearts.* Ventura, Calif.: Regal, 1981.

Samartha, Stanley J. *Between Two Cultures: Ecumenical Ministry in a Pluralist World.* Geneva: WCC Publications, 1996.

————. *One Christ, Many Religions: Toward a Revised Christology.* Maryknoll, N.Y.: Orbis, 1991.

Sanders, John. *No Other Name: An Investigation into the Destiny of the Unevangelized.* Grand Rapids: Eerdmans, 1992.

————, ed. *What About Those Who Have Never Heard? Three Views on the Destiny of the Unevangelized.* Downers Grove, Ill.: InterVarsity Press, 1995.

Schnabel, Eckhard J. *Early Christian Mission.* 2 vols. Downers Grove, Ill.: InterVarsity Press, 2004.

Shedd, William G. T. *Dogmatic Theology,* 3rd ed., edited by Alan Gomes. Phillipsburg, N.J.: Presbyterian & Reformed, 2003.

Strange, Daniel. *The Possibility of Salvation Among the Unevangelised: An Analysis of Inclusivism in Recent Evangelical Theology.* Paternoster Biblical and Theological Monographs. Carlisle, U.K.: Paternoster, 2002.

Tiessen, Terrance L. *Who Can Be Saved? Reassessing Salvation in Christ and World Religions.* Downers Grove, Ill.: InterVarsity Press, 2004.

Tillich, Paul. *Christianity and the Encounter of the World Religions.* New York: Columbia University Press, 1962.

Visser't Hooft, W. A. *No Other Name: The Choice Between Syncretism and Christian Universalism.* Philadelphia: Westminster Press, 1963.

Wells, David F. *God the Evangelist: How the Holy Spirit Works to Bring Men and Women to Faith.* Grand Rapids: Eerdmans, 1987.

Wright, Christopher J. H. "The Christian and Other Religions: The Biblical Evidence." *Themelios* 9 (January 1984): 4-15.

————. *The Mission of God: Unlocking the Bible's Grand Narrative.* Downers Grove, Ill.: InterVarsity Press, 2006.

Yong, Amos. *Beyond the Impasse: Toward a Pneumatological Theology of Religions.* Grand Rapids: Baker, 2003.

————. "Discerning the Spirit(s) in the World of Religions: Toward a Pneumatological Theology of Religions." In *No Other Gods Before Me? Evangelicals and the Challenge of World Religions,* edited by John G. Stackhouse Jr., pp. 37-64. Grand Rapids: Baker, 2001.

Name Index

Subject Index

Scripture Index

VOCABULARY

EXCLUSIVISM -

INCLUSIVISM -

PLURALISM -

Pg # 15 (FIVE MAJOR ARGUMENTS OF INCLUSIVIST.)